Transactions of the Royal Historical Society

SIXTH SERIES

XXI

CAMBRIDGE
UNIVERSITY PRESS

Published by the Press Syndicate of the University of Cambridge
The Edinburgh Building, Cambridge CB2 8RU, United Kingdom
32 Avenue of the Americas, New York, NY 10013-2473, USA
477 Williamstown Road, Port Melbourne, VIC 3207, Australia
C/Orense, 4, Planta 13, 28020 Madrid, Spain
Lower Ground Floor, Nautica Building, The Water Club,
Beach Road, Granger Bay, 8005 Cape Town, South Africa

First published 2011

A catalogue record for this book is available from the British Library

ISBN 9781107019317 hardback

SUBSCRIPTIONS. The serial publications of the Royal Historical Society, *Royal Historical Society Transactions* (ISSN 0080–4401) and Camden Fifth Series (ISSN 0960–1163) volumes, may be purchased together on annual subscription. The 2011 subscription price, which includes print and electronic access (but not VAT), is £121 (US $ 203 in the USA, Canada, and Mexico) and includes Camden Fifth Series, volumes 38, 39 and 40 (published in April, July and December) and Transactions Sixth Series, volume 21 (published in December). Japanese prices are available from Kinokuniya Company Ltd, P.O. Box 55, Chitose, Tokyo 156, Japan. EU subscribers (outside the UK) who are not registered for VAT should add VAT at their country's rate. VAT registered subscribers should provide their VAT registration number. Prices include delivery by air.

Subscription orders, which must be accompanied by payment, may be sent to a bookseller, subscription agent, or direct to the publisher: Cambridge University Press, The Edinburgh Building, Shaftesbury Road, Cambridge CB2 8RU, UK; or in the USA, Canada, and Mexico: Cambridge University Press, Journals Fulfillment Department, 100 Brook Hill Drive, West Nyack, New York, 10994–2133, USA.

SINGLE VOLUMES AND BACK VOLUMES. A list of Royal Historical Society volumes available from Cambridge University Press may be obtained from the Humanities Marketing Department at the address above.

Printed and bound in the United Kingdom at the University Press, Cambridge

CONTENTS

Transactions of the RHS 21 (2011), pp. 1–38 © Royal Historical Society 2011
doi:10.1017/S0080440111000028

TRANSACTIONS OF THE

ROYAL HISTORICAL SOCIETY

PRESIDENTIAL ADDRESS

By Colin Jones

FRENCH CROSSINGS: II. LAUGHING OVER BOUNDARIES

READ 26 NOVEMBER 2010

ABSTRACT. Under the generic title, 'French Crossings', this Presidential Address explores the history of laughter in French society, and humour's potential for trangressing boundaries. It focuses on the irreverent and almost entirely unknown book of comic drawings entitled *Livre de caricatures tant Bonnes que mauvaises* (Book of Caricatures, both Good and Bad), that was composed between the 1740s and the mid-1770s by the luxury Parisian embroiderer and designer, Charles-Germain de Saint-Aubin, and his friends and family. The bawdy laughter that the book seems intended to provoke gave it its nickname of the *Livre de culs* (Book of Arses). Yet despite the scatological character of many of the drawings, the humour often conjoined lower body functions with rather cerebral and erudite wit. The laughter provoked unsparingly targeted and exposed to ridicule the social elite, cultural celebrities and political leaders of Ancien Régime France. This made it a dangerous object, which was kept strictly secret. Was this humour somehow pre- or proto-Revolutionary? In fact, the work is so embedded in the culture of the Ancien Régime that 1789 was one boundary that the work signally fails to cross.

Jean-Georges Wille was a Parisian engraver. He kept a diary. And in that diary in June 1770 he recorded: 'We dined at the home of M. Basan with the family of Chereau and with the elder Saint-Aubin. We laughed a lot.'[1] Pierre-François Basan and Jacques Chereau were also engravers.

[1] G. Wille, *Mémoires et journal*, ed. G. Duplessis (2 vols., Paris 1857), I, 440. On another occasion Wille notes the two men being together again in 'un festin' where 'nous sommes restés assez longtemps à table de fort bonne humeur'. *Ibid.*, 578. (Note that the editor mistakenly takes this second reference to be to Charles-Germain's brother Augustin.)

The 'elder Saint-Aubin' was Charles-Germain de Saint-Aubin. He was
by vocation an embroiderer, an artisan working in a luxury trade; but he
also dabbled in much else besides, including engraving – and laughter.
His family would retain the memory of him as 'likeable, witty, clever, very
caustic, very satirical, very gallant with the ladies, and never out of place
wherever he went'. Witty, clever, satirical, caustic, never out of place in
society – he was thus a good man to spend an evening with, an evening
laughing with.

For much of Charles-Germain de Saint-Aubin's adult life, seemingly
from the 1740s through to the 1770s, in an atmosphere of scrupulous
secrecy, he maintained, developed and shared with a small group of
cronies a collection of nearly 400 drawings that he entitled *Livre de caricatures
tant Bonnes que mauvaises* (Figure 1: 675.1).[2] As its title suggests, it is a book
of humorous drawings, a visual joke book. This extraordinary document,
which is almost wholly unknown, testifies to that taste for festive sociability,
that gift of laughter, that Wille's diary evokes. It not only offers a striking
visual perspective on the culture and politics of Paris during the middle
decades of the eighteenth century, it also provides a unique prism on the
nature of laughter in France of the Ancien Régime, a society organised
around those boundaries, frontiers and divisions which Charles-Germain,
a man 'never out of place', it would seem, was adept at crossing.

Charles-Germain de Saint-Aubin, whom we can take to be the
principal author of the *Livre de caricatures*, is an obscure figure, in whom
historians have expressed little interest (Figure 2: 675.386).[3] Born in 1721
under the Regency, he lived all his adult life – down to his death in 1786 –
in pre-Revolutionary, Ancien Régime, Enlightenment France. Among
historians of art, he is far less-known than his brothers, Gabriel, the odd-
ball artist and proto-*flâneur* of the streets of Paris, whose star is currently
rising in art-historical circles, and Augustin, one of the most celebrated
engravers of the late eighteenth century.[4] Charles-Germain too may well

² *Livre de caricatures tant Bonnes que mauvaises*, Charles-Germain de Saint-Aubin, *c.* 1740 –
c. 1775, 187 × 132mm, Waddesdon Manor, Classmark 675. It is currently located in the library
of Waddesdon Manor, Bucks. In conjunction with colleagues from Waddesdon Manor,
Juliet Carey and Pippa Shirley, and research assistant, Emily Richardson, I have recently
completed an AHRC grant devoted to this volume. Note that to make references more
manageable, I have included references to particular images in the text using Waddesdon
Manor's classification. The digitised images plus critical commentary – may be accessed on
Waddesdon's website: see the Waddesdon Saint-Aubin Project at www.waddesdon.org.uk.
For all that follows, the curatorial commentary for each image mentioned is recommended.
   ³ Victor Advielle, *Renseignements intimes sur les Saint-Aubin, dessinateurs et graveurs d'après les
papiers de leur famille* (Paris, 1896), contains the fullest account of Charles-Germain's life and
draws on autobiographical and biographical fragments described below, n. 5.
   ⁴ Advielle, *Renseignements intimes*, has until recently offered the best description of the lives
of Gabriel and Augustin. For Gabriel, see now *Gabriel de Saint-Aubin, 1724–1780*, ex. cat. The
Frick Collection, 30 Oct. 2007 – 27 Jan. 2008, Musée du Louvre, 28 Feb. – 26 May 2008

have nurtured artistic ambitions. Like the rest of his family, he had painted and drawn from childhood and he dabbled in engraving. From the age of fifteen, he maintained a book of drawings and paintings of flowers – the *Recueil de plantes* – which he prized highly.[5] Flower designs were staple features of the rococo style which adorned the clothes in whose design he came to specialise. In 1748, he produced a set of engravings of *papillonneries*, the human antics of butterflies, which seemed to presage an academic career in the art world – which then fizzled out completely.[6]

Charles-Germain probably made the right decision in renouncing a career in fine art and in following his father, who was *brodeur du roi* (royal embroiderer) into the trade of fancy, high-end embroidery. He enjoyed almost instantaneous success. In 1747, when he was still in his twenties, he designed the dauphin's wedding costume.[7] He was already accounted as among the very best in the business. He went on to prosper, and to have children, whom he tried to marry well. Flowers and design remained at the core of the 40,000 drawings which he claimed to have completed in the course of his lifetime.[8] His *Recueil de plantes*, to which he was adding even on the eve of his death, would pass into the hands of his daughter on his death, as did a family album that he had composed in the last years of his life, known as the *Livre des Saint-Aubin*. These two books are now in the possession of the Oak Spring Garden Library in Virginia and the Louvre respectively.[9] The travels of his *Livre de caricatures* are more obscure. The volume is mentioned in no private document nor public record before the middle of the nineteenth century. It was fleetingly seen

---

(Paris, 2007). More generally, cf. E. Dacier, *Gabriel de Saint-Aubin. Peintre, dessinateur et graveur (1724–80), l'homme et l'œuvre* (2 vols., Paris, 1929–31), which contains much material on the brothers.

[5] *Receuil [sic] de plantes copiées d'aprés [sic] nature par de Saint Aubin, dessinateur du Roy Louis XV, 1736–1785*, by Charles-Germain de Saint-Aubin, 365 × 245mm, Oak Spring Garden Library, Upperville, Virginia. See also Lucia Tongiori Tomasi, *An Oak Spring Flora: Flower Illustrations from the 15th Century to the Present Time: A Selection of Rare Books and Manuscripts in the Collection of Rachel Lambert Mellon* (Upperville, VA, 1997), and Adrien Moreau, 'Recueil des plantes de Charles-Germain de Saint-Aubin', *L'Art*, 73–8 (1903), 129–34. It is from the *Recueil des Plantes* that the description of Charles-Germain's character evoked in the first paragraph of this paper derives.

[6] P. Mauriès, *Les papillonneries humaines* (reprint edn; Paris, 1996). Charles-Germain also was involved with brother Gabriel in preparing a pornographic novel in the mid-1740s. For details on this and on other biographical data, see Juliet Carey and Colin Jones, 'Introduction', to *eadem, idem* and Emily Richardson, eds., *Charles-Germain de Saint-Aubin and his 'Livre de culs'* (forthcoming Studies in Voltaire and the Eighteenth Century, Voltaire Foundation, Oxford, 2012).

[7] Charles-Germain de Saint-Aubin, *L'Art du brodeur* (Paris, 1770). The text and accompanying illustrations have been reprinted as *The Art of Embroidery*, translated and annotated by Nikki Scheuer (Los Angeles, 1983).

[8] The reference is in the autobiographical fragments in the *Recueil de plantes*.

[9] See above, n. 4, and also Pierre Rosenberg, *Le Livre des Saint-Aubin* (Paris, 2002), for the Louvre volume.

by the Goncourt brothers, before it arrived at Waddesdon Manor in the 1890s – where it has been very little viewed.[10] It was evidently a book that the brothers Saint-Aubin did not wish to become public in their lifetime. They preferred to keep strictly to themselves and their closest intimates what was known in their family – with reason, as we shall see – as their *Livre de culs*, their 'Book of Arses'.[11]

My series of presidential lectures, which I have entitled, 'French Crossings', has as its motif the act of crossing – crossing territorial boundaries (I am a British historian of France; France is the framework for my talks), crossing disciplinary frontiers and exploring the act of crossing, and the meaning of crossing, in the lives of my subjects. Last year, I used the Channel hoppings of Charles Dickens to explore issues of personal and national identity focused around his great novel about the French Revolution, *A Tale of Two Cities*. I suggested that understanding the act of constantly travelling between two cities and two cultures was crucial to grasping Dickens's relationship with, and the underlying meanings of, his famous novel.[12] In this paper, I shall be studying an individual who, in contrast to Dickens, was almost wholly obscure yet who was similarly adept at crossing – though over social rather than national boundaries – and for whom, as we shall see, that act was a key, until now a hidden key, to his identity.

Coming to terms with the unusual laughing book that is the focus of this paper requires thinking about how as historians we deal with the subject of laughter. In recent years, this slippery phenomenon has enjoyed something of a vogue among historians, who have done their best to seek explanatory traction from other fields of scholarly endeavour, including philosophy, psychology, physiology, sociology, anthropology, literary criticism and visual theory.[13] Yet whatever its disciplinary livery, there is one virtually universal characteristic of scholarly studies of

---

[10] For the book's history, see Carey and Jones, 'Introduction'. This collection comprises essays on the work from very wide-ranging and divergent perspectives. The Goncourts provide the only substantial comment on the work before the present day: see their *L'Art du XVIIIe siècle*, 3rd edn (Paris, 1882).

[11] This in a loose-leaf page located in the *Livre de caricatures* at Waddesdon Manor. It is in the hand of Pierre-Antoine Tardieu, the husband of one of Charles-Germain's grand-daughters, who inherited the book in the early 1820s and seems to have been party to a number of family traditions.

[12] Colin Jones, 'Presidential Address: I. Tales of Two Cities', *Transactions of the Royal Historical Society*, 20 (2010), 1–26.

[13] To focus solely on eighteenth-century France, particularly recommended on laughter, from a list which could be much extended, are Anne Richardot, *Le rire des Lumières* (Paris, 2002); 'Le rire', ed. Lise Andries, *XVIIIe siècle*, 32 (2000); Antoine de Baecque, *Les éclats du rire: la culture des rieurs au XVIIIe siècle* (Paris, 2000); Jean Goldzink, *Les Lumières et l'idée du comique* (Fontenay-aux-Roses, 1992); *idem*, *Comique et comédie au siècle des Lumières* (Paris, 2002); and Elizabeth Bourguinat, *Le siècle du persiflage, 1734–1789* (Paris, 1998). For slightly earlier periods, see Daniel Ménager, *La Renaissance et le rire* (Paris, 1995), and Dominique Bertrand, *Dire le*

humour. They are very, very rarely amusing. 'Those who seek the metaphysical causes of laughter', Voltaire noted, presciently, 'are rarely jolly.'[14] Present-day researchers beating their paths towards such works can be certain they will leave them with the straightest of faces. Indeed, there may even be something about the subject which attracts the constitutionally morose. The psychologist Vicky Bruce, author of important work on visual cognition and facial recognition, remarks in one of her books, 'I am forever passing people in the street who say "Cheer up, it might never happen"' – sadly going on to note, 'Clearly though quite unintentionally I tend to wear a troubled face.'[15]

The apparent attraction of the topic of humour to the serious-minded and lugubrious of countenance seems quite amusing in fact, as though just talking seriously and academically about humour was comic in itself. Warming to the notion of the unwittingly comic aspect of serious work on the topic of humour, the sociologist Peter Berger has remarked that

> writing a book about the comic could be construed as *prima facie* evidence of ... humourlessness. Conversely, the witness to such an endeavour may well find it funny. It calls for a humorous antithesis as occurs when a philosopher lecturing on metaphysics loses his trousers ... – the physical taking comic revenge on the pretensions of the metaphysical.[16]

An image from the *Livre de caricatures* appositely and punningly illustrates the point: the hot air of a musicology lecturer is met full on by wind of an altogether different kind emerging from a 'fundamental bass' (Figure 3: 675.63). The academic pretension to truth-telling finds itself subverted by the more earthy truth of the body, indeed in this case from this book of arses, the truth of the arse. This is a dimension of the comic, of which any academic researcher needs to remain acutely aware. Although I shall approach the subject of humour with due academic seriousness, I will be braced and tightly belted against the ironical realisation that just trying to be funny about the funny is supremely funny because the effort must needs be quintessentially unfunny.

Of course, one reason why historical studies of laughter are rarely amusing is that humour is both culture-bound and time-specific and

---

rire à l'âge classique: représenter pour mieux contrôler (Aix-en-Provence, 1995). Very useful general works include Georges Minois, *Histoire du rire et de la déraison* (Paris, 2000); Robert Favre, *Le rire dans tous ses éclats* (Lyon, 1995); Dominique Bertrand and Véronique Gély-Ghedira, eds., *Rire des dieux* (Clermont-Ferrand, 2000); C. Biondi *et al.*, eds., *La quête du bonheur et l'expression de la douleur dans la littérature et la pensée françaises* (Geneva, 1995); and Maurice Lever, *Le sceptre et la marotte: histoire des fous de cour* (Paris, 1983). For a helpful comparative angle, see Jan Verberckmoes, *Laughter, Jestbooks and Society in the Spanish Netherlands* (Basingstoke, 1999).

[14] Voltaire, *Dictionnaire philosophique*, article 'rire'.

[15] Vicki Bruce, *Recognising Faces* (1988), 23.

[16] Peter Berger, *Redeeming Laughter: The Comic Dimension of Human Experience* (New York, 1991), xiv.

consequently travels very badly. By the time a joke is explained in all its intricacy, any thought of laughter will probably have long vanished. Aristotle once remarked that surprise is an indispensable feature of laughter. But surprise cannot be patiently dissected and expounded at length. 'A joke explained', to cite Voltaire again, 'stops being a joke'.[17] Laughter theory thus travels as badly as humour itself. This point is all the more pertinent in that since the late nineteenth century, theories of laughter with scientific claims have been dominated by two disciplines, psychology and evolutionary biology, neither of which is very receptive to historical analysis. In psychology, Henri Bergson's influential 1899 lectures on laughter, and the work of Freud, stress the transhistorical universality of humour.[18] Following in the footsteps of Charles Darwin's work on the expression of emotion, evolutionary biology offers categories whose ultra-long time-frame also makes them recalcitrant to chronological periodisation. Neo-Darwinian theorists of the emotions in our own day such as Paul Ekman and his school espouse an evolutionist viewpoint which is difficult to reconcile with historical analysis.[19]

The starting point for this essay on eighteenth-century laughter is that we will be in a better posture for understanding something like the *Livre de caricatures* if we accept that laughter and laughter theory simply do not travel, are indeed radically incommensurable, and that humour from another period or another society is just basically not funny any longer. In this, I am taking further the methodological path mapped out by Robert Darnton, in his wonderful essay on the 'Great Cat Massacre', which appeared in 1984.[20] Darnton argued that the historian should be particularly interested in areas of opacity about past societies. It was precisely when historians could not see anything even faintly amusing in what people in the past found funny that one could be certain that there was something being transacted that was worthy of investigation. In the case that Darnton studied, it was the mass slaughter of neighbourhood cats by young apprentices in the neighbourhood of the Rue Saint-Séverin in Paris in the 1720s, a mass slaughter that, it was recorded, provoked unparalleled hilarity among the group. What indeed – Darnton nodded towards the phrasing of his Princeton colleague, the cultural anthropologist Clifford Geertz, with whom he collaborated – was

---

[17] Voltaire, *Lettres philosophiques*.

[18] H. Bergson, *Le rire: essai sur la signification du comique* (Paris, 1900); for Freud, see esp. his *The Joke and its Relation to the Unconscious* (1905).

[19] Charles Darwin, *The Expression of the Emotions in Man and Animals*, ed. P. Ekman, 3rd edn (1998). Besides the introductory material by Ekman in this edition, see too Ekman, *What the Face Reveals*, 2nd edn (Oxford, 2005); *idem*, *Emotion in the Human Face*, 2nd edn (Cambridge, 1982). Ekman appears to have never failed not to laugh at a historical joke

[20] Robert Darnton, 'Workers Revolt: The Great Cat Massacre of the Rue Saint-Séverin', in his *The Great Cat Massacre and Other Episodes in French Cultural History* (1984).

going on here? And understanding what indeed was going on – getting the joke in fact, understanding the laughter – would, Darnton wagered, permit us to gauge precisely what was specific, non-transferable, truly and intractably historical about a past society. Darnton wrote a brilliant essay, then a wonderful book, around this one grisly, surely unfunny, eighteenth-century 'comic' episode. Scholars of Charles-Germain de Saint-Aubin's *Livre de caricatures* will gulp at the prospect: for we have not one joke to decipher. We have nearly 400 comic drawings whose humour we have to unravel, whose capacity for eliciting laughter we have to understand.

In the daunting task of identifying the character of the humour to be found in the *Livre de caricatures*, it seems wisest to eschew laughter theories of the present day and to look for some guidance at least to those of the author's past. It is comforting that if we today lack the conceptual equipment to say just what people found funny in the eighteenth century and why, so did they. Laughter in the eighteenth century was almost as much of a puzzle and a conundrum as laughter theory is to us. For the era of Enlightenment which prided itself on coming up with rational answers to questions about the natural and social worlds, laughter was annoyingly difficult to pin down, as indeed Voltaire's comments highlight. Louis Poinsenet de Sivry, the author of a learned disquisition on laughter published in 1768, the *Traité des causes physiques et morales du rire*, agreed with Aristotle that laughter was the special privilege and province of humanity.[21] There was, it seemed, no individual in history who had never laughed. In antiquity even the supremely serious and virtuously po-faced Cato was known to have indulged once in his life, when he saw an ass eating thistles ... .[22] Poinsenet de Sivry, who could catalogue over a dozen forms of laughter (the gracious laugh, the silly laugh, the civil laugh, the forced laugh, the belly-laugh and so on), concluded that it was shocking that, despite the ubiquity of laughter and the existence of theories of laughter going back to antiquity, mankind had still to reach a real understanding of the essence of the phenomenon.[23] Yet this did not stop mankind from trying.

Early modern discussions of laughter invariably referred back to a sixteenth-century treatise on laughter written by Laurent Joubert, the *Traité du ris* or *Traité du rire* (the 'Treatise on Laughter'). Written in 1560, published in French in 1579, Joubert's treatise is a kind of ur-text of early modern discussions of laughter.[24] Its influence was very evident, for example, in Poinsenet de Sivry's 1768 text. Joubert is a helpful

---

[21] Louis Poinsenet de Sivry, *Traité des causes physiques et morales du rire, relativement à l'art de l'exciter* (Amsterdam 1768; reprint edn, Exeter 1986, ed. W. Brooks).

[22] The Cato example is given in Joubert (see references at n. 24): 228.

[23] Poinsenet de Sivry, *Traité des causes physiques*, 9.

[24] Laurent Joubert, *Traité du ris* (Slatkine reprint, Paris, 1970). See the English translation (with a helpful introduction): Laurent Joubert, *Treatise on Laughter*, ed. and trans. G. David

guide, supplying a whole agenda for considering laughter physiologically and aesthetically, medically and morally, culturally and socially. Joubert himself was a Montpellier medical professor by vocation, as indeed François Rabelais had been. The latter's *Gargantua* and *Pantagruel* could be taken as a faithful exemplification of Joubert's treatise – had the latter not in fact predated them by several decades. No matter.[25] For both Rabelais and Joubert viewed the issues of laughter along similar lines, as pitched between the disciplines of natural philosophy and medicine. (Evolutionary theory was two centuries distant, the psychological turn in laughter studies 300 years away.) Joubert expressed particular interest in questions such as: what happens to the human body when we laugh? What triggers off that laughter? And what was the experience of laughing like? He provided, for example, a kind of comparative acoustic typology of the laugh, noting a wide range of behavioural tics. Thus there were, he suggested, individuals who laugh like geese hissing, goslings grommeling, wood pigeons sighing, chicks peeping, horses neighing, strangulated dogs yapping and so on, through to individuals whose laugh resembles a pot of cabbage on the boil.[26] Joubert's physiology had it that laughter originates in the heart and radiates throughout the body by the muscles in the diaphragm, causing the chest to shake, the voice to tremble, the mouth to widen and open. Air coming up through the chest becomes too much for nostrils to handle, causing the mouth to open, setting off a range of facial movements as the eyes wrinkle, the cheeks expand and dimples form on and around the chin.

> Certainly [he states] there is nothing that gives more pleasure and recreation than a laughing face, with its wide, shining, clear and serene forehead, eyes shining, resplendent from any vantage point, and casting fire as do diamonds; cheeks vermillion and incarnate, mouth flush with the face, lips handsomely drawn back, . . . chin drawn in, widened and a bit recessed. All this is in the smallest laugh and in the smile, amidst salutations, caresses and greetings, favours an encounter of much grace.[27]

Joubert and his disciples were well aware, however, that, among the wide, gradated range of laughter forms that he could identify, less benign forms of laughter also existed. Two in particular stood out. First, there was sardonic laughter, which Joubert showed had been much described in antiquity.[28] It drew sustenance from Aristotle's proclamation that laughter

de Rocher (Alabama, 1980); and G. David de Rocher, *Rabelais's Laughers and Joubert's* Traité du Ris (Alabama, 1979).

[25] The works in the series appeared from 1532 to 1564 (Rabelais had died in 1553).

[26] Joubert, *Traité du ris*, 221. Following this cue, one later author maintained that four Galenic humours – melancholic, bilious, phlegmatic and sanguine temperaments – could be exactly mapped on to the different forms of laughter: hi-hi, hé-hé, ha-ha and ho-ho. *Ibid.*, *Épître*, no page number.

[27] Joubert, *Traité du ris*, 221.

[28] *Ibid.*, 225ff.

derived from 'the joy we have in observing the fact that we cannot be hurt by the evil at which we are indignant', and was characterised as an involuntary sneering laugh, often displaying the canine teeth. It feigned a true, sincere laugh. And it characterised the liar, the embittered and the ill-willed.

Ugly, rude and indecorous, sardonic laughter should be steered clear of. The same caution should be exercised by another non-benign form of laughter. Joubert painted a frightening picture of laughter when it gets out of hand, instancing

> the great opening of the mouth, the notable drawing back of the lips, the broken and trembling voice, the redness of the face, the sweat that sometimes comes out of the entire body, the spraying of the eyes with the effusion of tears, the rising of the veins in the forehead and throat, the coughing, the expelling of what was in their mouth and nose, the shaking of the chest, shoulders, arms, thighs, legs and the whole body, like a convulsion, the great pain in the ribs, sides and abdomen, the emptying of the bowels and the bladder, the weakness of the heart for want of breath, and some other effects.[29]

Joubert itemised some of the other effects as convulsions, fainting, apoplexy and indeed death. The death claim was repeated in the mid-seventeenth century by the physician Cureau de La Chambre who made this kind of 'vehement' laughter sound uncomfortably like orgasm.[30] Joubert's description and this evocation of what was, literally, a killer laugh was much drawn on throughout the seventeenth and eighteenth centuries. The vivacious, life-enhancing, attractive, salubrious laugh highlighted by Joubert thus had its dark avatar in mortiferous, uncontrollable, convulsive, body-shaking, sputum-spraying, self-soiling laugher. The latter form of laughter was also, as Joubert puts it, 'ugly, deformed, improper, indecent, unfitting and indecorous'.[31]

Joubert's basic physiology stood up relatively well to changes in medical knowledge in the seventeenth and eighteenth centuries, even as the credibility of the Galenic system of the humours on which it had been based began to erode. In his *Treatise on the Passions* (1649), for example, René Descartes would introduce a Harveian acceleration in the circulation of the blood as a predisposing factor to laughter as conceptualised by Joubert.[32] This mechanistic approach was elaborated further during the Enlightenment by post-humoral, anatomically minded physicians. The article on laughter in Diderot's *Encyclopédie*, for example, showed the continuing influence of Joubert's descriptions, but also sought a more precise, mechanistic understanding of laughter in terms

---

[29] Joubert, *Taité du ris*, 160–1.
[30] M. Cureau de La Chambre, *Les caractères des passions* (2 vols., Paris, 1658), I, 58.
[31] Joubert, *Traité du ris*, 52.
[32] René Descartes, *Traité des passions* (1649).

of the facial muscles.[33] Moreover, the laugh was only one form in the broad taxonomy of mouth behaviours with which medical writers now concerned themselves: laughter took its place in advanced mouth morphology alongside the yawn, the smile, the hiccup, the rictus, the grimace.[34] Though also following a mechanistic approach, the great German physiologist Haller in addition highlighted the importance of the nervous system, as one would expect from one of the key theorists of the cult of sensibility.[35] For Haller, the laugh was essentially an alteration in the respiratory system. He twinned it with the equally involuntary cough. But the human mind was somehow engaged in laughter, he noted, except of course in cases of tickling (a practice in which Joubert had been particularly interested in fact).[36] The cult of sensibility developing across the eighteenth century highlighted how certain types of individual were particularly prone to laughter. The hyper-nervous constitution of women pushed them towards hysterical, pathological laughter, for example, while the crude nervous system of the common people predisposed them to coarse rough Rabelaisian mirth.[37]

Much of Joubert's physiology of the laugh remained recognisably in place; yet shifts were going on in the semiotics of laughter. In the middle of the seventeenth century, as Quentin Skinner has noted, Thomas Hobbes picked up the darker aspect of Laurent Joubert's account of occasions for laughter. Whereas for Joubert mocking, sardonic laughter was only one form among many, for Hobbes all laughter came down to rejoicing in the misfortunes of others. 'The passion of Laughter is nothyng but a suddaine Glory arising from the suddaine Conception of some Eminency in our selves by Comparison with the Infirmityes of others.' For Hobbes, all laughter was derision.[38]

This view became highly influential in France as well as in England in the late seventeenth century. It was buttressed in France by the political and religious conjuncture, which predisposed towards a highly pessimistic evaluation of laughter. The Catholic Church after the Council of Trent had a gloomy predilection for avoiding humour at all costs. By the late seventeenth century, Bishop Bossuet would be defining laughter as 'a

---

[33] *Encyclopédie, ou Dictionnaire raisonné des sciences, des arts et des métiers, par une société de gens de lettres* (17 vols., Geneva, 1754–72), XIV, 298ff.

[34] See the excellent M. Guédron, *L'art de la grimace: cinq siècles d'excès de visage* (Paris, 2011).

[35] *Dr. Albert Haller's Physiology; Being a Course of Lectures upon the Visceral Anatomy and Vital Oeconomy of Human Bodies*, 2nd edn (1772), I, 346.

[36] 'Sis problemes du chatoulemant', in Joubert, *Traité du ris*, 201.

[37] A. Vila, *Enlightenment and Pathology: Sensibility in the Literature and Medicine of Eighteenth-Century France* (1998); L. Wilson, *Women and Medicine in the French Enlightenment: The Debate over 'Maladies des Femmes'* (1993).

[38] Thomas Hobbes, *The Elements of Law Natural and Politic*, ed. F. Tonnies, 2nd edn (1969), 42 (original 1634). Cf. Quentin Skinner, 'Hobbes and the Classical Theory of Laughter', in *idem, Visions of Politics*, III: *Hobbes and Civic Science* (Cambridge, 2002).

deplorable sickness of our hearts'.[39] 'Did Jesus laugh?' was a question that had divided theologians back to the early church fathers.[40] The answer in absolutist France appeared to be absolutely not. The abbé Thiers's 1686 treatise on games must, for example, rank as a high-water mark in this post-Tridentine age of humour-phobia. It was quite legitimate to laugh and joke, Thiers maintained, but he then went on to list such a wide range of taboo areas and inappropriate times for laughter that his conclusion, 'it is best not to undertake a joke at all', came as no surprise. 'It is not excessive joking that we must avoid, but joking of any sort.'[41]

Divine-Right Bourbon monarchy added its weight to the religious condemnation of laughter. The state not only supported the Church's teachings, but also led an onslaught on existing forms of humour and laughter in its own right. Molière was banned from Louis XIV's court for simply being funny, as, later, was the Comédie Italienne. Carnivalesque popular festivities such as the Feast of Fools and other parodic rituals which offered a forum for laughter were a particular target.[42] Versailles court culture did not prize laughter. Indeed, La Bruyère, subtle analyst of court mores in the late seventeenth century, noted that Rabelais had become simply unintelligible.[43] Court behaviour affected a stiff solemnity in which any kind of laughter (save arguably the cruellest) was out of place. The ancient position of court fool was placed in mothballs. One simply did not laugh at the Sun King, whose regime seemed wholeheartedly dedicated to the erasure of simple fun.[44]

The early eighteenth century brought a lightening of the mood, however, and a revival in the fortunes of that more benign form of laughter also sketched by Laurent Joubert. This more optimistic account of laughter originated across the Channel in writings by Shaftesbury, Steele, Addison, Hutcheson and others. For Shaftesbury, humour had a sort of civilising mission; its task was to 'polish one another and rub off our corners and rough sides by a sort of amicable collision'.[45] Raillery, mockery and sardonic laughter should be avoided. And decorous, polite laughter should replace both negative forms of laughter identified by Joubert – sneering, sardonic, Hobbesian laughter and also plebeian, quasi-mortiferous uproariousness. The preachers of

---

[39] Bossuet in his *Maximes et réflexions sur la comédie* (cited in Richardot, *Le rire des lumières*, 37).

[40] J. Le Goff, 'Jésus a-t-il ri?', *L'Histoire*, 158 (1992), 72–4.

[41] Jean-Baptiste Thiers, *Traité des jeux* (Paris, 1686), cited in Minois, *Histoire du rire*, 305–6.

[42] Sara Beam, *Laughing Matters: Farce and the Making of Absolutism in France* (Ithaca, NY, 2007); cf. Minois, *Histoire du rire*, 307ff.

[43] Cited in Minois, *Histoire du rire*, 369.

[44] Cf. Colin Jones, 'The King's Two Teeth', *History Workshop*, 65 (2008), 79–95.

[45] Shaftesbury cited in Vic Gatrell, *City of Laughter: Sex and Satire in Eighteenth-Century London* (2006), 169. Gatrell provides an excellent account of this optimistic whiggish reading of laughter, targeting Hobbesian pessimism.

politeness added to Joubert's physiology of the laugh a sense that laughter reflected not just social status but also the temperamental organisation of the self – as Voltaire put it, 'laughter arises from a gaiety of disposition, absolutely incompatible with contempt and indignation', an anti-Hobbesian statement if ever there was one.[46] It also had a collective history and social function. A progressive meta-narrative shaped up, which saw mankind emerging purposively from a Dark Age of Miserabilism. A nostalgic picture was painted of a kind of 'Merry France' that had been laid low by the forces of humourlessness that were the post-Tridentine church and the absolutist state.

How did these laughter debates, these early modern outcrops of laughter theory, play out in Charles-Germain de Saint-Aubin's *Livre de caricatures*? Before exploring the book's contents, I want first briefly to highlight a point about the nature of the drawings, and to consider key features in the book's production and audience. The book's title may lead us to expect something which picks up the caricatural genre which English satirists exploited and which in France Daumier would later develop as a fine art.[47] This is misleading. The term 'caricature' derives from the Italian, 'caricare', meaning to load, as in, in the case of portrait caricature, to exaggerate or to put emphasis upon some distinguishing feature of the subject. The term and its practice had allegedly been brought into France in 1665 when the Italian sculptor Bernini was visiting Louis XIV's court.[48] Yet it did not catch on either as a social practice or cultural form within France. It would not be until 1762 – a full century after the Bernini episode – that the word entered a French dictionary.[49] Diderot's *Encyclopédie* noted that the word applied to 'grotesque and extremely

---

[46] Voltaire, *L'enfant prodigue* (1738), preface, no page numbers.

[47] Werner Hofmann, *Caricature from Leonardo to Picasso* (1957), offers a good introduction to the origins of caricature, as, more recently, do Diana Donald, *The Age of Caricature: Satirical Prints in the Reign of George III* (New Haven and London, 1996), introduction; and T. Porterfield, ed., *The Efflorescence of Caricature, 1759–1838* (2010). See too E. Gombrich and E. Kris, *Caricature* (Harmondsworth, 1940); and Gombrich's two essays, 'The Cartoonist's Armoury' (in *idem, Meditations of a Hobby Horse* (1963)) and 'The Experiment of Caricature' (in *idem, Art and Illusion: A Study in the Psychology of Pictorial Representation* (1959)). Although many publications have been devoted to specifically French traditions of caricature, these tend to cut off at the end of Louis XIV's reign only to restart at the opening of the Revolution in 1789. Few texts concern caricature during the early and middle decades of the eighteenth century. One exception, which does cover the period of the Saint-Aubin drawings is André Blum, 'L'Estampe satirique et la caricature en France au XVIIIe siècle', *Gazette des Beaux-Arts*, 52 (1910), 379–420, 53 (1910), 69–87 – which, however, has scant mention of Charles-Germain.

[48] Irving Lavin, 'Bernini and the Art of Social Satire', *History of European Ideas*, 4 (1983), 365–420, and *idem*, 'High and Low before their Time: Bernini and the Art of Social Satire', in *Modern Art and Popular Culture: Readings in High and Low*, ed. Kirk Varnedoe and Adam Gopnik (New York, 1990), 18–50.

[49] *Dictionnaire de l'Académie Française*, 4th edn (1762) ('Caricature, s.f. Terme de peinture, emprunté de l'italien. C'est la meme chose que Charge en peinture'). Word searches in

disproportionate figures . . . that a painter, a sculptor or an engraver does in order to amuse or to make people laugh', adding sniffily, 'it is a kind of libertinage of the imagination that one should really only allow oneself for relaxation'.[50] And this seems to get the mood of the Saint-Aubin volume: comic drawings that displayed a 'libertinage of the imagination', and that constituted a pursuit appropriate for leisure-time.

Such a definition certainly chimes with the principal author of the *Livre de caricatures*'s description of the book's function. On the first page of the book, Charles-Germain recorded that in 1740,

> I found this volume on the quais [i.e. he purchased it from a Parisian *bouquiniste*] with figures naively drawn into it. My friends added captions and got me to continue this miscellany of follies which are not good enough to be shown to reasonable people. Fortunately there are still some empty headed people (*des crânes vides*) around. (675.1b)

Analysis suggests that around a third of the images in the book are fairly crude comic pictures which may have originally been drawn in another hand and then developed in ink and paint by the Saint-Aubin circle, and captions added. This 'miscellany of follies' was a kind of collective bricolage.[51]

Most of the finished drawings are by Charles-Germain himself, but we can also detect more than a dozen other hands, both in the drawings and in the captions which were an important ingredient in the book's humour. There are certainly contributions by Charles-Germain's two brothers, Gabriel and Augustin. In addition, a number of the jokes relate knowingly to individuals with links to the Saint-Aubin family drawn from the worlds of art, theatre, publishing and public administration. It seems plausible that such individuals were the 'empty heads' who composed the audience for Charles-Germain's inspiration, and this 'laughing group' may well have fitfully contributed their ideas to it too.[52] Yet if the making of the *Livre de caricatures* was something of a collective social event, Charles-Germain himself was principal contributor to the book's contents and overall impresario of its mirth.

The laughing group around Charles-Germain was an enduring one, for the contents of the *Livre de caricatures* suggest a facture over around three decades – from the 1740s through to the mid-1770s. Our strong sense is that this was a joke-book that Charles-Germain would bring out on festive occasions as a custom involving close friends and family. There is indeed

Frantext (USA: ARTFL) reveal less than a score of hits. These include Mirabeau's *L'ami des hommes*, Diderot's *Essais sur la peinture*, Voltaire's *Correspondance* and Mercier's *Tableau de Paris*.

[50] *Encyclopédie*, II, 684.

[51] On these issues of authorship, materiality and use, see Colin Jones and Emily Richardson, 'Materiality and Archaeology', in *Charles-Germain de Saint-Aubin*, ed. Carey, Jones and Richardson.

[52] On such 'laughing groups', see de Baecque, *Les éclats du rire*.

a whole thematic within the book of special days, such as Mardi Gras and also of *étrennes*, the jokes, riddles and gift-giving practices associated with New Year's Day. Many of the drawings have a kind of quizzing, puzzling quality. One drawing, for example, depicts a figure composed of sheets of music. 'Guess who?' asks the caption – and a later hand has added 'Rameau', the visual reference apparently to one of the characters in Rameau's opera *Platée*, first performed in 1745 (Figure 4: 675.56). This helping hand is very welcome. The in-joke character of the humour of our little laughing society makes it difficult to prise open the meanings of many of the drawings.⁵³

We should make clear one additional reason why the whole book remained an elaborate in-joke. Charles-Germain and his brothers can have been under no illusion that not everyone would find its humour very funny. In fact they would have been absolutely certain that had their book of jokes fallen into the hands of the legal or police authorities, its authors would have been thrown into prison and their precious book would have been publicly burned.⁵⁴ A great many of the 387 comic drawings were innocuous and mild, whimsical and harmless. Yet a fair proportion were rude, crude, offensive and irreverent, and carried a whiff of danger about them. Some, in the context of Ancien Régime France, were political dynamite. A man who publicly portrayed a naked Madame de Pompadour performing her intimate ablutions astride a bidet, while sundry Jesuits grovelled at her feet, would not be going anywhere fast in Ancien Régime France – except to the Bastille, that is (Figure 5: 675.282). Nor would the marquise have been anything but scandalised by the shrine to her radiant arse that Charles-Germain touchingly imagined (Figure 6: 675.281).

As these examples suggest, this volume of drawings is a book of surprises, and one surprise is to encounter political satire in Ancien Régime France in this visual form. This is extremely rare. Before 1789, France lacked the dynamic, explosively outspoken visual satire that Hogarth, Gillray, Rowlandson and many others provided for their English peers. France would only go down this route after 1789. There were some

⁵³ Pierre-Antoine Tardieu, husband of Charles-Germain's grand-daughter, who inherited the book in the 1820s, added captions explaining the jokes. The Rameau example is a case in point – though sometimes he got the jokes wrong. Jones and Richardson, 'Materiality and Archaeology'.

⁵⁴ On censorship, see esp. George Minois, *Censure et culture sous l'Ancien Régime* (Paris, 1995); Barbara de Negroni, *Lectures interdites: le travail des censeurs au XVIIIe siècle, 1723–1774* (Paris, 1995); and essays by Daniel Roche, Robert Darnton and Raymond Birn in Robert Darnton and Daniel Roche, eds., *Revolution in Print: The Press in France, 1775–1800* (Berkeley, Los Angeles and London, 1989). On the censorship of visual material, see ch. 3, 'Censorship of Caricature before 1830', in Robert Justin Goldstein, *Censorship of Political Caricature in Nineteenth-Century France* (Kent, OH, and London, 1989).

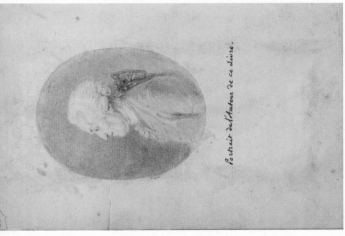

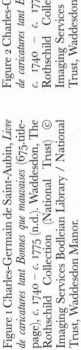

Figure 1 Charles-Germain de Saint-Aubin, *Livre de caricatures tant Bonnes que mauvaises* (675.title-page), *c.* 1740 – *c.* 1775 (n.d.). Waddesdon, The Rothschild Collection (National Trust) © Imaging Services Bodleian Library / National Trust, Waddesdon Manor.

Figure 2 Charles-Germain de Saint-Aubin, *Livre de caricatures tant Bonnes que mauvaises* (675.386), *c.* 1740 – *c.* 1775 (n.d.). Waddesdon, The Rothschild Collection (National Trust) © Imaging Services Bodleian Library / National Trust, Waddesdon Manor.

Figure 3 Charles-Germain de Saint-Aubin, *Livre de caricatures tant Bonnes que mauvaises* (675.63), *c.* 1740 – *c.* 1775 (n.d.). Waddesdon, The Rothschild Collection (National Trust) © Imaging Services Bodleian Library / National Trust, Waddesdon Manor.

Figure 4 Charles-Germain de Saint-Aubin, *Livre de caricatures tant Bonnes que mauvaises* (675.56), *c.* 1740 – *c.* 1775 (n.d.). Waddesdon, The Rothschild Collection (National Trust) © Imaging Services Bodleian Library / National Trust, Waddesdon Manor.

Figure 5 Charles-Germain de Saint-Aubin, *Livre de caricatures tant Bonnes que mauvaises* (675.282), *c.* 1740 – *c.* 1775 (n.d.). Waddesdon, The Rothschild Collection (National Trust) © Imaging Services Bodleian Library / National Trust, Waddesdon Manor.

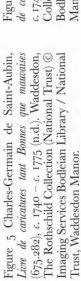

Figure 6 Charles-Germain de Saint-Aubin, *Livre de caricatures tant Bonnes que mauvaises* (675.281), *c.* 1740 – *c.* 1775 (n.d.). Waddesdon, The Rothschild Collection (National Trust) © Imaging Services Bodleian Library / National Trust, Waddesdon Manor.

Figure 7 Charles-Germain de Saint-Aubin, *Livre de caricatures tant Bonnes que mauvaises* (675-99), *c.* 1740 – *c.* 1775 (n.d.). Waddesdon, The Rothschild Collection (National Trust) © Imaging Services Bodleian Library / National Trust, Waddesdon Manor.

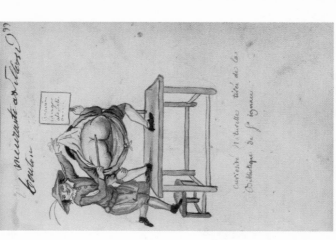

Figure 8 Charles-Germain de Saint-Aubin, *Livre de caricatures tant Bonnes que mauvaises* (675-144), *c.* 1740 – *c.* 1775 (n.d.). Waddesdon, The Rothschild Collection (National Trust) © Imaging Services Bodleian Library / National Trust, Waddesdon Manor.

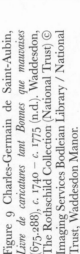

Figure 9 Charles-Germain de Saint-Aubin, *Livre de caricatures tant Bonnes que mauvaises* (675.288), *c.* 1740 – *c.* 1775 (n.d.). Waddesdon, The Rothschild Collection (National Trust) © Imaging Services Bodleian Library / National Trust, Waddesdon Manor.

Figure 10 Charles-Germain de Saint-Aubin, *Livre de caricatures tant Bonnes que mauvaises* (675.153), *c.* 1740 – *c.* 1775 (n.d.). Waddesdon, The Rothschild Collection (National Trust) © Imaging Services Bodleian Library / National Trust, Waddesdon Manor.

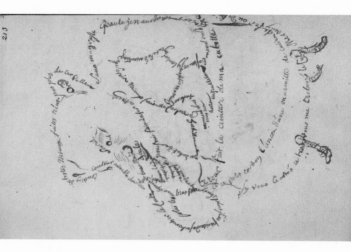

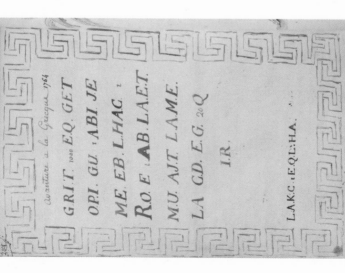

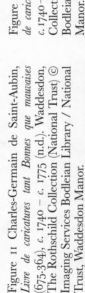

Figure 11 Charles-Germain de Saint-Aubin, *Livre de caricatures tant Bonnes que mauvaises* (675.364), *c.* 1740 – *c.* 1775 (n.d.). Waddesdon, The Rothschild Collection (National Trust) © Imaging Services Bodleian Library / National Trust, Waddesdon Manor.

Figure 12 Charles-Germain de Saint-Aubin, *Livre de caricatures tant Bonnes que mauvaises* (675.213), *c.* 1740 – *c.* 1775 (n.d.). Waddesdon, The Rothschild Collection (National Trust) © Imaging Services Bodleian Library / National Trust, Waddesdon Manor.

Figure 14 Charles-Germain de Saint-Aubin, *Livre de caricatures tant Bonnes que mauvaises* (675-248), *c.* 1740 – *c.* 1775 (n.d.), Waddesdon, The Rothschild Collection (National Trust) © Imaging Services Bodleian Library / National Trust, Waddesdon Manor.

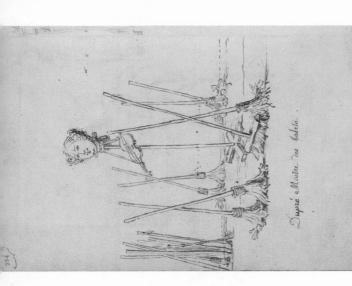

Figure 13 Charles-Germain de Saint-Aubin, *Livre de caricatures tant Bonnes que mauvaises* (675-384), *c.* 1740 – *c.* 1775 (n.d.), Waddesdon, The Rothschild Collection (National Trust) © Imaging Services Bodleian Library / National Trust, Waddesdon Manor.

Figure 16 Charles-Germain de Saint-Aubin, *Livre de caricatures tant Bonnes que mauvaises* (675.138–9), *c.* 1740 – *c.* 1775 (n.d.). Waddesdon, The Rothschild Collection (National Trust) © Imaging Services Bodleian Library / National Trust, Waddesdon Manor.

Figure 15 Charles-Germain de Saint-Aubin, *Livre de caricatures tant Bonnes que mauvaises* (675.198–9), *c.* 1740 – *c.* 1775 (n.d.). Waddesdon, The Rothschild Collection (National Trust) © Imaging Services Bodleian Library / National Trust, Waddesdon Manor.

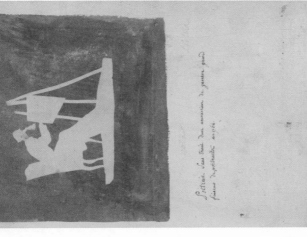

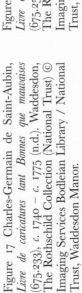

Figure 17 Charles-Germain de Saint-Aubin, *Livre de caricatures tant Bonnes que mauvaises* (675-253), *c.* 1740 – *c.* 1775 (n.d.). Waddesdon, The Rothschild Collection (National Trust) © Imaging Services Bodleian Library / National Trust, Waddesdon Manor.

Figure 18 Charles-Germain de Saint-Aubin, *Livre de caricatures tant Bonnes que mauvaises* (675-253), *c.* 1740 – *c.* 1775 (n.d.). Waddesdon, The Rothschild Collection (National Trust) © Imaging Services Bodleian Library / National Trust, Waddesdon Manor.

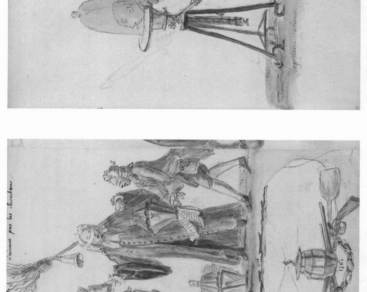

Figure 19 Charles-Germain de Saint-Aubin, *Livre de caricatures tant Bonnes que mauvaises* (675.374), *c.* 1740 – *c.* 1775 (n.d.). Waddesdon, The Rothschild Collection (National Trust) © Imaging Services Bodleian Library / National Trust, Waddesdon Manor.

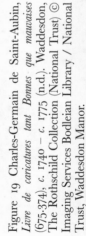

Figure 20 Charles-Germain de Saint-Aubin, *Livre de caricatures tant Bonnes que mauvaises* (675.209), *c.* 1740 – *c.* 1775 (n.d.). Waddesdon, The Rothschild Collection (National Trust) © Imaging Services Bodleian Library / National Trust, Waddesdon Manor.

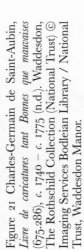

Figure 21 Charles-Germain de Saint-Aubin, *Livre de caricatures tant Bonnes que mauvaises* (675.286), *c.* 1740 – *c.* 1775 (n.d.). Waddesdon, The Rothschild Collection (National Trust) © Imaging Services Bodleian Library / National Trust, Waddesdon Manor.

Figure 22 Charles-Germain de Saint-Aubin, *Livre de caricatures tant Bonnes que mauvaises* (675-339), *c.* 1740 – *c.* 1775 (n.d.). Waddesdon, The Rothschild Collection (National Trust) © Imaging Services Bodleian Library / National Trust, Waddesdon Manor.

Figure 23 Charles-Germain de Saint-Aubin, *Livre de caricatures tant Bonnes que mauvaises* (675.356), *c.* 1740 – *c.* 1775 (n.d.). Waddesdon, The Rothschild Collection (National Trust) © Imaging Services Bodleian Library / National Trust, Waddesdon Manor.

Figure 24 Charles-Germain de Saint-Aubin, *Livre de caricatures tant Bonnes que mauvaises* (675.276), *c.* 1740 – *c.* 1775 (n.d.). Waddesdon, The Rothschild Collection (National Trust) © Imaging Services Bodleian Library / National Trust, Waddesdon Manor.

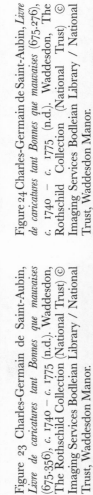

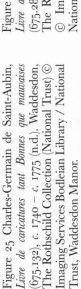

Figure 25 Charles-Germain de Saint-Aubin, *Livre de caricatures tant Bonnes que mauvaises* (675.132), *c.* 1740 – *c.* 1775 (n.d.). Waddesdon, The Rothschild Collection (National Trust) © Imaging Services Bodleian Library / National Trust, Waddesdon Manor.

Figure 26 Charles-Germain de Saint-Aubin, *Livre de caricatures tant Bonnes que mauvaises* (675.285), *c.* 1740 – *c.* 1775 (n.d.). Waddesdon, The Rothschild Collection (National Trust) © Imaging Services Bodleian Library / National Trust, Waddesdon Manor.

pre-1789 French exceptions, it is true: historians have milked all they can out of a niche market in pornography, on occasion relating to the royal family, which was political in scope.[55] But political satire in Bourbon France simply lacked a solid base in the visual arts. Censorship of the image seems to have worked even more effectively than censorship of the word. This is one reason our book is such a rarity.

In order to analyse the forms that the humour of the book takes, it is helpful to turn again to our friend Laurent Joubert. In his laughter treatise, Joubert derives from Aristotle the idea that there can be humour in words and humour in deeds.[56] Taken together, these sub-categories give a good sense of the range of Saint-Aubin humour. The first two of Joubert's five sub-categories of humour in deeds are the exposure of the shameful parts and the exhibiting of the behind. The Madame de Pompadour examples highlight this. There are dozens of arses in the *Livre des culs*. The fairgound wonder-arse at 675.99 (Figure 7), for example, given an anti-Jesuit spin by the caption, highlights scatological humour (for the shameful parts are almost always anal rather than genital or erotic in focus) as one of the most significant registers in which Saint-Aubin works. The third group of occasions for laughter cited by Joubert is the comic fall – the familiar prat-fall in essence – examples of which do not lack in the *Livre de caricatures* (Figure 8: 675.144). The fourth occasion for laughter is the misapprehension of taste – as, in Joubert's words, 'when one mistakes stinking smells for sweet'.[57] This kind of misprision is evident, to give a single example, in this drawing of perfumed lips (Figure 9: 675.288). Joubert's fifth category is the somewhat indeterminate 'light damage', or inconsequential harm, of which there are any number of examples. In drawing 675.153, for example, blind Belisarius is about to fall down the hole (Figure 10).[58]

Besides his five sub-categories of laughter through deeds, Joubert, taking his cue from Aristotle, also underlined the role of words in stimulating laughter. He cited a whole slew of linguistic devices which could provoke laughter, including puzzles, metaphors, allegories and innuendoes. The *Livre de caricatures* is full of such devices, ranging from

[55] The English tradition is superbly encapsulated by Gatrell, *City of Laughter*. For post-1789 France, see esp. James Cuno, ed., *French Caricature and the French Revolution, 1789–99*, ex. cat., Grunwald Center for the Graphic Arts, Wight Art Gallery, University of California (Los Angeles, 1988); Antoine de Baecque, *La caricature révolutionnaire* (Paris, 1988); and Claude Langlois, *La caricature contre-révolutionnaire* (Paris, 1988). For the pornographic tradition, see Robert Darnton, *The Devil in the Holy Water, or the Art of Slander from Louis XIV to Napoleon* (Philadelphia, 2010).

[56] Joubert, *Traité du ris*, ch. 2, 'Des fais ridicules', 16ff, and ch. 3, 'Des propos ridicules', 29ff.

[57] *Ibid.*, 26.

[58] Cf. 675.3, 675.305.

puzzles like the Rameau example cited earlier (Figure 1), through to forms such as the rebus (Figure 11: 675.364), jokey textualised drawings (Figure 12: 675.213), allegories and all manner of puns. The celebrity dancer Dupré is represented as master of the ballet – or is it master of the brooms (*balais*) (Figure 13: 675.384)? Then again, the caption, the '3 synonyms of the abbé Gouget', is deliberately misleading, for depicted are only two forms of crane (or *grue*), the bird and the lifting gear (Figure 14: 675.248). Where is the third? *Grue* was a slang word for whore. It may well be Madame de Pompadour who is being invisibly targeted.[59]

Many of the linguistic triggers of laughter are deliberately set up to work through contrast between text and the accompanying image. Thus the rule of Polykleitos, the measure of ideal human beauty derived from Ancient Greece, is illustrated with a small, dumpy, weeble-like figure (675.39). Similarly, the drawing of an ancient vessel – which was in fact copied from the *Recueil d'antiquités* of the polymathic proto-archaeologist, the comte de Caylus – is made to look ridiculous by a caption which states that what went on to become a pomade pot for Queen Christina of Sweden and holy water stoup for the pope started life as the chamberpot of Queen Semiramis of Babylon (675.126).[60] The practice of linking images on facing pages also allows the potential for such incongruities to be exploited. Thus the images at 675.198–9 show a bare-arsed couple blowing farts at each other in a mock instantiation of civilised politesse (Figure 15). Such matching farts are evident in a similar, punning couplet (Figure 16: 675.138–9). Here, the *propositions de paix* could be either peace (*paix*) or fart (*pet*) proposals. Meanwhile the enema-syringe-wielding Dutch Stadtholder is poised to administer his own radical solutions to both. These drawings refer to the inglorious peace negotiations leading to the Treaty of Aix-la-Chapelle after the War of Austrian Succession in 1748.

In these last two sets of images, the crudeness of the body, specifically the arse, seems to be an implicit critique of both high-falutin politesse and diplomatic claims to glory. The truth of the arse finds out the hollow portentousness of elite culture. This charge brings us close to the influential notion of grotesque realism expounded by the Russian formalist critic, Mikhael Bakhtin.[61] Bakhtin analysed Renaissance popular culture by way of the writings of Rabelais, and he highlighted how the collective and festive deployment of the crude and obscene body

---

[59] On this point, see the discussion in Colin Jones, *Madame de Pompadour: Images of a Mistress* (2002), 141.

[60] Cf. Perrin Stein, 'The Vase as a Site for Satire', in *Charles-Germain de Saint-Aubin*, ed. Carey, Jones and Richardson.

[61] M. Bakhtin, *Rabelais and his World* (Cambridge, MA, 1968).

humour of the streets offered a parodic critique of elite culture. Certainly within the *Livre de caricatures* there is more than enough arsiness to suggest a willing embrace of this aspect of Rabelaisian humour. The Rabelaisian reference point is also evident in a number of images which depict scenes from the author or else foreground images that had accompanied past editions of his works.[62] Many of the comic drawings which lack an obvious humorous point also celebrate good and riotous living in a way of which Rabelais would doubtless have approved.

Although the *Livre de caricatures* is thus ironic about politeness, the spirit of the book does overlap with the meta-narrative developed by theorists of politeness according to which Merry France of yore had been wrongly turned away from the paths of happiness by the dark forces of politico-religious miserabilism. The book not only presides over a kind of Rabelaisian Second Coming. On a related note, it also makes particular reference to long-defunct provincial convivial associations and ceremonies linked to the old Feasts of Fools such as the convivial group of the Mère Folle (the 'Mad Mother'), which had flourished in Dijon from the late Middle Ages before being snuffed out by central government in the 1630s.[63]

As well as drawing inspiration from the archaeology of French laughter, the Saint-Aubin circle was also probably influenced by more recent laughter societies, such as the Régiment de la Calotte. Formed in 1702, and coming to prominence under the freer mores of the Regency after 1715, the Régiment de la Calotte had been dedicated to ridiculing pretensions and tyranny in high Parisian society, selecting as the butts of its humour those who needed to be laughed into better, saner ways.[64] This 'aristocratic comicocacry'[65] used patrician wit in order to laugh down at its pretentious social and upwardly-mobile inferiors through the publication of contemptuous and humorous attacks. Though initially protected by high state officials, the group over-reached itself by publishing obscene verbal ditties about the king's new mistress, Madame de Pompadour, in the late 1740s and was dissolved forthwith by royal fiat.[66]

---

[62] See e.g. 675.75 and 675.111 for direct Rabelaisian citations. For a generally 'Rabelaisian' spirit, cf. 675.72–3 and 675.271.

[63] The Saint-Aubins derived much of their material on the topic from the antiquarian work, *Mémoire pour servir à l'histoire de la fête des fous* published by the antiquarian, du Tilliot: Jean-Bénigne Lucotte du Tilliot, *Mémoire pour servir à l'histoire de la fête des fous* (Lausanne and Geneva, 1751). There had been an earlier 1741 edition. For related drawings, see 675.161, 675.372.

[64] De Baecque, *Les éclats du rire*, esp. ch. 1, 'Le Régiment de la Calotte, ou les stratégies aristocratiques du rire bel esprit (1702–52)'.

[65] *Ibid.*, 44.

[66] There is a good account of the episode in Evelyne Lever, *Madame de Pompadour* (Paris, 2000), 145ff. See too Robert Darnton, *Public Opinion and Communication Networks*

The two laughter groups shared much in common, notably festive sociability, a firm belief in alcohol as a life-giving force and as a stimulus for jollity, and deep antagonism towards Madame de Pompadour. Many of the motifs mentioned in the writings of the Régiment de la Calotte – the *calotte* (or ecclesiastical skullcap), the jester's stick or *marotte*, the caps and bells of folly, whirligigs, antlers and rats – are also echoed in the *Livre de caricatures*. Yet whereas the Régiment operated largely through text, the Saint-Aubin circle preferred visual imagery. And while the pronouncements of the Régiment were published openly, the Saint-Aubins in contrast kept their humour secret and under wraps. Nor was there much that was aristocratic about the Saint-Aubins' sense of humour either. The Régiment's sense of humour had been very *de haut en bas*, and seemed closer to the cruel Hobbesian ethic than was the case with the altogether more benign Saint-Aubin circle. There is little overt patrician refinement in the *Livre de caricatures*, literary or otherwise. Indeed, the book glories in the transgression of refinement in all its forms. As the *Livre des culs* label and its overall, all-round arsiness suggests, it claimed to be 'popular' rather than elitist.

The principal author of a joke-book in which a fart is never far away was something of a hybrid, who was well situated to cross both generic and social boundaries. Charles-Germain de Saint-Aubin worked in trade – a luxury trade, it is true – but this still placed him irredeemably outside the French status elite. In autobiographical fragments in his *Recueil de plantes*, he evoked his great-grandfather who had been a clog-wearing peasant from the Beauvaisis. But that was in the distant past. The Saint-Aubin family may not have been patrician but they were emphatically not plebeian. Charles-Germain was a pillar of bourgeois respectability, a frequenter of the royal court, who held his head high among the most elevated company, a member of the public (to use a classic Enlightenment distinction) but not one of the people. It would be foolish to imagine the *Livre de caricatures* somehow channelling Rabelaisian-esque popular culture in a direct and unmediated form. Its elaborate word games and engagement with antiquarian scholarship on humour back to Rabelais show that. Rather, the work engages with popular culture at a meta level, playing with the plebeian, making jokes through it, offering visual evocations of it, trying to chart its history – in short slumming with it to some degree. There may be a lot of arsiness in the Saint-Aubin *Livre de*

in *Eighteenth-Century Paris*, www.historycooperative.org/ahr/darnton_files/darnton/pocn/, especially sub-section entitled 'Court Politics'. Further examples can be found in Marie André Alfred Emile Raunié, *Chansonnier historique du XVIIIe siècle ... Recueil Clairembault-Maurepas...* (10 vols., Paris, 1879–84), esp. VII: 'Le règne de Louis XV: Madame de Châteauroux et Madame de Pompadour, 1743–1763'.

caricatures – but it is cerebral arsiness, developed in the interests of a very idiosyncratic sense of humour.[67]

The *Livre de caricatures* thus reveals its authors as individuals capable of crossing the social boundary from bourgeois to plebeian, and of appropriating traits and features of the culture of the streets, turning them into something that, if not high art, was not low art either. The simple, sometimes even rough and crude, execution of the drawings and colouring is likewise a bit of a pose. In fact the *Livre de caricatures* contains numerous visual cues to the history of art. There are quotations from or homages to Arcimboldo (Figure 17: 675.233) and Lyotard (Figure 18: 675.253) – as also to Bosch, Jacques Callot, Della Bella, Poussin, Watteau and Boucher – and doubtless others.[68] A lot of these drawings may look vulgar – but probably only to the vulgar. It is very erudite vulgarity.

Capable of crossing generic boundaries between high and low, the *Livre de caricatures* also ceaselessly switches from reality to fantasy. The latter half of the volume appears to offer many insights into Parisian street-life, most notably in the 1750s and 1760s. Thus we are shown, by way of example, the new Paris street lighting system (Figure 19: 675.374), the abolition of cumbersome shop signs, new taxes on street traders, and the invention of a city postal system.[69] Talking points and *causes célèbres* of the Parisian public sphere are also present: the publication of the *Encyclopédie*, for example, elections to the Académie française and Académie des sciences, lectures from the Academy of Painting, the furore caused by La Mettrie's 'man machine' and musical polemics between Rameau and the supporters of Lully.[70] Yet as these images hint, Saint-Aubin transcends the simple chronicle. He invariably includes a choice artistic trait, a satirical barb, a humorous nudge, a smidgeon of fantasy. Invariably, the truth of the arse implicitly subverts any intellectual claims being made.

It would thus be misguided to take the *Livre de caricatures* at the face value it disingenuously presents. Street-traders, for example, might be shown uttering their customary cries in a way that was only too familiar to Charles-Germain, who lived in the parish of Saint-Eustache, next

[67] As was the case, it must be said, with Rabelais.

[68] See as follows: Bosch, 675.102; Callot, 675.11; Della Bella, 675.27; Poussin, 675.379; Watteau, 675.26 and Boucher, 675.303. These are only single examples; in some cases there are multiple quotations. Besides the pastoral style and evidence of heraldry (e.g. 675.2, 675.181), there is a lot of chinoiserie throughout. Charles-Germain's *papillonneries* and his botanical drawings are also referenced (675.163; 675.320; 675.160).

[69] For shop-signs, 675.358; for street traders, 675.348; for the post, 675.347.

[70] For the *Encyclopédie*, 675.162 and 675.313; for the Académies, 675.266, 675.341 and 675.355; for La Mettrie, 675.202; plus many on Rameau, including 675.239 and 675.241.

to Les Halles.[71] But such images are as much a commentary on the artistic genre of the *cris de Paris*, which went back to the Renaissance, as a verisimilitudinal description of life on the streets.[72] Similarly, representations of street theatre reference *commedia dell'arte*, but more in regard to artistic tradition than to real life players.[73] Then again, shepherds evoke the mock pastoral not the authentically rustic. Similarly, the Savoyard beggars and manual workers who composed a significant part of the Parisian immigrant labour force are here too, but more often than not in the guise of stage Savoyards, who look fancy and wear high heels.[74]

If the *Livre de caricatures* sardonically and whimsically theatricalises Parisian street life and culture, it also presents a fascinating perspective on the Parisian stage. The Saint-Aubins had numerous contacts within the theatrical world, and, like many of their social level, would have been avid theatre-goers. Stage celebrities – the ballet-dancers Dupré (Figure 13), Gaetan Vestris, Mademoiselle Heinel, the actor Le Kain and the poet and dramatist Sedaine – all receive particular attention, and some indeed may well have formed part of the Saint-Aubin circle.[75] Other polite public spectacles also get a mention: the scientific demonstrations of the abbé Nollet, for example, who is captured suffocating himself in his own air-pump (Figure 20: 675. 209), the physics experiments of the comte de Lauraguais and the ocular harpischord of the abbé Castel.[76] The underlying theme of many of these drawings is the need to puncture the pretentious showiness of urban spectacle, so as to reveal the somewhat humdrum underlying reality. Thus while Charles-Germain transmutes the realism of the streets to urban fantasy, he also draws on the mock heroic mood to collapse the purposively spectacular into the drab and everyday.

Overall, the *Livre de caricatures* is a very Parisian book – and no doubt this is only to be expected from someone who strayed beyond city walls

---

[71] Cf. 675.24, 675.330.

[72] V. Milliot, *Les cris de Paris, ou le peuple travesti: les représentations des petits métiers parisiens (XVIe–XVIIIe siècles)* (Paris, 1995).

[73] E.g. 675.17.

[74] E.g. 675.98, 675.232. Cf. E. Munhall, 'Savoyards in Eighteenth-Century French Art', *Apollo*, 87 (1968), 86–94.

[75] For Vestris, 675.380; for Heinel, 675.102; for Le Kain, 675.283; and for Sedaine, 675.353, 675.360. For plays, see too 675.142, 675.222–3, 675.352, 675.384. On Charles-Germain's theatrical links, see M. Ledbury, *Sedaine, Greuze and the Boundaries of Genre* (Oxford, 2000); *idem*, 'Theatrical Life', in *Charles-Germain de Saint-Aubin*, ed. Carey, Jones and Richardson.

[76] For Lauraguais, 675.176; for Castel, 675.302. See also 675.175 for the panic about the 'Beast' of the Gévaudan, and 675.377 for the papal conclave of 1774. The latter images are rare for being outside the Paris–Versailles axis which frames the volume as a whole.

almost only so as to get to the royal court at Versailles.[77] Yet Charles-Germain evidently enjoyed switching elements and crossing boundaries of all kinds. The *Livre de caricatures* is a work which reveals a sensibility comprehensively transformed by knowledge of – and, ultimately, disdain towards – the showy ostentation of court life at Versailles, which of course was shadowed in the fashion business in which Charles-Germain made his living. The crown and the court aristocracy were among the best clients for his fancy embroidery. This meant that he and, for related reasons, his brothers were perfectly situated within networks of courtly patronage to be on the receiving end of current courtly tittle-tattle, and to be able to grasp the essence of court mores. No doubt in order to prosper at court, Charles-Germain had to play the court games. Yet the *Livre de caricatures* is full of references to the dark side of court life – its sex, its lies, its propaganda. The 1756 alliance between France and Austria, arranged by Madame de Pompadour and the Austrian envoy Starhemberg (Figure 21: 675.286) for example, is given satirical treatment, as are the military campaign of 1757, the melting down of court silver to finance the war effort (Figure 22: 675.339), the torture of Louis XV's would-be assassin Damiens in the same year, the suppression of the Jesuit Order and the ups and downs of the Jansenist conflict pitting the archbishop of Paris against the Paris parlement. Though the book seems to end in 1775, this just leaves enough time to note the rumours about the sexual frigidity of the duc de Berry, the future Louis XVI, and his Austrian bride, Marie-Antoinette (Figure 23: 675.356).[78]

The social boundary-crosser who brought a sense of Versailles culture to his depiction of Parisian cultural life thus applied a very frondeur-ish Parisian sensibility to court life at Versailles. We see this most spectacularly in his treatment of Madame de Pompadour, Louis XV's official mistress from 1745 to her death in 1764.[79] The marquise was one of the great patrons of the arts and of the luxury trades in the eighteenth century, and in her way a fashion icon. Saint-Aubin knew her personally rather well, and dedicated a book of flower drawings to her; he encouraged her to draw, particularly flower designs; and he humbly received the gifts she made him of inks imported from China and baubles and porcelain from Japan.[80] He enjoyed terms of some intimacy with the marquise, visiting her home, the present-day Elysée palace, and its gardens. Yet despite

---

[77] Charles-Germain's autobiographical fragments in the *Recueil des plantes* reveal that his father forbade him to go to Lyon as a youth to learn silk design; and that he only made trips outside the city in the early 1770s to Flanders and Provence.

[78] For the 1757 campaign, 675.354; Damiens affair, 675.262–263; Jesuits, 675.354; Jansenist issues, 675.357.

[79] Lever, *Madame de Pompadour*; Jones, *Madame de Pompadour*.

[80] The documents on the settlement of the estate, discussed in Advielle, *Renseignements intimes*, are located at Archives Nationales, ET LIV 1029; and the 1780 will at ET XI 736.

these close bonds between the two, Charles-Germain revealed himself a scabrous and abrasive critic of the marquise as soon as he picked up his pencil or prepared his palette. Around a dozen drawings make direct reference to Pompadour. All are hostile and critical, sometimes scandalously so. Matching the bidet scene cited above is an equally obscene rendition of a Pompadour in full cardinal's apparel, crudely and scatologically shattering the dreams of preferment of her one-time favourite, the abbé de Bernis (Figure 24: 675.276).[81]

The attacks on Madame de Pompadour highlighted particularly vehemently her *arrivisme*. Pompadour came from trade – her critics never allowed her to forget her family name (Poisson – 'fish' in French) (Figure 25: 675.132).[82] She had used her beauty and cunning to gain a social niche way above her station. To the author of the *Livre de caricatures*, her promotion of a circle of parvenu financiers threatened the state with ruin. She feminised the aristocracy and the king, who turned to cooking and tapestry-making.[83] The reign of *la Pompadour* was one where the whole establishment made a god of money, and was riddled with moral failings. Besides mistresses on the make, there were greedy financiers avid for gain at anyone's expense, ministers flying too high for their abilities, power-mad Jesuits out to take over the world, and uppity parlements thinking they were intelligent enough to rule. Politics was a game of ins and outs, ups and downs on the wheel of fortune (Figure 26: 675.285).[84] In Charles-Germain's vision, Madame de Pompadour was a perfect representation of the ferment of corruption which was rotting traditional values and producing a risible inauthenticity. Anything of value in this world was likely to be as fragile and as ephemeral as the butterflies which were Charles-Germain's special signature.

Let us move from butterflies to cats. In the 'Cat Massacre' article that I mentioned earlier and that I have used as a heuristic device in this paper, Robert Darnton's analysis of the Saint-Séverin cat-slaughter highlights underlying class tensions between workers and their masters.[85] One of the reasons that the artisans of the Rue Saint-Séverin found cat-killing so funny, he argues, was that they were enjoying a joke at the expense of their social betters. Killing their master's cats and the laughter that this instigated was social revolt, metaphorised. It was if, in other

Much of the detail on Charles-Germain's relations with Madame de Pompadour come from the fragments in the *Recueil de plantes*.

[81] Other anti-Pompadour drawings include drawings at 225, 316–17, 322, 328, 339, 359.

[82] Cf. 675.235.

[83] 675.165, 675.359. On the latter drawing, see Juliet Carey, 'The King and his Embroiderer', in *Charles-Germain de Saint-Aubin*, ed. Carey, Jones and Richardson.

[84] Making a god of money, 675.308; greedy financiers, 675.294; ministers, 675.103, 675.121, 675.318; Jesuits, 675.277, 675.354; and parlements, 675.357.

[85] See above, p. 8.

words, this cat-killing somehow prefigured the aristocrat-killing of the same neighbourhoods in the radical phase of the French Revolution: social revolt first as farce and second as tragedy, to reverse the more usual Marxian sequence. Using the same logic, we might wonder: was Charles-Germain de Saint-Aubin a proto-Revolutionary?

A by now venerable current of historiography places great store by an alleged 'desacralisation' of attitudes towards the crown in particular and the social and political elite over the course of the eighteenth century.[86] Certainly it is tempting to rank the *Livre de caricatures* alongside other evidence of desacralisation, and to suppose that the attitudes found within the volume must have been widespread, but that similar works have simply not survived. Yet such a move is perhaps too easy, and certainly fails to do justice to this extraordinary work and the idiosyncratic sensibility of its principal author. Moreover, even leaving aside some of the presuppositions of the 'desacralisation thesis' (to what extent, for example, had attitudes to the crown in the past ever been homogeneously 'sacralised'?), it is difficult not to conclude that Charles-Germain's proto-Revolutionary credentials are not strong. He closed the *Livre de caricatures* in 1775. He died in March 1786, before the pre-Revolution, let alone the Revolution, had started. There was very little about the situation in 1786 which would allow anyone – let alone an ageing royal embroiderer – to think a Revolutionary process was about to unfold. Faced with what he knew, Charles-Germain seems to have accepted the follies of the world as, precisely, the follies of the world. If they excited anything in him, it was not a yearning for a new political world, but an ingenuity in finding ways of responding to them, critically, yes – but also artistically, philosophically, ideologically, wittily and humorously. He drew on the cultural resources at hand and operated within inherited frameworks of humour coloured, as I have suggested, by a range of influences from Laurent Joubert, François Rabelais and the Feast of Fools through to the more-recent Régiment de la Calotte, so as to create a very original and unusual book of jokes, that revelled in contradicting all available narratives and theories of humour. It is true that in his humour, disdain emerges, but it is invariably for his social superiors, and there is little resembling systematic Hobbesian contempt for inferiors. There are glimpses in the work of the civilising humour of the sensibility school that opposed Hobbesian pessimism. Yet as we have seen, current politeness was also a target for his humour too,

---

[86] The desacralization thesis is laid out in Jeffrey Merrick, *The Desacralisation of the French Monarchy in the Eighteenth Century* (Baton Rouge, 1990); and Dale Van Kley, 'The Religious Origins of the Revolution, 1560–1791', in Peter R. Campbell, *The Origins of the French Revolution* (Houndmills, 2006), 160–90. See too the critique of Jens Ivo Engels, 'Désigner, espérer, assumer la réalité: le roi de France perçu par ses sujets, 1680–1750', *Revue d'histoire moderne et contemporaine*, 50 (2003), 96–126, and *idem*, 'Beyond Sacral Monarchy: A New Look at the Image of the Early Modern French Monarchy', *French History*, 15 (2001), 139–58.

and he revelled in Rabelais-style slumming in popular culture. Far from looking forward to a new age of reason and good manners, moreover, Saint-Aubin looked fondly back on a rumbustious and fictive 'Merry France', and sought to effect its recovery, anachronistically of course. If there was anything of the Revolutionary about him, it was the backward-looking Revolutionary. Revolutionary, Charles-Germain de Saint-Aubin? *Son cul* is the more obvious response.

Furthermore, we lose much about Charles-Germain in seeking to slot him into any prefabricated social or political identity. What is most striking about his humour was its deliberate predilection for crossing borders and denying stable identities – even and especially that most stolid bourgeois identity which everything else that we know about his life proclaims. His 'laughing over boundaries' operated in contradictory, paradoxical ways. His laughter transcended boundaries; but boundary-breaking was also the subject of much of his humour. Social (and sexual) climbing was for him a cardinal sin, and he reserved his most acerbic laughter for those (like his patron, Madame de Pompadour) who thought they could cross boundaries with impunity – but were found out, so to speak, and commonly mocked for their pretentiousness. Charles-Germain was a serial boundary-breaker, and the crossing of boundaries of every sort – from social frontiers through to artistic styles and genres, and the very distinction between the world and the imagination, and between reality and fantasy – were hard-wired into his being. But he refrained from revealing his views and evaded being ever found out to be the author of these drawings. Secrecy was not only a pragmatic lifeline. Coming out with such drawings would have transformed him and them into something they emphatically were not.

It is probably more profitable, in conclusion, to rank the Saint-Aubin *Livre de caricatures* less as a case-history than as a microhistory, drawing its value not from any putative representative value but from its stubborn exceptionalism. Our French royal embroiderer, in this estimation, would be the same frame as Menocchio, the wild, heterodox Friulian miller at the centre of Carlo Ginzburg's classic microhistorical study *The Cheese and the Worms*.[87] We find in both figures not the fixed and replicable *mentalité* of a preexistent social category, but rather a quirkily individual temperament, invaluable to the historian precisely because of its untypicality and its exceptionality. Yet Menocchio never laughed – or if he did Carlo Ginzburg kept quiet about it. Spending time in the company of Charles-Germain de Saint-Aubin was (and is) fun. He made people laugh. And although my whole approach in this paper has been to argue that humour is radically incommensurable between time periods – that it just does not travel – I

---

[87] Carlo Ginzburg, *The Cheese and the Worms: The Cosmos of a Sixteenth-Century Miller*, English trans. (Baltimore, MD, 1980).

hope in a way that my argument has not been totally convincing. For it is difficult not to come away from the *Livre de caricatures* without a contagious sense of the idiosyncratic warmth, charm, humour and humanity of a figure – 'likeable, witty, clever, very caustic, very satirical, very gallant with the ladies, and never out of place wherever he went' – whose *Livre de caricatures* challenges us to think more deeply about a very serious question: how can we hope to write the history of laughter – without crossing boundaries?

Transactions of the RHS 21 (2011), pp. 39–57 © Royal Historical Society 2011
doi:10.1017/S008044011100003X

THINKING WITH BYZANTIUM*

By Averil Cameron

READ 5 FEBRUARY 2010

ABSTRACT. It is well known that the history of Byzantium does not fit comfortably
with mainstream medieval history. This paper returns to the problem in the light
of two recent, if opposing, historiographical trends: first, the emphasis on the
Mediterranean as a unifying factor, and second, the turn towards the comparative
history of western and eastern Eurasia. Neither emphasis accommodates Byzantium
well, and it is argued that however difficult it may seem to some historians, any broad
approach to medieval history will be inadequate if it does not make space for the
history of Byzantium.

Visitors to the recently extended and reorganised Ashmolean Museum in
Oxford will not find Byzantium mentioned in the leaflet giving the floor
plans and layout. Instead, the Museum's significant Byzantine collections
are dispersed – coins under the heading of 'Money' (into a new Cyprus
gallery) and icons and other objects into a new (and stunning) gallery
on the 'Mediterranean world', which is itself part of a grouping under
the heading of 'Asian crossroads'. Byzantium is thus placed with the east,
indeed with the far east. 'Rome' has a gallery, but Byzantium does not.
Yet the Museum's Byzantine collection is an important one, and in terms
of numbers and interest among graduate students, Byzantine studies in
Oxford is booming: an attendance of forty or so is not uncommon at
a regular seminar, and since 'late antiquity' attracts Byzantinists as well,
and the boundary between the two periods (if such they are) is fuzzy in the
extreme, there are often many more. A seminar on one or the other takes
place virtually every day, and packed audiences are becoming the norm.[1]
It is perhaps not surprising, given that the end of the Roman empire and
the transition to the medieval world is again a topic of such appeal, if

---

* This is an adapted version of a paper read to the Society in February 2010, and I
am grateful for comments received then; some of the material was included, though with
different emphasis, in the Syme Lecture at Wolfson College, Oxford, and the John W. Pope
Lecture at the University of Carolina, Chapel Hill, both given in November 2010.
[1] This is aided by the recent creation of an Oxford Centre for Late Antiquity and an
Oxford Centre for Byzantine Research.

we spend time debating about periodisation and definitions. But this also points to some real problems about Byzantium. They were evident also in 2008 when visitors to a spectacular exhibition on Byzantium in London came away bemused, admiring the objects but wondering what it was all about.[2] Non-Byzantinists have been surprised when I have explained that a historian of Byzantium even if not an art historian needs to be familiar with the main repertoire of surviving objects, and more than that, to keep up as far as possible with the latest interpretations and of course datings. Visitors to the exhibition (in my experience) needed a good deal of context, not only on chronology but also about Byzantine society and religion in order to appreciate many of the objects, and in many cases non-specialists come armed with preexisting and unhelpful assumptions. Conversely (since some of the most spectacular objects in the exhibition came from Venice, where they had been taken by the Crusaders and subsequently in some cases adapted for western use), a young Greek academic colleague, brought up in an Orthodox country but not a Byzantinist, said she was amazed to see the 'Byzantine' objects from western collections, and asked if it was really true that Catholics had done the adaptation and remodelling.

Those of us who work on Byzantine history are well aware of these problems. The real Byzantium is nowhere near as user-friendly as the field of late antiquity, which has literally exploded since Peter Brown published his *World of Late Antiquity* in 1971.[3] Judith Herrin has addressed this problem in her last book, and a range of recent handbooks and companions to Byzantium all show awareness of it.[4] I can only ruefully concur when she says that (except for enthusing over icons) telling anyone you are a Byzantinist is a total conversation stopper.

It is therefore intriguing to find a section about Byzantium in a volume of essays by the distinguished strategist Edward Luttwak,[5] and the same author has now published a whole book on Byzantium.[6] Luttwak is not a Byzantinist either, and reviewers have pointed out deficiencies in his book, including the use he makes of various Byzantine military

[2] See Robin Cormack and Maria Vassilaki, eds., *Byzantium 330–1453* (Royal Academy of Arts, London, 2008).

[3] Peter Brown, *The World of Late Antiquity* (1971).

[4] Judith Herrin, *Byzantium: The Surprising Life of a Medieval Empire* (2007); see Cyril Mango, ed., *The Oxford History of Byzantium* (Oxford, 2002); Elizabeth Jeffreys, ed., *The Oxford Handbook of Byzantine Studies* (Oxford, 2008); Paul Stephenson, ed., *The Byzantine World* (2010); Liz James, ed., *A Companion to Byzantium* (Chichester, 2010), and cf. Averil Cameron, *The Byzantines* (Oxford, 2006).

[5] Edward Luttwak, *The Virtual American Empire: War, Faith and Power* (New Brunswick, 2009); for the phrase 'faith and power' (explicitly acknowledged) see Helen C. Evans, ed. *Byzantium: Faith and Power (1261–1557)* (Metropolitan Museum of Art, New York, 2004), the catalogue of another of the several major Byzantine exhibitions in recent years.

[6] Edward Luttwak, *The Grand Strategy of the Byzantine Empire* (Cambridge, MA, 2009).

manuals.[7] In 1976 he published *The Grand Strategy of the Roman Empire*, which was at the time controversial among Roman historians: it argued, indeed it assumed, that the Roman empire actually did have a grand strategy, whereas Roman historians at the time and later argued in the main that Roman military policy did not work like that.[8] The Byzantine book follows on with this model, and in fact an appendix briefly discusses the reception of his earlier book. Luttwak argues that all states have a grand strategy, even if they do not realise it themselves, and that the Byzantine preferred strategy was defensive and relied on diplomacy wherever possible against aggressive warfare or pitched battles. Not surprisingly, Luttwak draws some ideological messages from this, with frequent references to 'discredited Marxist history', disparaging references to historical theory in general, and use of the term 'jihad' for any and every Muslim military initiative. One reviewer regarded this as playful anachronism,[9] but that does not seem adequate.

I wonder what it was that interested Luttwak in Byzantium, beyond the fact that here is another good topic for a continuation of his book on Rome, and that he had (evidently) been to a recent major exhibition at the Metropolitan Museum, New York? The Byzantine section in *The Virtual American Empire* consists of three essays. One is a review of the Metropolitan Museum exhibition of 2004 dealing with the last period of Byzantium; another is evidently also a review (though this is not stated) of a major book, *Byzantine Court Culture from 829 to 1204*, which came out in 1997.[10] The first may perhaps have arisen from a review of Warren Treadgold's *History of the Byzantine State and Society*, also of 1997, a book which aimed at replacing the standard work by George Ostrogorsky (on which more below). Luttwak admires Treadgold's *History* as a book for the general reader, but he also takes the opportunity to express his own view that the Byzantine empire lasted because it had a grand strategy, military strength subordinated to diplomacy and used to contain and punish.[11] This ignores the many examples of when Byzantium did prefer military action, as well as its habitual civil wars. But Luttwak's stress on containment is intended as a lesson for contemporary America, and that is behind the longer book

---

[7] See the detailed review by Anthony Kaldellis, *Bryn Mawr Classical Review*, 2010.01.49; for a different approach see the comments of the distinguished scholar of late antiquity Glen Bowersock, *London Review of Books*, 32.3, 11 Feb. 2010, 17–18. See also Luttwak in *Foreign Policy*, 2009, cited by Bowersock (*ibid.*, 18); the concept of an 'operational code' was developed in connection with the Politburo during the cold war period, and depended on the idea of a stable and closed system.

[8] Edward Luttwak, *The Grand Strategy of the Roman Empire from the First Century* A.D. *to the Third* (Baltimore, 1976); see for instance Benjamin Isaac, *The Limits of Empire: The Roman Army in the East* (Oxford, rev. edn, 1992).

[9] *FT Weekend*, 27–9 Nov. 2009.

[10] Henry Maguire, ed., *Byzantine Court Culture from 829 to 1204* (Washington, DC, 1997).

[11] Luttwak, *Virtual American Empire*, 150.

as well. He further takes an unashamedly synchronic view of Byzantium: 'I recognize that the very different circumstances of subsequent centuries left their marks on Byzantine strategy' – but 'there was enough continuity to define an "operational code" [of warfare], and in thus conflating eight centuries I am reassured by eminent predecessors'.[12] This essentialist approach, seeing Byzantium as an unchanging entity, is exactly one of its problems.

We are currently in an age of agonising about the end of empires. In the literature on late antiquity, which is of course also the early Byzantine period, the fall of the Roman empire has made a comeback as a main topic, as has the role of violence. The concept of holy war in Byzantium is another obvious example of a topic driven by contemporary concerns. Comparisons with contemporary conditions are indeed all the rage, and no less in relation to the history of Byzantium. Cullen Murphy's 2007 book, called in the US *Are We Rome? The End of an Empire and the Fate of America*, is only one in a current genre, of which James O'Donnell's recent book, *The Ruin of the Roman Empire*, is perhaps the most thoughtful and unexpected example.[13] From O'Donnell, a distinguished student of late Latin authors, who has written previously on Augustine, Boethius and Cassiodorus, we have the view from the west: the sixth-century eastern, that is, Byzantine, emperor Justinian is the villain of the piece, with his religious obsession, his unnecessary and destructive wars and his failure to secure Mesopotamia (for which read Iraq), while in contrast Theodoric the Ostrogoth is the unexpected hero and real heir to Roman values. 'Barbarians' here are the true guardians and continuators of Rome, while the Byzantine emperor based in Constantinople is an invader and occupier. Put another way, Rome (that is, America) has declined and fallen, and the east is trying to assert itself. This is Rome's story; Byzantium does not fit.

There does seem to be a problem about where Byzantium is placed in the broad spectrum of historical thinking. One problem lies with the boundary between the classical past and the Byzantine world, the former, that is the classical world, usually being preferred, and certainly having a generally higher status in western scholarship. As Edward Luttwak observes, Byzantium has not only been neglected by western European scholars brought up on the classical tradition; it has been denigrated.[14] The very term 'Byzantine' was originally (and still is) pejorative. After all, during nearly all their long history the Byzantines called themselves

---

[12] Luttwak, *Grand Strategy*, 418.

[13] Cullen Murphy, *Are We Rome? The End of an Empire and the Fate of America* (Boston, MA, 2007); cf. *idem, The New Rome: The End of an Empire and the Fate of America* (Thriplow, 2007); cf. also Adrian Goldsworthy, *The Fall of the West: The Slow Death of the Roman Superpower* (2009); James J. O'Donnell, *The Ruin of the Roman Empire* (2009).

[14] Luttwak, *Virtual American Empire*, 154.

Romans. This was so even though a high-level form of Greek remained their language of culture, government and religion throughout; only latterly did Byzantine writers begin to recognise their Greek past under the term 'Hellene'.[15] So why do we call them Byzantines, if not to deny their own claims? As an undergraduate studying classics I was taught to despise the 'Byzantine' scholars who made bold conjectures in classical texts, instead of appreciating the revival of editorial and textual scholarship in later Byzantium.[16] In traditional scholarship on Byzantium, the reception of the classical tradition has always been a privileged theme, as though Byzantium had nothing of its own and only preserved the classical past. *Mimesis*, or imitation, a term applied to the Byzantine appropriation of classical literary language, style, motifs and genres, has been a key theme in secondary literature,[17] and scholars of Byzantine literature have only recently begun to work towards an evaluation not based on the assumption of inferior imitation of the classical past.[18] That attitude is still with us, and Byzantinists still struggle with it. The deeper question of how Byzantines viewed their own past does not permit of a simple answer, given the changes in Byzantine culture over the long history of Byzantium, and clearly Byzantines themselves approached the issue in different ways; this too is a subject which has often been impeded by modern negative assumptions.[19]

Now that the later Roman empire has been re-invented as 'late antiquity', Byzantinists also struggle with encroachment into their subject by the far more numerous band of late antique specialists, many of whom now carry their subject well into the Islamic period and as late in time as the eighth century or even later.[20] Some Byzantinists have reacted by

---

[15] See Anthony Kaldellis, *Hellenism in Byzantium: The Transformation of Greek Identity and the Reception of the Classical Tradition* (Cambridge, 2007); Claudia Rapp, 'Hellenic Identity, *Romanitas* and Christianity in Byzantium', in *Hellenism, Culture and Ethnicity from Antiquity to Modernity*, ed. Katerina Zacharia (Aldershot, 2008), 127–47; Gillian Page, *Being Byzantine: Greek Identity before the Ottomans* (Cambridge, 2008). The Greek term 'Hellene' referred to pagans in most Byzantine literature and was only gradually used for 'Greek', mainly from the eleventh century AD onwards.

[16] For the Byzantine approach see Michael Jeffreys, 'Textual Criticism', in *The Oxford Handbook of Byzantine Studies*, ed. Jeffreys, 86–94, who points out that the standard manuals of textual criticism are designed for and written by classicists.

[17] See on this H. Hunger, 'On the Imitation (Mimesis) of Antiquity in Byzantine Literature', *Dumbarton Oaks Papers*, 23–4 (1969–70), 17–38; Margaret Mullett and Roger Scott, eds., *Byzantium and the Classical Tradition* (Birmingham, 1981).

[18] See P. Agapitos, 'Literary Criticism', in *The Oxford Handbook of Byzantine Studies*, ed. Jeffreys, 77–85.

[19] See Anthony Kaldellis, 'Historicism in Byzantine Thought and Literature', *Dumbarton Oaks Papers*, 61 (2007), 1–24.

[20] See G. W. Bowersock, Peter Brown and Oleg Grabar, eds., *Late Antiquity: A Guide to the Post-Classical World* (Cambridge, MA, 1999). The first issue of the new *Journal of Late Antiquity* in 2008 carried three papers discussing this periodisation from the point of view of late

making 'Byzantium' begin only in the seventh century with the aftermath of the Arab conquest.[21] But with a huge outpouring of handbooks, companions and histories of both late antiquity and Byzantium also appearing, there is in effect a culture war going on between Byzantinists and the much more numerous students of late antiquity over claims to these early centuries. This is further complicated by the fact that in some national or academic traditions, for instance among Israeli archaeologists, the term 'Byzantine' is simply the standard usage for the period from Constantine to the Arab conquest.[22]

Two other themes in current scholarship also both raise problems for the historiography of Byzantium. The first is the question of Byzantium and the Mediterranean, or of 'Mediterraneanism', as it has been termed. The other is the question of how Byzantium might fit into the much broader conception of Eurasian history, and the east/west axis which sets Europe on the one side and (typically) Asia, or specifically China, on the other. From an even broader perspective, how might Byzantium fit into a conception of 'global history', or 'the global Middle Ages'?

I will start with the second, the Eurasian model, according to which Byzantium, and indeed Rome, should be seen in the context of the whole of Eurasia, not just of Europe and the Mediterranean. This is of course a reaction against what has been seen by Jack Goody and many others as an excessive Eurocentrism.[23] On the other hand, a growing concentration on the history of Europe, in the sense of western Europe, also poses problems about the inclusion of Byzantium.

As we will see, comparative history is integral to the project of presenting Rome and Byzantium within a Eurasian perspective, but it is also integral in Christopher Wickham's important book, *Framing the Early Middle Ages*.[24] Its sub-title invites us to think about Europe and

---

antiquity (not Byzantium). Brown, *The World of Late Antiquity*, covers the period AD 150–750 and has as its sub-title *From Marcus Aurelius to Muhammad*.

[21] See Mark Whittow, *The Making of Orthodox Byzantium, 600–1025* (1996); Jonathan Shepard, ed., *The Cambridge History of the Byzantine Empire c. 500–1492* (Cambridge, 2008) begins *c.* 500; for discussion of this choice of date see *ibid.*, 21–6.

[22] French scholarship is also readier to make Byzantium start with Constantine, and the majority of publications on Byzantine art in English also start there: see Cameron, *The Byzantines*, ch. 1; the first volume of *Le monde byzantin*, ed. Cécile Morrisson (Paris, 2004), is entitled *L'Empire romain d'Orient 330–641*, that is, from the dedication of Constantinople to the end of the reign of Heraclius.

[23] See e.g. *The Theft of History* (Cambridge, 2006); *The Eurasian Miracle* (Cambridge, 2010); *Renaissances – The One or the Many?* (Cambridge, 2010); see also J. M. Hobson, *The Eastern Origins of Western Civilization* (Cambridge, 2004), and for the current valency of 'Eurasia': also J. P. Arnason and B. Wittrock, eds., *Eurasian Transformations, Tenth to Thirteenth Centuries: Crystallizations, Divergences, Renaissances* (Leiden, 2004).

[24] Christopher Wickham, *Framing the Early Middle Ages: Europe and the Mediterranean 400–800* (Oxford, 2006).

the Mediterranean in the fifth to eighth centuries, rather than Eurasia, and it was followed by another large book, in the Penguin History of Europe series, *The Inheritance of Rome: A History of Europe from 400 to 1000*.[25] *Framing the Early Middle Ages* is highly unusual in bringing an explicitly comparative approach to the period and dealing with both east and west, Byzantium and western Europe. It explicitly refuses to tell a story or provide a narrative. Most of the book is specific and comparativist, but the conclusion tentatively identifies seven tendencies or 'trends' which Wickham finds happening across both western Europe and the Byzantine world and which 'together mark the distinctiveness of the period 400–800'.[26] These trends or tendencies are: (1) a simplification of fiscal structures; (2) a period of relative aristocratic weakness; (3) greater peasant autonomy; (4) a shift among the aristocracy from birth to military identity; (5) greater regional diversity; (6) social fluidity; and finally (7) the end of Roman imperial unity, in the west in the fifth century, in the east in the seventh.

The breadth of coverage and the inclusion of Byzantium in such a way in the history of Europe is, as I have said, highly unusual. Nevertheless one reviewer[27] took Wickham to task for being too narrow, for writing, in fact, about a 'Roman Mediterranean system', or MWS ('Mediterranean World System') which, he believed, was already being reconfigured before the end of Wickham's chosen period, in 'a great geo-political shift', while the MWS itself entered a period of fragmentation. In fact *Framing the Early Middle Ages* is a remarkable feat of comparative history. One could reasonably say that it rests on the conception of an east and west linked in certain ways by trade, economic exchange and social ties, even if those ties were weakening towards the end of the period covered. The 'east' here is the world of the early Byzantine empire, and indeed that world shrank very dramatically in the seventh century with the loss of its eastern provinces and part of Anatolia to the Arabs – following on from an occupation of most of the same area by the Persians and a hard-fought even if ultimately successful war against them.[28] Other historians, including some historians of late antiquity, already think in terms of a separated western Europe, and vigorously reemphasise the traditional

---

[25] *Idem, The Inheritance of Rome: A History of Europe from 400 to 1000* (2009). The first volume in the same series, with a telling title, is by Simon Price and Peter Thonemann, *The Birth of Classical Europe: A History from Troy to Augustine* (2009), and ends in AD 425; what does this imply for Byzantium?

[26] Wickham, *Framing the Early Middle Ages*, 827–31.

[27] Brent D. Shaw, 'After Rome: Transformations of the Early Mediterranean World', *New Left Review*, 51 (May/June 2008), 89–114, cf. 112.

[28] For the latter see James Howard-Johnston, *Witnesses to a World Crisis: Histories and Historians of the Middle East in the Seventh Century* (Oxford, 2010), with a robust defence of the reliability of the Arabic sources.

'fall' of the western empire in the fifth century.[29] This is a return to western European history without Byzantium, and stands in sharp contrast to the inclusiveness of Wickham.

One can point to many other western medieval histories, or books on the origins of Europe, which have dealt with the west more or less to the exclusion of Byzantium, so much so indeed that this has in the past been the default situation. The late Evelyne Patlagean, a Byzantinist whose work was marked by its unusual breadth and the connections it made between Byzantium and the west, pointed in an article of 2005 to a famous saying of the great medievalist Georges Duby, according to which 'Il n'y a pas de Moyen Âge byzantin',[30] that is, Byzantium had nothing to do with the western Middle Ages – it was simply itself, and, perhaps, it is implied, fossilised. More recently, I would contend, a renewed focus on 'Europe' has intensified the trend,[31] and it is interesting to note that Niall Ferguson's book *Colossus*, on the decline of the American empire, actually has a chapter called 'Europe between Brussels and Byzantium'.[32] Against this, Patlagean argued powerfully against Duby in her controversial last book that Byzantium was not to be separated from the 'medieval west', but on the contrary to be seen as integrally connected with it.[33] How far these issues are politically sensitive can be seen from the reserve with which this book was received in France, as well as from the fact that when I myself argued in a Greek monthly for the integration of Byzantium into discussions of the development of Europe, the paper immediately elicited a range of responses from other scholars, mainly Greek, published in subsequent issues.[34]

The now notorious Samuel Huntington also had a view: Byzantium (and 'modern Slavic states') represented a third, middle ground between west and the far east – 'Orthodox civilisation'. The characteristics of this so-called 'Orthodox civilisation' are, according to Huntington, the *absence* of the following defining 'western' characteristics: the Renaissance, the Reformation, the Enlightenment and overseas colonialism rather than contiguous expansion. The west – in contrast to 'modern Slavic states' is,

[29] See Peter Heather, *Empires and Barbarians* (Oxford, 2009); Peter Heather, *The Fall of the Roman Empire* (Oxford, 2005); Bryan Ward-Perkins, *The Fall of Rome and the End of Civilization* (Oxford, 2005).

[30] Evelyne Patlagean, 'Byzance dans le millenaire médiéval', *Annales HSS*, 60.4 (2005), 721–9, at 723.

[31] See Averil Cameron, 'The Absence of Byzantium', *Nea Hestia* (Jan. 2008), 4–59, at 42–3.

[32] Niall Ferguson, *Colossus: The Rise and Fall of the American Empire* (2004).

[33] Evelyne Patlagean, *Un Moyen Âge grec* (Paris, 2007); the interpretation of changes in Byzantium in the eleventh century is crucial, and has undergone major revision in the last decades; current excavations at Sagalassos and Euchaita (Avkat) in Anatolia focusing on the relation of urban sites and their hinterlands are providing more relevant information.

[34] Cf. Cameron, 'The Absence of Byzantium'.

according to him, characterised by the infusion of classical culture through Rome rather than mediated by the Byzantine empire.[35] Thus Byzantium seems to be characterised by negatives – the absence of 'western' characteristics like Renaissance, Reformation and Enlightenment. In this scenario, the 'Orthodox civilisation' of Byzantium and its successors was centred on Russia and the Balkans. There are all too obvious contemporary issues about defining a 'culture' or a 'civilisation' by reference to a single religious label, and the analogy with similar characterisations of Islam is obvious[36] – except of course that Orthodoxy has always featured as such a defining characteristic of Byzantium. It is interesting to find that the Eurasianist or neo-Eurasianist agenda means something different in post-Soviet Russia than as used by the scholars referred to here, and that some Russian writers are also laying great stress on religion (i.e. Orthodoxy) as the foundation of civilisations.[37] In relation to Byzantium, one of the most urgent desiderata is surely an analysis of Byzantine society which applies some modern theoretical understanding of religion. This stands in sharp contrast to the huge amount of current writing about religion in the Roman empire, and especially late antiquity, where it is now very well realised that the religious situation was far more complex and contradictory than how it has so often seemed, and that it requires and repays a highly sophisticated analysis in terms of the history of religion.[38]

With these preliminaries, we can return to the tendency to recast the Roman empire and by extension Byzantium within a Eurasian framework. This thinking has shown itself in variety of places. It also appeared in Brent Shaw's review of Wickham's *Framing the Early Middle Ages*, already mentioned. Jack Goody's books on the subject can certainly be criticised in relation to their presentation of ancient history, not least

---

[35] Samuel Huntington, *The Clash of Civilizations and the Remaking of the World Order* (New York, 1996); see Cameron, 'The Absence of Byzantium', 32. J. P. Arnason, 'Parallels and Divergences: Perspectives on the Early Second Millennium', in *Eurasian Transformations*, ed. Arnason and Wittrock, 13–40, writes of the 'Byzantine/Orthodox sphere' (21), and allows for a partial corrective of earlier negative views (30), while still stressing eventual failure (30–2).

[36] See for instance Jack Goody, *Islam in Europe* (Cambridge, 2004); Aziz al-Azmeh, *Islams and Modernities*, 3rd edn (2009).

[37] See Marlène Laruelle, *Russian Eurasianism: An Ideology of Empire*, Eng. trans. (Washington, DC, 2008), 100–1, on Aleksandr S. Panarin's concept of Orthodox civilisation; unlike Eurasianists or neo-Eurasianists who looked towards the east and Russia's Turkic Muslim heritage, Panarin focused on Christianity, even though not emphasising Kievan Rus with its strong Byzantine connection.

[38] See meanwhile Averil Cameron, 'Byzantium and the Limits of Orthodoxy', Raleigh Lecture in History, *Proceedings of the British Academy*, 154 (2008), 139–52; see also *eadem*, 'Enforcing Orthodoxy in Byzantium', in *Discipline and Diversity*, ed. Kate Cooper and Jeremy Gregory, Studies in Church History 43 (Woodbridge, 2007), 1–24.

for relying on an outmoded, or at least not up-to-date, model. But the point is the prevalence of this kind of argument, and its evident attraction for Roman and medieval historians. The debate is partly about teleology, and specifically the desirability of avoiding the western European (and in a different sense also Marxist) notion of linear progress. In the view of Brent Shaw, the kind of material assembled through comparative history (eschewing narrative and chronology) demonstrates 'that the dominant Austro-German model of historical evolution is so fundamentally flawed and misleading that it must surely be abandoned'.[39] He goes on to argue that this teleology, which is not only Marxist but also embedded in a deeply rooted western historiographical and intellectual tradition, which envisages classical antiquity leading to the Middle Ages and then leading to modernity, must be replaced by considering 'what was actually happening', and 'what specific forces were involved in the transmutations of global systems'.[40] Wickham too is much exercised to avoid teleology – hence the 'trends' gently summarised at the end of his book – but the chronological frame of *Framing the Early Middle Ages* comes to an end before the crucial developments in the eleventh- and twelfth-century west. The question here is whether Byzantium can be accommodated to either of the two models I have discussed, namely the western European model or the Eurasian one. There are difficulties with both. In the case of Europe, Evelyne Patlagean has attempted to rescue the medieval model of Byzantium by reasserting a type of Byzantine feudalism, very different, it is true, from older models of feudalism in the west, but still of its nature controversial. Other Byzantinists have addressed themselves to questions of economic growth and the rise of towns, and to the intellectual stirrings in Byzantium and its contacts with western intellectuals in the early fourteenth and fifteenth centuries. But the ever-present consciousness of the fall of Constantinople in 1453 (not to mention the sack by the Fourth Crusade in 1204) has laid a dead hand on much modern Byzantine history-writing. If therefore it is difficult, and perhaps misguided, to fit Byzantium into the western European model, the question is whether it would fare any better with the newer Eurasianist approaches.

In fact, it is striking that the 'Eurasianists' focus primarily on China, not Byzantium or the Middle East. However, the comparison between the empires of Rome and China has its own history. It was pursued in the 1970s by Keith Hopkins, and it is a feature of an influential work of the 1980s, Michael Mann's *Sources of Social Power*.[41] It has been taken up more recently by ancient historians, especially through the Stanford Ancient Chinese

[39] Shaw, 'After Rome', 113.
[40] *Ibid.*, 113–14.
[41] Michael Mann, *The Sources of Social Power*, I: *A History of Power from the Beginning to* AD *1760* (Cambridge, 1986); Mann's Eurocentric approach has already been noted by others.

and Mediterranean Empires comparative history project, now with two published books,[42] and with a 2007–8 Mellon–Sawyer seminar based at Stanford.[43] The project is focused on comparative methodology, using largely quantitative and demographic data, particularly in comparing western and eastern Eurasia. As its title implies, one of the volumes has a chapter on Byzantium by John Haldon, which is indeed very welcome. But the question of where Byzantium fits into the overall concept still needs to be asked.

For example, these books deal with comparison between empires, which raises the issue of Byzantium's own status as an empire. For parts of its history it would surely fit the requirement that an empire must have the ability to unify disparate elements; it also maintained, if with great difficulty at certain times, the capacity to raise taxes and support an army.[44] The Stanford project focuses also on state-formation and structures, and while Byzantium can certainly be compared with other examples, its state structures changed substantially over its long history, so that the timespan needs to be carefully defined.[45] It is difficult (though commonly done) to write about Byzantium as if this were not so, and indeed it can hardly claim the status of an empire in its last Palaeologan phase (which may be why Edward Luttwak does not extend his coverage later than 1204). Comparative history also poses special problems of its own. The Stanford project statement tellingly says of its wide Rome-China comparative approach that 'macro-causal analysis obviates the need to provide coherent narratives', and a stated objective of the related seminar was to find key variables between the comparanda, with a demographic emphasis and with plague and large-scale migrations to the fore. A primary interest is indeed on state formation and unification (certainly still a primary concern of the young Chinese graduate students I met when I visited a few years ago). Thus in general the emphasis is on structures, not narrative. But is it really possible to dissolve Byzantium, categorised so often as exotic and exceptional, not least by the visitors to the great exhibitions of recent years, into such a Eurasian model?

---

[42] Ian Morris and Walter Scheidel, eds., *The Dynamics of Ancient Empires: From Assyria to Byzantium* (Stanford, 2009), and Walter Scheidel, ed., *Rome and China: Comparative Perspectives on Ancient World Empires* (Oxford, 2009).

[43] Entitled *The First Great Divergence: China and Europe, 500–800 CE*; the Stanford–Princeton Working Papers on the Classics (*PSUWP*), available on the web, include this material, as well as an earlier version of Shaw's review of Wickham.

[44] On the issues of definition see Jack A. Goldstone and John F. Haldon, 'Ancient States, Empires and Exploitation: Problems and Perspectives', in *Dynamics of Ancient Empires*, ed. Morris and Scheidel, 3–29; Thomas J. Barfield, 'The Shadow Empires: Imperial State Formation along the Chinese–Nomad Frontier', in *Empires: Perspectives from Archaeology and History*, ed. Susan E. Alcock *et al.* (Cambridge, 2001), 10–41, at 28–39.

[45] See also John F. Haldon, *The State and the Tributary Mode of Production* (1993).

It is time to turn my other theme, that of Byzantium and the Mediterranean. What does it mean to place Byzantium in the context of the Mediterranean? And what *period* of Byzantium? As we saw, Byzantium, or the 'Byzantine empire', was subject to dramatic geographical change during its long history. Yet although it was based, with only a short interlude from 1204 to 1261, on Constantinople (not a Mediterranean city), there is a sense in which it inherited the position of the Roman empire as a Mediterranean empire. Justinian tried to reestablish this Mediterranean unity in the sixth century, when the western provinces had already given way to the barbarian kingdoms of the early medieval west. The Byzantine armies easily recovered North Africa from the Vandals, and reimposed taxation, gaining control of a province which had previously supplied Rome with its food supply and was to impress the Arabs with its oil production in the seventh century; despite the defeat of a Byzantine army and exarch by the Arabs in the mid-seventh century and the foundation of an Arab settlement at Kairouan, Constantinople held on to Carthage and may even, as a coin hoard from Rougga may suggest, have put its own resources into North Africa in the second half of the seventh century. However, the cost of the arrangements needed for the imposition of Byzantine rule in both Africa and Italy was very high. The reconquest of Italy was more difficult, and only small parts of Italy and Spain were regained; Italy after the Byzantine 'reconquest' was reduced to a far poorer state.[46] It was not simply the Arab conquests that rendered the dream of restored Mediterranean unity impossible. There were also threats from the north and west: Avars, Slavs and Bulgars threatened Constantinople and Thessaloniki as well as Greece and the Balkans in the late sixth and seventh centuries. The Persians occupied Anatolia, Syria, Palestine and Egypt in the early seventh century and the success of the Emperor Heraclius in his desperate campaign against them was followed immediately by the Arab conquests, resulting in a catastrophic loss of territory in the east. The grain imports across the Mediterranean from Egypt, on which Constantinople depended for its food supply, stopped when Egypt came under Persian rule, and with the Arab conquests there was undoubtedly a falling off of the long-distance trade and exchange that had been the basis of the prosperity of the eastern Mediterranean provinces. The Mediterranean was no longer safe; with the sharp reduction of territory, damage to the water supply as a result of the great siege of Constantinople in 626, and loss of the grain from Egypt, the population of the capital dropped drastically, and Constantinople

---

[46] In 1981, Christopher Wickham wrote: 'The holocaust in Italy came in the great age of wars, 535–93: the shifts of balance under the German rulers, first Odoacer (476–93) and then the Ostrogothic kings (490–553) were trivial by contrast' (*Early Medieval Italy: Central Power and Local Society, 400–1000* (1981), 15).

reinvented itself by looking in a different direction, relying for its food supply on its own hinterland in Thrace and western Asia Minor,[47] while militarily and diplomatically it turned to the Balkans and the north.

In the next centuries, the Mediterranean was a dangerous place, frequented by pirates and Arab raiders. For all that, travel and trade did not stop; but tenth-century Byzantium looked for its boasted 'family of nations' to the Balkans, the Slavic world and the north, not across what David Abulafia has called 'the Classic Mediterranean'.[48] That changed with changes in the Arab world and the fragmentation that followed the end of the Abbasids. Byzantium had recovered eastern territory meanwhile, but by the eleventh century the stakes were different. Various western players impinged on Byzantium – Crusaders, traders, ambitious new city-states – and were usually greeted with ambivalence. Byzantium became home to Italian merchants from Venice, Genoa and Pisa, but in a fit of xenophobia the people of Constantinople turned on the Latins in the late twelfth century and the city, now a staging post on the way to the east, fell victim in a catastrophic manner in 1204 to the Fourth Crusade.[49] Palaeologan Byzantium was tiny and localised, certainly not Mediterranean, and squeezed between the Ottoman threat and the contemptuous west whose aid it desperately needed.

We need to be clear what we mean by 'Mediterranean'. Abulafia writes of 'sub-Mediterraneans', and 'multiple Mediterraneans'.[50] The first term, positing the existence of sub-Mediterraneans of the 'Classic Mediterranean', denotes for example the Adriatic and the Aegean; the latter, 'multiple Mediterraneans', something quite different – other seas edged by land, literally, seas 'between the lands'. Thus the North Sea and the Baltic, the 'northern Mediterranean', even the Atlantic;[51] but this is not much to do with Byzantium. In this global set of 'Mediterranean' seas, Byzantium fades from view. Nor indeed for much of its history does it have much purchase with the 'Classic Mediterranean' with which we are more familiar.

In this 'Mediterranean' way of thinking, focusing on the sea itself rather than the societies around it, the level of trans-Mediterranean trade and travel has been a fundamental marker since Henri Pirenne;

---

[47] See J. Durliat, 'L'approvisionnement de Constantinople, in *Constantinople and its Hinterland*, ed. Cyril Mango and Gilbert Dagron, with the assistance of Geoffrey Greatrex (Aldershot, 1995), 19–33.

[48] See especially David Abulafia, ed., *The Mediterranean in History* (2003).

[49] On which see Angeliki E. Laiou, ed., *Urbs Capta. The Fourth Crusade and its Consequences* (Paris, 2005).

[50] David Abulafia, 'Mediterraneans', in *Rethinking the Mediterranean*, ed. W. V. Harris (Oxford, 2005), 64–93.

[51] *Ibid.*, 76–80; cf. R. S. Lopez, *The Commercial Revolution of the Middle Ages, 950–1350* (Englewood Cliffs, NJ, 1971).

Pirenne placed the end of the ancient world, and thus of the unified Mediterranean, at the time of the Arab conquests – the end of late Roman long-distance trading systems – in his famous words, 'without Mahomed, no Charlemagne'.[52] Long-distance exchange, that is, trade and exchange across the Mediterranean, above all in grain, wine and olive oil, is still what preoccupies historians of late antiquity, though with many proponents of the 'long late antiquity' seeing Mediterranean unity as lasting for longer and the rise of Islam as less of a break than in Pirenne's model. But from the later seventh and eighth centuries, if not before, long-distance trade and exchange on the previous scale fell away,[53] and Byzantium was largely out of long-distance exchange for several centuries. The importance of this exchange across the Mediterranean in late antiquity is a key theme in Wickham's book, and has been so for the last generation of scholars of late antiquity, following the mass of evidence gathered by archaeologists since the 1970s, when Andrea Carandini and his school of Italian archaeologists were trailblazers.[54] While the extent and nature of this long-distance exchange is still much debated, and Horden and Purcell have made a case for continuing small-scale traffic at all periods, it was nevertheless fundamental to the prosperity of the east in late antiquity.[55] In a later period, while Shlomo Goitein's great work based on the documentary record of Jewish traders preserved in the Cairo Geniza reveals a connectedness in which Constantinople made a temporary reappearance,[56] this was not the kind of long-distance trade or exchange familiar from the late Roman world; the commodities changed, and the documents show that its geographical range was different too,

[52] Henri Pirenne, *Mahomet et Charlemagne* (Paris, 1937); see the review by Peter Brown, 'Mohammed and Charlemagne by Henri Pirenne', in *idem, Society and the Holy in Late Antiquity* (Berkeley, 1982), 63–79. As Brown points out, though the book appeared only in 1937, Pirenne had expressed his ideas from as early as 1922.

[53] So also Michael McCormick, *Origins of the European Economy: Communications and Commerce AD 300–900* (Cambridge, 2001), and see Peregrine Horden and Nicholas Purcell, *The Corrupting Sea: A Study of Mediterranean History* (Oxford, 2000), 169–72, 365–76, with 153–60 (an 'early medieval depression'); Brent D. Shaw, 'Challenging Braudel: A New Vision of the Mediterranean', *Journal of Roman Archaeology*, XIV (2001), 419–53.

[54] Cf. the memorable review by Christopher Wickham, 'Marx, Sherlock Holmes and Late Roman Commerce', *Journal of Roman Studies*, 78 (1988), 183–93.

[55] See Bryan Ward-Perkins, 'Specialisation, Trade and Prosperity. An Overview of the Economy of the Late Antique Eastern Mediterranean', in *Economy and Exchange in the Eastern Mediterranean during Late Antiquity*, ed. Sean Kingsley and Michael Decker (Oxford, 2001), 167–78; against excessive emphasis on 'shipping lanes', Horden and Purcell, *The Corrupting Sea*, 153–60. See the other papers in Kingsley and Decker, eds., *Economy and Exchange*, for trade and exchange as factors in the prosperity of the eastern Mediterranean in late antiquity, and cf. also Sean A. Kingsley, ed., *Shipwreck Archaeology of the Holy Land: Processes and Parameters* (2004), and Marlia Mundell Mango, ed., *Byzantine Trade, 4th–12th Centuries* (Farnham, 2009).

[56] S. D. Goitein, *A Mediterranean Society: The Jewish Communities of the Arab World as Portrayed in the Documents of the Cairo Geniza* (6 vols., Berkeley, 1967–93).

focused on a now Islamic Mediterranean. The entry of the Italian trading cities and the concessions they were granted in Constantinople changed the picture even more.[57]

In any case, there are, as is clear, problems with the 'Mediterranean' concept. Is it about the sea and the connections across it; or is it about the people and societies who lived around it? It is certainly fashionable: an article of 2005 counted up the extraordinary number of new journals and serials appearing especially since the 1980s which have Mediterranean in their title, and commented on the looseness with which the term is used.[58] That does not apply to the most important recent book on the subject, *The Corrupting Sea*, by Peregrine Hordern and Nicholas Purcell (2000), which eschews *histoire événementielle* for ecology, continuity and 'connectedness' on a small scale, and speaks of a 'Mediterranean society' based on enduring anthropological models of honour and shame. But again, while much discussion has taken place among Greek and Roman historians on the latter concept,[59] it does not seem to help much with Byzantium. The anthropologist Michael Herzfeld has indeed pointed out problems with this kind of analysis but also seen the 'Mediterranean' emphasis as a kind of 'Mediterraneanism'.[60] The concept of honour has been applied to the governing structures of the Roman empire,[61] but those structures were modified greatly under Diocletian and Constantine and the late Roman administrative system which then emerged did not survive the pressures of the seventh century. The question for Byzantium must be how far the anthropological concepts of honour and shame perceived in Greek

[57] See the survey by Angeliki E. Laiou, 'Exchange and Trade, Seventh–Twelfth Centuries', in *The Economic History of Byzantium: From the Seventh through the Fifteenth Century*, ed. Angeliki E. Laiou (3 vols., Washington, DC, 2002), II, 697–768; M. Balard, 'A Christian Mediterranean', in *The Mediterranean in History*, ed. Abulafia, 183–213. For Byzantium and the concept of a Mediterranean agrarian economy see P. Toubert, 'Byzantium and the Mediterranean Agrarian Economy', in *The Economic History of Byzantium*, ed. Laiou, I, 377–91 (with a section on 'Byzantine Specificities', 387–91).

[58] Susan E. Alcock, 'Alphabet Soup in the Mediterranean Basin: The Emergence of the Mediterranean Serial', in *Rethinking the Mediterranean*, ed. Harris, 314–36.

[59] Honour and shame: Horden and Purcell, *The Corrupting Sea*, 487–523; J. K. Campbell, *Honour, Shame and Patronage: A Study of Institutions and Moral Values in a Greek Mountain Community* (Oxford, 1964); J. G. Peristiany, ed., *Mediterranean Family Structures* (Cambridge, 1976); J. G. Peristiany, ed., *Honour and Shame: The Values of Mediterranean Society* (1965); D. D. Gilmore, ed., *Honour and Shame and the Unity of the Mediterranean* (Washington, DC, 1987); cf. Seth Schwarz, *Were the Jews a Mediterranean Society? Reciprocity and Solidarity in Ancient Judaism* (Princeton, 2010). See also V. Burrus, *Saving Shame: Martyrs, Saints and Other Abject Subjects* (Philadelphia, 2008).

[60] M. Herzfeld, 'Practical Mediterraneanism: Excuses for Everything, from Epistemology to Eating', in *Rethinking the Mediterranean*, ed. Harris, 45–63; Herzfeld is noted as an 'anti-Mediterraneanist' by Horden and Purcell (*The Corrupting Sea*, 20, 486; see also M. Herzfeld, *Anthropology through the Looking- Glass: Critical Ethnography on the Margins of Europe* (Cambridge, 1987)).

[61] J. E. Lendon, *Empire of Honour: The Art of Government in the Roman World* (Oxford, 1997, 2001).

mountain society and elsewhere also applied during the long centuries of Christian Byzantium;[62] there are obvious and major issues of continuity not merely with classical Greece but (even more acutely in the case of Byzantium) with modern Greece.[63]

There is indeed a particular problem in seeing Byzantium in the context of the *longue durée*, just because this is a culture which has suffered particularly badly from an excessive stress on continuity. There are also problems enough in seeing modern Mediterranean societies through the spectacles of ancient Greece, or in seeing too readily in the culture of the villages studied by anthropologists a set of ageless 'Mediterranean' values, and Byzantium has commonly been branded with the opposite, with the whole mental apparatus of decline and inferiority with which Greece itself was invested in the Ottoman period.[64] The intense controversy aroused by nineteenth-century assertions of Byzantine continuity in the history of the modern Greek state is well known. Yet Byzantium is evoked routinely in current discussions of modern Greece or Russia; for example a *Guardian* leader about Greece in late October 2010 was headed 'The Byzantine shroud' – the point being apparently that contemporary Greece has as many bureaucrats as Byzantium.

In fact Byzantium was constantly changing, and it especially changed its geographical and geopolitical footprint. If modern Istanbul does not exactly feel like a Mediterranean city, neither did medieval Constantinople, surrounded by water yet having to go to considerable lengths to secure its own water supply,[65] dependent on its Thracian and Macedonian hinterland and with its face set towards the Black Sea, the source of the fish on which it lived for much of its existence,[66] and outlet of the great rivers that provided a passage to the Vikings and connected Byzantium with the Slav lands of the north.

So Byzantium seems not to fit very well with either of these two models for understanding ancient and medieval society, the Eurasian model and

---

[62] The considered and detailed discussion of the issue in Horden and Purcell, *The Corrupting Sea*, ranges widely both chronologically and geographically, but without dealing with Byzantium, which gets no special treatment in the book.

[63] On this fraught subject see recently John Koliopoulos, 'Modern Greece: An Old Debate', in *Networks of Power in Modern Greece: Essays in Honour of John Campbell*, ed. Mark Mazower (2008), 129–35.

[64] Well brought out by Suzanne Saïd, 'The Mirage of Greek Continuity: On the Uses and Abuses of Analogy in Some Travel Narratives from the Seventeenth to the Eighteenth Century', in *Rethinking the Mediterranean*, ed. Harris, 268–93, at 276–9.

[65] See James Crow, Jonathan Bardill and Richard Bayliss, *The Water Supply of Byzantine Constantinople* (2008).

[66] See the brilliant paper by Gilbert Dagron on the arrangements made in the Middle Byzantine period to secure the supply of fish from the Black Sea, 'Poissons, pêcheurs et poissoniers de Constantinople', in *Constantinople and its Hinterland*, ed. Mango and Dagron, 57–76.

the Mediterranean model. It is not very easy to think with Byzantium when applying them.

It is not very easy to think with Byzantium either when in so many countries of the Balkans and eastern Europe the standard textbook is still George Ostrogorsky's *History of the Byzantine State*, originally published in 1940 by a Russian émigré who was a student in Germany and had moved to Belgrade in 1933, where he spent the rest of his career.[67] The book has a Slavist agenda and asserts Byzantine feudalism; despite numerous revised editions, it is obviously very out of date now and it does not of course reflect any of the archaeological and epigraphic work that is currently so immensely important. But it is still in every central European and Balkan bookshop, and it is hard to point to a comprehensive replacement.[68] The volume devoted to Byzantium in the first edition of the Cambridge Medieval History appeared only a decade after the English translation of Ostrogorsky's history, and was edited by its translator, the English Byzantinist Joan Hussey.[69] We now have substantial chapters devoted to Byzantium in the new edition (though not a dedicated volume as such), and a history of the Byzantine empire which draws on those chapters.[70] But we still have alive and well in many popular books and in the popular imagination the Byzantium of intrigue, exoticism and weakness.

You have to think *about* Byzantium before you can think *with* Byzantium. Some basic points need to be emphasized. First, change, a theme I have already stressed – the sheer amount of change that happened during the long period we call 'Byzantine'. It does not make sense to talk about Byzantium without specifying which part of this long period we mean – the early part, up to about the seventh century, when at first the eastern empire was just that, part of the whole Roman empire, and then after the 'fall of the western empire' in the fifth century, still had much of the organisation and administration of the later Roman empire; or the obscure time after the Arab conquests when Constantinople lost so much of its territory (and thus its taxpayers and its centres of education) and the city itself shrank to perhaps only a quarter or even less of its former

---

[67] G. Ostrogorski, *Geschichte des byzantinischen Staates* (Munich, 1940); Eng. trans. by Joan Hussey, *History of the Byzantine State* (Oxford, 1956); on Ostrogorsky see also Patlagean, *Un Moyen Âge grec*, 49–51.

[68] Though see Warren T. Treadgold, *A History of the Byzantine State and Society* (Stanford, 1997); Timothy E. Gregory, *A History of Byzantium* (Malden, MA, 2005).

[69] J. M. Hussey, with the editorial assistance of D. M. Nicol and G. Cowan, *The Cambridge Medieval History*, IV: *The Byzantine Empire* (Cambridge, 1966–7); here the starting point is AD 717.

[70] Shepard, ed., *The Cambridge History of the Byzantine Empire*, including sixteen out of twenty-four chapters from various volumes of the *New Cambridge Medieval History* (as explained at ch. 10, n. 24). See also Michael Angold, ed., *Cambridge History of Christianity*, V: *Eastern Christianity* (Cambridge, 2006).

size, with large parts deserted; or the revival that started in the ninth century and reached a peak, at least in its own publicity, in the tenth, when territory was regained in the east and Constantine Porphyrogenitus claimed Byzantium as heading a family of nations; or the eleventh century, which now seems a time of growth, not the decline and crisis of earlier narratives; or Byzantium in the time of the Crusades, culminating in the shock of the sack of Constantinople by the Fourth Crusade 1204 and the fragmentation that followed; or finally the Paleologan period, after the Byzantine recovery of Constantinople in 1261, when the state had drastically shrunk, and the emperor became a vassal of the Ottomans, yet which also produced some of the best Byzantine art, notable buildings and intellectuals in the whole Byzantine period. The geographical changes in the extent of the empire were as dramatic as the economic and social ones.

I would also want to emphasise the question of identity – who were 'the Byzantines'? The term is wide. It is certainly not an ethnic term; it means only the inhabitants of the state, or empire, who might come from all kinds of different backgrounds or indeed different regions, bearing in mind the territorial changes. In some areas 'Byzantines' found themselves coming under Muslim rule, and vice versa. Populations were also transplanted from one part of the empire to another.[71] These are phenomena that have been as yet very little studied, but which have obvious resonances nowadays. Finally, civil war and usurpation were regular features of Byzantine life, and at almost every period, Byzantium was at war with itself.

One of the usually cited hallmarks of Byzantine culture is the life of the court, and its ceremonial, but these changed too. The emperors built on to the Great Palace, and later moved away from it altogether; new ceremonies were invented as well. Western travellers marvelled at the ceremonies of Palaeologan Constantinople, but these were not the same as they would have experienced earlier – new ones came into being. The aristocracy of the Comnenian period was also not the same as that of the tenth century, with its elaborate system of state-paid offices, and that of Palaeologan Byzantium was different again.

Finally, that other hallmark of Byzantium, its Orthodoxy. It is almost impossible to look at Byzantium without reading back the characteristics of Orthodoxy in the modern world. It is equally hard to think of any theme more likely to produce an essentialist response than that of Byzantium as an Orthodox society. After all, for much – though not all – of its history

---

[71] See M. Balard and A. Ducellier, eds., *Migrations et diasporas méditerranéennes (Xe–XVIe siècles)* (Paris, 2002); multi-ethnicity in the Byzantine empire: H. Ahrweiler and Angeliki E. Laiou, eds., *Studies on the Internal Diaspora of the Byzantine Empire* (Washington, DC, 1998); for the period after 1204 see e.g. Benjamin Arbel, Bernard Hamilton and David Jacoby, eds., *Latins and Greeks in the Eastern Mediterranean after 1204* (1989).

it was indeed a Christian medieval society. It also famously exported Orthodox Christianity to the Slavs, and, especially crucially, to Russia, and bequeathed it – not without contention and fierce argument – to modern Greece. Even if the Byzantine 'missions' to the Slavs were not quite the official state initiatives they have usually been thought to be,[72] we are still living with that situation today. The Byzantine church also found a way to continue the Orthodox presence – even if in a very different form – during the Ottoman period, and today's situation with the ecumenical patriarchate in Istanbul, poised in an uneasy equilibrium with the Turkish state, is a reminder of that.

Byzantium does not fit easily into this diachronic Orthodox model either. It is not so easy to say when it became 'Orthodox', in the generally accepted sense. The emperor was never the head of the church, and often quarrelled with or was openly challenged by the patriarch. The year of the 'Great Schism' of 1054 was not the event it is often made out to be, and many later Byzantines were prepared to agree to union with Rome. Internal religious argument did not cease with the end of iconoclasm in 843, though that was represented as the 'Triumph of Orthodoxy'; and a vast amount of effort had to be expended at every period on the attempt to say what Orthodoxy was and to beat off rival formulations.[73] A variety of vested interests all laid claim to be 'orthodox'. In the face of this deluge of contemporary polemical and apologetic writing, it is becoming common to say that that was the preserve of only a few, and a concentration among some historians is now on the diversity of Byzantine religious practice, rather than the politics of doctrinal dispute;[74] in a parallel move, designed to avoid falling into the trap of appealing to Byzantine spirituality, religious practice is often presented as if it were reducible to the study of material culture. These developments alone underline what is surely true, namely that the subject of Byzantine religion desperately needs more theoretical and sociological analysis than it has had to date.

Why should anyone want to 'think with Byzantium'? I hope to have shown that thinking *without* Byzantium is a dangerous procedure; for all the awkwardness that might be involved in including Byzantium, not to include it leaves a gap that matters. But to think *with* Byzantium will be even more difficult than it is already if Byzantium itself is not normalised and brought fully within mainstream history.

---

[72] Cf. C. Raffensperger, 'Revisiting the Idea of the Byzantine Commonwealth', *Byzantinische Forschungen*, 28 (2004), 159–74; S. Ivanov and V. Vavřínek, in Elizabeth Jeffreys, ed., *21st International Congress of Byzantine Studies*, II: *Abstracts of Panel Papers* (Aldershot, 2006), 32–3, 34–5.

[73] See Cameron, 'Enforcing Orthodoxy in Byzantium'.

[74] So for instance Derek Krueger, ed., *A People's History of Christianity*, III: *Byzantine Christianity* (Minneapolis, MN, 2006).

Transactions of the RHS 21 (2011), pp. 59–91 © Royal Historical Society 2011
doi:10.1017/S0080440111000041

WHY WERE SOME TENTH-CENTURY ENGLISH KINGS PRESENTED AS RULERS OF BRITAIN?*

The Alexander Prize Essay

By George Molyneaux

ABSTRACT. Some tenth-century English kings, especially Æthelstan and Edgar, were commonly presented as rulers of Britain. The basic reason for this is that they had a loose but real hegemony over the other rulers on the island. This hegemony did not collapse in subsequent centuries, but English kings were less often described as rulers of Britain. The intensification of royal rule within the English kingdom in the second half of the tenth century made kings' power inside the kingdom increasingly unlike their power elsewhere in Britain: it consequently became harder to think of Britain as a single political unit.

In this year [927] appeared fiery lights in the northern part of the sky, and Sihtric died, and King Æthelstan gained the Northumbrian kingdom (*feng to Norðhymbra rice*); and he had power over (*gewylde*) all the kings who were on this island: first Hywel, king of the West Welsh, and Constantine, king of the Scots, and Owain, king of the people of Gwent, and Ealdred son of Eadwulf of Bamburgh. And they established peace (*fryþ*) with pledge and oaths (*mid wedde 7 mid aþum*) in the place which is called Eamont [near Penrith] on 12 July and renounced all idol-worship (*deofolgeld*) and afterwards departed with friendship (*mid sibbe*).[1]

From the latter part of the reign of Alfred (871–99) to the beginning of that of Æthelstan (924–39), the West Saxon king's style in charters was usually some variant of *Angul Saxonum rex*, reflecting his domination

---

* I am grateful to Thomas Charles-Edwards, George Garnett, Rory Naismith, Alice Taylor, Chris Wickham and Alex Woolf for comments on drafts, and to Nick Karn for supervising the undergraduate dissertation in which I first explored some of the themes of this article.

[1] *Anglo-Saxon Chronicle (ASC)* D 927. The *ASC* is cited from S. Keynes, D. N. Dumville *et al.*, eds., *The Anglo-Saxon Chronicle: A Collaborative Edition* (9 vols. so far, Cambridge, 1983–). Citations are by manuscript and year, as corrected by D. Whitelock, D. C. Douglas and S. I. Tucker, *The Anglo-Saxon Chronicle: A Revised Translation* (1961). It is possible that the Cumbrian king Owain was also present: William of Malmesbury, *Gesta Regum Anglorum*, II.134, ed. and trans. R. A. B. Mynors, R. M. Thomson and M. Winterbottom (2 vols., Oxford, 1998–9), I, 214.

over both Saxon Wessex and Anglian Mercia.[2] After the seizure of York and the meeting at Eamont in 927, Æthelstan was frequently styled *Rex Anglorum* and also presented as the ruler of Britain: a clear majority of his extant charters articulate such a claim. Following Æthelstan's death and the succession of Edmund (939–46), Hiberno-Scandinavian rule was reestablished at York until 944: this probably explains why Edmund was (so far as we know) not described as a ruler of Britain except in the last two years of his reign.[3] During the reigns of Eadred (946–55) and Eadwig (955–9), an assertion of rulership of Britain appears in a fair proportion of royal diplomas, and it is very common in the charters of Edgar (959–75). The idea was not confined to charters: many coins in Æthelstan's name call him *Rex totius Britanniae*, a poem probably written just after the Eamont meeting alludes to him readying for battle *per totum Bryttanium*, Æthelweard styled Edgar *monarchus Brittannum* and Byrhtferth of Ramsey referred to the same king as *totius Albionis imperator*, *Albion* being a synonym for *Britannia*. Similar examples could be multiplied.[4]

Claims to rulership of Britain became less pervasive after the late tenth century. They by no means disappeared, but the proportion of eleventh-century diplomas in which they appear was lower than for Æthelstan or

[2] S. Keynes, 'The West Saxon Charters of King Æthelwulf and his Sons', *English Historical Review*, 109 (1994), 1109–49 especially 1147–9. My comments on the relative frequencies of different charter styles are based upon Susan Kelly's unpublished catalogue of royal styles (a copy of which she kindly sent to me) and H. Kleinschmidt, 'Die Titulaturen englischer Könige im 10. und 11. Jahrhundert', in *Intitulatio III. Lateinische Herrschertitel und Herrschertitulaturen vom 7. bis zum 13. Jahrhundert*, ed. H. Wolfram and A. Scharer (Vienna, 1988), 75–129.

[3] S. Keynes, 'England, *c.* 900–1016', in *The New Cambridge Medieval History*, III: *c. 900 – c. 1024*, ed. T. Reuter (Cambridge, 1999), 456–84 at 472–3; C. Downham, 'The Chronology of the Last Scandinavian Kings of York, AD 937–954', *Northern History*, 40 (2003), 25–51. For Edmund as king of *Albion* in 945 and 946, see P. H. Sawyer, *Anglo-Saxon Charters: An Annotated List and Bibliography* (1968), revised S. E. Kelly, *The Electronic Sawyer*, accessible at www.trin.cam.ac.uk/chartwww/eSawyer.99/eSawyer2.html, accessed 8 June 2011 (hereafter cited as 'S'), nos. 505, 509.

[4] E. John, *Orbis Britanniae and Other Studies* (Leicester, 1966), 46–63, and, for the examples cited, C. E. Blunt, 'The Coinage of Athelstan, 924–939: A Survey', *British Numismatic Journal*, 152 (1974), 35–160 at 47–8; M. Lapidge, 'Some Latin Poems as Evidence for the Reign of Athelstan', *Anglo-Saxon England*, 9 (1981), 61–98 at 98; Æthelweard, *Chronicle*, IV.9, ed. and trans. A. Campbell (Edinburgh, 1962), 56; Byrhtferth of Ramsey, *Life of St Oswald*, IV.17, ed. and trans. M. Lapidge (Oxford, 2009), 136. On *Albion*, see J. Crick, 'Edgar, Albion and Insular Dominion', in *Edgar, King of the English, 959–975*, ed. D. Scragg (Woodbridge, 2008), 158–70. It may or may not be coincidence that the tenth-century English revival of the word *Albion* followed fairly closely the adoption by Gaelic writers of *Alba* as a term for the Scottish kingdom. *Alba* had originally meant 'Britain', but it is unlikely that Scottish kings were propounding a claim to the whole island: D. Broun, *Scottish Independence and the Idea of Britain from the Picts to Alexander III* (Edinburgh, 2007), 20–4, 71–97. Edgar sometimes appears as *rex totius Britanniae* on coins, but less commonly than Æthelstan: C. E. Blunt, B. H. I. H. Stewart and C. S. S. Lyon, *Coinage in Tenth-Century England from Edward the Elder to Edgar's Reform* (Oxford, 1989), 173–8.

Edgar. Moreover, the number of diplomas being issued declined sharply during the eleventh century; writs, which simultaneously proliferated, did not articulate such claims. Nor was the idea prominent in eleventh-century narrative sources. The *Life* of Edward the Confessor occasionally hints that Edward's sphere of authority extended across Britain, but more often characterises him as ruler of the English alone.[5] The *Encomium Emmae Reginae* states that Cnut was *imperator* of England, Wales and Scotland (as well as Denmark and Norway), rather than depicting Britain as a single political unit.[6] After the Norman Conquest, as Rees Davies pointed out, claims to rule Britain became rarer still, despite increasingly frequent English interventions in Wales and Scotland.[7]

It is often noted that tenth-century English kings were presented as rulers of Britain, but the question of why this was so has received little extended comment, probably because the answer appears obvious. The island is a definite physical unit and had long been recognised as such: its geography had been described by Pliny, Orosius, Isidore and Bede, to name but four particularly influential writers.[8] There was, moreover, venerable precedent for the idea that one man might be presented as the preeminent figure on the island. Bede had described the power of Edwin and Oswald, seventh-century Northumbrian kings, in such terms.[9] Æthelbald and Offa, eighth-century Mercian kings, had appeared in charters as *rex Britanniae* and *rex et decus Britanniae*.[10] Asser had portrayed Alfred as the *rector* of all the Christians of the island of Britain.[11] Given

---

[5] F. Barlow, ed. and trans., *The Life of King Edward who Rests at Westminster Attributed to a Monk of Saint-Bertin*, 2nd edn (Oxford, 1992), 6, 10, 12, 14, 16, 18, 40, 116 (English), 18, 20, 34 (Britain).

[6] A. Campbell, ed. and trans., *Encomium Emmae Reginae*, II.19 (1949), 34. In this context, *Britannia* clearly means 'Wales', since *Anglia* and *Scothia* are also listed.

[7] R. R. Davies, *The Matter of Britain and the Matter of England* (Oxford, 1996); R. R. Davies, *The First English Empire: Power and Identities in the British Isles, 1093–1343* (Oxford, 2000). For an exceptional post-Conquest use of the style *Dei gracia tocius Brittanie monarches*, see D. Bates, ed., *Regesta Regum Anglo-Normannorum: The Acta of William I (1066–1087)* (Oxford, 1998), no. 286.

[8] Pliny, *Natural History*, IV.16, ed. and trans. H. Rackham, W. H. S. Jones and D. E. Eichholz (10 vols., Cambridge, MA, 1938–63), II, 196–8; Orosius, *Historiarum Adversum Paganos Libri VII*, I.2, ed. C. Zangemeister (Vienna, 1882), 28; Isidore, *Etymologiarum sive Originum Libri XX*, XIV.vi.2, ed. W. M. Lindsay (2 vols., Oxford, 1911); Bede, *Ecclesiastical History of the English People*, I.1, ed. and trans. B. Colgrave and R. A. B. Mynors (Oxford, 1969), 14–16. On the Roman idea that Britain constituted another world (*alter orbis*), separate from the *orbis Romanus*, see C. Erdmann, *Forschungen zur politischen Ideenwelt des Frühmittelalters* (Berlin, 1951), 8–9, 40, 42.

[9] Bede, *Ecclesiastical History*, II.5, II.9, III.6 (148–50, 162, 230). Cf. Adomnán, *Life of Columba*, I.1, ed. and trans. A. O. and M. O. Anderson (Oxford, 1990), 16.

[10] S 89, 155. Cf. Alcuin, *Letters*, ed. E. Dümmler (Monumenta Germaniae Historica, Epistolae Karolini Aevi, II, Berlin, 1895), no. 64.

[11] Asser, *Life of King Alfred*, preface, ed. W. H. Stevenson and revised D. Whitelock (Oxford, 1959), 1.

that the *Chronicle* states (in the extract quoted at the outset) that Æthelstan had subordinated all other kings on the island, there is, on the face of it, little need to explain why he too was presented as the ruler of Britain. The matter is not, however, quite so simple, since few historians would now claim that any tenth-century (or earlier) English king had much more than a loose hegemony over the other kings in Britain: one could say that English power in Wales and northern Britain was 'extensive', rather than 'intensive'.[12] Why then were several tenth-century English kings nonetheless presented as rulers of Britain? And why, moreover, did such pretensions become less ubiquitous after Edgar's reign?

Before addressing these questions, we should note two long-running historiographical controversies. The first revolves around whether documents in the names of tenth-century kings were commonly written by permanent members of the royal household. The king might alternatively have commissioned people to write documents *ad hoc*, or indeed have expected the beneficiaries of royal grants to arrange the drawing up of diplomas themselves.[13] I cannot resolve this debate here (or, for that matter, elsewhere) but, for the purposes of my argument, it can be sidestepped. Whoever produced a diploma, it is unlikely that the draftsman would use a style of which the king disapproved, as royal backing was fundamental to the future security of the grant. But given that a wide variety of titles was used in tenth-century charters, it does not appear that kings routinely stipulated (at least in detail) how they were to be described: charter styles thus probably reveal most about how the king's position was perceived by literate churchmen who, whether working in a royal writing office or not, were almost certainly those who drafted diplomas.

The second debate concerns the significance of 'imperial' terminology. There are a couple of dozen cases of kings from Eadred to Cnut being

---

[12] Cf. M. Mann, *The Sources of Social Power*, I: *A History of Power from the Beginning to A.D. 1760* (Cambridge, 1986), 7, who defines 'extensive power' as 'the ability to organize large numbers of people over far-flung territories in order to engage in minimally stable cooperation' and 'intensive power' as 'the ability to organize tightly and command a high level of mobilization or commitment from the participants, whether the areas and numbers covered are great or small'. The terms 'intensive' and 'extensive' represent ideal types, or poles on a spectrum of intensity/extensity, not a binary division.

[13] R. Drögereit, 'Gab es eine angelsächsische Königskanzlei?', *Archiv für Urkundenforschung*, 13 (1935), 335–436; P. Chaplais, 'The Origin and Authenticity of the Royal Anglo-Saxon Diploma', *Journal of the Society of Archivists*, 3.2 (1965), 48–61; P. Chaplais, 'The Anglo-Saxon Chancery: From the Diploma to the Writ', *Journal of the Society of Archivists*, 3.4 (1966), 160–76; S. Keynes, *The Diplomas of King Æthelred 'the Unready', 978–1016: A Study in their Use as Historical Evidence* (Cambridge, 1980); P. Chaplais, 'The Royal Anglo-Saxon "Chancery" of the Tenth Century Revisited', in *Studies in Medieval History Presented to R.H.C. Davis*, ed. H. Mayr-Harting and R. I. Moore (1985), 41–51; S. E. Kelly, *Charters of Abingdon Abbey* (2 vols., Oxford, 2000–1), I, pp. lxxi–cxxxi; S. Keynes, 'Edgar, *rex admirabilis*', in *Edgar*, ed. Scragg, 3–59 at 12–23.

styled *imperator*. Edmund Stengel and Carl Erdmann interpreted these as manifestations of a 'nichtrömische Kaiseridee', and similar connotations have sometimes been imputed to other titles, most notably *basileus*, which crops up frequently from the reign of Æthelstan to that of Edward the Confessor. The title *imperator* could be conferred by the pope (e.g. to Charlemagne in 800), but Stengel and Erdmann demonstrated that papal coronation was not a prerequisite for a man to be styled *imperator* or described as exercising *imperium* in the early medieval west. Even when a ruler had no particular connection to Rome, such terms were sometimes used if his power extended over several subordinate kingdoms or peoples.[14] We should not, however, assume that any particular political idea lay behind each use of a word like *imperator* or *basileus*. Tenth-century Anglo-Latin was marked by attempts to exhibit erudition through obscure vocabulary, and calling the king *basileus* may have been more about displaying knowledge of a grecism than likening him to a Byzantine emperor: that *basileus* was glossed *rex* suggests that it did not necessarily evoke 'imperial' associations.[15] Even *imperator* might have been used for the sake of lexical variety and a general air of grandeur, rather than because the writer associated the term with a specific 'imperial' ideology: one could translate it 'commander', as well as 'emperor'.[16]

While the contemporary import of words like *imperator* and *basileus* cannot be ascertained with confidence, it is not unlikely that some people were thinking along the lines sketched by Stengel and Erdmann, since tenth-century English kings were frequently presented as ruling a collection of peoples. The *ordo* that was probably first used for Æthelstan's consecration referred to the king ruling two peoples (i.e. the Saxons and the Mercians), and in later versions this was increased to three, who were

---

[14] E. E. Stengel, 'Kaisertitel und Suveränitätsidee: Studien zur Vorgeschichte des modernen Staatsbegriffs', *Deutsches Archiv für Geschichte des Mittelalters*, 3 (1939), 1–56; Erdmann, *Forschungen*, 1–51 especially 37–43. See also S. Fanning, 'Bede, *Imperium*, and the Bretwaldas', *Speculum*, 66 (1991), 1–26. The notion that a man might be called *imperator* on the grounds that he possessed two (or more) *regna* is particularly clearly expressed in *Annales Fuldenses*, 869, ed. F. Kurze and revised R. Rau, in *idem*, *Quellen zur karolingischen Reichsgeschichte*, 2nd edn (3 vols., Darmstadt, 1968–9), III, 74–6. R. Drögereit, 'Kaiseridee und Kaisertitel bei den Angelsachsen', *Zeitschrift der Savigny-Stiftung für Rechtsgeschichte. Germanistische Abteilung*, 69 (1952), 24–73 especially 57–73, argued that *imperator* only occurs in forged documents. His case is countered by E. E. Stengel, 'Imperator und Imperium bei den Angelsachsen. Eine wort- und begriffgeschichtliche Untersuchung', *Deutsches Archiv für Erforschung des Mittelalters*, 16 (1960), 15–72 especially 54–66; John, *Orbis Britanniae*, 52–5. S 392, 404, 406 are not reliable evidence that Æthelstan was styled *imperator*.

[15] Drögereit, 'Kaiseridee und Kaisertitel', 57–8; F. M. Stenton, *Anglo-Saxon England*, 3rd edn (Oxford, 1971), 353; M. Lapidge, 'The Hermeneutic Style in Tenth-Century Anglo-Latin Literature', *Anglo-Saxon England*, 4 (1975), 67–111.

[16] R. E. Latham et al., eds., *Dictionary of Medieval Latin from British Sources* (Oxford, 1975–), s.v. *imperator*.

named as the Saxons, the Mercians and the Northumbrians.[17] Edgar's *obit* in the D and E texts of the *Chronicle* calls him 'ruler of the Angles, friend of the West Saxons and protector of the Mercians'.[18] Especially in the mid-tenth century, charter styles quite frequently assert that kings ruled both the English and unnamed neighbouring peoples, as in *rex Anglorum ceterarumque gentium in circuitu persistentium gubernator et rector* ('king of the English and governor and ruler of other peoples dwelling round about').[19] It is particularly notable that the largest cluster of occurrences of the word *imperator* is in a group of mid-tenth-century charters that refer to an assemblage of peoples, using styles like *rex Ængulsæxna ond Norðhymbra imperator paganorum gubernator Brittonumque propugnator* ('king of the Anglo-Saxons and *imperator* of the Northumbrians, governor of the pagans and defender of the Britons').[20] The notion of rulership of Britain is often mentioned in the context of analyses of possible 'imperial' claims, but these two pretensions should be distinguished. The examples just cited show that a king did not need to claim authority throughout Britain to be understood as the ruler of several peoples and therefore a potential *imperator*. Equally, a claim to rulership of Britain would not require an 'imperial' ideology. Since my argument is not predicated upon the presence or absence of any 'imperial' conception of kingship, I leave that slippery and probably irresolvable issue open, and focus on the question of why it was claimed that certain kings ruled the whole island.

There is reason to think that charter styles did not merely reflect drafting fashions, but also bore some relation to political reality: the presentation of Æthelstan as ruler of Britain began quite soon after the Eamont meeting, and Edmund was not thus described while York was under Hiberno-Scandinavian rule. To understand why English kings were sometimes styled rulers of Britain, we therefore need to assess the nature of their relationships with neighbouring rulers in the late Anglo-Saxon period, focusing initially on the century or so between Alfred and Edgar. The extant contemporary evidence is sparse and almost all English in origin: as is often pointed out, there is a risk that this may tempt us to overstate English domination. Each reference to contact between English and neighbouring kings has been extensively picked over, and there are

---

[17] C. E. Hohler, 'Some Service-Books of the Later Saxon Church', in *Tenth-Century Studies: Essays in Commemoration of the Millennium of the Council of Winchester and Regularis Concordia*, ed. D. Parsons (Chichester, 1975), 60–83, 217–27 at 67–9; J. L. Nelson, 'The Second English *Ordo*', in *eadem, Politics and Ritual in Early Medieval Europe* (1986), 361–74 at 361–9; J. L. Nelson, 'The First Use of the Second Anglo-Saxon *Ordo*', in *Myth, Rulership, Church and Charters: Essays in Honour of Nicholas Brooks*, ed. J. Barrow and A. Wareham (Aldershot, 2008), 117–26.

[18] *ASC* DE 975. Cf. *ASC* BC 959.

[19] For references, see Kleinschmidt, 'Titulaturen', 93–8, 106, 110–11, 112. Cf. *Regularis Concordia*, I, ed. and trans. T. Symons (Edinburgh, 1953), I.

[20] For references, see Kleinschmidt, 'Titulaturen', 99–103.

many hypotheses about what was demanded or agreed on particular occasions. My intention here is neither to assemble a complete corpus of the evidence nor to dwell on the detail of what may have happened in any individual incident. Rather, I aim to assess the general character of English kings' dealings with their neighbours, within the severe constraints of the extant sources.

Charter attestations constitute the clearest evidence that English kings were at least sometimes dominant over other rulers. We may begin with the only attendee of the Eamont meeting to whom the *Chronicle* does not accord the title *cyning* ('king'), Ealdred of Bamburgh. Between 930 and 932, an Ealdred *dux*, very probably the man who was at Eamont, attested several of Æthelstan's charters, most of which were issued south of the Thames: that Ealdred travelled far from his base on the Northumbrian coast to attend assemblies shows his acknowledgement of Æthelstan's superiority.[21] Ealdred probably died in 934, but his family retained power in north-eastern Northumbria for over a century and continued to witness diplomas from time to time, which indicates that they recognised the dominance of Æthelstan and his successors, at least intermittently.[22] Men whom English sources at least sometimes styled 'king' also appear in witness lists. Five Welsh kings, the most famous of whom is the Hywel who was present at Eamont, witnessed several charters from between 928 and 935, the majority of which were issued well within Æthelstan's heartlands. Constantine II, the Scottish king and another Eamont attendee, is known to have attested at Buckingham and Cirencester in 934 and 935, immediately after an English campaign in Scotland; Owain, the king of Cumbria or Strathclyde (the terms are interchangeable), appears at Worthy, Cirencester and Dorchester in 931 and 935. These men were styled *subregulus* ('subordinate ruler'), which was at least one notch below the titles sported by the English king, such

---

[21] S 403, 412, 413, 416, 418, 418a, 1604. In all but two of these witness lists, the name directly after Ealdred is Uhtred *dux*. This strengthens the identification with Ealdred of Bamburgh, who had a brother called Uhtred: *Historia de Sancto Cuthberto*, XXII, ed. and trans. T. Johnson South (Cambridge, 2002), 60. See also S 379, 417.

[22] The likely year of Ealdred's death can be inferred from the *Annals of Clonmacnoise*, which survive only in a seventeenth-century English translation. The death of 'Adulf m^cEtulfe king of North Saxons' is recorded under 928, along with Æthelstan's Scottish campaign, which sources with more reliable absolute chronology place in 934: D. Murphy, ed., *The Annals of Clonmacnoise* (Dublin, 1896), 149. Ealdred's successors attested S 407, 425, 434, 520, 544, 546, 550, 552a (Osulf, in the first three with Uhtred), 766, 771, 779, 806 (Eadulf), 881 (Waltheof), 921, 922, 926, 931, 931b, 933, 934 (another Uhtred). Cf. D. Whitelock, 'The Dealings of the Kings of England with Northumbria in the Tenth and Eleventh Centuries', in *The Anglo-Saxons: Studies in Some Aspects of their History and Culture Presented to Bruce Dickens*, ed. P. Clemoes (1959), 70–88 at 76–84.

as *rex* or *basileus*.[23] Like Ealdred of Bamburgh, the *subreguli* journeyed far into the core territories of the English king, thereby recognising his superiority. No genuine extant charter is witnessed by a Scottish king after 935, and the only possible subsequent attestation by a Cumbrian ruler is the *Malcolm dux* who appears in a dubious diploma dated 970, but there is another clutch of Welsh attestations between 946 and 956.[24] Save for Malcolm's possible appearance in 970, all the Welsh, Cumbrian and Scottish attestations occur in two distinctive groups of diplomas, the so-called 'Æthelstan A' and 'alliterative' charters.[25] That these rulers' presence was recorded may be a result of the foibles of the draftsmen responsible for these particular series: Welsh, Cumbrian and Scottish rulers could have attended assemblies at other times without being noted in extant witness lists, and the lack of attestations after 956 need not indicate that English domination of Wales and northern Britain had loosened.[26] In this regard, it is interesting to note that no extant witness list records the presence of any Welshman at Edmund's court in 945, but a Welsh king apparently aided his ravaging of Cumbria that year.[27]

The best-known occasion on which a tenth-century English king met with neighbouring rulers was in 973, when the D and E texts of the *Chronicle* state that Edgar went with a naval force to Chester, where six kings met him and 'with him they all pledged (*getreowsodon*) that they would be cooperators (*efenwyrhtan*) on sea and on land (*on sæ 7 on lande*)'.[28] The twelfth-century re-workings of this passage by John of Worcester and William of Malmesbury supply the names of eight men, who can plausibly be identified with Scottish, Cumbrian, Hiberno-Scandinavian and Welsh (or Breton) potentates active in the 970s. The discrepancy in the number of kings need not be suspicious, since the compiler of the *Chronicle* could have regarded two of those present as sub-regal. John and William may

---

[23] S 400, 407, 413, 416, 417, 418a, 420, 425, 426, 427, 434, 1792. For Strathclyde/Cumbria, see P. A. Wilson, 'On the Use of the Terms "Strathclyde" and "Cumbria"', *Transactions of the Cumberland and Westmorland Antiquarian and Archaeological Society*, new series, 66 (1966), 57–92; A. Woolf, *From Pictland to Alba, 789–1070* (Edinburgh, 2007), 152–7.

[24] Malcolm's attestation is in S 779. The Welsh attestations are in S 520, 544, 550, 552a, 566, 633, 1497.

[25] S. Keynes, *An Atlas of Attestations in Anglo-Saxon Charters, c. 670–1066* (Cambridge, 2002), Table XXXVI.

[26] Cf. A. Williams, 'An Outing on the Dee: King Edgar at Chester, A.D. 973', *Mediaeval Scandinavia*, 14 (2004), 229–43 at 236 n. 35; Woolf, *Pictland to Alba*, 174; Keynes, 'Edgar', 26–7, 50–1.

[27] The campaign is mentioned in *ASC* ABCDEF 945, but Welsh involvement is known only from Roger of Wendover, *Flores Historiarum*, ed. H. O. Coxe (5 vols., 1841–4), I, 398. Roger wrote in the thirteenth century, but his knowledge of Edgar's coin reform demonstrates that he had access to material on the tenth. For an attempt to identify the Welsh king, whom Roger names as 'Leolin', with Hywel, see A. Breeze, 'Armes Prydein, Hywel Dda, and the Reign of Edmund of Wessex', *Études Celtiques*, 33 (1997), 209–22 at 218–22.

[28] *ASC* DE 973.

well have drawn on some early account of those who gathered at Chester, although their lists could alternatively reflect an eleventh- or twelfth-century guess as to who was likely to have attended a meeting in 973.[29] We can, however, be reasonably confident that the king of Scots was one of those present, since Ælfric, writing no more than about twenty-five years later, stated that 'all the kings who were on this island, of *Cumeras* and of *Scottas*, came to Edgar – once, on one day, eight kings – and they all bowed (*gebugon*) to Edgar's rule (*wissunge*)'.[30] The meaning of *Cumeras* is doubtful: it could be a reference to the Welsh, the Cumbrians or perhaps both. The precise identities of those present are not critical here: the key point is simply that the king of Scots and a number of other insular rulers met Edgar at Chester. It has been claimed that Chester, which was frequented by merchants from around the Irish Sea, constituted a neutral venue.[31] It was not. It was a town with which Edgar had a longstanding connection: one of his earliest extant charters granted six estates in western Cheshire to a minster in Chester.[32] That Chester was firmly under Edgar's control in the last years of his reign is demonstrated by the minting there of coins of his reformed type. The reform was associated with a marked reduction in the number of moneyers active in Chester; the suddenness of this change is suggestive of an administrative imposition, rather than a shift in popular demand for coins.[33] As in Æthelstan's reign, neighbouring kings were in 973 acknowledging the superiority of an English king by meeting him on his own ground, clearly at his instigation.

In guessing what Edgar wanted to achieve at Chester, we should bear in mind two events that happened earlier the same year. The first is well known: shortly before the Chester meeting, Edgar was consecrated at Bath at Pentecost. Janet Nelson argues persuasively that he had already been consecrated near the beginning of his reign, and that the Bath consecration was intended to stress his rule of Britain, rather than merely of the English: the *ordo* most likely followed in 973 was very similar to that which was probably used for Edgar's first consecration, but a prayer that the king be honoured *pre cunctis regibus terrae* ('above all kings

[29] John of Worcester, *Chronicle*, 973, ed. and trans. R. R. Darlington, P. McGurk and J. Bray (2 vols. so far, Oxford, 1995–), II, 422–4; William of Malmesbury, *Gesta Regum*, II.148 (I, 238–40); D. E. Thornton, 'Edgar and the Eight Kings, AD 973: *textus et dramatis personae*', *Early Medieval Europe*, 10 (2001), 49–79; Williams, 'Outing on the Dee'; A. Breeze, 'Edgar at Chester in 973: A Breton Link?', *Northern History*, 44 (2007), 153–7.

[30] Ælfric, *Life of St Swithun*, XXVIII, ed. and trans. M. Lapidge, *The Cult of St Swithun* (Oxford, 2003), 590–609 at 606 with discussion of the date of composition at 577.

[31] J. Barrow, 'Chester's Earliest Regatta? Edgar's Dee-Rowing Revisited', *Early Medieval Europe*, 10 (2001), 81–93.

[32] S 667; C. P. Lewis, 'Edgar, Chester, and the Kingdom of the Mercians, 957–9', in *Edgar*, ed. Scragg, 104–23.

[33] K. Jonsson, *The New Era: The Reformation of the Late Anglo-Saxon Coinage* (1987), 128–30; D. M. Metcalf, *An Atlas of Anglo-Saxon and Norman Coin Finds, 973–1086* (1998), 208.

of the land') was changed to *pre cunctis regibus brittaniae*.[34] If Nelson is correct that the Bath consecration was concerned with articulating pan-British pretensions, the Chester gathering would serve to prove that these were far from empty pomp. The second event is less familiar to most English historians. It occurred seven weeks before the Bath consecration, at Quedlinburg in eastern Saxony: Otto I, who had recently conquered much of Italy and whom the pope had crowned emperor in 962, celebrated Easter in the company of the dukes of Poland and Bohemia, along with legates from the Greeks, Beneventans, Hungarians, Bulgars, Danes and Slavs. Shortly before, Edgar had sent an embassy to Otto and surely learned of plans for the Quedlinburg gathering, to which the Chester meeting presents clear parallels.[35] Whatever specific promises of cooperation Edgar wanted to secure at Chester, it is hard to avoid the inference that a large part of the meeting's purpose was to demonstrate Edgar's strength and to ape the most powerful ruler in Europe. If displaying power was indeed a central objective, Edgar may have selected Chester as the venue because its visible Roman remains, like those of Bath, would call to mind an earlier Britain-wide hegemony.

The superiority of English kings was at certain times demonstrated in various other ways, besides visits to their courts. We have already seen that a Welsh king assisted Edmund in his ravaging of Cumbria in 945, and charter attestations suggest that Æthelstan may have received military aid from three Welsh kings on his Scottish expedition of 934.[36] Referring to this campaign, the *Chronicle* merely records that Æthelstan ravaged much of Scotland with both land and naval forces, but John of Worcester, quite possibly reproducing an earlier source, adds that Constantine then handed over his son as a hostage, along with 'worthy gifts', presumably tribute in some form.[37] There is firmer evidence of the

---

[34] H. A. Wilson, ed., *The Benedictional of Archbishop Robert* (1903), 145; D. H. Turner, ed., *The Claudius Pontificals* (Chichester, 1971), 93; J. L. Nelson, 'Inauguration Rituals', in *Early Medieval Kingship*, ed. P. H. Sawyer and I. N. Wood (Leeds, 1979), 50–71 at 63–70; Nelson, 'Second English *Ordo*', 369–74.

[35] Thietmar of Merseburg, *Chronicon*, II.31, ed. R. Holtzmann (*Monumenta Germaniae Historica, Scriptores Rerum Germanicarum*, new series, IX, Berlin, 1955), 77–8. On Edgar's embassy, see K. J. Leyser, 'The Ottonians and Wessex', in *idem, Communications and Power in Medieval Europe: The Carolingian and Ottonian Centuries*, ed. T. Reuter (1994), 73–104 at 95–8; Keynes, 'Edgar', 49.

[36] Three Welsh kings who witnessed a charter at Winchester on 28 May 934 (S 425) attested at Nottingham ten days later (S 407): they appear to have been accompanying Æthelstan as he headed for Scotland.

[37] *ASC* ABCDEF 934; John of Worcester, *Chronicle*, 934 (II, 388–90). In the section of John's *Chronicle* concerning the period before about 970, verifiable sources are usually rendered with reasonable accuracy: R. R. Darlington and P. McGurk, 'The "Chronicon ex Chronicis" of "Florence" of Worcester and its Use of Sources for English History before 1066', *Anglo-Norman Studies*, 5 (1982), 185–96.

Welsh paying tribute: *Armes Prydein,* a prophetic poem that could plausibly date from almost any time between the mid-ninth and eleventh centuries, bemoans the rapacity of the stewards of an unnamed English king.[38] Spiritual patronage could be used to express superiority and to create or reinforce reciprocal bonds of obligation: Asser states that Alfred stood sponsor to Anarawd ap Rhodri at his confirmation and, less reliably, William of Malmesbury reports that Æthelstan ordered the baptism of Constantine's son and became his (the son's) godfather in 927.[39] English kings also used spiritual patronage in their dealings with Scandinavians: Alfred became the godfather of both Guthrum and a son of Hæsten, and Edmund sponsored Olaf Sihtricson at his baptism and Ragnald at his confirmation.[40]

References to encounters between English and neighbouring kings often allude to some kind of agreement of common purpose. Thus, the *Chronicle* states that those who assembled at Eamont in 927 renounced idolatry, that the Scottish king agreed in 945 to be Edmund's cooperator (*his midwyrhta* – literally 'his together-worker') and that the kings who met at Chester in 973 likewise promised to be cooperators (*efenwyrhtan*).[41] It is important to remember that cooperation is not the same as equality. Aside from the references in the D and E texts of the *Chronicle* for 973, there are four extant occurrences of *efenwyrhta, efenwyrcend* and *emnwyrhta.* All appear in Old English translations of Latin texts and all translate Latin *cooperator* or *operator.* In the two occurrences in the *Old English Bede,* the cooperators are an abbot and a monk (Benedict Biscop and Ceolfrith) and an archbishop and an abbot (Theodore and Hadrian): in neither case were the men who worked together equals in power or status.[42] The

[38] I. Williams and R. Bromwich, ed. and trans., *Armes Prydein: The Prophecy of Britain from the Book of Taliesin* (Dublin, 1982), especially lines 17–22, 69–86. For discussion, see D. N. Dumville, 'Brittany and "Armes Prydein Vawr"', *Études Celtiques,* 20 (1983), 145–58; Breeze, '*Armes Prydein*', 209–18; C. Etchingham, 'North Wales, Ireland and the Isles: The Insular Viking Zone', *Peritia,* 15 (2001), 145–87 at 183–6. Dumville favours a date between *c.* 935 and *c.* 950, but perhaps as late as *c.* 980. Breeze contends that the poem was written in 940. Etchingham extends the date range into the eleventh century.

[39] Asser, *Life of King Alfred,* LXXX (66–7); William of Malmesbury, *Gesta Regum,* II.134 (I, 214). Cf. J. H. Lynch, *Christianizing Kingship: Ritual Sponsorship in Anglo-Saxon England* (Ithaca, NY, 1998), 189–228. For an intriguing suggestion about the baptismal name of Constantine's son, see Woolf, *Pictland to Alba,* 192–3.

[40] *ASC* 878, 893, ABCD 943.

[41] *ASC* D 927, ABCD 945, DE 973.

[42] T. Miller, ed. and trans., *The Old English Version of Bede's Ecclesiastical History of the English People,* IV.20, V.18 (4 vols. in 2, 1890–8), I, 314, 464; H. Magennis, ed. and trans., *The Old English Life of Saint Mary of Egypt* (Exeter, 2002), lines 119, 402. Cf. Bede, *Ecclesiastical History,* IV.18, V.20 (388, 530); Paul the Deacon, *Life of St Mary of Egypt,* ed. and trans. Magennis, *Old English Life of Saint Mary,* lines 134, 416. I identified this corpus through searches of A. Cameron, A. C. Amos and A. diP. Healey, eds., *Dictionary of Old English* (Toronto, 1986–), consulted at http://oxlip.ouls.ox.ac.uk/doe/, accessed 8 June 2011; A.diP.

same point can be made about *midwyrhta*: the *Old English Soliloquies* states that God is a *mydwyrhta* to each well-working person.[43] Cooperation need not be voluntary and parties can cooperate in pursuit of an objective that is for one party's benefit: it is quite conceivable that English, Welsh, Cumbrian and Scottish kings agreed to work together to further a largely English agenda. It is likely that the key demand that English kings made was that their counterparts should not support Hiberno-Scandinavians seeking to maintain or establish a position in Northumbria. The exclusion of Hiberno-Scandinavians was not necessarily congruent with Welsh, Scottish or Cumbrian interests: Hiberno-Scandinavian rule at York might reduce the number of footloose raiders in the Irish Sea and would provide a buffer against northward West Saxon expansion. Indeed, Welsh, Cumbrian and Scottish rulers sometimes allied with Scandinavians: Anarawd of Gwynedd appears to have cooperated with Guthfrith of Northumbria in the late ninth century, and in 937 Æthelstan defeated an alliance of Olaf Guthfrithson, Constantine and (probably) a Cumbrian king.[44] The *Armes Prydein* poet dreamed of an even grander anti-English coalition, encompassing the Welsh, Dubliners (i.e. Hiberno-Scandinavians), Bretons, Cornish, Irish, Cumbrians and Scots.[45]

Why did Welsh, Cumbrian and Scottish kings recognise English superiority, particularly if this involved handing over hostages and tribute, or promising to forsake potentially attractive Hiberno-Scandinavian alliances? The obvious answer is that English kings were in all probability the wealthiest and most militarily powerful men on the island and could therefore coerce their neighbours. The clearest instance of this is Æthelstan's ravaging of Constantine's kingdom in 934: immediately after, Constantine attested charters at Buckingham and Cirencester, and quite possibly paid tribute and gave his son as a hostage. Having regained York in 944, Edmund demonstrated that he too could inflict destruction in northern Britain: the next year, he ravaged Cumbria and blinded two sons of its king.[46] It is clear that Edgar likewise had formidable coercive

---

Healey, ed., *The Dictionary of Old English Corpus in Electronic Form* (Toronto, 2009), consulted at http://weblearn.ox.ac.uk/site/human/english/materials/chronology/oldenglish/, accessed 8 June 2011. It is also notable that *efenwyrhtan* is translated *cooperatores* by John of Worcester, *Chronicle*, 973 (II, 422).

[43] T. A. Carnicelli, ed., *King Alfred's Version of St. Augustine's Soliloquies* (Cambridge, MA, 1969), 69.

[44] Asser, *Life of King Alfred*, LXXX (66–7); *ASC* ABCD 937; Symeon of Durham, *Libellus de Exordio atque Procursu istius, hoc est Dunhelmensis, Ecclesie*, II.18, ed. and trans. D. Rollason (Oxford, 2000), 138.

[45] *Armes Prydein*, especially lines 9–11, 131, 147–54.

[46] *ASC* ABCDEF 945; Roger of Wendover, *Flores Historiarum*, I, 398. Edmund may well also have been involved in the death of the king of Gwynedd, who was killed 'by the Saxons' in 942: D. N. Dumville, ed. and trans., *Annales Cambriae, A.D. 682–954: Texts A–C in Parallel* (Cambridge, 2002), 16.

capabilities: in the decades after his death, several writers remarked upon his naval strength and there is good circumstantial evidence that he employed a powerful mercenary fleet.[47] If Edgar's neighbours wished to avoid their lands being ravaged, the invitation to Chester was probably not one that they could decline. It is, moreover, interesting that the *Chronicle* notes that Edgar was accompanied to Chester by his *scipfyrd* or *sciphere* (naval force), which presumably served to focus the mind of any visitor who had contemplated refusing to cooperate.[48]

Certain historians of Wales and especially Scotland have sought to explain away evidence that 'their' kings recognised English superiority.[49] Some others accept that submissions were made, but protest that they were forcibly extracted, thus exonerating Welsh and Scottish kings from the charge that they cravenly sucked up to the English.[50] While the threat of coercion was important, we should not assume that kings were reluctant to acknowledge English domination. There is no reason why they 'ought' to have seen themselves as on a par with militarily stronger English kings: indeed, Dauvit Broun argues that it was only in the first half of the thirteenth century that Scottish kings began to assert that they were of equal status to their English counterparts.[51] Submission need not have been humiliating: when Welsh, Cumbrian and Scottish rulers visited the English king, they appear to have been treated with honour, attesting above the non-royal English lay witnesses and, in the 'Æthelstan A' charters, also above the bishops and sometimes the archbishops.[52] Nor need the burdens associated with submission have been particularly onerous. The English king might demand non-alliance with Hiberno-Scandinavians, tribute, hostages and occasional military aid, but there is no evidence that a Welsh, Cumbrian or Scottish king's authority within his own kingdom was significantly compromised.

The 'costs' of accepting English domination are thus unlikely to have seriously undermined a king. The benefits, on the other hand, were not trivial and extended beyond being spared from attack. Asser spelled out some of these benefits in his account of Alfred's dealings with the Welsh. The passage in question is the most detailed extant description of a submission to a pre-Conquest English king, but its value does not lie merely in its detail. Since Asser was a Welshman in an English king's

---

[47] S. Jayakumar, 'Some Reflections on the "Foreign Policies" of Edgar "the Peaceable"', *Haskins Society Journal*, 10 (2001), 17–37.

[48] *ASC* DE 973.

[49] B. T. Hudson, *Kings of Celtic Scotland* (Westport, CT, 1994), especially 73–6, 97–101, is particularly tendentious.

[50] The clearest instance is D. P. Kirby, 'Hywel Dda: Anglophil?', *Welsh History Review*, 8 (1976–7), 1–13.

[51] Broun, *Scottish Independence*, 1–24, 161–212.

[52] S 400, 407, 413, 416, 417, 418a, 420, 425, 434, 520, 544, 550, 552a, 566, 633, 1497, 1792.

service, and may well have envisaged both Welsh and English readers for his work, his account is probably the nearest thing we have to a 'balanced' report of any relationship between English and neighbouring kings.[53] Asser emphasises the dignified nature of the submissions: the Welsh kings initiated contact, Alfred received Anarawd *honorifice* ('honourably') and their relationship was one of *amicitia* ('friendship').[54] It is, however, plain that the Welsh kings recognised Alfred's superiority: Hyfaidd of Dyfed 'submitted himself to [Alfred's] royal overlordship' (*regali se subdiderat imperio*), the kings of Glywysing, Gwent and Brycheiniog sought Alfred's *dominium* ('lordship') and Anarawd of Gwynedd agreed to be obedient to Alfred's will in all things (*in omnibus regiae voluntati sic oboediens*). Asser stresses the benefits that Alfred could offer the Welsh kings in return. One was *familiaritas* ('friendship' or 'intimacy'), the attraction of which should not be dismissed: there are plenty of examples from better-documented periods of dignitaries being keen to hobnob with foreign royalty. Submission to Alfred could also apparently lead to an increase in worldly power, perhaps because *familiaritas* with a powerful external figure boosted a king's prestige in the eyes of his own subjects. Furthermore, Asser states that the Welsh kings gained wealth and mentions the extravagant gifts that Alfred showered on Anarawd. The bestowal of presents would indicate Alfred's high esteem for his Welsh clients and give them resources with which to reward their followers, but would also underline Alfred's superiority, unless the Welsh kings gave him equivalent gifts. Asser implies, however, that the most important attraction of Alfred's lordship, at least for the southern Welsh rulers, was the possibility of protection from Ealdorman Æthelred of Mercia (Alfred's son-in-law) and from Anarawd and his brothers. Alfred had some capacity to restrain Æthelred, who had (according to Asser) promised obedience to Alfred, and Alfred could threaten to attack (or to have Æthelred attack) Gwynedd if Anarawd troubled the southern Welsh kings. The effectiveness of this protection is doubtful, since the *Annales Cambriae* records that in or around 893 Anarawd ravaged south-west Wales *cum Anglis*. The *Angli* involved could have been Mercians rather than West Saxons, but Alfred had failed to shield some

---

[53] The relevant section is Asser, *Life of King Alfred*, LXXX–LXXXI (66–7). On audience, see D. P. Kirby, 'Asser and his Life of King Alfred', *Studia Celtica*, 6 (1971), 12–35 at 17; J. Campbell, 'Asser's *Life of Alfred*', in *The Inheritance of Historiography, 350–900*, ed. C. Holdsworth and T. P. Wiseman (Exeter, 1986), 115–35 at 122–8; M. Kempshall, 'No Bishop, No King: The Ministerial Ideology of Kingship and Asser's *Res Gestae Aelfredi*', in *Belief and Culture in the Early Middle Ages: Studies Presented to Henry Mayr-Harting*, ed. R. Gameson and H. Leyser (Oxford, 2001), 106–27.

[54] That the parties to an *amicitia* agreement did not need to be equals is illustrated by Henry the Fowler's contracting *amicitiae* with men whose lord he was: G. Althoff, *Amicitiae und Pacta. Bündnis, Einung, Politik und Gebetsgedenken im beginnenden 10. Jahrhundert* (Hanover, 1992), 27–35. See also G. Althoff, *Family, Friends and Followers: Political and Social Bonds in Early Medieval Europe*, trans. C. Carroll (Cambridge, 2004), 67–90.

of his Welsh clients from assault; his domination in most of Wales may thereafter have been severely attenuated.[55] A promise of protection was not without value, however: even though a protégé could not rely on support, the mere possibility that his lord might intervene would likely make potential aggressors hesitate before attacking.

It is probable that tenth-century English kings likewise gave *familiaritas*, gifts and promises of protection in return for cooperation, and there are a couple of clear examples of Scottish kings deriving benefit from being on friendly terms with their English counterparts. The *Chronicle* reports that in 945 Edmund ravaged Cumbria and granted (*let*) it to Malcolm I on condition that Malcolm be 'his cooperator (*his midwyrhta*) both on sea and on land'. Contrary to what has sometimes been asserted, Cumbria (or Strathclyde) was at this time a distinct kingdom, not an apanage for the heir to the Scottish kingship: Edmund was helping one northern king to assert overlordship over another.[56] The second case is Edgar's alleged grant of Lothian (the area between the Forth and the Tweed or some part thereof) to Kenneth II, reported in an early twelfth-century Durham text. If the account is reliable, the 'grant' must have been made between Kenneth's accession in 971 and Edgar's death in 975, most probably in connection with the Chester meeting in 973, when Kenneth and Edgar likely promised to be *efenwyrhtan* 'on sea and on land'. Lothian had probably been under the *de facto* domination of the kings of Scots for some time and had never been subject to more than very loose West Saxon overlordship.[57] Edgar is thus unlikely to have regarded his 'grant' as a substantive concession, but the security afforded by English acceptance that Lothian was within the Scottish sphere will have been of some value to Kenneth. In both 945 and the 970s, English kings recognised and aided the extension of Scottish royal power in return for promises of cooperation on land and sea.

It thus appears that for much of the century or so between Alfred and Edgar, Welsh kings recognised the superiority of the West Saxon king, who was able to constrain and mould their actions through threats and promises. From at least about 927, and perhaps (as we shall see)

[55] Dumville, ed. and trans., *Annales Cambriae, A.D. 682–954*, 14, with discussion by T. M. Charles-Edwards, 'Wales and Mercia 613–918', in *Mercia: An Anglo-Saxon Kingdom in Europe*, ed. M. P. Brown and C. A. Farr (2001), 89–105 at 102–5.

[56] *ASC* ABCD 945; B. T. Hudson, '*Elech* and the Scots in Strathclyde', *Scottish Gaelic Studies*, 15 (1988), 145–9; Woolf, *Pictland to Alba*, 156–7, 182–5, 270–1.

[57] *De Primo Saxonum Adventu*, ed. T. Arnold, *Symeonis Monachi Opera Omnia* (Rolls Series, 75, 2 vols., 1882–5), II, 365–84 at 382. For discussion, see M. O. Anderson, 'Lothian and the Early Scottish Kings', *Scottish Historical Review*, 39 (1960), 98–112; G. W. S. Barrow, *The Kingdom of the Scots: Government, Church and Society from the Eleventh to the Fourteenth Century* (1973), 148–61; B. Meehan, 'The Siege of Durham, the Battle of Carham and the Cession of Lothian', *Scottish Historical Review*, 55 (1976), 1–19, especially 12–17; Woolf, *Pictland to Alba*, 211, 234–6.

slightly earlier, the same was so vis-à-vis the rulers of Bamburgh, and the Cumbrian and Scottish kings. But English overlordship was not continuous and did not create a troop of pliant acolytes. The clearest demonstration of this is the Scottish and Cumbrian kings' alliance with Olaf Guthfrithson against Æthelstan in 937, and it is likely that English kings' dominance in northern Britain was minimal at times when there was a Hiberno-Scandinavian kingdom in Northumbria. There are also references in the so-called *Chronicle of the Kings of Alba* to Scottish raids on Northumbria in *c.* 949, *c.* 971 and *c.* 972, and the possibility of similar forays by Welsh kings cannot be discounted.[58] But unless Welsh, Cumbrian and Scottish kings allied with each other or with a Hiberno-Scandinavian king, there is no sign that any of them could threaten the English king in any fundamental way. By contrast, it is implicit in Asser's account that already in the 880s Alfred was sufficiently powerful that the southern Welsh kings thought that he could constrain the king of Gwynedd in north-west Wales. By 934, moreover, the English king could cause serious problems to any ruler on the island: that year, Æthelstan's forces ravaged as far as Caithness, going further north than even Edward I is known to have ventured.[59] The campaign of 934 was not a campaign of conquest, intended to leave Æthelstan with any enduring capability to impinge directly upon the lives of the mass of the population of northern Britain. Rather, it enforced the English king's personal domination over another ruler, but only temporarily. Tenth-century English kings' power in Wales and (even more so) northern Britain was a loose and somewhat intermittent hegemony, 'extensive' rather than 'intensive'.[60] English kings were nonetheless quite capable of coercing neighbouring rulers: the terms upon which they dealt with their Welsh, Cumbrian and Scottish counterparts did not, *pace* some recent commentators, approach anything like equality.[61]

This assessment of the tenth-century evidence resembles Rees Davies's characterisation of how English kings kept Welsh and Scottish kings in line in the century after the Norman Conquest. From the late twelfth century, English domination became increasingly precise, onerous, threatening and sometimes humiliating: tacit understandings were replaced with written codifications, and English kings asserted tenurial

---

[58] The text is edited by B. T. Hudson, 'The Scottish Chronicle', *Scottish Historical Review*, 77 (1998), 129–61 at 148–51. Cf. Woolf, *Pictland to Alba*, 177–81, 209–11.

[59] *Historia Regum*, ed. Arnold, *Symeonis Monachi Opera Omnia*, II, 3–283 at 93. For a map, see Woolf, *Pictland to Alba*, 162.

[60] Cf. R. R. Davies, *Domination and Conquest: The Experience of Ireland, Scotland and Wales, 1100–1300* (Cambridge, 1990), especially 1–24.

[61] Contrast Thornton, 'Edgar and the Eight Kings', 77–9; Barrow, 'Chester's Earliest Regatta?'; Jayakumar, 'Some Reflections', 31–5.

and jurisdictional claims over subordinate rulers' territories. Before the latter part of the twelfth century, however, English kings' hegemony was rather less oppressive: their loose superiority was honourably acknowledged through intermittent visits to their courts, the handing over of hostages and tribute and the provision of occasional military aid.[62] It is quite likely that most post-Conquest English kings had somewhat more capacity than their tenth-century predecessors to intervene in Scottish and Welsh affairs, but, as in the tenth century, English domination of Wales and northern Britain was not continuous in the century after the Norman Conquest, collapsing during Stephen's reign. The tenor of English kings' relationships with Scottish and Welsh rulers does not seem to have been radically different between the Conquest and the late twelfth century from how it had been between c. 927 and c. 973.

The theme of English domination of Britain is less prominent in modern discussions of the years between c. 973 and c. 1066. For this period, we have a scattering of references to English magnates raiding in Wales, and to incursions by both Welsh and Scottish kings, but contemporary references to contacts between English kings and the Welsh, Cumbrians and Scots are even scarcer than in the period between Alfred and Edgar.[63] One might hypothesise that this near-silence reflects that English domination in Wales and northern Britain crumbled in the ninety years between Edgar and the Norman Conquest. Such a conjecture may have some substance, particularly with regard to the second half of the reign of Æthelred II (978–1016), who must have been preoccupied with attempting to resist Scandinavian attack. Even then, however, Æthelred was able to ravage Cumbria in 1000 and it is unlikely that the offensive capabilities of English kings were significantly weakened during the eleventh century.[64] Nor is it likely that the power of eleventh-century Welsh and Scottish rulers (with the possible exception of Gruffudd ap Llywelyn) was in a different league from that of their predecessors.[65] If English kings' domination did loosen in the ninety years after Edgar's death, this was probably at least as much a consequence of a change in the balance of power within Ireland as of any change in the balance of power within Britain. In 980, Máel Sechnaill, king of Mide, defeated Olaf Sihtricson, king of Dublin and sometime king of York. The Hiberno-Scandinavian kingdom of Dublin survived, but was thereafter a more minor political player, with

---

[62] Davies, *Domination and Conquest*, 47–108; R. R. Davies, '"Keeping the Natives in Order": The English King and the "Celtic" Rulers 1066–1216', *Peritia*, 10 (1996), 212–24.

[63] For references, see K. L. Maund, *Ireland, Wales, and England in the Eleventh Century* (Woodbridge, 1991), 120–41; Woolf, *Pictland to Alba*, 232–40, 254–5, 270.

[64] *ASC* CDE 1000. Cf. Woolf, *Pictland to Alba*, 222–3.

[65] W. Davies, *Patterns of Power in Early Wales* (Oxford, 1990), 41–7, 80–91; Woolf, *Pictland to Alba*, 342–50.

no realistic chance of obtaining a substantial foothold in Britain.[66] The principal reason why Edgar and his predecessors sought domination over Welsh, Cumbrian and Scottish rulers was probably to deter them from giving succour to anyone seeking to establish or maintain a Hiberno-Scandinavian kingdom in Northumbria, a prospect that receded after Olaf's defeat in 980. The Scandinavians who afflicted Æthelred primarily came across the North Sea and did not (so far as we know) attempt to ally with any king in Britain: the need for English kings to expend effort and resources on keeping neighbouring rulers in line thus became less pressing.

Even so, we should be wary of the conclusion that eleventh-century English kings were substantially less dominant over their Welsh, Cumbrian and Scottish counterparts than tenth-century kings had been. In or around 1031, Cnut went to Scotland and, according to the *Chronicle*, received some sort of recognition of superiority from Malcolm II, the king of Scots, and two other northern kings, Macbeth and Echmarcach.[67] In 1054, Earl Siward of Northumbria led an expedition into Scotland and defeated Macbeth, by now king of Scots. The D text of the *Chronicle* states that some of Edward the Confessor's housecarls were killed during this campaign, which indicates that it was undertaken with Edward's approval, and perhaps at his instigation. Unlike in Shakespeare's play, Macbeth did not die in battle against Siward, but was killed in 1058 by Malcolm III. What happened during the intervening four years is obscure, but it appears that Macbeth was replaced as king before his death by his stepson, whom Malcolm also killed in 1058. Siward was not necessarily seeking to set Malcolm in Macbeth's place, but defeat probably undermined Macbeth and played a major part in his downfall.[68] Something similar happened in Wales in 1063/4, when Earls Harold and Tostig attacked Gruffudd ap Llywelyn's territory. According to the C text of the *Chronicle*, Gruffudd had sworn in 1056 to be 'a loyal and faithful underking (*underkingc*) to King Edward', but two years later he aided the exiled Earl Ælfgar, a rival of Harold and Tostig. Following Harold and Tostig's campaign, Gruffudd 'was killed by his own men because of the fight he fought against Earl Harold'. Gruffudd's head was brought to Harold, who presented it to Edward. Edward and Harold then set up two of Gruffudd's half-brothers in his place; they gave hostages and swore oaths that they would pay tribute and 'be everywhere ready on water and

<hr/>

[66] Woolf, *Pictland to Alba*, 214–19.

[67] *ASC* DEF 1027. On the date and context, see B. T. Hudson, 'Cnut and the Scottish Kings', *English Historical Review*, 107 (1992), 350–60; Woolf, *Pictland to Alba*, 244–8; T. Bolton, *The Empire of Cnut the Great: Conquest and the Consolidation of Power in Northern Europe in the Early Eleventh Century* (Leiden, 2009), 136–50.

[68] *ASC* CD 1054; Woolf, *Pictland to Alba*, 260–70.

on land', presumably a promise of military assistance.[69] The English king, sometimes acting through his earls, could still represent a serious threat to any other ruler on the island.[70] Cnut and Edward perhaps gave practical expression to their superiority even more intermittently than their tenth-century predecessors or their twelfth-century successors, but looking across a long time span, the broad continuities between Æthelstan and Henry II are striking: while the extent of English kings' domination over their neighbours fluctuated, a loose but unmistakable overlordship over the other kings in Britain was a general feature of these two-and-a-half centuries.

With this in mind, we can now tackle the specific problem posed by my title, approaching it via the question of why claims to rule Britain became less ubiquitous after the tenth century. One could explain their reduced prominence in the eleventh century by pointing to the possible loosening of English overlordship, but this explanation would not account for the rarity with which Norman, Angevin and Plantagenet kings were described as rulers of Britain. Rees Davies's central concern in his Ford Lectures was to explain why twelfth- and thirteenth-century kings were by and large not presented as rulers of Britain, in spite of both their undoubted power and of post-Conquest writers' celebration of the pan-British pretensions of Æthelstan and Edgar. In proposing an explanation for this problem, Davies acutely observed that to explain how the English understood their relationship with Britain one 'must look towards England itself'.[71] Above all, he stressed the importance of a strong sense of English identity, which was often coupled with strident contempt for the allegedly barbarous Welsh and Scots: this, Davies argued, precluded the presentation of post-Conquest kings as rulers of Britain.[72] Furthermore, Davies drew attention to how the uniformity and ubiquity of royal administration within the English kingdom contrasted with the looser structures of central rule in other parts of Britain: since English kings' power was fundamentally

---

[69] *ASC* C 1056, D 1058, DE 1063. Cf. B. T. Hudson, 'The Destruction of Gruffudd ap Llywelyn', *Welsh History Review*, 15 (1990–1), 331–50; Maund, *Ireland, Wales, and England*, 125, 138–9.

[70] English military interventions in Wales are also known to have occurred in 967, 978, 983, 985, 992, 1012, 1035, 1046, 1055 and 1056. Some or all of these campaigns may well have had royal approval or support. For references to 992 and later, see Maund, *Ireland, Wales, and England*, 121–5. For earlier references, see J. Williams ab Ithel, ed., *Annales Cambriae* (Rolls Series, 20, 1860), 19, 20 and the annals for 967, 978, 983 and 985 in T. Jones, trans., *Brut y Tywysogyon or The Chronicle of the Princes: Peniarth MS. 20 Version* (Cardiff, 1952); T. Jones, ed. and trans., *Brut y Tywysogyon or The Chronicle of the Princes: Red Book of Hergest Version* (Cardiff, 1955); T. Jones, ed. and trans., *Brenhinedd y Saesson or The Kings of the Saxons* (Cardiff, 1971).

[71] Davies, *First English Empire*, 195.

[72] *Ibid.*, especially 48–53, 79–88, 113–71, 191–203.

different within the English kingdom from how it was elsewhere, it was hard to think of them as kings of Britain.[73]

Davies regarded analysis of the English kingdom as central to understanding the dealings of the English with other peoples in the British Isles, but also highlighted that understanding of the English kingdom itself can be sharpened through analysis of how the English related to their neighbours.[74] My object here is to use Davies's arguments about identity and administration in the twelfth and thirteenth centuries to ask questions about the English kingdom in the period when it was coming into being, the tenth century. Davies declared, following Patrick Wormald and Sarah Foot, that 'the medieval English state ... had already by the tenth century forged its identity, as the polity of the *gens Anglorum*, the *Angelcynn*', and that this identity was associated with a belief that the English were 'the new Israel'.[75] The logic of Davies's argument about the post-Conquest period does not seem to have led him to question these axioms that Anglo-Saxonists presented to him. But if Davies was correct that the chauvinistic rigidity of English identity was a prime reason why post-Conquest kings were not called rulers of Britain, and if this English identity was already deeply entrenched and coupled with an exclusivist ideology of divine election by the tenth century, would it not be odd that Æthelstan and Edgar were so often lauded as kings of Britain?

There is plenty of evidence from throughout the Anglo-Saxon period that the Germanic inhabitants of Britain could collectively be regarded as the *gens Anglorum*. From at least the second half of the ninth century, this expression was rendered in the vernacular as *Angelcynn*. But, as I have argued elsewhere, there are no good grounds to think that this English identity was tied to any particular political vision in the late ninth century: the conclusions of Wormald and Foot are predicated upon dubious assumptions about how Bede was received by later generations. There is no sound basis for believing that the English conceived of themselves as 'the new Israel', God's specially chosen people, at any time during the Anglo-Saxon period. There is scarcely more reason to think that Alfred and his successors set out to unify the English. The greatest cluster of occurrences of the word *Angelcynn* is in the *Old English Bede*. Once one recognises that this text is not concerned with promoting any notion of the English as a single special people, the argument that other instances of the word *Angelcynn* indicate a programme of nation-building and unification

---

[73] *Ibid.*, especially 89–112, 195–6, 198–9.

[74] See especially R. R. Davies, 'The English State and the "Celtic" Peoples 1100–1400', *Journal of Historical Sociology*, 6 (1993), 1–14.

[75] Davies, *First English Empire*, 199–200. Cf. P. Wormald, '*Engla Lond*: The Making of an Allegiance', *Journal of Historical Sociology*, 7 (1994), 1–24 at 10–18; S. Foot, 'The Making of *Angelcynn*: English Identity before the Norman Conquest', *Transactions of the Royal Historical Society*, 6th series, 6 (1996), 25–49.

dissolves.[76] That Edgar was content to recognise Scottish authority over Lothian implies that English unification was not a priority, since Lothian had been part of the old Northumbrian kingdom and long continued to be seen as in some sense 'English': Adam of Dryburgh, writing in what is now the Scottish Borders in 1179/80, regarded himself as living 'in the land of the English (*terra Anglorum*) and in the kingdom of the Scots (*regno Scotorum*)'.[77] The aim of Alfred and his tenth-century successors was not to create a kingdom of all the English, but to contain, subdue and ultimately expel the Scandinavian potentates who had gravely threatened Wessex. Welsh, Cumbrian and Scottish rulers did not present anything like the same level of menace: if English kings could secure their cooperation, the potential benefits of seizing their territory probably did not in most cases (including that of Lothian) appear commensurate with the effort that would have been required.

If one sets aside the idea that the West Saxon kings were seeking to unite the English, it is unsurprising that they were accorded a range of titles. As we have seen, Æthelstan and his successors could be the king of the English, or the king of Britain or Albion, or the king of a collection of peoples.[78] This variety reflects the fact that the geographical extent of West Saxon power was increasing greatly in the tenth century, and contemporaries did not know what form the expanding kingdom would take: draftsmen therefore experimented with different ways to conceptualise royal authority. In the tenth and eleventh centuries, the strident sense of English superiority that Davies saw as so inimical to any idea of a kingship of Britain remained inchoate at most. A couple of tenth-century charter styles alluded vaguely to the *barbari* who neighboured the English, and the *Life* of Edward the Confessor (probably written 1065–7) made a few disparaging remarks about the Scots and Welsh, but, as John Gillingham has shown, it was in the first half of the twelfth century that sustained contempt for the Scots and Welsh was first seriously articulated by English writers.[79] That Æthelstan and Edgar were frequently called rulers of Britain reflects that their kingship was not tied to a specifically

---

[76] G. Molyneaux, 'The *Old English Bede*: English Ideology or Christian Instruction?', *English Historical Review*, 124 (2009), 1289–323; G. Molyneaux, 'The Formation of the English Kingdom, c. 871 – c. 1016' (D.Phil. thesis, University of Oxford, 2010), 24–67.

[77] Adam of Dryburgh, *De tripartito tabernaculo*, II.13, in J. P. Migne, ed., *Patrologia Latina* (221 vols., Paris, 1844–64), CXCVIII, col. 723. Cf. D. Broun, 'Becoming Scottish in the Thirteenth Century: The Evidence of the Chronicle of Melrose', in *West over Sea: Studies in Scandinavian Sea-Borne Expansion and Settlement before 1300: A Festschrift in Honour of Dr Barbara E. Crawford*, ed. B. Ballin Smith, S. Taylor and G. Williams (Leiden, 2007), 19–32.

[78] For references, see Kleinschmidt, 'Titulaturen', 89–116.

[79] S 632, 725; *Life of King Edward*, 64–6, 86; J. Gillingham, 'The Foundations of a Disunited Kingdom', in *Uniting the Kingdom? The Making of British History*, ed. A. Grant and K. J. Stringer (1995), 48–64. This is but one of Gillingham's several articles bearing on this issue.

English ideology, let alone to a clearly formed belief in English moral superiority.

While Davies particularly emphasised the significance of English chauvinism, he also argued that it was difficult to think of post-Conquest kings as rulers of Britain because their loose and intermittent domination of Wales and Scotland was so unlike their intensive and arguably 'bureaucratic' rule within the English kingdom. Davies neither wholeheartedly endorsed nor seriously challenged the claims of James Campbell and Patrick Wormald about the administrative sophistication of 'the Anglo-Saxon state', but his argument again implicitly raises questions about the tenth century: if the intensity of royal administration within the English kingdom made it hard to conceive of post-Conquest kings as rulers of Britain, was Æthelstan called *rex totius Britanniae* in part because his administrative apparatus in the nascent English kingdom was rudimentary?[80] Was his power there not so very different in nature from in Wales and northern Britain?

It has been established beyond reasonable doubt that in the last century or so of the Anglo-Saxon period kings were capable of impinging as a matter of routine upon the lives of quite ordinary people living across most of what is now England.[81] Æthelred II raised vast sums to buy off Scandinavian attackers and to hire mercenaries, and an annual land tax appears to have been levied between 1012 and 1051. The assessment and collection of taxation must have required formidable coercive and administrative power: the division of the kingdom into shires and hundreds appears to have been crucial.[82] These same administrative units, and the network of local agents (especially sheriffs) associated with them, formed the basis of a judicial system through which the king

---

[80] For rather equivocal comments on the contentions of those whom one might call the 'Anglo-Saxon statesmen', see Davies, 'English State and the "Celtic" Peoples', 4; R. R. Davies, 'The Medieval State: The Tyranny of a Concept?', *Journal of Historical Sociology*, 16 (2003), 280–300 especially 286, 288–90.

[81] J. Campbell, 'The Late Anglo-Saxon State: A Maximum View', *Proceedings of the British Academy*, 87 (1994), 39–65, is one of many statements to this effect.

[82] *ASC* D 1051 states that Edward the Confessor abolished the *heregyld* in the thirty-ninth year after it had been instituted. He had previously dismissed at least some of his mercenary sailors (*ASC* C 1049, CE 1050). The reference to the thirty-ninth year corresponds to the record of forty-five Danish ships having entered Æthelred's service in 1012 (*ASC* CDE 1012). The tax may not, however, have been suspended for long: F. Barlow, *Edward the Confessor*, revised edn (New Haven, CT, 1997), 106 and n. 5. On the scale of taxation, see M. K. Lawson, 'The Collection of Danegeld and Heregeld in the Reigns of Æthelred II and Cnut', *English Historical Review*, 99 (1984), 721–38, with Lawson and Gillingham's subsequent debate in volumes 104 (1989) and 105 (1990). The role of shires and hundreds in tax assessment and collection is demonstrated by the Northamptonshire Geld Roll: A. J. Robertson, ed., *Anglo-Saxon Charters*, 2nd edn (Cambridge, 1956), 230–6.

could regulate society at a local level.[83] Similar conclusions about royal capabilities can be drawn from the coinage. From sometime towards the end of Edgar's reign onwards, a single design of coin was almost always struck throughout the kingdom at any one time, with the design being changed frequently. Since many hoards are composed of a single type, or a small number of chronologically close types, it appears that old coins were to a significant extent withdrawn from circulation, probably under some form of compulsion. That people could seemingly be induced to exchange their coins for the new type, very likely at disadvantageous rates, is again indicative of administrative sophistication and coercive strength.[84] Some of the more extravagant claims that have been made for Anglo-Saxon administrative genius are dubious: it is, for example, surely permissible to doubt that all variations in the weight and fineness of coins reflect a meticulous royal plan. But it is clear that late tenth- and eleventh-century kings, like their post-Conquest successors, ruled the English kingdom in an 'intensive' manner, quite different from their loose, intermittent, 'extensive' domination of Wales and northern Britain.

Much work on how kings ruled the early English kingdom suffers from a degree of chronological imprecision. Surveys of the means of royal rule typically treat the period between Alfred and the Norman Conquest as a block. While those who have written such accounts often allude to developments over the course of the period, they are usually vague about what changes are likely to have occurred when: in consequence, the tenth century seems broadly similar to the eleventh and Alfred's reign appears (at least implicitly) as the most decisive stage in the formation of the administrative basis of late Anglo-Saxon kingship.[85] Given the scarcity of sources, it is tempting to take a lengthy timespan and to construct a single

---

[83] P. Wormald, 'Charters, Law and the Settlement of Disputes in Anglo-Saxon England', in *The Settlement of Disputes in Early Medieval Europe*, ed. W. Davies and P. Fouracre (Cambridge, 1986), 149–68; P. Wormald, 'Giving God and King their Due: Conflict and its Regulation in the Early English State', *Settimane di studio del centro italiano di studi sull'alto medioevo*, 44 (1997), 549–90. Wormald's views on the marginalisation of feud should be treated with caution: P. R. Hyams, *Rancor and Reconciliation in Medieval England* (Ithaca, NY, 2003), 71–110.

[84] R. H. M. Dolley and D. M. Metcalf, 'The Reform of the English Coinage under Eadgar', in *Anglo-Saxon Coins: Studies Presented to F.M. Stenton on the Occasion of his 80th Birthday*, ed. R. H. M. Dolley (1961), 136–68; I. Stewart, 'Coinage and Recoinage after Edgar's Reform', in *Studies in Late Anglo-Saxon Coinage in Memory of Bror Emil Hildebrand*, ed. K. Jonsson (Stockholm, 1990), 456–85; Metcalf, *Atlas*.

[85] E.g. J. Campbell, 'Observations on English Government from the Tenth to the Twelfth Century', *Transactions of the Royal Historical Society*, 5th series, 25 (1975), 39–54; H. R. Loyn, *The Governance of Anglo-Saxon England, 500–1087* (1984), 81–171; P. Stafford, *Unification and Conquest: A Political and Social History of England in the Tenth and Eleventh Centuries* (1989), 134–49. A. Williams, *Kingship and Government in Pre-Conquest England, c. 500–1066* (Basingstoke, 1999), 73–150, is somewhat more nuanced in chronology. Campbell particularly acknowledged change over time in his 'Late Anglo-Saxon State', 53.

picture from the scattered fragments of evidence. Such an approach, however, risks fudging change over time.

A detailed analysis of how tenth-century kings ruled what was becoming the English kingdom is beyond this article's scope. Here we need only focus on two salient problems. The first is whether the northern extension of West Saxon power was accompanied by mass expropriation of existing landholders, with their estates being retained by the king or granted to his West Saxon associates. Since we have no tenth-century Domesday Book, and only a few diplomas concerning lands north of an imaginary line stretching from Worcester to the Wash, we can only make educated guesses. It is almost certain that a considerable quantity of land entered royal hands during the territorial expansion of the first half of the tenth century: this is the most obvious way to explain how kings had by 1066 acquired a fair amount of land in most shires north of the Thames. Ælfwynn of Mercia and the Hiberno-Scandinavian kings of Northumbria were deprived of power and it is likely that many or all of their lands were appropriated by the king.[86] But the evidence for widespread expropriation of persons below the highest social ranks is slight. The *Chronicle* refers time and again to people in the East Midlands, East Anglia and Essex 'turning' to Edward the Elder or 'choosing him as lord' after he showed up with his army. This may suggest that those who accepted Edward's lordship, albeit under threat of force, were allowed to retain at least some land.[87] Such a conclusion would accord with an account of a dispute about land in Huntingdonshire, which occurred soon after Edgar's death. The matter hinged on whether the claimants' uncle's grandmother had made a timely submission to Edward. Since she had not, she forfeited her land but, had she submitted, she would apparently have retained it: the case reveals expropriation, while simultaneously suggesting that it was far from universal.[88]

---

[86] For a map of Edward the Confessor's lands, as recorded by Domesday, see D. H. Hill, *An Atlas of Anglo-Saxon England* (Oxford, 1981), 101. Kings acquired much land that had once been in ecclesiastical possession, but the extent to which they directly expropriated churches is unclear: R. Fleming, 'Monastic Lands and England's Defence in the First Viking Age', *English Historical Review*, 100 (1985), 247–65; D. N. Dumville, *Wessex and England from Alfred to Edgar* (Woodbridge, 1992), 29–54.

[87] *ASC* ABCD 914, A 915, 917, 918. Edward the Elder's legislation states that harbourers of fugitives in the north and east must make amends in accordance with *friðgewritu*: II Ew, 5.2 (unless otherwise stated, legal texts are cited from F. Liebermann, ed., *Die Gesetze der Angelsachsen* (3 vols., Halle, 1903–16), using the system of reference set out at I, p. xi). These 'peace-writings' may have been the terms upon which submissions had been made to Edward, *pace* P. Wormald, *The Making of English Law: King Alfred to the Twelfth Century*, I: *Legislation and its Limits* (Oxford, 1999), 438–9.

[88] E. O. Blake, ed., *Liber Eliensis* (1962), 98–9. For interpretations that play up the extent of expropriation, see Dumville, *Wessex and England*, 152–3; C. R. Hart, *The Danelaw* (1992), 134–5, 226–7; Wormald '*Engla Lond*', 8. The text states that 'there was no land in the whole

Even scarcer than evidence of expropriation is evidence of the intrusion of people of West Saxon origin into newly acquired territory. It can hardly be doubted that some West Saxons gained lands north of the Thames, but the supposition that the upper aristocracy was overwhelmingly West Saxon is not founded on any secure evidence. It is sometimes stated that Æthelstan Half-King and Ælfhere, ealdormen north of the Thames and the two most powerful lay magnates of the mid-tenth century, hailed from Wessex.[89] The basis for this belief is that they are known to have held lands there, but one could just as well postulate that they were Mercians who had been granted estates south of the Thames. Such a possibility is suggested by Asser's account of how Wærferth and Plegmund, two Mercian churchmen who entered Alfred's service, were showered with honours and powers in Wessex, in addition to those that they had in Mercia.[90] On a balance of probabilities, it appears that West Saxon expansion was achieved primarily through a series of local agreements in which incumbent landholders were cowed into submission, rather than through widespread forcible expropriation.

The second fundamental issue that needs to be considered is the character of tenth-century royal rule in what was becoming the English kingdom. Much of the secondary literature implies (and sometimes states) that Alfred had a sophisticated administrative apparatus south of the Thames and that this was briskly replicated elsewhere, with shires and hundreds being rolled out as Edward the Elder and Æthelstan pressed north.[91] Even on grounds of general probability, one might doubt this: it would be surprising if kings could effect immediate and fundamental administrative reorganisation of newly acquired territories while simultaneously expending significant time and resources on campaigns to secure further submissions. Such a scenario would be even

of Huntingdonshire that was so free that it could not be lost through forfeiture (*tam libera que per forisfacturam non posset iri perditum*)' save for two hides at Bluntisham and two near Spaldwick. Hart renders this 'there was no free land but that was forfeited' except the hides at Bluntisham and near Spaldwick, a slight but possibly significant mistranslation.

[89] Stafford, *Unification and Conquest*, 157; Hart, *Danelaw*, 569–604 especially 570–2; C. Wickham, *Problems in Doing Comparative History* (Southampton, 2005), 25. Cf. the now-untenable assumption that the rise of the Carolingians led to a mass imposition of Austrasian magnates in Neustria: K. F. Werner, 'Important Noble Families in the Kingdom of Charlemagne – A Prosopographical Study of the Relationship between King and Nobility in the Early Middle Ages', trans. T. Reuter, *The Medieval Nobility: Studies on the Ruling Classes of France and Germany from the Sixth to the Twelfth Century* (Amsterdam, 1979), 137–202 at 146–73.

[90] Asser, *Life of King Alfred*, LXXVII (62). Cf. N. Banton, 'Ealdormen and Earls in England from the Reign of King Alfred to the Reign of King Æthelred II' (D.Phil. thesis, University of Oxford, 1981), 89, 96–100, 141; J. L. Nelson, '"A King Across the Sea": Alfred in Continental Perspective', *Transactions of the Royal Historical Society*, 5th series, 36 (1986), 45–68 at 60–1.

[91] Stenton's attribution to Edward the Elder of the shiring of the West Midlands has been particularly influential: Stenton, *Anglo-Saxon England*, 336–7. I develop the argument of this and the following four paragraphs much more fully at Molyneaux, 'Formation', 89–243.

more unlikely if incumbent landholders for the most part remained in place. To overcome the argument from basic probability, one would want firm evidence, which is altogether lacking. Except in the case of Essex, the first evidence that any part of the area north of the Thames was divided into shires is from the 970s.[92] Essex and the shires south of the Thames are attested before the end of the ninth century, but their only identifiable function at that time was as military units: there is no sign of the routine holding of shire meetings in any part of the kingdom before Edgar's reign.[93] It is also around this time that the sheriff, the king's key local agent in the eleventh century, made his earliest appearance.[94] Hundreds are first mentioned in the legislation of Edmund (939–46), but it is from Edgar's reign onwards that references to them become ubiquitous: whatever previous existence hundreds possibly had, it appears that it was in the second half of the tenth century that they became fundamental units of royal administration.[95]

Earlier in the tenth century, fortifications (*burhs*) built south of the Thames by Alfred, and in the Midlands by Edward the Elder and Æthelflæd, served as outposts of royal authority, but only a small proportion of the population lived in them. Edward and Æthelstan sought to ban or limit trade outside a *port*, and it appears that a *port* was much the same sort of place as a *burh*: this suggests that early tenth-century kings had administrative structures (most likely a network of reeves) through which to monitor transactions in *burhs*, but that kings lacked a comparable

---

[92] Lantfred, *Translatio et Miracula S. Swithuni*, VIII, ed. and trans. Lapidge, *Cult of St Swithun*, 252–333 at 290; *ASC* C 980; *Liber Eliensis*, 85, 98–9, 109, 116; W. D. Macray, ed., *Chronicon Abbatiæ Rameseiensis* (Rolls Series, 83, 1886), 50, 93. There are grounds to think that Norfolk and Suffolk were not established as shires until well into the eleventh century: L. Marten, 'The Shiring of East Anglia: An Alternative Hypothesis', *Historical Research*, 81 (2008), 1–27.

[93] For southern shires before the end of the ninth century, see *ASC* 757, 802, 840, 845, 851, 853, 860, ABCD 897. The earliest clear accounts of shire meetings are S 1454, 1456, 1458; *Liber Eliensis*, 85, 98–9, 109; *Chronicon Abbatiæ Rameseiensis*, 50. In the south, where shires are known to have existed earlier, the men of the shire may sometimes have assembled to address judicial matters (III As is suggestive in this regard), but there is no sign that they did so regularly before the latter part of the tenth century.

[94] S 1456, 1458. Cf. W. A. Morris, *The Medieval English Sheriff to 1300* (Manchester, 1927), 1–39 especially 18–21.

[95] III Em, 2; III Eg, 5, 7.1; IV Eg, 3.1–11; I Atr, 1.2–1.3; III Atr, 1.2, 3.1–3.3; II Cn, 15.2, 17–17.1, 19, 20–20a, 22–22.1, 25.1, 27, 30–30.2, 31a; A. G. Kennedy, 'Cnut's Law Code of 1018', *Anglo-Saxon England*, 11 (1983), 57–81 at 79 (cl. 26.3). Some of these references are to wapentakes, the equivalent of hundreds in areas of Scandinavian influence. The Hundred Ordinance is undated but cannot be earlier than Edmund's reign, since it refers to him: Hu, 2. For an attempt to trace hundreds back to the early tenth century, see H. R. Loyn, 'The Hundred in England in the Tenth and Early Eleventh Centuries', in *British Government and Administration: Studies Presented to S.B. Chrimes*, ed. H. Hearder and H. R. Loyn (Cardiff, 1974), 1–15 at 3–6.

apparatus elsewhere.[96] By contrast, Edgar's later legislation presupposed that the whole kingdom was divided into hundreds (or wapentakes), and ordered that transactions be witnessed either in a *burh* or in a hundred (or wapentake).[97] A similar shift from Æthelstan to Edgar can be detected with regard to royally ordained public meetings. Æthelstan's legislation implied that such meetings would be held in *burh*s, since the leading men of the *burh* were to seize the property of non-attenders.[98] Edgar's legislation contains a similar provision, but 'the leading men of the *burh*' are replaced with 'men from the meeting', the location of which is unspecified. That this is probably an allusion to hundred meetings can be inferred from the statement, not found in Æthelstan's legislation, that half of the non-attender's property was to go to the hundred.[99] With regard to both trade and meetings, there appears to have been a significant change between Æthelstan and Edgar: administrative structures that had formerly been restricted to *burh*s were extended into the countryside through hundredal organisation. Kings thus developed mechanisms for social regulation throughout the kingdom, rather than merely in particular fortified centres.

That 'absence of evidence is not evidence of absence' is a well-known mantra. But when we search (in vain) for evidence of a sophisticated and kingdom-wide royal administrative apparatus in the first half of the tenth century, we are to some extent dealing with silent sources, not with a straightforward absence of sources: it is particularly striking that the substantial corpus of legislation from Alfred to Æthelstan says nothing about hundreds, and indeed ascribes to *burh*s functions that *burh*s would later share with hundreds.[100] It is, moreover, notable that the Midland shires, routine shire assemblies and sheriffs appear almost simultaneously, around the time of Edgar's reign, and that the first descriptions of actual shire meetings occur very soon after the first reference to a *scirgemot* in royal legislation.[101] That different types of sources break their silence at the same time suggests that earlier silence indeed reflects absence.

The argument from silence is reinforced by numismatics. The ability of Edgar and his successors to enforce uniformity in coin design and

---

[96] I Ew, 1–1.1; II As, 12, 13.1 but cf. IV As, 2; VI As, 10. That a *port* was the same kind of place as a *burh* can be inferred from II As, 14–14.2, which states that no one may mint coins except in a *port*, allocates quotas of moneyers to certain towns and assigns each unnamed *burh* one moneyer. For the association of reeve and *burh*, see I As, prol. '*Burh*s' is so widely used that it would seem precious to insist on *byrig* as the plural.

[97] IV Eg, 2–12.1, which stresses that the provisions should apply in all parts of the kingdom.

[98] II As, 20–20.8.

[99] III Eg, 7–7.2. The other half was to go to a person known as the *landhlaford*, again a change from Æthelstan's legislation.

[100] The groups of one hundred men mentioned in VI As should not be confused with territorial hundreds.

[101] III Eg, 5.1.

frequent changes of type is one of the surest signs of the sophistication of royal administration in the last ninety years of the Anglo-Saxon period. Between Alfred's death and Edgar's reform, the situation was quite different: there were no kingdom-wide changes of type and different designs were struck simultaneously in different regions. There were also significant variations in weight and fineness, especially in the third quarter of the tenth century. Alfred appears to have had reasonably close control over minting in his kingdom south of the Thames and, from the late 870s, in western Mercia: his coinage was fairly uniform and he carried out changes of type.[102] His successors may well have maintained such control in the south, which displays a significant degree of coherence in terms of the type being struck. They were, however, either unable to enforce uniformity of minting in their newly acquired territories, or uninterested in doing so.[103] Edgar's reign saw major change in the coinage: this supports the conclusion that the breaking of the silence of the written sources around the same time reflects similarly substantial changes in other aspects of royal administration. The reasons for these changes cannot be explored here: for my present argument, it is enough to establish that the latter part of the tenth century was critical in the development of a fairly uniform and sophisticated administrative apparatus across the kingdom.

Without such an apparatus, earlier kings are unlikely to have been able to impinge as a matter of routine upon the lives of more than a small proportion of their subjects. They could, however, use their wealth to secure the loyalty of the majority of the greater aristocracy, the only politically significant social stratum. Through gifts of land, treasure, office and assistance in disputes, kings could buy magnates' support; in case of disloyalty, they could withdraw their favour. Even the most powerful men were vulnerable to forfeiture: a charter of Edward the Elder reveals that an ealdorman had been deprived of his land for breaching his oath to Alfred.[104] Kings' extensive landholdings almost

[102] M. A. S. Blackburn, 'Alfred's Coinage Reforms in Context', in *Alfred the Great: Papers from the Eleventh-Centenary Conferences*, ed. T. Reuter (Aldershot, 2003), 199–217.

[103] On regional variation, see I. Stewart, 'English Coinage from Athelstan to Edgar', *Numismatic Chronicle*, 148 (1988), 192–214. The fundamental reference work is Blunt, Stewart and Lyon, *Coinage in Tenth-Century England*, with analysis of metrology at 235–47. For debate on the extent of royal control of minting, see Jonsson, *New Era*, 31–78, 185–92; D. M. Metcalf, 'Were Ealdormen Exercising Independent Control over the Coinage in Mid Tenth Century England?', *British Numismatic Journal*, 57 (1987), 24–33; K. Jonsson, 'The Pre-Reform Coinage of Edgar – The Legacy of the Anglo-Saxon Kingdoms', in *Coinage and History in the North Sea World, c. 500–1250: Essays in Honour of Marion Archibald*, ed. B. Cook and G. Williams (Leiden, 2006), 325–46. I do not endorse Jonsson's contention that ealdormen restricted the movement of coin within the kingdom, but the argument for minimal royal control of minting is strong.

[104] S 362. Cf. Nelson, '"A King Across the Sea"', 53–5.

certainly enabled them to maintain bigger and better military retinues than any of their subordinates.[105] They could thus visit destruction upon those who displeased them: Eadred ordered a great slaughter in Thetford in 952 to avenge the killing of an abbot and Edgar had all Thanet ravaged in 969 as a reprisal for the mistreatment of some merchants.[106] Tenth-century royal 'justice' could be crude and arbitrary, but the mere threat of a visit from the king's goons was probably sufficient to induce compliance with the royal will. Kings did not cease to manipulate magnates or ravage the lands of the recalcitrant after the late tenth century, but it was then that these means of rule appear to have been supplemented by administrative structures through which royal power could be routinely projected at a local level throughout the kingdom.[107]

Until the latter part of the tenth century, royal power in the nascent English kingdom was based squarely upon using rewards and threats to secure the loyalty of the greater magnates, not upon regulating the lives of the mass of the population. Something similar could be said of English kings' domination in Wales and northern Britain: they coerced and cajoled neighbouring rulers into some measure of obedience, but did not impinge in any sustained way upon these rulers' subjects. It will have been easier for English kings to punish disobedience in Thanet or Thetford than in Wales or northern Britain, and they did not have *burh*s in the latter areas, but the means by which Æthelstan and his immediate successors enforced their will on Scottish, Cumbrian and Welsh rulers were not fundamentally dissimilar to the methods they used within most of what we think of as England: before the late tenth century, the variations in English royal power in different parts of Britain were more quantitative than qualitative. Contemporary writers implied as much. Asser stated explicitly that Anarawd submitted to Alfred on the same terms as Æthelred of Mercia.[108] Asser referred to Æthelred as *comes* while almost certainly thinking of Anarawd as *rex* (the title he accorded to weaker Welsh kings), but the practical power of a Welsh king and a leading English ealdorman may well have been fairly similar. A charter of Alfred from 889 styled Æthelred *subregulus et patricius Merciorum*, an obvious

---

[105] The extent of kings' lands cannot be determined before Domesday Book, but in 1066 Edward the Confessor was the greatest landholder in the kingdom: S. Baxter, *The Earls of Mercia: Lordship and Power in Late Anglo-Saxon England* (Oxford, 2007), 128–38.

[106] *ASC* D 952, DEF 969; Roger of Wendover, *Flores Historiarum*, I, 414–15. Roger assigns the punishment of Thanet to 974, but his chronology is unreliable: M. Dolley, 'Roger of Wendover's Date for Eadgar's Coinage Reform', *British Numismatic Journal*, 49 (1979), 1–11 at 3–7.

[107] For ravaging after Edgar's reign, see *ASC* CDE 986, CD 1041, E 1051; John of Worcester, *Chronicle*, 1041 (II, 532); W. E. Kapelle, *The Norman Conquest of the North: The Region and its Transformation, 1000–1135* (Chapel Hill, NC, 1979), 117–19.

[108] Asser, *Life of King Alfred*, LXXX (66–7).

parallel with the presentation of Scottish and Welsh rulers as *subreguli* in tenth-century diplomas.[109] A couple of writers are even known to have treated Æthelred as *rex*: Æthelweard twice styles him thus, and he appears as the final name in a regnal list that begins with Penda and is headed *de regibus Merciorum*.[110] Æthelred was not the only tenth-century ealdorman whose power was understood in quasi-regal terms: the most powerful English magnate of the second quarter of the tenth century was known as Æthelstan *semi-rex*.[111]

The words with which the *Chronicle* narrates English kings' dealings with Wales and northern Britain often echo those used with regard to the area that was becoming the English kingdom. The *Chronicle* uses the same verb, *oferhergian*, to refer to English kings ravaging Thanet (under English rule), 'between the dykes and the Ouse' (under Danish rule), a part of Northumbria that was under Hiberno-Scandinavian rule, Cumbria and eastern Scotland.[112] The *Chronicle*'s statement that peace was established by Æthelstan, Constantine, Hywel and others at Eamont 'with pledge and oaths' (*mid wedde 7 mid aþum*) is reminiscent of the legislation of Alfred and Edward the Elder: Alfred ordered that every man abide by *his að 7 his wed* and Edward prescribed the payment of compensation by any man who breached the *að* and *wæd* that the whole people (*ðeod*) had given.[113] The oaths of cooperation on sea and on land made in 945 and 973 echo the promise of the Danish army of East Anglia in 917 to keep the peace 'both at sea and on land', and the same couplet appeared in Edward the Elder's legislation.[114] The specific terms upon which cooperation was agreed surely varied, but they were not so divergent as to require different conceptual frameworks.

The *Chronicle* refers to people from Bedford, Northampton, Cambridge and Stamford seeking Edward the Elder's lordship in 914, 917 and 918, then goes on to say that the Welsh kings 'sought to have [Edward] as lord' in 918.[115] Two years later, the Scottish and Cumbrian kings, the rulers of Bamburgh and a Hiberno-Scandinavian potentate who had recently established himself at York 'chose [Edward] as father and lord'.[116] These

[109] S 346.

[110] Æthelweard, *Chronicle*, IV.3 (49, 50); T. Hearne, ed., *Hemingi Chartularium Ecclesiæ Wigorniensis* (2 vols., Oxford, 1723), I, 242. The regnal list is preserved in an early eleventh-century manuscript: N. R. Ker, 'Hemming's Cartulary: A Description of the Two Worcester Cartularies in Cotton Tiberius A. xiii', in *Studies in Medieval History Presented to Frederick Maurice Powicke*, ed. R. W. Hunt, W. A. Pantin and R. W. Southern (Oxford, 1948), 49–75 especially 55, 68–72.

[111] Byrhtferth of Ramsey, *Life of St Oswald*, III.14 (82–4).

[112] *ASC* ABCD 903, ABCDEF 934, 945, D 948, DEF 969.

[113] *ASC* D 927; Af, 1; II Ew, 5. Cf. *ASC* D 947.

[114] *ASC* A 917, ABCD 945, DE 973; II Ew, 1.1.

[115] *ASC* ABCD 914, A 917, 918.

[116] *ASC* A 920.

relationships can hardly have been identical, but lordship was a sufficiently elastic concept to encompass them all: it entailed one party recognising the other's superiority and both agreeing obligations to each other, but there was plenty of scope for variation in what these obligations might be.[117] By the latter years of Edward's reign, it was probably clear that the English king was the most powerful man on the island: it is by no means implausible that Welsh and northern rulers acknowledged Edward's superiority and agreed to further his interests, perhaps in return for promises of non-aggression and protection.[118] Æthelstan may therefore not have been the first tenth-century king to be recognised by other rulers as the preeminent man in Britain.[119] More importantly, a contemporary writer did not need to draw a conceptual distinction between Edward's relationship with the people of Bedford and his relationships with the men ruling at York and Bamburgh, or indeed with the Welsh, Cumbrian and Scottish kings: all these relationships could be understood in terms of lordship.

English royal power will never have been uniform across the island, but in the first half of the tenth century the variations were much less marked than they later became. Through a mix of fear and favour, Edward the Elder and Æthelstan secured some measure of obedience from Welsh, Cumbrian and Scottish rulers, as they had previously done in the Midlands, East Anglia and Northumbria: they had power across Britain, but this power was more 'extensive' than 'intensive'. The administrative reforms that appear to have been implemented in or around the reign of Edgar did not produce homogeneous administration within the new English kingdom: East Anglia may well not have been divided into shires until well into the eleventh century, and even at the end of the Anglo-Saxon period royal control was loose north of the Humber, and even looser north of the Tees.[120] But the reforms that took place around Edgar's time did make the king's rule within much of the English kingdom substantially more pervasive, routine and 'intensive', while English domination of Wales and northern Britain remained loose, intermittent and 'extensive'.

[117] Cf. R. R. Davies, *Lords and Lordship in the British Isles in the Late Middle Ages*, ed. B. Smith (Oxford, 2009), especially 1, 6–7, 15–18, 158–78, 197–217.

[118] Contrast M. R. Davidson, 'The (Non)submission of the Northern Kings in 920', in *Edward the Elder, 899–924*, ed. N. J. Higham and D. H. Hill (2001), 200–11.

[119] Since no genuine charters are extant from the second half of Edward the Elder's reign, it is impossible to say whether he was accorded styles that presented him as ruler of Britain. The probability is that he was not, since Æthelstan's early charters do not include such styles. On the hiatus in the charters, see Dumville, *Wessex and England*, 151–3; P. Wormald, '*On þa wæpnedhealfe*: Kingship and Royal Property from Æthelwulf to Edward the Elder', in *Edward the Elder*, ed. Higham and Hill, 264–79 especially 275.

[120] Marten, 'The Shiring of East Anglia'. There are grounds to suspect that even in the late eleventh century at least some people regarded the Tees as the northern limit of the English kingdom: Kapelle, *Norman Conquest*, 11–13.

The intensification of royal rule within the English kingdom fostered an increasingly strong sense that it was a single and discrete political unit, which was to be ruled by one *rex Anglorum*: Bishop Æthelwold (writing 964×84) condemned the partition between Eadwig and Edgar (957–9), and the *Encomium Emmae Reginae* (written 1041×2) presented the death of Edmund Ironside (1016) as an act of divine mercy since it ended the division of the kingdom between him and Cnut.[121] By the early eleventh century, the English kingdom had gained clearer definition: fundamental to this was the development of a marked difference in the nature of royal power inside and outside the kingdom.

While Æthelstan and Edgar were often described as plain *rex Anglorum*, or as rulers of the English and surrounding peoples, the great majority of their diplomas incorporated some explicit claim to rulership of Britain. These titles could be combined. Æthelstan was often *rex Anglorum per omnipatrantis dexteram totius Brytanie regni solio sublimatus* ('king of the English elevated by the right hand of the Almighty to the throne of the whole kingdom of Britain'), and many charters of Edgar style him *totius Brittannie basileus* in the dispositive section and *rex Anglorum* in the witness list.[122] After Edgar's reign, claims to rulership of Britain by no means disappeared, but the proportion of diplomas that mentioned Britain decreased. Changes within the nascent English kingdom itself are the key to understanding this shift in titles. The notion that Æthelstan was *rex totius Britanniae* was not a bombastic fantasy. He did have power throughout Britain, but that power seems almost everywhere to have been 'extensive', founded upon personal bonds with potentates who recognised his superiority, not upon an administrative network that would enable routine engagement with the mass of the population. Contemporaries could see him as *rex Anglorum*, since he was a member of the *gens Anglorum* and could most easily cajole and coerce those living in the part of Britain that this *gens* inhabited. But as yet it often did not seem necessary to think of the king's authority as varying in nature in different parts of Britain. By the end of the tenth century, this was changing: from around the time of Edgar, a major difference opened up between 'intensive' rule and 'extensive' overlordship, such that it became increasingly problematic to conceive of Britain as a unitary realm. As with the pan-British domination attributed to Edwin, Oswald, Æthelbald and Offa, the titles accorded to Æthelstan and Edgar reflect strength, relative to contemporary neighbours. But such titles also reflect weakness, relative to subsequent English kings. Æthelstan

---

[121] D. Whitelock, M. Brett and C. N. L. Brooke, eds., *Councils and Synods with Other Documents Relating to the English Church, I, A.D. 871–1204* (2 vols., Oxford, 1981), I, 146; *Encomium Emmae Reginae*, II.14 (30). Cf. Molyneaux, 'Formation', 17–24.

[122] Æthelstan: S 407, 412, 413, 416, 418, 419, 425, 426, 458. Edgar: S 700, 702, 706, 709, 716, 744, 762, 764, 767. These lists are not comprehensive.

and Edgar's successors, were, like them, in some sense overlords of Britain. These later kings, however, were also direct rulers of a kingdom that was more intensively governed than any other in the Latin west. This was not the case with Æthelstan's reign, and was only just becoming so in Edgar's time: until the late tenth century, intensive royal administration inside the English kingdom was not so entrenched as to impede the presentation of its kings as rulers of Britain.

Transactions of the RHS 21 (2011), pp. 93–121 © Royal Historical Society 2011
doi:10.1017/S0080440111000053

THE REFORMATION OF THE GENERATIONS: YOUTH, AGE AND RELIGIOUS CHANGE IN ENGLAND, *c.* 1500–1700

By Alexandra Walsham

SCHEDULED TO BE READ 7 MAY 2010

ABSTRACT. This exploratory essay adopts the life-cycle as a tool with which to investigate religious change in the sixteenth and seventeenth centuries. It examines how inherited tropes about youth and age were deployed and the ways in which the notion of generational strife was invoked at various stages of England's long Reformation. These provide insight into how contemporaries understood and experienced the theological and cultural upheavals of the era and the process by which Protestantism 'aged' as it progressed beyond its unruly protest phase and became institutionalised as the official faith.

In November 1635, a man reputed to be 152 years of age died in London and was accorded the honour of burial in Westminster Abbey. A native of the small hamlet of Winnington in Shropshire, Thomas Parr had lived a long and vigorous life in the countryside before being persuaded by a visiting nobleman to journey at his expense to the capital, where crowds flocked to see this remarkable example of human longevity. Shortly afterwards, however, affected by the impure urban air, the celebrated centenarian expired. Parr's body was examined by the famous physician William Harvey and the story of this 'monument and almost miracle of nature' became the subject of a catchpenny pamphlet by the water poet John Taylor (Figure 1). In a postscript, Taylor described 'the changes of manners, the variations of customes, ... the alterations of religions, the diversities of sects, and the intermixture of accidents' that had happened since Parr's alleged birth in 1483. His lifetime had spanned the era of England's protracted and idiosyncratic Reformation. Brought up in the Catholic faith, by the time of the Henrician break with Rome he was fifty years old – in an era of limited life expectancy already a rather elderly man. He had witnessed the succession of theological and liturgical upheavals and reversals of the reigns of Edward VI, Mary and Elizabeth I and had lived to see the steady entrenchment of the Protestant religion under their early Stuart successors James and Charles. According to Taylor, Parr had

Figure 1 'The Old, Old, Very Old Man', Thomas Parr: John Taylor, *The Old, Old, Very Old Man: Or, The Age and Long Life of Thomas Par* (1635), frontispiece. © British Library Board (shelfmark C. 34. f. 43).

borne the religious turbulence of his times with equanimity; he had not been troubled by the dissolution of the monasteries, nor murmured at the replacement of the Latin mass by vernacular prayers. He was unperturbed by the royal supremacy, had observed the passing of old Catholic customs and rituals and the rise of puritanical scruples about remnants of popery with cool indifference, and outlived many sectaries and heretics executed for their unorthodox opinions. 'He held it safest to be of the Religion of the King or Queen that were in being, for he knew that hee came raw into the world, and accounted it no point of Wisedome to be broiled out of it.' No martyr or zealot, at least in the witty pen portrait provided by Taylor, Parr was a temporiser by instinct. A bemused bystander rather than active participant in five generations of religious change, he died on the eve of the tumultuous new stage of the English Reformation precipitated by the outbreak of civil war in 1642.[1]

The case of Thomas Parr provokes a series of intriguing questions. Did age matter in the Reformation? How was the life-cycle implicated in the movements for religious renewal that marked the sixteenth and seventeenth centuries? What consequences did these developments have for generational relations: for interactions between children and adults in a hierarchical society that clung tightly to the patriarchal assumption that young people should defer submissively to their elders? And to what extent did the Reformation itself age as it progressed beyond its initial unruly phases and became institutionalised as the official faith? These are issues that have been largely neglected by historians to date. The debate about the Reformation has revolved around alternative polarities: whether it sprang up spontaneously from below or was imposed on the populace from above, whether it was fast or slow, whether it was enthusiastically welcomed or fiercely resented, whether it was a dismal failure or a resounding success, whether it created a nation of convinced Protestants or merely a Protestant nation. Somewhat surprisingly, the consensus that has emerged from the historiographical controversies of the last thirty years that England experienced a long and incremental Reformation has not prompted very much interest in how people at the various points in the life-cycle reacted to it and how far the religious developments of the period can be said to have had a generational complexion, though interventions by Susan Brigden and Norman Jones represent partial and notable exceptions.[2]

---

[1] John Taylor, *The Old, Old, Very Old Man: Or, The Age and Long Life of Thomas Par* (1635), sigs. D3r–v.

[2] Susan Brigden, 'Youth and the English Reformation', *Past and Present*, 95 (1982), 37–67; Norman Jones, 'Living the Reformations: Generational Experience and Political Perception in Early Modern England', *Huntington Library Quarterly*, 60 (1999), 273–88; idem, *The English Reformation: Religion and Cultural Adaptation* (Oxford, 2002), 196–8 and *passim*. For Europe, see

Such questions have also been somewhat marginal to the concerns of the social historians who have focused attention upon groups at either end of the age spectrum, intrigued by a society with an age profile sharply contrasting with our own, in which those under twenty-one comprised some 40–50 per cent of the population,[3] and by the apparent paradox of a gerontocratic culture that revered the authority of the elderly despite the fact that they were numerically in the minority. The work of Keith Thomas, Paul Griffiths, Steven Smith, Ilana Ben-Amos, Lynn Botelho and Pat Thane among others has illuminated key questions about the autonomy and dependence, perception, identity and regulation of the young and old and enhanced our understanding of the ambiguous mixture of agency and vulnerability that shaped the experience of these groups in the two centuries between 1500 and 1700.[4] However, the connections between these tendencies and trends and the mental and cultural sea changes brought about by the Reformation are still under-investigated.

Nor has the Reformation been the subject of ambitious studies of the role of generational difference and conflict as critical forces in history. From the early work of Auguste Comte in the 1830s and 1840s to the fruitful theoretical insights developed by Karl Mannheim in the 1920s and the spasm of intellectual activity on this theme fostered by the youth movements of the 1960s, the primary focus of scholarly attention has been the twentieth century.[5] Whether conceived of as a cohort of people linked by biology or as a group of coevals bound by a common

Amy Nelson Burnett, 'Generational Conflict in the Late Reformation: The Basel Paroxysm', *Journal of Interdisciplinary History*, 32 (2001), 217–42. See also Peter Marshall, '(Re)defining the English Reformation', *Journal of British Studies*, 48 (2009), 564–86, esp. 567–8, 576–7.

3 See E. A. Wrigley and R. S. Schofield, *The Population History of England 1541–1871* (Cambridge, 1989 edn), 528, and see 215–19.

4 On youth, see Steven R. Smith, 'The London Apprentices as Seventeenth-Century Adolescents', *Past and Present*, 61 (1973), 149–61; *idem*, 'Religion and the Conception of Youth in Seventeenth-Century England', *History of Childhood Quarterly*, 2 (1975), 493–516; Keith Thomas, 'Children in Early Modern England', in *Children and their Books: A Celebration of the World of Iona and Peter Opie*, ed. Gillian Avery and Julia Briggs (Oxford, 1989), 45–77; Paul Griffiths, *Youth and Authority: Formative Experiences in England 1560–1640* (Oxford, 1996); Ilana Krausman Ben-Amos, *Adolescence and Youth in Early Modern England* (New Haven and London, 1994). On old age, see Keith Thomas, 'Age and Authority in Early Modern England', *Proceedings of the British Academy*, 62 (1976), 205–48; Steven R. Smith, 'Growing Old in Early Stuart England', *Albion*, 8 (1976), 125–41; Pat Thane, *Old Age in English History: Past Experiences, Present Issues* (Oxford, 2000), chs. 2–4; Susannah R. Ottaway, L. A. Botelho and Katharine Kittredge, eds., *Power and Poverty: Old Age in the Pre-industrial Past* (Westport and London, 2002); L. A. Botelho, *Old Age and the English Poor Law, 1500–1700* (Woodbridge, 2004); Pat Thane, ed., *The Long History of Old Age* (2005), chs. 3–4; Lynn Botelho and Susannah R. Ottaway, eds., *The History of Old Age in England, 1600–1800* (8 vols., 2008).

5 Karl Mannheim, 'The Problem of Generations', in *Essays on the Sociology of Knowledge: Collected Works*, V, ed. Paul Keeskemeti (1952), 276–320; Herbert Butterfield, *The Discontinuities between the Generations in History: Their Effect on the Transmission of Political Experience* (Cambridge,

consciousness shaped by shared experience, the problematic concept of the generation has not been widely exploited by early modern historians. For all its attendant pitfalls, the idea that there may be some kind of correlation between the inexorable cyclical succession of fathers and mothers by daughters and sons and momentous processes of historical change arguably still has considerable potential as a heuristic tool. In the guise of the influential scheme of the Seven Ages of Man the notion that people in different stages in life (infancy, childhood, youth, manhood, old age and decrepit old age) had distinct characteristics, temperaments and instincts and that these corresponded typologically with particular eras of human history was deeply embedded in sixteenth- and seventeenth-century culture itself (Figure 2).[6] Assimilating the vocabulary of the bible, contemporaries conceived of their world in terms of a series of 'generations' to whom God had displayed mercy when they followed His commandments and against whom He would certainly rise up in wrath and judgement if they disobeyed Him.[7]

Three further preliminary points must be made. The first is that concepts of age in this culture were not fixed and immutable but relative, fluid and flexible; although there were conventions about where childhood ended (typically fourteen) and when old age began (commonly fifty or sixty), the boundaries between youth and age were often imprecise. Furthermore, the words were often utilised metaphorically to describe a stage of mental maturity, moral degeneracy or spiritual development; one could be old in years, but young in faith or display a childish piety but be aged and grey in iniquity. Age was and is both a biological fact and a cultural construct.

Secondly, attitudes towards youth and age were fundamentally ambivalent. Drawing on the reservoir of Scripture and classical culture, the former was linked with both ignorance and innocence. It was seen as a phase in the life-cycle singularly prone to sin, insubordination and idleness but simultaneously as one in which people were particularly receptive to salutary religious influences. Old age had a similarly equivocal quality, being linked on the one side with wisdom, gravity and experience and on

---

1971); Alan B. Spitzer, 'The Historical Problem of Generations', *American Historical Review*, 78 (1973), 1353–85; Anthony Esler, ed., *The Youth Revolution: The Conflict of Generations in Modern History* (Lexington, 1974); Annie Kriegel and Elisabeth Hirsch, 'Generational Difference: The History of an Idea', *Daedalus*, 107 (1978), 23–38; Hans Jaeger, 'Generations in History: Reflections on a Controversial Concept', *History and Theory*, 24 (1985), 273–92.

[6] See, e.g., Henry Cuffe, *The Differences of the Ages of Mans Life* (1607). For the medieval heritage of this scheme, see J. A. Burrow, *The Ages of Man: A Study in Medieval Writing and Thought* (Oxford, 1986); Elizabeth Sears, *The Ages of Man: Medieval Interpretations of the Life Cycle* (Princeton, NJ, 1986).

[7] See *Oxford English Dictionary*, 'generation', 5a, for uses of the word in this sense, which date from the Wycliffite bible of 1382.

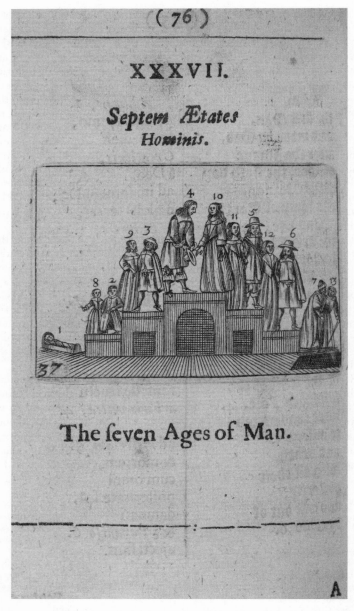

Figure 2 The Seven Ages of Man: Johann Amos Comenius, *Orbis Sensualium Pictus* (1659), 76. © British Library Board (shelfmark E 2116 (1)).

the other with folly, depravity and senility. These negative and positive elements coexisted in contemporary mentalities without contradiction.[8]

A third caveat concerns the intractable difficulty of accessing the experience of the young and the elderly in an unmediated form. We mainly see them refracted through the spectacles of the adults who described them or through the equally distorting lenses of recollection and memory. Fiction and fact are inextricably entangled in the prescriptive texts, eulogistic biographies, diaries and other ego-documents upon which we are compelled to rely. It is as pointless as it is impossible to unravel the lives depicted in these texts from the lives lived in the flesh they purportedly describe. Even so, as I hope to show, the manner in which inherited tropes about youth and age were deployed and the ways in which the notion of generational strife was invoked at various stages of England's long Reformation may cast fresh light on the contours and repercussions of this movement.

I

The language of youth and age pervades the polemical literature engendered by the Reformation and was central to the process of confessional identity formation. Those who resisted the tide of change proudly claimed to have antiquity on their side. Catholicism was the 'old religion'; its roots in the ancient Christian past and its durability over so many centuries were certain signs of its truth and legitimacy. Insisting that their religion alone had the imprimatur of history, a long succession of Catholic controversialists from Thomas Harding and John Rastell to Matthew Kellison and Richard Broughton castigated Protestantism as a new-fangled and upstart religion invented from scratch and stuffed with 'gross absurdities' and 'rotten rags' by a recent faction. Taunting their enemies with the question 'where was your church before Luther?', they hurled the damaging charge of novelty against them with venom.[9] In reply, Protestant propagandists deftly turned the tables and proclaimed that their church rather than that of the papists was the real incarnation of the primitive religion of Christ and his disciples. The Reformation had not given birth to a new faith but had resurrected an apostolic and indeed an Abrahamic one. As Thomas Bell, Robert Abbot, Josias Nicholls and

---

[8] See the references in n. 4.

[9] Thomas Harding, *A Confutation of a Booke Intituled An Apologie of the Church of England* (Antwerp, 1565), fos. 15v, 42r–v; John Rastell, *A Replie against an Answer (Falslie Intitled) in Defence of the Truth* (Antwerp, 1565), fos. 168v–191r; Matthew Kellison, *A Survey of the New Religion Detecting Manie Grosse Absurdities which it Implieth* (Douai, 1603); Edward Maihew, *A Treatise of the Groundes of the Old and Newe Religion* ([English secret press, 1608]); Richard Broughton, *The Conviction of Noveltie, and Defense of Antiquitie. Or Demonstrative Arguments of the Falsitie of the Newe Religion in England* ([Douai, 1632]).

many others declared, it was the medieval papacy and clergy who were guilty of introducing a false and bastard child into the world, riddled with fabricated superstitions disguised under the title of ancient 'traditions'.[10]

Protestantism also liked to present itself as the religion of those who had cast aside the puerile beliefs and practices of their benighted forefathers and embraced a system of faith befitting those who had reached the age of discretion and reason. Alluding to the text of 1 Corinthians 13, godly ministers such as Edward Dering described it as the doctrine of those who no longer needed the swaddling bands and mother's milk of signs, wonders and miracles to be persuaded of the truth and who relied solely on the word of God rather such 'poore and childish conceits'.[11] Simultaneously, and somewhat inconsistently, Protestants increasingly connected Catholicism with the stubborn conservatism of those in their dotage. Castigating elderly nurses and dames for indoctrinating children with 'idle fables' and 'lying vanities', they summarised their contempt for this process of generational transmission in the disparaging phrase 'old wives' tales'.[12] The misguided nostalgia of the aged for the pre-Reformation era likewise became a commonplace enshrined in sentences such as 'it was never merry England since the mass was put down' or 'the Bible came abroad'.[13] Catholicism was at once the faith of those reduced to imbecility by age and those who had failed to transcend their natural infantile state.

By contrast, Catholics were all too willing to exploit the topos of childhood to recall heretics to the bosom of the mother church.[14] Spokesmen for the Marian Counter-Reformation including Cardinal Pole systematically employed it as a symbol of the attitude English Christians should adopt, urging those seduced by Protestantism humbly to submit

[10] Miles Coverdale, *The Old Faith, an Evident Probacion out of the Holy Scripture, that the Christian Fayth (which Is the Right, True, Old and Undoubted Fayth) Hath Endured Sens the Beginnyng of the Worlde* (1547); Christopher Rodsell, *A Godly and Short Discourse ... Whereby May Appeare, Howe the Reformation at this Day in England is not a Bringing in of a Newe Religion, but a Reducing Againe of the Olde and Auncient Fayth* (1589), sigs. A2r–3v and *passim*; Josias Nicholls, *Abrahams Faith: That is the Old Religion* (1602), sig. B2v and *passim*; Robert Abbot, *A Defence of the Reformed Catholicke of M. W. Perkins ... Wherein ... their Religion is Dismasked of that Antiquity which they Pretend for it* (1606); Thomas Bell, *The Tryall of the New Religion. Contayning a Plaine Demonstration, that the Late Faith and Doctrine of the Church of Rome, is Indeede the New Religion* (1608). See also Joseph Hall, *The Olde Religion. A Treatise, Wherin is Laid Downe the True State of the Difference betwixt the Reformed, and Romane Church* (1628).

[11] Edward Dering, *XXVII Lectures or Readings, upon Part of the Epistle Written to the Hebrues* (first publ. 1576), repr. in *Maister Derings Workes* (1590), 116–17.

[12] Adam Fox, *Oral Culture and Literate Culture in England 1500–1700* (Oxford, 2000), ch. 3, esp. pp. 175–6.

[13] See, e.g., the words of the Marian sumner, Father Atwell: John Foxe, *Actes and Monuments* (1576 edn), 1462.

[14] Warren W. Wooden, 'The Topos of Childhood in Marian England', *Journal of Medieval and Renaissance Studies*, 12 (1982), 179–94.

themselves to the instruction of their spiritual elders and heed Christ's admonition in Matthew 18 that unless they became like 'little children' and 'young babes' they would never enter the kingdom of heaven. In a further paradox, Catholic polemicists often blamed the pernicious spread of heresy in the earliest phases of the Reformation on the fickleness of youth. Writers such as William Peryn, Miles Huggarde and John Feckenham attributed the apostasy they saw occurring around them to the inherent tendency of 'yonglinges' to be buffeted by 'every puffe of wynd' and to their predeliction towards disorder and insolence. They branded Protestantism as a movement of 'lewd laddys' and 'beardless boys'.[15] The fruits of this new-fangled doctrine were the disobedience of children and the turning of the established hierarchy of youth and age upside down. Writing in 1554, John Christopherson deplored the young evangelicals who made a mocking stock of their 'papisticall' parents saying 'my father is an old doting foole, and will fast upon the fryday, and my mother goeth always mumblinge on her beades'.[16]

For their part, early Protestants acknowledged that these were extraordinary times in which youth might indeed teach or facilitate the conversion of their elders. Nicholas Ridley recalled how during Edward's reign 'the aged folk, which had been brought up in blindness, and in ignorance of those things which every Christian is bound to know' absorbed reformed tenets by 'hearing their children and servants repeating the same'; the illiterate Welsh fisherman Rawlins White learned the complete text of the bible by listening to his son ('a special minister appoynted by God (no doubt) for that purpose') read it aloud; and a court case from John Hooper's diocese of Gloucester in 1551 describes how the prowess of a small girl who perfectly recited the catechism was used to shame a recalcitrant parishioner unable to declare the ten commandments and articles of faith despite his more advanced years.[17]

Snippets of evidence confirm the picture Susan Brigden has painted of the energetic involvement of youth in the early Reformation. They show that adolescent apprentices often played a critical role in the spectacles of demystification by which miraculous images like the Rood of Boxley were exposed as fraudulent: after breaking the crucifix in two in the pulpit John Hilsey handed the idol over to 'the rude people and boyes' to

[15] For these writers, see Brigden, 'Youth', 38–9, and *passim*.

[16] John Christopherson, *An Exhortation to all Menne to Take Hede and Beware of Rebellion* (1554), sig. C2r–v.

[17] Foxe, *Actes and Monuments* (1576 edn), 1474; F. D. Price, 'Gloucester Diocese under Bishop Hooper 1551–3', *Transactions of the Bristol and Gloucestershire Archaeological Society*, 60 (1938), 51–151, at 145.

smash to smithereens.[18] They hurled snowballs at popish priests, made the trumpery of the mass the subject of satirical jests and carnivalesque games, and like the grammar school pupil John Davis of Worcester composed ballads against the Catholic clergy with provocative titles such as 'Come down, for all your shaven crowne.'[19] At Buxton in Derbyshire, with the connivance of a local evangelical gentleman, they profaned the chapel associated with the former holy well of St Anne with irreverent tippling, drinking, piping, dancing and hopping and reproved older parishioners who called upon them to desist from these 'foolish youthful fashions'.[20]

The pages of John Foxe's *Actes and Monuments* celebrate the inversion of patriarchal structures of deference to which this revolutionary moment gave rise. They dwell on the fervour of fresh-faced youths who outshine learned doctors of theology with whom they dispute; their presumption in lecturing their elders is excused because it is divinely inspired. The template here is Jesus taking on the rabbis in the Temple at Jerusalem. Julius Palmer is rebuked by his interrogator as 'a beardless boy, start[ed] up yesterday out of the schools'; the nineteen-year-old apprentice William Hunter arrested for bible-reading and his denial of transubstantiation is angrily reprimanded as a 'naughty boy' by an official whom he discomfits with his deep knowledge of scripture, while the blind boy from Gloucester who engages impressively with the chancellor of the diocese overcomes his disability as well as his age.[21] Such stories represent a reinvigoration of the medieval hagiographical trope of *puer senex*, the godly child who transcends his stage in the life-cycle and displays the spiritual sagacity of the aged. Nowhere is this more evident than in the evolving myth of England's young Josiah, Edward VI. Present in embryo soon after his premature death in 1547, by the late seventeenth century it was firmly entrenched in patriotic legend. Preaching at the Guildhall chapel in 1699, John Strype invoked the memory of the precocious boy king, who 'tho he were but a Child, he was a Father, a true Nursing Father, to God's Church and People'.[22]

[18] Charles Wriothsley, *A Chronicle of England during the Reigns of the Tudors, from* A.D. *1485 to 1559*, ed. William Douglas Hamilton (2 vols., Camden Society, new series 11, 1875–7), I, 76. See Susan Brigden, *London and the Reformation* (Oxford, 1989), 534–5, 598–9.

[19] John Gough Nichols, ed., *Narratives of the Days of the Reformation, Chiefly from the Manuscripts of John Foxe the Martyrologist* (Camden Society, old series, 77, 1859), 60–8, at 63.

[20] The National Archives, C 1/1322, fo. 57r. See also Ethan H. Shagan, *Popular Politics and the English Reformation* (Cambridge, 2003), 267.

[21] Nichols, ed., *Narratives*, 18–20; John Foxe, *Actes and Monuments* (1576 edn), 1462–4. See also Sarah Covington, '"Spared not from Tribulation": Children in Early Modern Martyrologies', *Archiv für Reformationsgeschichte*, 97 (2006), 165–83.

[22] John Strype, *Lessons Moral and Christian, for Youth and Old Age* (1699), 48–56, at 51. For an earlier expression, see John Champneys, *The Harvest is at Hand Wherein the Tares Shall Be Bound and Brent* (1548), sig. A7r–v. For the medieval trope, see Shulamith Shahar, *Childhood in the Middle Ages* (London and New York, 1990), 15–16.

Young people who place confession of the truth above obedience to their elders are also acclaimed for their bravery in martyrological texts. The Chelmsford lad William Maldon boldly defies his father's insistence that he abandon his heretical opinions, saying 'Forsouthe ... I have no scholmaster but God.' Viciously whipped for his temerity, he rejoices in the punishment inflicted upon him by his own parent for Christ's sake.[23] In the early heady years of the Reformation some children felt compelled in conscience to cast filial duty in order to save the souls of their loved ones: young Robert Plumpton wrote to his 'worshipfull mother' in 1536 saying 'it is my dutie to instruct you, most principallie of all other' and sent her a copy of Tyndale's New Testament.[24] Such examples of role reversal and generational dissension were not deplored so much as heralded as signs of the Almighty at work. More generally, Foxe highlighted the youthfulness of those who suffered for their faith: the courage of young maids such as Joan Warren, who was burned at Smithfield with seven other 'godly and constant martirs', far exceeded what would normally be expected of their tender years. He similarly celebrated the stoicism of Rose Alline of Colchester, whose hand was gratuitously burned with a candle by Sir Edmund Tyrell 'til the very sinowes crackte in sonder' after she dared to answer back to his exhortation to counsel her parents to be 'better catholicke people' saying 'Sir, they have a better instructor then I' (Figure 3).[25]

In turn, accounts of the courageous deaths of elderly evangelicals at the hands of the Marian regime highlight the childlike simplicity displayed by such martyrs as they went to the stake. In their final moments, they rise above the physical degeneration attendant upon their age and regain their youthfulness in the eyes of spectators; 'whereas in hys clothes' (a threadbare gown and penny leather girdle), Hugh Latimer had 'appeared a withered and crooked sely old man', stripped of his shroud in readiness for making the ultimate sacrifice in 1555, 'he now stode bolt upryght, as comely a father as one might lightly behold'. At Cardiff, Rawlins White 'seemed in a manner to be altered in nature' as he awaited the fire: 'For wheras before he was wont to go stowping ... through the infirmitie of age, havyng a sad countenance and a very feeble complexion, and withal very soft in speache and gesture. Now he wente and stretched up hym selfe' and acquired the stature and countenance of a man in his prime, his white hair and beard lending him an angelical appearance.[26] Assimilated to ancient prototypes, these eye-witness accounts do not provide us with access to the real experiences of young and old so much as evidence of the

---

[23] Nichols, ed., *Narratives*, 348–51.
[24] Joan Kirby, ed., *Plumpton Correspondence* (Camden Society, 5th series, 8, 1996), 232–4.
[25] Foxe, *Actes and Monuments* (1570 edn), 2199–200.
[26] *Ibid.* (1570 edn), 1928; (1576 edn), 1476.

Figure 3 The godly maid, Rose Alline, of Colchester: John Foxe, *Actes and Monuments* (1583), II, 2006. Reproduced by kind permission of the Syndics of Cambridge University Library (shelfmark Young 200).

vitality of rhetorical devices that play on the ambivalence of early modern images of age. They highlight the early Reformation as a time when contemporaries anticipated and accepted that the settled hierarchies of their society would be overturned temporarily.

It is worth stressing the surge of pedagogic activity and optimism about the transfiguring effects of education that marked the 1540s and 1550s. Instruction of the young was seen as a key priority for achieving the spiritual regeneration of sixteenth-century England. John Colet, founder of St Paul's School in London, believed that the nation's chief hope lay in having the rising generation trained in good principles. Without the godly education of yeoman's sons, concurred Latimer in a sermon preached before Edward VI in 1549, 'ye pluck salvation from the people, and utterly destroy the realm'.[27] As Philippa Tudor has shown, the early

[27] Desiderius Erasmus, *The Lives of Jehan Vitrier ... and John Colet*, ed. J. H. Lupton (1883), 28; George Elwes Corrie, ed., *Sermons by Hugh Latimer, Sometime Bishop of Worcester, Martyr, 1555* (Parker Society, Cambridge, 1844), 102.

reformers developed an ambitious programme of religious instruction for children and adolescents, especially in the guise of catechising. This was to precede their full admission to the church when they reached 'the yeres of discrecion' and could affirm with their own mouths the promises made on their behalf by their godparents at their baptism.[28] Like their counterparts in Lutheran Germany, they were convinced that this was a singularly powerful method of weaning the population from superstition.[29]

II

These convictions persisted, but by the 1570s and 1580s it is possible to detect a growing sense of disillusionment about the receptiveness of the young to the Protestant Gospel. By now, ironically, the children who were the subject of clerical endeavours had been born and baptised in the Protestant church and never known the days in which popery had reigned. This coincided with a developing anxiety about the failure of the Reformation as an engine of evangelical conversion more generally and an awareness of the reluctance of many elderly people to internalise the new faith. One measure of this is the outpouring of printed catechisms and works of practical divinity that Ian Green has dated to these decades. Directed both to 'children in yeeres and children in understanding', they provided 'milke for babes' not merely in age but also in knowledge of Christ. They reflected a recognition that many older parishioners lacked even a basic understanding of Protestant dogma and required a form of adult education. The weaknesses of such catechumens were to be corrected by clergymen young enough to be their sons.[30]

As the first generation of the Reformation gave way to the second and third and Protestantism progressively cemented its hold on English society, the pattern of the young deferring to their elders vigorously reasserted itself. Dozens of seventeenth-century tracts adopted the form of didactic dialogues, 'monitors' and 'remembrancers' in which Old Age tutored the Young Man on his pilgrimage through life: spiritual maturity was once more in, rather than out of step with biological age. In a text translated from Dutch in 1659, for instance, Youth submits gratefully to the superior wisdom and experience of Age in matters of faith and acknowledges that

[28] Philippa Tudor, 'Religious Instruction for Children and Adolescents in the Early English Reformation', *Journal of Ecclesiastical History*, 35 (1984), 391–413. For the rite of confirmation, see *The First and Second Prayer Books of Edward VI* (1910), 404–9.

[29] Gerald Strauss, *Luther's House of Learning: Indoctrination of the Young in the German Reformation* (Baltimore and London, 1978).

[30] Ian Green, '"For Children in Yeeres and Children in Understanding": The Emergence of the English Catechism under Elizabeth and the Early Stuarts', *Journal of Ecclesiastical History*, 37 (1986), 397–425; Ian Green, *The Christian's ABC: Catechisms and Catechizing in England c. 1530–1740* (Oxford, 1996). For examples, see William Crashaw, *Milke for babes. Or, A North-Countrie Catechisme* (1618); John Stalham, *A Catechisme for Children in Yeeres and Children in Understanding* (1644); Robert Abbot, *Milk for babes, or, A mothers catechism for her children* (1646).

without such guidance 'by reason of my ignorant Child-hood' he would 'perish in blindness and misery'.[31]

This was accompanied by a fresh emphasis on the innate vanity and depravity of the young and on the necessity of strict parental discipline that finds clear expression in the burgeoning genre of books of household governance. These works capture the tension between the deeply pessimistic anthropology that lay at the heart of Protestant theology and its lingering hope that training and education might have a redemptive effect by bridling the froward, refractory and 'brutish' impulses to which youth were instinctively prone. Predicated on Calvin's precept that children carried 'an innate corruption from the very womb', they insist that sharp correction is essential if children are not to slide down the slippery slope into inveterate sin and become, in the words of the Jacobean divine Robert Shelford, 'the Divels drudges' and 'packe-horse'. It was best, they declared, to begin when the plant was pliable and tender and when the minds of the young were still like soft wax and easiest to imprint with the lessons of righteousness.[32] The diligent efforts of parents to instruct their offspring in godliness, wrote William Gouge in his bestselling manual *Of Domesticall Duties*, were 'an especiall means of propagation of true religion from age to age, and from generation to generation'.[33] Neglect of these obligations was the readiest route to anarchy within the family and the dissolution of Christian society, for, as the Sussex divine John Maynard averred in 1669, 'Satan's kingdom' was built 'upon the ruines of the younger sort'.[34]

Such sentiments coexisted with the idea that youth and childhood comprised a time when individuals might enjoy special spiritual insight. The later sixteenth and seventeenth centuries throw up many instances

---

[31] *A Spiritual Journey of a Young Man, Towards the Land of Peace . . . With some Proverbs or Sentences, which the Old-Age Spake to the Young Man* (1659), 40, and see 43. See also W. P., *The Young-Mans Guide to Godlinesse* (1619); Samuel Burrowes, *Good Instructions for all Youngmen and Maids* (1642); Samuel Crossman, *The Young Mans Monitor, or, A Modest Offer Toward the Pious, and Vertuous Composure of Life from Youth to Riper Years* (1664); Roger Hough, *The Young Man's Duty: or Good Council for Young-Men* (1677).

[32] John Calvin, *Institutes of the Christian Religion*, trans. Henry Beveridge (2 vols., Grand Rapids, MI, 1989), I, 214 (bk II, ch. 1); Robert Shelford, *Lectures or Readings upon the 6. Verse of the 22 Chapter of the Proverbs, Concerning the Vertuous Education of Youth* (1606), esp. 134 [*vere* 123]–128. See also Gervase Babington, *A Very Fruitful Exposition of the Commandements by Way of Questions and Answers for Greater Plainnesse* (1596), 88–102; John Dod and Robert Cleaver, *A Plaine and Familiar Exposition of the Ten Commandments* (1612), 183–216. On Protestant attitudes towards upbringing, see John Morgan, *Godly Learning: Puritan Attitudes towards Reason, Learning and Education 1560–1640* (Cambridge, 1986), ch. 8; Anthony Fletcher, 'Prescription and Practice: Protestantism and the Upbringing of Children, 1560–1700', in *The Church and Childhood*, ed. Diana Wood, Studies in Church History 31 (Oxford, 1994), 325–46.

[33] William Gouge, *Of Domesticall Duties: Eight Treatises* (1622), 538, and treatise 6 'Of Parents Duties' *passim*.

[34] John Maynard, *A Memento to Young and Old* (1669), 17.

of young boys and girls of exemplary piety who died before they reached adulthood. '[E]ven from his bairnlie age', William Michel, the son of a Scottish pastor, who passed away in 1634, 'had the wit of a Man, the knowledge of a Scholler, & the carriage of a Christian'.[35] As described by her biographer Henry Wilkinson, Margaret Corbet 'was young in years, yet ... old in Grace' when she died aged twenty-eight in 1656, while the devout New England youth Nathanel Mather, brother of the more famous Cotton, had displayed 'a sign of Ninety at Nineteen'.[36] Twelve-year-old Cicely Puckering, celebrated in a funeral sermon published in 1640, had likewise 'excelled all others of her sexe and age'.[37] Her profound utterances during her final sickness, which amazed those who assembled at her deathbed, bear comparison with the prodigious pronouncements of the succession of young children who were recognised as prophets in the course of this period – children such as the Suffolk husbandman's son William Withers, who fell into a coma on Christmas Eve 1580 and awoke ten days later to deliver a series of vehement denunciations of sin and immorality, and the eleven-year-old 'wise virgin' Martha Hatfield, whose trance-like revelations made her a celebrity in puritan London in 1653 (Figure 4). These episodes reflected the idea, rooted in the text of Psalm 8 v. 2 ('Out of the mouths of babes and sucklings ...'), that the young were sensitive radio-transmitters of divine messages from heaven. These prophets' short-lived usurpation of the role of preachers was sanctioned by God, who resorted to making the young his mouthpieces when people would not heed the impassioned calls of ordained ministers and/or when the apocalypse was nigh.[38] These, however, were exceptions to a more general rule summed up by William Perkins. Where self-proclaimed seers were young rather than old, 'babling and talkative', 'unruly and disordered' rather than 'quiet' and 'silent with wisdome', he declared, 'suspicion may be gathered' that their premonitions were 'an illusion of Satan. For in the weaker sort he most prevaileth.'[39] Symptomatic of what Max Weber might have

[35] M. R. B., *Epitaphs upon the Untymelie Death of that Hopefull, Learned, and Religious Youth, Mr William Michel* (Aberdeen, 1634), sig. E2r.

[36] Henry Wilkinson, *The Hope of Glory or Christs Indwelling in True Believers Is an Evident Demonstration of their Hope of Glory. As it Was Set Forth in a Sermon ... at the Funerall of that Eminently-Religious-Gentlewoman M[ist]ris Margaret Corbet* (Oxford, 1657), p. 75; Cotton Mather, *Early piety, exemplified in the life and death of Mr. Nathanael Mather, who ... changed earth for heaven, Oct. 17. 1688* (1689), 60.

[37] John Bryan, *The Vertuous Daughter. A Sermon Preached at Saint Maries in Warwick, at the Funerall of the Most Vertuous and Truly Religious Yong Gentlewoman, Mistris Cicely Puckering* (1640).

[38] Alexandra Walsham, 'Out of the Mouths of Babes and Sucklings: Prophecy, Puritanism and Childhood in Elizabethan Suffolk', in *The Church and Childhood*, ed. Diana Wood, Studies in Church History 31 (1994), 285–99; Nigel Smith, 'A Child Prophet: Martha Hatfield as the Wise Virgin', in *Children and their Books*, ed. Avery and Briggs, 79–93.

[39] William Perkins, *A Fruitfull Dialogue concerning the End of the World* (1631), 468.

Figure 4 Martha Hatfield, 'the wise virgin': James Fisher, *The Wise Virgin or, A Wonderfull Narration of the Hand of God* (1653), frontispiece and title-page. Reproduced by kind permission of the Syndics of Cambridge University Library (shelfmark 8. 41. 37).

called the routinisation of the Church of England's charisma,[40] the dominant tendency of late Tudor and early Stuart Protestantism was towards scepticism about the capacity of youth to function as vessels and vehicles of divine enlightenment. Such figures represented a threat to the monopoly on religious authority claimed by the ecclesiastical hierarchy, and the more typical response was to dismiss them as victims of diabolical delusion.

The rash of cases of demonic possession that spread from the middle years of Elizabeth's reign is significant here. In many such episodes, possessed adolescents and children oscillate between blaspheming and preaching; the voices that emanate from them as from ventriloquists' dolls come from God as well as the devil. Thus, in between his fits, the

[40] Max Weber, *The Sociology of Religion*, trans. Ephraim Frischoff, intro. Talcott Parsons (1971 edn), esp. 60–79.

Derbyshire boy Thomas Darling displayed an attachment to Scripture and wished he might live 'to thunder out the threatenings of Gods word', while John Starkie cried out against the 'straunge sinnes of the land committed in all estates & degrees of people' like an accomplished Paul's Cross preacher.[41] The diagnosis of possession that prevailed on these occasions represented a defeat for the afflicted and the triumph of a perspective that regarded their disturbing behaviour as an unwarrantable upsetting of the natural order in which children were subservient to their parents, and laypeople to the clergy.[42] With Jim Sharpe, we might see the impious outbursts and irreverence towards Scripture with which these edifying speeches were intermixed as an index of youthful rebellion against a rigid puritan upbringing. Attributing their misconduct to the work of Satanic forces was a convenient way of explaining disruption in the well-ordered and somewhat claustrophobic households of godly patriarchs, which were widely regarded as microcosms of the Christian commonwealth at large.[43] By the later sixteenth century, generational conflict was often intra- rather than inter-confessional in character.

Such incidents reflect the pronounced stress that was developing in post-Reformation culture on the fifth commandment, 'Honour thy father and mother.' Popular treatises on the Decalogue such as those produced by Gervase Babington and John Dod and Robert Cleaver exhorted the young to show an 'awful respect and filial or child like feare' to their parents and masters because they bore the 'print' or 'image of God'.[44] As Matthew Griffith remarked in his 1633 handbook for family management, *Bethel*, old men represented the antiquity and eternity of the Almighty, who had ordained obedience to them in Leviticus 19 ('Thou shalt rise up before the hoarie head, and honour the face of the old man').[45] The consequences of defying this element of the Mosaic code were underlined in Thomas Beard's *Theatre of Gods Judgements* (1597), which regaled its readers with gory anecdotes of the retributive punishments visited upon ungrateful and wayward daughters and sons throughout the ages, from Absolom's rebellion against David onwards. The case of twelve-year-old

---

[41] Jesse Bee, *The Most Wonderfull and True Storie, of a Certaine Witch Named Alse Gooderige of Stapen hill . . . As also a True Report of the Strange Torments of Thomas Darling*, ed. J. Denison (1597), 2; George More, *A True Discourse concerning the Certain Possession and Dispossession of 7 Persons in One Family in Lancashire* (1600), 25.

[42] David Harley, 'Explaining Salem: Calvinist Psychology and the Diagnosis of Possession', *American Historical Review*, 101 (1996), 307–30.

[43] J. A. Sharpe, 'Disruption in the Well-Ordered Household: Age, Authority and Possessed Young People', in *The Experience of Authority in Early Modern England*, ed. Paul Griffiths, Adam Fox and Steve Hindle (Basingstoke, 1996), 187–212.

[44] Gouge, *Of Domesticall Duties*, 430, 482; Dod and Cleaver, *Plaine and Familiar Exposition*, 247. See also John Ayre, ed., *The Catechism of Thomas Becon, S.T.P.* (Parker Society, Cambridge, 1844), 358.

[45] Matthew Griffith, *Bethel: Or, A Forme for Families* (1633), 45–6.

Denis Benfield, struck dead the day after calling the Almighty 'an old doting foole', served a triple purpose: as an example of divine vengeance against those who showed contempt for the deity and for the aged, and as a warning to parents who suffered 'their young ones to growe up in blindnesse'.[46]

The Reformation of Manners, which gathered pace in the last quarter of Elizabeth's reign, may be interpreted as a further index of Protestantism's advance into middle age. As Patrick Collinson has argued, the sins and vices which magistrates and ministers joined forces to combat were less those of the poor than the young. The dancing, drinking and other pastimes against which the authors of the literature of moral complaint railed were the delinquencies of people living out the contemporary proverb that 'youth must have its swing'.[47] Several of these books, including John Northbrooke's treatise reproving dicing, dancing, plays and other 'idle pastimes' of 1579, were framed as conversations between Youth and Age. Asked why he disdains parish worship for foolish recreations, the former declares that the church is a 'place more fitte for suche olde fatherly men as you are than for such young men as I am'. By the end, he heartily thanks the latter for his 'fatherly instructions', which have corrected his errors and led him out of his evil ways.[48] It is also revealing that the majority of offenders from the Essex village of Earls Colne hauled before the church courts of Essex for moral and especially sexual misdemeanours were in their teens and early twenties.[49] In its second generation, Protestantism became a mechanism for enforcing patriarchal authority and repressing a vigorous adolescent subculture that fiercely resented the interference of parents and other 'busy controllers' in its activities. While the polarities implied in moralising tracts of the time are belied by the mid-seventeenth-century Lancashire apprentice Roger Lowe, who combined sermon-gadding with regular trips to dances and alehouses, they nevertheless reflect shifting perceptions of the nature of generational relations.[50] Their resurgence hints at a sea change in Protestant culture that found expression in its partial repudiation of the catchy popular media such as plays, pictures and songs which young people had exploited to subvert the Catholic establishment in the early

[46] Thomas Beard, *The Theatre of Gods Judgements* (1631 edn), 184, and see 214–26.

[47] Patrick Collinson, *The Religion of Protestants: The Church in English Society 1559–1625* (Oxford, 1982), 224–30.

[48] John Northbrooke, *Spiritus est Vicarius Christi in Terra, A Treatise Wherein Dicing, Dauncing, Vaine Plaies or Enterludes with other Idle Pastimes, &c ... are Reprooved* (1579), fos. 1r, 72r.

[49] Robert von Freideburg, 'Reformation of Manners and the Social Composition of Offenders in an East Anglian Cloth Village: Earls Colne, Essex, 1531–1642', *Journal of British Studies*, 29 (1990), 347–85.

[50] William L. Sachse, ed., *The Diary of Roger Lowe of Ashton-in-Makerfield, Lancashire 1663–74* (London and New York, 1938).

Reformation. Protestantism lost its youthful gloss and ceased to be at ease in the inns and bowling alleys in which the young habitually spent their free time.[51]

By the 1580s, the old Marian priests who had survived the Elizabeth settlement and perpetuated conservative religious practices in England's rural parishes were dying out and being replaced by younger ministers trained in seminaries of godly piety like Emmanuel and Christ's. The ignorant 'dumb dogs' denounced by puritan surveyors of the ministry were giving way to a breed of clerical youngsters whose intemperate zeal rubbed some of their elders up the wrong way. We catch one glimpse of this in John Earle's deft caricature of the 'young raw preacher': 'a bird not yet fledg'd, that hath hopt out of his nest to be Chirping on a hedge' who 'takes on against the Pope without mercy' and whose 'action is all passion, & his speech interjections'.[52] A second is the sharp exchange between Archbishop Whitgift and a nonconforming minister from Kent whom he furiously upbraided with the words 'Thou boy, beardless boy, yesterday bird, new out of shell.'[53]

Some members of this emerging cohort were the products of religiously divided households. Arthur Hildersham had been 'brought up in the Popish manner' and 'taught to say his Prayers in Latine'; his defiance of repeated parental attempts to send him overseas to train for the priesthood in Rome led to him being cast off. Laurence Chaderton's conservative father had 'sent him a Poke with a groat in it' when he exhibited Protestant proclivities, signifying his intention to disinherit him.[54] Increasingly, though, the clerical ranks of the Church of England were filled by men of impeccably reformed lineage. A growing number, moreover, came from hereditary dynasties of ministers. Andrew Willet, for instance, was the progeny of a Marian Protestant exile who returned to England at the accession of Elizabeth to the parsonage of Barley in Hertfordshire, a living he passed on in his old age directly to his son.[55] And many of these divines tied the knot with the daughters of neighbouring preachers whom they admired. The increasingly incestuous and endogamous character of the post-Reformation ministry was one of the side-effects of Protestantism's endorsement of clerical marriage, though also of its ambivalent status in post-Reformation society, which

[51] Patrick Collinson, *The Birthpangs of Protestant England: Religious and Cultural Change in the Sixteenth and Seventeenth Centuries* (New York, 1988), ch. 4.

[52] John Earle, *Micro-cosmographie. Or, A Peece of the World Discovered in Essayes and Characters* (1628), sigs. B3r–5r.

[53] Quoted in Patrick Collinson, *The Elizabethan Puritan Movement* (1964), 254.

[54] Samuel Clarke, *A General Martyrologie . . . Whereunto is Added the Lives of Thirty Two English Divines* (1677 edn), 114–15, 145.

[55] Thomas Fuller, *Abel Redevivus: Or, The Dead Yet Speaking. The Lives and Deaths of the Moderne Divines* (1651), 565–75.

limited the pool from which the female offspring of the clergy could choose husbands. It was also a by-product of its studied cultivation of the ideology of the godly household. Many children reared in the hot-house atmosphere that prevailed in such families found it impossible to resist receiving its imprint.[56]

Plentiful evidence of these trends can be found in the 'testimonies' and 'commendations' of deceased worthies appended to funeral sermons and in biographical works like Samuel Clarke's *Lives* of eminent divines and Thomas Fuller's *Abel Redevivus* (1651) which fed parasitically off these encomiastic discourses, albeit refracted through the filter of Erasmian convention and an Aristotelian ideal of moderation. These texts were 'magazeens of religious patterns' which conceived of their subjects as living 'commentaries' on abstract Protestant doctrine and as walking 'sermons'.[57] Two tropes can be detected in their accounts of the childhood and youth of the future lights of the church. The first is an emphasis on precocious piety. As a schoolboy Julines Herring was noted for his prodigious diligence in reading the holy Scriptures and was so religiously disposed that instead of playing he would pray with one or two devout friends, recite the catechism and repeat sermons.[58] '[E]ven from his infancy', Herbert Palmer, later Master of Queen's College, Cambridge, had been 'addicted to the serious study of both Religion and Learning' and exhibited 'Symptoms of Grace and Piety ... so that we may not without good ground, esteem him sanctified even from the Womb'.[59] The zeal of the young Jeremy Whitaker was such that he regularly travelled 'eight or ten miles to hear a wakening soul-warming sermon'; he was a 'plant of Gods own setting, [which] did both blossome, and put forth fruit quickly, which Providence did afterwards make a very fruitful Tree'.[60]

Rooted in the *Confessions* of St Augustine, the second trope is that of the casting aside of a misspent youth to embrace evangelical piety. Samuel Fairclough's moment of spiritual awakening followed an episode in which he robbed an orchard and gorged himself on pears; a week later he listened to a sermon by Samuel Ward which pierced him to the heart like a dart.[61] Robert Bolton had loved the theatre, gambling, Christmas merrymaking, swearing and Sabbath-breaking until one day God had smote him to the ground, 'running upon him as a gyant, taking him by

[56] See Michelle Wolfe, 'The Tribe of Levi: Gender, Family and Vocation in English Clerical Households, Circa 1590–1714' (Ph.D. thesis, Ohio State University, 2004).

[57] See Patrick Collinson, '"A Magazine of Religious Patterns": An Erasmian Topic Transposed in English Protestantism', in his *Godly People: Essays on English Protestantism and Puritanism* (1983), 499–525.

[58] Clarke, *Lives of Thirty Two Divines*, 190 [*vere* 160].

[59] *Ibid.*, 183–4.

[60] *Ibid.*, 264.

[61] Samuel Clarke, *The Lives of Sundry Eminent Persons in this Later Age* (1683), 154.

the necke and shaking him to peeces'.[62] And in her girlhood the godly gentlewoman Jane Ratcliffe had been 'too much delighted with dancing, Stage-playes, and other publick vanities, according to the fashion of young folkes' until it pleased God to call her by the ministry of Nicholas Byfield to a full assurance of her election to grace.[63]

III

The theme of a sudden or more gradual revelation of the divine spirit working within one is more commonly associated with the conversion narrative, the full emergence of which coincides with the rise of the spiritual autobiography in the seventeenth century. It is present, for instance, in the voluminous personal notebooks that the London woodturner Nehemiah Wallington began to write in 1621 in his early twenties, in which he recorded how despite 'being brought up in the waies of God from a childelike yong Timothi', he had lived in 'a vile and sinfull condition', being 'a very froward and disobedient crying childe' and 'given to pelfering and stelling'. His conversion was a gradual process, involving a pricking of his conscience and the purchase of a Geneva bible, interspersed with bouts of suicidal temptation as well as moral backsliding.[64] The early pages of the Presbyterian Richard Baxter's well-known *Reliquiae* likewise list the adolescent addiction to gluttonous eating of fruit and love of romances, fables and old tales 'which corrupted my affections' and the Baptist John Bunyan's *Grace Abounding to the Chief of Sinners* describes how he had been 'the very ringleader of all the Youth that kept me company, into all manner of vice and ungodliness' prior to seeing the light.[65]

Underpinning such stories is another paradoxical passage from St Paul: the exhortation in Ephesians 4:22–4 that the sincere follower of Christ cast off 'the old man, which is corrupt according to the deceitful lusts' and take on 'the new man, which after God is created in righteousness and true holiness'. Repeatedly invoked by sixteenth- and seventeenth-century preachers as a metaphor for the process of metamorphosis experienced by real believers,[66] this was the root of the concept of spiritual rebirth that

[62] Edward Bagshaw, 'The Life and Death of Mr Bolton', bound with Nicholas Estwick, *A Learned and Godly Sermon Preached on the XIX. Day of December, Anno Dom. MDCXXI. at the Funerall of Mr Robert Bolton* (1633), sig. b5r.

[63] Clarke, *Lives of Thirty Two Divines*, 377.

[64] David Booy, ed., *The Notebooks of Nehemiah Wallington, 1618–1654: A Selection* (Aldershot, 2007), 31, 265, 266–9, and see 40–1.

[65] J. M. Lloyd Thomas, eds., *The Autobiography of Richard Baxter Being the Reliquiae Baxterianae* (London and Toronto, 1925), 5; John Bunyan, *Grace Abounding with Other Spiritual Autobiographies*, ed. John Stachniewski with Anita Pacheco (Oxford, 1998), 7.

[66] See Thomas Becon, *A Comfortable Epistle too Goddes Faythfull People in Englande* (Strassburg [Wesel?], 1554), sig. B3r; John Bradford, 'A comparison betweene the old man and the

permeated the evangelical conversion narrative in its eighteenth-century heyday. It is worth noting the belated appearance (or reappearance) of the genre in its fully blown form: Judith Pollmann has commented on the partial hiatus in this longstanding tradition that can be observed in the first phase of the Reformation.[67] Glimpses of it appear in the midst of some apologetic texts, including the case of Thomas Bilney, who dated his conversion to a casual reading of a verse from the New Testament, which 'one sentence' exhilarated his heart and brought him to 'a marvelous comfort and quietnesse, in so much, that my brused bones leapt for joy'.[68] But it remains conspicuous by its relative absence in the sixteenth century. Pollmann explains this interruption by reference to early Protestantism's desire to claim the sanction of antiquity and dissociate itself from the taint of novelty. Its vigorous reemergence in the seventeenth century may be seen as a measure of generational change and the institutionalisation of reform: once Protestantism had firmly established itself as the official faith, the notion of breaking with the past seemed not only less drastic but actually necessary as an expression of personal spiritual development. The conversion narrative told of the process by which people gained a sense of the excitement of the Gospel in an age of settled and complacent Protestant orthodoxy. The change of heart described in such autobiographies did not represent a rebellion against filial piety but an outworking of the struggle for assurance and sanctification that was central to experimental predestinarianism and a sign of the discovery of the inner light that lay behind so much of the sectarian enthusiasm that flourished in the 1640s and 1650s.[69] Some writers adopted the device of counting their age from the date at which they had been born again in the faith of the Lord. In 1536, a Dominican friar who was a disciple of the charismatic Hugh Latimer was known as 'Two-Year-Old', and Ignatius Jurdain, the renowned puritan mayor of Exeter, died in 1640 in the 79th year of his life, but the 65th 'according to

new', in *Godly Meditations uppon the Ten Commaundementes, the Articles of the Fayth, and the Lords Prayer* (1567), fos. 91r–66r [*vere* 96r]; George Abbot, *An Exposition upon the Prophet Jonah* (1600), 476; Thomas Adams, *The Happines of the Church* (1619), 198; Nicholas Beare, *Metamorphosis Christiana: or, the Old Man Changed into the New* (1679).

[67] Judith Pollmann, 'A Different Road to God: The Protestant Experience of Conversion in the Sixteenth Century', in *Conversion and Modernities: The Globalization of Christianity*, ed. Peter van der Veer (New York and London, 1996), 47–64. But cf. the evidence assembled by Peter Marshall, 'Evangelical Conversion in the Reign of Henry VIII', in *The Beginnings of English Protestantism*, ed. *idem* and Alec Ryrie (Cambridge, 2002), 14–37.

[68] Foxe, *Actes and Momuments* (1583 edn), 1005.

[69] See D. Bruce Hindmarsh, *The Evangelical Conversion Narrative: Spiritual Autobiography in Early Modern England* (Oxford, 2005).

his account for the new-birth', 'For so long he reckoned since the time of his effectual Calling.'[70]

By the 1650s, Protestantism was edging towards a form of gerontocracy. To adhere to it was no longer an act of youthful rebellion against the time-honoured ways of one's forebears; it was an act of conformity with the status quo and its elder statesmen. It is revealing that the average age at which seventeenth-century archbishops of Canterbury were appointed was sixty.[71] Earle's character of the 'grave [Anglican] divine' has several decades of pastoral duty, serious study, and sensible judgement behind him: he 'is a maine pillar of our Church, though not yet Deane nor Canon, and his life our Religions best Apologie: His death is his last Sermon, where in the Pulpit of his Bed hee instructs men to dye by his example'.[72] Many of the puritan ministers commemorated in Clarke's *Lives* exemplify the religious and moral virtues early modern culture prized in old age. In the winter of their life, they continue to demonstrate an indefatigable devotion to duty despite their disintegrating health and display a quasi-divine kind of wisdom. Thomas Cartwright, who died at sixty-eight, was greatly troubled with the stone and gout 'yet would he not intermit his labours, but continued preaching when many times he could scarce creep up into the Pulpit'. John Carter 'was as fit for service in Gods Harvest-field at fourscore, as he was at forty' and a visitor to Suffolk 'heard him discourse with such holy gravity, and a mixture of all kinde of learning, solidity, and wit, that he stood amazed at it, and said . . . I see you are like unto the Palm and Cedar Tree, you bring forth more fruit in your Age.'[73] These divines are venerable figures who physically as well as spiritually resemble the prophets and patriarchs of the Old Testament, whose longevity was seen as a sign of divine approbation: Abraham had lived until the age of 175 and the legendary Methuselah, son of Enoch and grandfather of Noah, 969. 'Towards his latter end in his visage' William Gouge was reputed to have resembled the 'the Picture that is usually made for Moses' and to be his 'exact Effiges' in spirit, and the old-fashioned clothing of John Carter and his wife persuaded some visitors that they had seen 'Adam and Eve, or some of the old Patriarchs'. Thomas Gataker had gone prematurely grey, 'which made him to be thought elder than he was, because he had long appeared ancient in the eyes of the world'.[74] Some actively cultivated these comparisons: John More, the so-called 'Apostle

[70] Cited in Susan Wabuda, '"Fruitfull Preaching" in the Diocese of Worcester: Bishop Hugh Latimer and his Influence 1535–1539', in *Religion and the English People 1500–1640*, ed. Eric Josef Carlson (Kirksville, MO, 1998), 49–74, at 68; Clarke, *Lives of Thirty Two Divines*, 407.

[71] Cited in Smith, 'Growing Old', 126.

[72] Earle, *Micro-cosmographie*, sigs. B5v–7v.

[73] Clarke, *Lives of Thirty Two Divines*, 21, 138–9.

[74] *Ibid.*, 135, 242 (and see the illustration on 234).

of Norwich' allegedly grew the longest beard of his generation so that 'no act of his life might be unworthy of the gravity of his appearance' (Figure 5).[75] Though images of God the father as a bearded old sage were technically anathema to the hottest sort of Protestants, more than a few preachers were depicted in a strikingly similar guise.

Devout laypeople who lived to a ripe old age were also immortalised in funeral sermons and godly *Lives*. Martha Hasselborn, who expired in 1696, at ninety-five, was celebrated as 'an aged servant of the Lord' and 'Old Disciple of Christ'. Like Sarah in the bible, who had died aged 127, she was 'a long example of Piety, to the very last step of Humane Life'.[76] It was a commonplace that the liminal phase immediately before death was a time when human beings were vouchsafed an ability to prophesy. The valedictory exhortations they made to friends and family were listened to with respect and written down as pearls of wisdom for the benefit of their posterity. The belief that old age brought individuals into closer communion with God and that their debilitated bodies contained youthful souls also explains the credence given to reports of the appearance of ancient seers predicting the future and threatening divine vengeance; a ballad of 1657 recorded the 'strange speeches' uttered by the 155-year-old Margaret Hough from Cheshire foretelling the fall of the Cromwellian commonwealth, while a pamphlet from the late 1670s told the news of two Frenchmen who declared themselves 'to be above a thousand years old a piece' and preached repentance to the world.[77]

IV

By 1700, Protestantism was the faith of those with the wrinkles, creases and grey hairs of experience. The mantle of youthful illegitimacy had passed to other quarters as early as the 1570s and 1580s, when young men and women in their hundreds left England for continental seminaries and convents in search of foreign adventures and in pursuit of a religious vocation. Others stayed at home and risked their lives assisting seminary priests and Jesuits whose very presence in the country after 1585 was an act of treason. As Susan Brigden remarked, now it was Catholicism that had 'the appeal of exotic and forbidden fruit'. In the mid-Tudor period, youth were the great white hope of the evangelical Protestant movement; half a century later, they were heralded as the best prospect for achieving

---

[75] See *Oxford Dictionary of National Biography*, s.n., 'John More'.

[76] Timothy Rogers, *The Happiness of a Quiet Mind both in Youth and Old Age ... In a Discourse Occasioned by the Death of Mrs Martha Hasselborn, Who Died March 13th, 1695/6 in the 95th Year of her Age* (1696), at 93, 104.

[77] *A New Prophesie: Or Some Strange Speeches Declared by an Old Woman Living Now in Cheshire, in Ranna* ([1657]); *The Worlds Wonder: Giving an Account of Two Old Men ... Who Declare Themselves to be Above a Thousand Years Old a Piece, and Preach Repentance to the World* ([1675–80]).

IOANNES MORVS S: Theo: Prof.

Ergo age Magne morj nil tandem More morare
Hic totus viues, nescic More morj
Corpore mente Simul te More hac tabula pingit
Hic absens aderis non moriture More

Figure 5 John More, 'the Apostle of Norwich', who grew the longest beard of his generation so that 'no act of his life might be unworthy of the gravity of his appearance': Henry Holland, *Herωologia Anglica* ([Arnhem], [1620]), 209. Reproduced by kind permission of the Syndics of Cambridge University Library (shelfmark SSS. 40. 19).

England's restoration to the Roman fold and for securing the survival of the Old Religion.[78]

Once again, this was a phase marked by inversions of the age hierarchy – by examples of children who heroically disobeyed their Protestant parents and refused to attend Calvinist worship or entered into religious orders without their consent, children whose pious disobedience was celebrated in missionary memoirs and Annual Letters – children such as the Wisbech boy Thomas Dowlton who reasoned with officials in the port of Rye with adult-like defiance when he was arrested in 1595 and Alice Harrison, who was 'corporally chastised' after she converted to Catholicism, 'and when this would not reclaim her, . . . turned adrift by her father'.[79] It was a time when the young had the audacity to reprehend and instruct their misguided elders in letters modelled on Robert Southwell's famous *Epistle to his Father* and when middle-aged men like the Benedictine Augustine Baker could lament the lukewarm piety of their elderly church papist parents, whom conformity had reduced to mere 'neutrals in religion'.[80] And it was a juncture at which thirteen-year-old girls like Elizabeth Orton of Flintshire could acquire spiritual authority in the eyes of clergy and laity alike as prophets and seers: the visions she experienced in 1580 involved a vigorous endorsement of proscribed Catholic doctrine and a spirited denunciation of the 'naughtie Religion now used' as 'moste abhominable in Gods sight'.[81] Recent work on the *Responsa Scholarum* of the English College at Rome promises to reveal more about how Catholic youths conceived of momentous life decisions that often involved an overturning of patriarchal norms and how far these patterns of religiously inspired juvenile delinquency declined over time as Catholicism became an increasingly endogamous and inward-looking community.[82]

---

[78] Brigden, 'Youth', 67. On this theme, see also Alison Shell, '"Furor Juvenilis": Post-Reformation English Catholicism and Exemplary Youthful Behaviour', in *Catholics and the 'Protestant Nation': Religious Politics and Identity in Early Modern England*, ed. Ethan H. Shagan (Manchester, 2005), 185–206.

[79] Philip Caraman, trans. and ed., *William Weston: The Autobiography of an Elizabethan* (1955), 152, 242–4; John Kirk, *Biographies of English Catholics in the Eighteenth Century*, ed. John Hungerford Pollen and Edwin Burton (1909), 111–12, 262–3.

[80] Robert Southwell, *An Epistle of a Religious Priest unto his Father: Exhorting him to the Perfect Forsaking of the World* ([London?], 1597); J. McCann and H. Connolly, eds., *Memorials of Father Augustine Baker and Other Documents Relating to the English Benedictines* (Catholic Record Society 33, 1933), 15–19.

[81] Barnaby Rich, *The True Report of a Late Practise Enterprised by a Papist, with a Yong Maiden in Wales* (1582), sig. D1r and *passim*.

[82] Anthony Kenny, ed., *The Responsa Scholarum of the English College, Rome, 1598–1685* (2 vols., Catholic Record Society 54–5, 1962–3). Lucy Underwood has studied these extensively as part of her forthcoming Cambridge Ph.D. on post-Reformation Catholicism and childhood.

Finally, the same tendencies can be traced within the mid-seventeenth-century sects, notably the Society of Friends. Early Quakerism was also a movement that revelled in its carnivalesque reversal of the roles of youth and age. It was a movement of unruly antinomian rebellion against institutionalised religion by individuals who described themselves as the 'children of light', who frequently spoke of the process of receiving the Holy Spirit in terms of the displacing of the Old Man by the New, and who engaged in behaviour like 'going naked for a sign' and refusing to doff their hats as a mark of respect that conservative contemporaries regarded as immature and insubordinate in the extreme.[83] It was led by young men like James Parnell, who boldly pitted themselves against the authority of ordained clergymen and compared their encounters with the biblical combat between the little 'stripling' David and the 'proud boaster' Goliath. In a tract written to refute Thomas Drayton, 'an ancient Country Minister' from Huntingdon, Parnell quoted the words of Solomon that 'a poor and wise Child, is better then an old foolish King' and that 'the honourable age is not that which is of long time, neither that which is measured by the Number of years; but wisdom is the gray hair: and an undefiled life is old Age'. He responded to Drayton's condescending comment that he had felt obliged to refute the young Quaker 'lest the Boy should be highly conceited of himself, and falsely boast, That he understand more then the Ancients' with the impertinent retort that even 'a Babe may comprehend thee, and tell thee of they foly, and when thou thinkest of thy beard or age (as thou sayest) confusion of face may cover thee'.[84] Quakers too initially took pride in their status as agents of household division and intergenerational tension; Parnell wrote of how Christ had now come 'to set at Variance, Father against Son, and Son against Father . . . and to turn the World upside down' and he and others urged their followers to shun older relatives who tried to bribe or browbeat them into withdrawing from the sect as 'Instruments of Satan'.[85] Eager young converts played up their bravery in defying parental opposition in their autobiographies: Thomas Ellwood recorded how he had received several 'buffets' about the head and 'whirrets on the ear' for refusing to remove his hat in his father's presence, and travelled on foot to meetings when the latter impounded his horse.[86] They replaced their own natural

---

[83] For the rhetoric of casting off the old man and becoming a 'babe' through a new 'spiritual birth', see Robert Barclay, *An Apology for the True Christian Divinity, as the Same is Held Forth, and Preached by the People, Called, in Scorn, Quakers* (1678), 37, 154, 169.

[84] James Parnell, *Goliahs Head Cut off with his own Sword* (1655), title-page, 2, 12, and *passim;* Thomas Drayton, *An Answer According to Truth, that Trembles not, nor Quakes, nor Quayleth* (1655), 1. See also Kate Peters, *Print Culture and the Early Quakers* (Cambridge, 2005), 162.

[85] James Parnell, *A Collection of the Several Writings Given Forth from the Spirit of the Lord* (1675), 67–8; Adrian Davies, *The Quakers in English Society 1655–1725* (Oxford, 2000), 195–201.

[86] Henry Morley, ed., *The History of Thomas Ellwood Written by Himself* (1885), 53–6, 59, 62.

progenitors with surrogate 'spiritual parents' who were their elders in this fledgling faith.

Over time, like Protestantism, Quakerism lost the spontenaity and tamed the wild enthusiasm that had marked its early years. As it moved into middle age and donned the garb of sober respectability and self-discipline, it looked back on the exploits of the first Friends with growing embarrassment. George Foxe's own journal was carefully edited in the final years of the seventeenth century to eliminate some of his more outrageous reminiscences, that 'it might not sound uncouth and unfashionable to nice ears'.[87] This was not just a strategy for surviving persecution and securing the support and sympathy of their orthodox neighbours; it may also be seen as a symptom of generational change. By the 1680s, the Society's heroes were no longer disorderly adolescents and youths but men and women like seventy-eight-year-old Loveday Hambly, the 'Cornish Quaker saint' who had maintained their faith over many decades in the face of severe trials and tribulations: the 'last words and departure' of this 'ancient and honourable' lady from St Austell who had endured several stints in gaol for her refusal to pay tithes, together with 'farther Testimonies concerning her life and conversation', were recorded by Friends who had gathered around her deathbed and printed for the edification of others scattered across the realm.[88]

This paper has merely set down a series of signposts and opened up various avenues of enquiry that require further investigation. Its conclusions are accordingly cautious and provisional. It is necessary to reiterate the difficulties of accessing the experience of those at either end of the age spectrum and to underline the extent to which our knowledge of it is refracted through the prisms of literary convention and biblical dictum and distorted by the vagaries of selective memory and sentimental retrospection. The old and young people we have encountered are merely representations, projections of the ideals, hopes and anxieties of those who described them and end-products of carefully studied acts of religious self-fashioning. At one level, they are no more than optical illusions. Nevertheless, the ways in which ancient *topoi* about youth and age were invoked and manipulated during the long Reformation has disclosed much about how this movement was perceived by outsiders and understood by its adherents. The recycling of negative and positive

---

[87] Norman Penney, ed., *The Journal of George Fox* (2 vols., New York, 1973 edn), I, xvi, xxxix. For the transformation of Quakerism in its second generation, see Barry Reay, *The Quakers and the English Revolution* (1985), ch. 6; Rosemary Moore, *The Light in their Consciences: The Early Quakers in Britain 1646–1666* (University Park, PA, 2000), ch. 17.

[88] *A Relation of the Last Words and Departure of that Antient and Honourable Woman Loveday Hambly of Trigangeeves, in the Parish of Austell in the County of Cornwal* ([1683]).

images of these age groups, of the inherited polarities of innocence and wisdom, irresponsibility and senility, illuminates both its initial impact and its later ramifications. It shows that contemporaries expected religious revolution to be accompanied by an overturning of parental authority and by episodes of youthful rebellion. And it demonstrates that the steady entrenchment of Protestantism coincided with a reassertion of the patriarchal hierarchy and a renewed emphasis on deference to those advanced in physical years and spiritual understanding that may qualify suggestions about the progressive marginalisation of the elderly in early modern society.[89] As we have seen, these processes were fraught with fruitful paradox and further complicated by the ingrained instincts of a culture that honoured antiquity and distrusted the new. Claims that evangelicalism, post-Reformation Catholicism and Quakerism engendered generational conflict may be exaggerated, but we need to ask ourselves why our sources choose to frame events in these terms and what this might mean. While few contemporaries lived as long as Thomas Parr and witnessed as many phases of revolution, reversal and renewal as he, the evidence assembled in this exploratory essay suggests that the life-cycle is likely to prove a versatile and valuable tool for investigating religious change in sixteenth- and seventeenth-century England.

---

[89] Cf. Thomas, 'Age and Authority', 248 and *passim*.

Transactions of the RHS 21 (2011), pp. 123–45 © Royal Historical Society 2011
doi:10.1017/S0080440111000065

MARKETS AND CULTURES: MEDICAL SPECIFICS AND THE RECONFIGURATION OF THE BODY IN EARLY MODERN EUROPE

By Harold J. Cook*

READ 14 APRIL 2010 AT GLASGOW CALEDONIAN UNIVERSITY

ABSTRACT. The history of the body is of course contested territory. Postmodern interpretations in particular have moved it from a history of scientific knowledge of its structure and function toward histories of the various meanings, identities and experiences constructed about it. Underlying such interpretations have been large and important claims about the unfortunate consequences of the rise of a political economy associated with capitalism and medicalisation. In contradistinction, this paper offers a view of that historical process in a manner in keeping with materialism rather than in opposition to it. To do so, it examines a general change in body perceptions common to most of the literature: a shift from the body as a highly individualistic and variable subject to a more universal object, so that alterations in one person's body could be understood to represent how alterations in other human bodies occurred. It then suggests that one of the chief causes of that change was the growing vigour of the market for remedies that could be given to anyone, without discrimination according to temperament, gender, ethnicity, social status or other variables in the belief that they would cure quietly and effectively. One of the most visible remedies of this kind was a 'specific', the Peruvian, or Jesuits' bark. While views about specific drugs were contested, the development of a market for medicinals that worked universally helped to promote the view that human bodies are physiologically alike.

The views presented here are meant to be speculative, in order to address some well-known changes in views of the body in early modern Europe so as to remind us of materialist possibilities within what have tended to become histories of 'culture'. The examples are taken from the history of medicine simply because that is a field I happen to know best, but the kinds of historical problems addressed through such examples will, I hope, speak to some elements of the general crisis historians currently face in making meaningful statements about the past. Perhaps more than in recent decades, the looming political, economic and ecological

* I would like to thank John Stewart and Colin Jones for inviting me to speak at the conference on 'Science and the Human Subject in History' at Glasgow Caledonian, and to the members of the audience for their thoughtful comments, and the same to the members of the Harvard Working Group on the History of Medicine, with whom I also discussed a version of the paper.

catastrophes of the moment are entangled in systems of production, exchange and coercion which exhibit the hard edges that sometimes seem to generate fear more than hope. At such moments, the double-meaning of 'culture' as a manifestation both of self-expression and collective behaviour seems to place it in the category of secondary effects, or to use an older terminology, of 'superstructure' built upon other foundations, the relationships of which call for analysis. The methods of historians, like others, have undoubtedly benefited enormously from the ethnographic turn, which has reminded us of the power of the forces that bind, even as our discipline has never lost sight of the materially real any more than anthropology, or art history, or other subjects that investigate the human. And yet, this seems an appropriate moment to advocate again the probing for connections between forms of culture and ways of living that are characterised as economic, so as to observe the effects of metal on flesh. The object of the inquiry is not to reject what we have learned about the power of culture, but to link it to other processes as well. The history of the body as viewed through transformations in medicine is an excellent vantage-point for such musings.

The account below therefore takes a situational approach to what has been considered by some to be a fundamental change in bodily perceptions: that is, it frames the changes in terms of a multitude of criss-crossing long-term trends and collective outlooks rather than in terms of causal chains. At the same time, many of the persons and events have an almost accidental relationship to one another, coming and going to form a narrative that is something more like a picaresque than a romance. Such accounts might well be knit together by referring to the culture in which they occurred. But other pressures had to do with commerce, for some kinds of articulations about the body were pressed on the public because they simplified treatments that used medicines that would have similar effects on anyone. In other words, moving from considerations of the body individual to the body universal had advantages in the medical marketplace.[1]

It is well known that over the past two or three decades, the history of the body has become a subject of much interest to historians of many kinds. Many of the descriptive and explanatory frameworks deployed in this literature have been guided by the kind of cultural studies which emerged from the debates of the late 1960s about how systems of power dominated their subjects without the need to resort to physical coercion, in which the views of Michel Foucault were formative. For instance, Barbara Duden's *Geschichte unter der Haut* (1987), translated into English in 1991 as *The Woman beneath the Skin*, was inspired by contemporary discourses about

---

[1] For a discussion of the analytical uses of the term, see Mark S. R. Jenner and Patrick Wallis, 'The Medical Marketplace', in *Medicine and the Market in England and its Colonies, c. 1450 – c. 1850*, ed. Mark S. R. Jenner and Patrick Wallis (Basingstoke, 2007).

how general assumptions and even personal expectations were rooted in ways of life. While other historians of the time might have referred to Gramsci's 'hegemony', or employed Michel Foucault's *episteme* or the Annalists' *mentalité* even more than she does, Duden also took much from both contemporary feminism and the circle around Ivan Illich (who was associated with Latin American liberation theology and found modern institutions such as state schooling and medicine to be disciplinary perversions of the authentic human spirit). But Duden also recruited support from sources such as the doctoral dissertation of Rudolph zur Lippe, which examined relationships between the geometrisation of space and body disciplines such as military drills, fencing and dancing.[2] A student of Theodor Adorno's, it is not surprising that Zur Lippe himself intended to explore some of the ways in which the beginnings of capitalism changed the senses and experiences of Europeans.[3] From other perspectives, Roy Porter's reposts to Foucault also emphasised a social history giving special attention to the ordinary person's or patient's voice with the market very clearly involved.[4] In other words, there is much in early work on the history of the body to suggest that its practitioners were concerned with intellectual cultures because they indicated the powerful effects of materialism. It was a process that, in one form, was called 'medicalisation'.

But as the New Left fractured due to violent militancy and state policing, to say nothing of the revelations of the Soviet Gulag and Chinese Cultural Revolution, and in light of the shifting focus of attention to the problems of gender, race and class, as well as human rights, much analysis moved toward seeking the roots of culture and power in more ideological and even philosophical terms. This is, of course, how Foucault came to be read, but other instances abound, such as Thomas Laqueur's deservedly influential *Making Sex* (1990). As his subtitle indicated, it explored 'body and gender from the Greeks to Freud'. The new enterprise represented by such a work attracted much attention for questioning the analytical categories that had been assumed to derive from nature itself, showing that they were, rather, located in 'cultural' space and time rather than being fixed.[5] Comparative studies such as Shigehisa Kuriyama's *The*

---

[2] Barbara Duden, *The Woman beneath the Skin: A Doctor's Patients in Eighteenth-Century Germany*, trans. Thomas Dunlap (Cambridge, MA, 1991), 44.

[3] Rudolf Zur Lippe, *Naturbeherrschung Am Menschen* (2 vols., Frankfurt am Main, 1981). For Anglo-American versions of the theme see, for example, Robert M. Young, *Mind, Brain and Adaptation in the Nineteenth Century: Cerebral Localization and Its Biological Context from Gall to Ferrier* (Oxford, 1990); Karl Figlio, 'Chlorosis and Chronic Disease in Nineteenth-Century Britain: The Social Construction of Somatic Illness in a Capitalistic Society', *Social History*, 3 (1978), 167–97.

[4] For example, Roy Porter, *Mind-Forg'd Manacles: A History of Madness in England from the Restoration to the Regency* (Cambridge, MA, 1987).

[5] Thomas Laqueur, *Making Sex: Body and Gender from the Greeks to Freud* (Cambridge, MA, 1990).

Expressiveness of the Body and the Divergence of Greek and Chinese Medicine (1999) located differences of medical concepts in varying experiences of the body related to incommensurable cultural environments.[6] Studies such as this were widely interpreted to support studies in the social or cultural construction of science,[7] which were in turn associated with versions of postmodernism. They turned studies of the growth of objectivity into the making of subjectivities.

While suspicion about biology as the only thing that counts was liberating, doubts about scientific answers to historical questions have also had an additional consequence: some have felt free to overlook the material constraints on bodily life – including those that come through in examples of people trying out new drugs to see if they worked. Many of the ideological arguments of the so-called science wars of the late 1980s and early 1990s arose from objections to postmodern views that subsumed the body and other aspects of nature within the cultural or social, seeming to make a mockery of what was known to be real and fundamental.[8] As one of the proponents of postmodernist analysis, Fredric Jameson, put it,

> In modernism, ... some residual zones of 'nature' or 'being', of the old, the older, the archaic, still subsist; culture can still do something to that nature and work at transforming that 'referent.' Postmodernism is what you have when the modernization process is complete and nature is gone for good. It is a more fully human world than the older one, but one in which 'culture' has become a veritable 'second nature.' Indeed, what happened to culture may well be one of the more important clues for tracking the postmodern: an immense dilation of its sphere (the sphere of commodities), an immense and historically original acculturation of the Real, a quantum leap in what Benjamin still called the 'aestheticization' of reality.[9]

For our purposes here, we can simply note that while Jameson saw postmodernism itself as the 'cultural logic' of late capitalism his point was that it had become possible to think about the world without regard to its material foundations.

There has been a strong push back, not only from scientists concerned about how cultural studies seems to demean their work by relativising all

---

[6] Shigehisa Kuriyama, *The Expressiveness of the Body and the Divergence of Greek and Chinese Medicine* (New York, 1999). Also see the exchange between Sandra Harding, 'Is Science Multicultural? Challenges, Resources, Opportunities, Uncertainties', *Configurations*, 2 (1994), 301–30, and Shigehisa Kuriyama, 'On Knowledge and the Diversity of Cultures: Comment on Harding', *Configurations*, 2 (1994), 337–42.

[7] For instance, note that in the first (1979) edition of Bruno Latour and Steve Woolgar, *Laboratory Life: The Construction of Scientific Facts* (Princeton, 1986) the subtitle read 'the social construction of scientific facts'.

[8] For example, Paul R. Gross and Norman Levitt, *Higher Superstition: The Academic Left and its Quarrels with Science* (Baltimore, 1994), and the discussions about the 'war' in Jay A. Labinger and H. M. Collins, eds., *The One Culture?: A Conversation About Science* (Chicago, 2001).

[9] Fredric Jameson, *Postmodernism: Or, the Cultural Logic of Late Capitalism* (Durham, NC, 1991), ix.

forms of knowledge, but from proponents of cultural studies of science who remained attentive to its materialist foundations. For instance, in the brilliant and mainly constructionist interpretation of colonial bodies offered by Megan Vaughan, she 'kept intact' some aspects of the history of diseases and bodies as 'material reality' despite feeling that by doing so she was committing what constructivists would consider a 'cardinal sin'.[10] More recently, Bruno Latour wondered who his allies had become, finding especially troubling the example of powerful US neo-cons adopting arguments about science as a mere cultural construction in their attack on the 'theory' of global warming.[11] Similarly, objections have come from some of the historians concerned about how 'culture' has dulled the edge of critiques of transnational capitalism. For instance, one group has not only attacked the development policies of the United Nations and World Bank, but implicated the cultural studies movement in their growing power: 'Despite the evidence that culture is subordinate to economic interests and phenomena, scholars in cultural studies continue to avoid confrontation of material realities out of an anxiety about "metanarratives" or "foundational" principles.' In other words, postcolonialism and postmodernism

> encourage preoccupation with identity and subjectivity, but only by displacing into the realm of culture the kind of self-knowledge that comes with the confrontation of historically circumscribed material realities. The end result is not so much self-knowledge as the denial of the possibility of knowledge of any kind and the re-reification of identities that produces a liberal relativism, and on the other hand, murderous separation of human beings.

In shying away from questions of material interest, then, 'structural power' goes unexamined, hence 'disguising, if not celebrating, contemporary forms of power'.[12]

For the moment, it is not necessary to engage further in contemporary polemics, only to remind ourselves of the following point: while the history of the body is – of course – strongly contested ground, among its original purposes were the exploration of questions about the cultural effects of economic formations. Such problems are worth another look.

The main shift in attitudes toward the body to be investigated here is well known: a shift from a discourse about how each person was unique to one in which all people were more or less interchangeable. Neither

---

[10] Megan Vaughan, *Curing their Ills: Colonial Power and African Illness* (Stanford, 1991), 7; her 'introduction' (1–28) remains a brilliant negotiation with the current literature.

[11] Bruno Latour, "Why Has Critique Run out of Steam? From Matters of Fact to Matters of Concern', *Critical Inquiry*, 30 (2004), 225–48.

[12] Arif Dirlik *et al.*, eds., *History after the Three Worlds: Post-Eurocentric Historiographies* (Lanham, MD, 2000), 5, 8, 10. For an example of a recent work that does not shirk the questions of power and domination, see Pratik Chakrabarti, *Materials and Medicine: Trade, Conquest and Therapeutics in the Eighteenth Century* (Manchester, 2010).

alternative was uncontested, since in some instances classical medicine allowed for the same thing to affect many different kinds of bodies (as in epidemics, for instance), while even the most modern clinicians are alert to individual characteristics when they are dealing with particular patients. But it is generally agreed that at earlier periods the dominant expectation was that the health and illness of each person emerged from their humours, age, sex, habits of life, environment, personal interactions and passions, probably together with their horoscopic signs, whereas in a more modern period health and illness have to do with the things all people share in common, such as certain kinds of bodily tissues, or certain kinds of caloric or nutritional inputs, or exposures to biological or chemical threats, and so on. The historical debate about the timing and causes of the change is broad and deep, running from how William Harvey's discovery of the circulation of the blood undermined classical physiology, to the rise of 'mechanical' physiology, to the Paris School and Xavier Bichat's pathology of tissues, to the rise of statistics, to cell theory and germ theory, to laboratory and hospital medicine, and so on – and that list simply includes a history of ideas, when state interventions for the control of human and animal diseases and many, many other kinds of causes could be invoked. Not surprisingly, the indefinable nature of the change is matched by the indefinable nature of the cause. But in a wide range of historical work, from Marxist-inspired historical sociology to professionally orientated accounts of the development of scientific medicine, there is wide agreement that a shift from seeing any person as naturally unique to naturally common is one of the marks of modernity.[13]

Exploring the rise of the modern body is obviously a problem too large to tackle in a short article. But one way of narrowing the problem is to consider the causes of the recognised change from a physiological to an ontological view of disease. That is, on the one hand, disease may be considered to arise from the individualised physiology of someone when responding to their unique circumstances, or, on the other hand, to occur because of the encounter with, or introduction of, or 'invasion' or 'attack' of, a substance that disrupts the normal activities of the body,

[13] To note only a few examples of this sense of historical process that can be found almost everywhere in the literature of the past few decades: Erwin H. Ackerknecht, *Medicine at the Paris Hospital 1794–1848* (Baltimore, 1967); William Coleman, 'Health and Hygiene in the Encyclopedie: A Medical Doctrine for the Bourgeoisie', *Journal of the History of Medicine*, 29 (1974), 399–421; N. D. Jewson, 'The Disappearance of the Sick-Man from Medical Cosmology 1770–1870', *Sociology*, 10 (1976), 225–44; Caroline Hannaway, 'From Private Hygiene to Public Health: A Transformation in Western Medicine in the Eighteenth and Nineteenth Centuries', in *Public Health*, ed. Teizo Ogawa (Tokyo, 1980); and David Weatherall, *Science and the Quiet Art: Medical Research and Patient Care* (Oxford, 1995). Foucault is among those who place this modernity in the rise of the 'Paris school' of the early nineteenth century: Michel Foucault, *The Birth of the Clinic: An Archaeology of Medical Perception*, trans. A. M. Sheridan Smith (New York, 1973).

this later entity being the identifiable cause.[14] Duden's *Woman beneath the Skin*, with its emphasis on the experience of mysterious metamorphoses in female bodies in the eighteenth century, with protean afflictions that transform themselves from one manifestation to another, is a fine example of the articulation of the first, while Christoph Gradmann's *Laboratory Disease*, tracing out the ramifications of Robert Koch's encounter with bacteriology, is a distinguished example of the second.[15] I do not propose to define further either view, nor to offer an account of change that reduces past discourses and debates about the body and disease to a single cause. (In many histories of medicine, for instance, the iatrochemists of early modern Europe, especially those who followed Van Helmont, are often identified as the main proponents of the ontological view.[16]) But an example of what was at stake is the famous claim made in 1676 by the well-known English physician, Thomas Sydenham, that diseases could be described in ontologically clear and distinct fashion according to their symptoms just as species of plants, such as an African violet, could be known by their attributes. Each might have individualistic variables but was clearly enough of the same kind.[17] Such orientations were supported in coming decades by Herman Boerhaave's call for careful distinctions between diseases, and the new subject of classifying diseases – nosology – exemplified by Linnaeus's *Genera morborum* (1763) and François Boissier de Sauvages de Lacroix's *Nosologia methodica* of the same year, with its classes of disease divided into orders, and genera, down to 2,400 species.[18]

But this view of diseases was promoted by the medical marketplace, in which remedies were offered that would counteract diseases in anyone whomsoever. I do not wish to reduce newer ideas about disease to economic processes, but to argue that among the significant causes of change was commodification, a process that helped to give rise to a certain form of objectivity – one based on the careful description and

[14] For thoughtful commentary on the almost timeless paring of these two modes of thought, see Owsei Temkin, 'The Scientific Approach to Disease: Specific Entity and Individual Sickness', in *Scientific Change*, ed. A. C. Crombie (New York, 1963); Peter H. Niebyl, 'Sennert, Van Helmont, and Medical Ontology', *Bulletin of the History of Medicine*, 45 (1971), 115–37.

[15] Duden, *Woman beneath the Skin*; Christoph Gradmann, *Laboratory Disease: Robert Koch's Medical Bacteriology*, trans. Elborg Forster (Baltimore, 2009). Megan Vaughan often uses the term 'unitised' when referring to the biomedical view of the body: *Curing their Ills*.

[16] For example, Walter Pagel, 'Prognosis and Diagnosis: A Comparison of Ancient and Modern Medicine', *Journal of the Warburg Institute*, 2 (1938), 382–98; Walter Pagel, *Paracelsus: An Introduction to Philosophical Medicine in the Era of the Renaissance* (New York, 1958); Andrew Wear, *Knowledge and Practice in Early Modern English Medicine, 1550–1680* (New York, 2000).

[17] Sydenham makes the point in the *Observationes medicae* (1676) which has been translated several times. For an careful and appreciative commentary, Lester S. King, *Medical Thinking: A Historical Preface* (Princeton, 1982), 110–17.

[18] Lester S. King, *The Medical World of the Eighteenth Century* (Chicago, 1958), 193–226.

analysis of objects. The medical literature of the early modern period is full of examples of medicines being tried out on human subjects to determine their universal efficacy, and this had implications for how contemporaries objectified the body. In other words, the causes for the increasing preference for the ontological experience of disease was not due to shifting medical ideas or 'European culture' alone, but was given a strong push from the development of a consumer market for medicines that would have similar effects on anyone who used them. Taking a look at how medicines were used is both an instance of the interconnections of ideas and practices, mind and body, and a reminder of the power of commerce.

We can begin such reflections about the interconnections between bodies, diseases and remedies with an illuminating special case: the acceptance in early modern Europe of medical 'specifics'. It is only when diseases were well-defined entities rather than protean expressions of the state of the body at any moment that there might be hope for their elimination by the powers of specific remedies. As Sydenham put it, a specific could counteract a particular disease not by acting on a particular organ or humour but in general, and without 'visible evacuation' such as purging or sweating – or as his acquaintance Robert Boyle put it, specifics 'are neither obvious to the sense, nor evacuate any gross, or at least sensible matter'.[19] To modern eyes, accustomed to taking tablets and pills intended to maintain or restore health insensibly, the use of specifics may seem like common sense; but to early modern ones, since most medicines 'worked' by producing dramatic physiological effects, and since they were usually supported by altered diet and regimen, while staying their 'course' might take many days, the subject could have no doubt about having been dosed.

One might say, then, that one ideal of 'modern' medicine is that its treatments be comfortable, targeted and available. And that they be good for any potential purchaser. Indeed, the medical advertisements of the period are rife with promises that pills could be had for a certain price that would infallibly cure this or that disease in anyone, and, as one of them put it, 'may be taken in the hottest or coldest Weather, and hinder no business'. Or as another had it: 'Speedy and Absolute Cure for the French Pox without Fluxing, or Confinement.'[20] Such remedies also helped to support a more private bodily space, since medicines could be used without anyone

---

[19] G. G. Meynell, *Materials for a Biography of Dr. Thomas Sydenham* (Folkestone, 1988), 52–3, quoting Sydenham, 1848, Thomas Sydenham, *The Works of Thomas Sydenham, M.D.*, translated from the Latin edn of Dr Greenhill with a life of the author, trans R. G. Latham (2 vols., 1848), I, 210 and Robert Boyle, *The Works . . . in 6 Volumes* (1772), V, 77.

[20] From a bound collection of 231 advertisements, British Library shelfmark 551.a.32, nos. 9 (probably by John Pechey) and 14.

else being the wiser. Although most intended specifics failed to convince established physicians of their intended benefit, hopes abounded. Robert Boyle, for instance, thought that many specifics were already known but needed to be sought out by learned people like himself:

> Nor should we onely expect some improvements to the Therapeutical part of Physick, from the writings of so ingenious a People as the Chineses; but probably the knowledge of Physitians might not be inconsiderably increased, if Men were a little more curious to take notice of the Observations and Experiments, suggested partly by the practice of Midwives, Barbers, Old Women, Empericks, and the rest of that illiterate crue, that presume to meddle with Physick among our selves; ... [For] where the Practitioners of Physick are altogether illiterate, there oftentime Specificks, may be best met with.[21]

He was seconded in 1752 by Pierre-Louis Moreau de Maupertuis, president of the Berlin Akademie der Wissenschaften: 'It is quite by accident and only from savage nations that we owe our knowledge of specifics; we owe not one to the science of physicians.'[22] And indeed, some of the most famous remedies of the period, from cinchona bark to digitalis, and inoculation to vaccination, arose from the kinds of sources Boyle and Maupertuis had in mind.

It is probably therefore no accident that in the same text in which Sydenham wrote of diseases like species, he also wrote favourably about a specific, the Peruvian bark. Also known simply as the bark or cortex, or Jesuit's bark or, later, cinchona bark, it remains the most famous specific of the seventeenth century, no doubt because of its recent use. Knowledge of the bark can be found in Spanish texts of the sixteenth century by Juan Fragoso and Nicolas Monardes,[23] but from the 1650s the bark became renowned for its curative effects against powerful intermittent fevers, then termed 'agues' in English and which we would today often call malaria, a frequent complaint.[24] While shrouded in obscurity, the most likely origin of the medicinal uses of the bark in Europe is that one or more Jesuit missionaries in Loja (modern Ecuador, then part of the viceroyalty of Peru) reported the indigenous uses of the bark to Juan de Vega in Lima, physician to the count of Chinchon, who used it successfully and in turn sent boxes of it to Seville for sale.[25] But the Jesuits themselves sent it on to Rome and began to market it – Jesuit pharmacies helped to underwrite the costs of the Society – and Jesuits were administering the bark in Rome by

---

[21] Robert Boyle, *Usefulnesse of Experimental Naturall Philosophy* (Oxford, 1663), Part II, 220–1.

[22] Quoted in Londa Schiebinger, 'Prospecting for Drugs: European Naturalists in the West Indies', in *Colonial Botany: Science, Commerce, and Politics in the Early Modern World*, ed. Londa Schiebinger and Claudia Swan (Philadelphia, 2004), 119.

[23] Fernando I. Ortiz Crespo, 'Fragoso, Monardes, and Pre-Chinchonian Knowledge of Cinchona', *Archives of Natural History*, 22 (1995), 169–81.

[24] Mary J. Dobson, *Contours of Death and Disease in Early Modern England* (Cambridge, 1997).

[25] Saul Jarcho, *Quinine's Predecessor: Francesco Torti and the Early History of Cinchona* (Baltimore, 1993), 1–11.

the mid-1640s.[26] It made its way into the Spanish Netherlands and in 1652 was used to treat Archduke Leopold, who was relieved of his fever but, when a relapse occurred a month later and he would not take it again, he died. The various controversies and commentaries that followed indicate that by the mid-1650s the bark was becoming well known throughout Europe as a specific.[27]

In his first book, *Methodus curandi febres* (1666), Sydenham had agreed that the bark was a specific in cases of ague, although also expressing caution about its use because of the possibility of dangerous relapses if it were not used carefully; ten years later, in his *Observationes medicae*, he endorsed it heartily while by implication condemning all other touted specifics: 'I am sure of this, that the only specific is the Peruvian bark.'[28] In August 1678, he gave advice to his friend John Locke on how to use it, with particular attention to how to prevent the fits of the agues from returning by further dosing. 'Thus you shall be sure to cure, for I never affirmed anything to you which failed.'[29] Two years later still, his elaborated method for using the bark appeared in a published letter to Dr Robert Brady, in which Sydenham says that its use was his 'sheet anchor'.[30] But he also explains there that when the bark had been introduced to London twenty-five years before (about 1655), it had been held responsible for the death of an alderman and a captain – because, he thought, it had wrongly been administered just before an expected fit instead of afterward and was not administered for long enough after the first missed fit, which caused relapses – but guarding against both of these problems, he found it to yield perfect cures.[31] Other of his associates also came to take a keen interest in the bark, such as Charles Goodall, who was later mocked for his extensive direct sale of the bark in powdered form despite being one of the foremost physicians in attacking medical empirics.[32] Indeed, the bark had such powerful specific properties that by

[26] Sabine Anagnostou, 'Jesuits in Spanish America: Contributions to the Exploration of the American Materia Medica', *Pharmacy in History*, 47 (2005), 3–17; Sabine Anagnostou, 'The International Transfer of Medicinal Drugs by the Society of Jesus (Sixteenth to Eighteenth Centuries) and Connections with the Work of Carolus Clusius', in *Carolus Clusius: Towards a Cultural History of a Renaissance Naturalist*, ed. Florike Egmond *et al.* (Amsterdam, 2007).

[27] Jarcho, *Quinine's Predecessor*, 12–43.

[28] Meynell, *Materials for a Biography of Sydenham*, 52.

[29] Letter of 3 Aug. quoted in Kenneth Dewhurst, *Dr. Thomas Sydenham (1624–1689:, His Life and Original Writings* (Berkeley, 1966), 59; Kenneth Dewhurst, *John Locke (1632–1704): Physician and Philosopher: A Medical Biography* (1963), 59. He also gives further particulars in a letter to Locke of 30 Aug. 1679, Dewhurst, *Sydenham*, 172.

[30] Jarcho, *Quinine's Predecessor*, 52.

[31] First Epistle in *Epistolae responsoriae duae* (1680), English translation reprinted in *Source Book of Medical History*, ed. Logan Clendening (New York, 1960), 202–3.

[32] Harold J. Cook, 'Goodall, Charles', in *Oxford Dictionary of National Biography*, www.oxforddnb.com/view/article/10949, accessed 1 Feb. 2011; two quarto satirical

1692 Richard Morton was proposing that it could be used to differentiate diseases, with those yielding to it being true agues and those that did not being something else.[33]

Another reason why Sydenham may have decided to make his views about the bark better known was its increased availability in the 1670s. Apparently a near monopoly on the supply of the bark via Jesuit sources had recently been broken, making it more affordable and so more popular. A book published in 1682 in Paris and immediately translated into English stated that 'When it was only in the hands of the Jesuits, it was sold at Rome and Paris for Eight or Nine Shillings Sterling the Dose, which consisted only of Two Drachms' (a quarter of an ounce). 'But so soon as Droguists began to Trade in it, it began to fall in Price, so that Three or Four years ago, the best might have been had for about Forty Shillings the Pound weight' (a drop of over sixfold). The market quickly rebounded, however, for 'no sooner had the English Remedy to be in vogue, but men began every where to make Experiments with the Bark of Perus, which much enhanced the value of it'. M. Audry and M. Vilain, the two most famous druggists in Paris, sold out their supplies even 'at the Rate of about Fifteen Pound the pound-weight' (about the same as the original price of the Jesuits). 'Nevertheless some small quantity came at length, but it was held up so dear, that it was like to have gone off at the rate of an Hundred Crowns the pound-weight' (up to a far higher rate than the original), before regular shipments from Spain and Portugal and less demand stabilised the price at '4 or 5 pound the pound-weight' (about a threefold drop from the initial price).[34] Whatever the exact figures may be, the lowered purchase price would indicate a new source of supply beyond channels controlled by the Jesuits causing the bark to be far more widely available from the later 1670s, while at the same time there was pent-up demand awaiting it.

Sydenham may have been pressed into further endorsements of the bark not only because it was becoming popular, but because of the success of Robert Tabor (or Talbor). While in 1677 Sydenham failed to mention the bark after hearing from his friend John Locke that he had been suffering from the ague,[35] a year later he wrote to Locke, still in France, with general advice about how to use the remedy. In doing so, he seems to be asking Locke to remember that he had found its benefits first: 'Understanding how much Tabor, now knighted here,

[33] Dobson, *Contours of Death and Disease*, 316, referring to Morton's *Pyretologia*.

[34] *The English Remedy: Or, Talbor's Wonderful Secret, for Cureing of Agues and Feavers*, (1682), 7–10.

[35] E. S. De Beer, ed. *The Correspondence of John Locke* (8 vols., Oxford, 1976), I, 488–9, letter no. 337, 4 June 1677.

hath been admired for his skill in curing agues, I thought fitt to let you know' how to use the bark, 'if you have not allready observed it in my book, page 99.'[36] He obviously expressed jealousy and possibly suggested plagiarism in further commenting that 'I never gott 10£ by it, he hath gott 5000. He was an Apothecary in Cambridge wher my booke and practices never much obtenyed.'[37] However Tabor had learned of the bark – and having apprenticed with an apothecary it certainly need not have been from Sydenham's book – he had perfected his method in the ague-infested Essex marshes, which brought him to the attention of the English king, gaining him an appointment as a royal physician; a book explaining his method (without revealing the details) quickly followed.[38] The knighthood that provoked Sydenham's letter to Locke came on 27 July 1678. A year later, Charles II sent Tabor on a tour of the courts of Europe, apparently because of the rising interest in the bark. In Paris, he attempted to corner the market by buying up 'all the Quinquina, that he could find at Paris, and the other chief Towns in France, and of England also', but other practitioners began to obtain supplies via Rouen and Bordeaux, undermining his plans.[39] He had more notable successes in curing the dauphine of France and the queen of Spain, Louisa Maria, of their fevers, while during Tabor's absence Charles himself had a fit of the ague at Windsor and recovered after being given the bark at the urging of Dr Thomas Short (one of Sydenham's acquaintances). In return for curing such people and revealing his secret, Louis XIV awarded Tabor the huge sum of 48,000 livres plus a pension of 2,000, along with the title of chevalier. He died a very wealthy man in 1681.[40]

Not everyone agreed that the bark was a specific, however. The response of the notoriously conservative physicians of France shows that

---

[36] Referring to the *Observationes medicae* (1676). In later letters, Sydenham expresses some slight irritation at Locke for not following his directions exactly, which was the reason that 'your exhibiting the Cortex hath not met with the same success as here': *Correspondence of John Locke*, II, 80–1, letter no. 496, 30 Aug. 1679; also II, 94–5, letter no. 500, 6 Sept. 1679.

[37] *Correspondence of John Locke*, I, 601–2, letter no. 398, 3 Aug. 1678; and Dewhurst, *Sydenham*, 171.

[38] *Pyretologia: A Rational Account of the Cause and Cure of Agues; with their Signs Diagnostick and Prognostick: Also Some Specifick Medicines Prescribed for the Cure of all Sorts of Agues. Also a Short Account of the Cause and Cure of Fevers, and the Griping in the Guts* (1672). I suspect that although the title page bears the date 1672, it was not published until late in that year, since it is listed in Robert Clavel, *The General Catalogue of Books. To. 1674* (1675) (as a small octavo priced at 1s, but not in Robert Clavel, *A Catalogue of All the Books. To. 1672* (1673). On 3 May 1678, the London College of Physicians discussed a letter from the lord chamberlain, Arlington, informing that Tabor had been made a royal physician because he cured the ague so well, and that they should not trouble him: Royal College of Physicians Annals, 128b.

[39] *The English Remedy*, 7–8.

[40] Mary Dobson, 'Sir Robert Tabor' in *Oxford Dictionary of National Biography*, www.oxforddnb.com/view/article/26910, accessed 1 Feb. 2011; Laurence Brockliss and Colin Jones, *The Medical World of Early Modern France* (Oxford, 1997), 292, 623.

clearly. Although the French king had ordered the publication of Tabor's practice, the book describing it actually reestablishes the authority of the king's senior physician by treating the specific as an ordinary simple (i.e. a single herb used medicinally). Published in French and immediately translated as *The English Remedy: Or, Talbor's Wonderful Secret, for Cureing of Agues and Feavers* (1682), the long version of the French title page hints at the alteration: *With the Observations of Monsieur the Premier Physician to his Majesty on the Composition, Vertues, and Uses of this Remedy.*[41] Authored by an entrepreneurial surgeon, Nicolas Blégny, the work not only presented Tabor's secret but added Blégny's own comments together with those of the premier physician Antoine d'Aquin (one of his patrons).[42] Its contents treat the bark not as a specific but as an ordinary herb, beginning with a thorough discussion of its nature and a list of all the problems it was good for. For example, the bark 'often' extinguishes the heat of hectic fevers and 'all other internal Inflamations' and generally acts 'against all extraordinary and preternatural Fermentations; in a very short time it rectifies the depraved motion and the altered consistency of the mass of Blood, and it many times occasions . . . salutary evacuations'.[43] Elsewhere, Blégny lists its usefulness in many conditions: 'The most wonderful effects of this Febrifuge appears in all intermittent Feavers, which are its true object; for it stops, and in fine wholly Cures Quotidian Agues, Tertian, double Tertian, Quartans, double and tripple Quartans, and sometimes also other kinds of Feavers.'[44] He also believes that a causal explanation is important, criticising Thomas Willis for saying that because the bark's action was not open to experiment 'all that is to be done is to endeavour to understand and well observe the phœnomina that depends thereon, without troubling ones self with the efficient principles thereof'. Others, who did offer an account of how the bark worked, such as Nicolas Lemery's *Cours de chimie* (1675), had not got the explanation quite right.[45] D'Aquin, however, had no trouble in offering a Galenic explanation: since fevers were caused by 'depraved Chylification', and the bark is 'very Stomachical', its action lay in how it helped digestion.[46]

As for recommendation on the bark's use, Blégny and d'Aquin also altered Tabor's practice considerably, reincorporating it within a

---

[41] *The English Remedy; Le remède anglais pour la guérison des fièvres: publié par ordre du roy. Avec des observations de monsieur le premier médecin de sa majesté sur la composition, les vertus, et l'usage de ce remède* (Paris, 1682).

[42] On Blégny and d'Aquin – who apparently learned Tabor's secret as early as October 1679, shortly after the latter arrived at the French court – see Brockliss and Jones, *Medical World*, 301, 320, 625.

[43] *The English Remedy*, 18–19.

[44] *Ibid.*, 51.

[45] *Ibid.*, 20–6.

[46] *Ibid.*, 55–6.

Galenic system of individualisation, complexity and continual alteration depending upon the state of the patient's constitution. While Tabor had argued for simplicity of practice, the authors commented that the dose should be altered in consideration of the age of the patient, whether they have 'a hot constitution', and whether they are 'much accustomed to Wine'.[47] Thus, while the book continues to use the word 'specifick' for the bark, d'Aquin especially continually altered its use to accord with the individualist methods of treatment, regimen and diet that many learned physicians continued to defend. Indeed, he even complements Tabor on coming up with a more complex method of administering the remedy than the Jesuits had recommended (simply adding the powdered bark to wine). At the same time, however, he believed that Tabor had 'disguised' the bark, as other empirics did their drugs. Because he followed his rules 'indifferently for both Sexes', Tabor even had a misfortune in administering it to the dauphin, 'whose Feaver proceeding from Vomiting and the weakness of his Stomach, was encreased considerably by the use of the Febrifuge'. D'Aquin also believed that Tabor erred in giving the bark 'indifferently in all times of the Feaver', and even killed people when he administered it to those suffering from continual fevers. Instead, it is necessary to use it together with 'Diet, Blood Letting, and especially Purging'.[48] D'Aquin not only gave recommendations for using it Galenically, but went on to advocate his own compound remedy as superior, mixing the bark with opium.[49] 'Hence one may judge how dangerous it is to trust the life and health of men, to the conduct of such kind of People' as Tabor, 'whose knowledge is always too much limited, to reach beyond the general Rules and Directions contained in their Receipts, and to descend into the exceptions that are indicated by sound judgment, experience, and the Principles of a judicious Doctrine'.[50] In short, the *English Remedy* is not really about the bark as a specific but about D'Aquin's adaptation of it to the world of simples so as to bring it back within the older method of individualised dietetic medicine.

The division between physicians who continued to give great weight to dietetic medicine and those who gave more emphasis to universalised therapeutics created one of the most fundamental medical controversies of the period.[51] Of course, many did their best to straddle the fence by incorporating the best of both worlds,[52] while even a supporter of

[47] *Ibid.*, 29–46.
[48] *Ibid.*, 51, 60–1, 65, 68, 69.
[49] *Ibid.*, 74–90.
[50] *Ibid.*, 65–6.
[51] Harold J. Cook, *The Decline of the Old Medical Regime in Stuart London* (Ithaca, NY, 1986).
[52] One example of a multitude: Everard Maynwaring, *Tutela Sanitatis. Sive Vita Protracta. The Protection of Long Life, and Detection of its Brevity, from Diatetic Causes and Common Customs* (1663).

Sydenham might decide that the bark was not a specific but rather 'the greatest Catholicon, or Panacea extant'.[53] But ranged against the people like D'Aquin were those like Robert Boyle, who despite his caution commented that 'it were to be wished, that there were fewer learned Men that think a Physitian hath done enough when he hath learnedly discoursed of the seat and nature of the Disease, foretold the event of it, and methodically imployed a company of safe, but languid remedies' and dietetic advice, and more who were able to find and use 'powerful Medicines'. The pursuit of new remedies would make treatment not only more effective but easy and painless.[54] The bark fitted such ambitions perfectly.

While it would certainly be possible to explore further the debate about whether the bark was a true specific or not, or the full implications of the argument between individualist dietetics and universal therapies, there is for the moment one additional wrinkle to note: it was becoming common to decide on the merits of a therapy by trying it out on anyone. In such cases, almost any body would do. General conclusions were drawn, *pace* Blégny and D'Aquin, without concern to the temperament, status or conditions of the person(s) used for the experiment. A good example is how the emperor of China was convinced of the efficacy of the bark. Jean de Fontenay, who led a famous group of French Jesuits to China in the late seventeenth century, set down an account of what happened in a letter to father François de la Chaise, father confessor to Louis XIV, which was published in 1707. When Fontenay was called to the Chinese court at the end of 1692, he found the Kangxi emperor to be ill with a malignant fever. The Kangxi emperor is well known for having had a longstanding interest in European science, and he clearly had an interest in European medicine as well. He had already taken some of the lozenges that Louis distributed as a remedy to the poor in France, and felt better, but he continued to have fits of the ague. He therefore sent out a proclamation seeking to be informed of all cures for his condition and announcing that those suffering from ague could come to the palace to seek a remedy. Such patients were then subjected to trials of remedies, some of which were even made under the supervision of members of the emperor's family. In Fontenay's case, he and a fellow Jesuit, Claude de Visdelou, brought along a pound of the Peruvian bark that they had obtained from their brethren in India on the way to China, which they prepared according to their special methods. Three ordinary people who had suffered from ague were given it the next day, one of whom no longer had the fits, another who was given it in the midst of a fit and the third who was still suffering

---

[53] Walter Harris, *Pharmacologia Anti-Empirica: Or, a Rational Discourse* (1683), 165; the chapter on the bark is XII, 165–92, with praises of Sydenham's account at 188.

[54] Boyle, *Usefulnesse*, 118–19, and Part II generally, esp. Essay 5 on therapeutics, 117–304.

from periodic fits but was not experiencing one at the time he was given the remedy. After a period of observation at the palace, all three were pronounced cured. The four noblemen of the court who had supervised the trial then tried the bark on themselves to make sure that it had no ill effects on the healthy, and they afterward felt perfectly well and slept soundly. After these trials, the emperor himself took the bark and quickly recovered his health. In gratitude, the Jesuits were given many important privileges, including an edict of toleration and a residence inside the walls of the imperial palace.[55]

Such trials were clearly meant to be a form of public demonstration rather than professional discourse. That is, they were subject to consensus about the outcome based on what all the witnesses could know through their experience of the events rather than anything to do with private perception or learned categories. New drugs were tried out experientially because early modern people, at least, thought this was a good way to determine the effects of drugs. For them, common bodies spoke the truth. The phenomenon can be seen in many instances.

Although the precedents for experimenting on patients are very old indeed, the practice was certainly alive in the sixteenth century. For instance, Antonio Barrera-Osorio has carefully described how in the first decade of that century, a Spanish medical practitioner on the Caribbean island of Santo Domingo asserted he had found a local balsam that was the equal of, or even better than, the wonderful balsam known to classical medicine, and the Spanish crown itself became deeply involved in experimental trials to assess his claims.[56] Another example from the same island is better known in the secondary sources: guaiacum wood, which was brought to Europe soon after Columbus founded Santo Domingo in the mid-1490s. It, too, was a remedy used by the indigenous people of the island to treat a common disease, and was adopted by the Spaniards following their example. According to legend, the local people of Hispanola who suffered from the chancres and other signs of what the Europeans would soon call syphilis were cured by water sprinkled from the branches of the guaiacum tree; Europeans came to associate the

[55] *Lettres edifiantes et curieuses, ecrites des missions etrangeres par quelques missions de la Compagnie de Jesus* (34 vols., Paris, 1703), VII, 222–32. A fuller account and the translated passages are given in Harold J. Cook, 'Testing the Effects of Jesuit's Bark in the Chinese Emperor's Court', *James Lind Library Bulletin* (2010), www.jameslindlibrary.org/illustrating/articles/testing-the-effects-of-jesuit's-bark-in-the-chinese-emperor' and www.jameslindlibrary.org/illustrating/records/letter-to-f-de-la-chaise-from-cheu-chan-a-port-in-the-province/key_passages, accessed 1 Feb. 2011.

[56] Antonio Barrera, 'Local Herbs, Global Medicines: Commerce, Knowledge, and Commodities in Spanish America', in *Merchants and Marvels: Commerce, Science, and Art in Early Modern Europe*, ed. Pamela H. Smith and Paula Findlen (New York and London, 2002); Antonio Barrera-Osorio, *Experiencing Nature: The Spanish American Empire and the Early Scientific Revolution* (Austin, 2006).

practice with the worship of Apollo, but imported the wood, shavings of which were taken in an infusion. In 1519, the noted humanist, Ulrich von Hutten, made it famous in literary circles by publishing a book about his own successful cure by the use of it: *De guiaci medicina et morbo Gallico*.[57]

Another example, that of the drug that replaced guaiac wood in the European pharmacopoeia as a remedy for syphilis – China root – in some ways prefigures the acceptance of Peruvian bark. The root of a deciduous climbing vine (*Smilax*) still widely used in traditional Chinese medicine, according to one mid-seventeenth-century account, 'This Root was first known' to Europeans 'when the Chinese brought the same to be sold in the City of Goa, in India', in 1535, from where the Portuguese shipped it back.[58] The famous anatomist, Andreas Vesalius, wrote something similar three years after the first edition of his more famous *De fabrica*, in his *Letter on the China Root* (published in 1546): 'It is imported by those who import pepper, cloves, ginger, and cinnamon, by Portuguese as well as by imperial seafarers.' When Vesalius first arrived in Venice in 1537, he says, China root was used by many of the great medical professors. But there were two cases with 'unhappy results', which led to it falling into disuse before a physician arrived from Antwerp (Venice's great commercial rival with better access to Portuguese commodities), who said he knew the best method for preparing it, which revived its use. But the bishop of Verona died after starting on a course of China root, although the reason for his death was probably due to other causes, and it fell into disrepute again. Its popularity was then revived again, this time in Brussels, at the imperial court, where it was used in several cases against syphilis, although Vesalius himself thought it less successful against the disease than guaiac wood. Emperor Charles V himself had used the wood to treat his gout and generally poor health, but several Spanish bishops praised the root very highly, and thought the wood to be in disfavour, and (Vesalius implies) because the emperor was able to control his appetite only with difficulty – while the regimen that went with the use of the root was shorter in duration and less restrictive of his diet – they convinced the emperor to try it. Charles's successful use of it secured its fame.[59]

The famous Portuguese physician of Goa, Garcia da Orta, was undoubtedly one of those involved in the trade in China root. The famous book he published on the medicines of the east, published in Goa in 1563, explained that the root was very good against syphilis, but also helped

[57] Sigrid C. Jacobs, 'Guaiacum: History of a Drug; a Critico-Analytical Treatise' (Ph.D. thesis, University of Denver, 1974).

[58] Jan Nieuhof, *An Embassy from the East India Company of the United Provinces to the Grand Tartar Cham Emperor of China*, trans. John Ogilby (1669; facsimile, Menston and Harrogate, 1972), 245.

[59] Charles D. O'Malley, *Andreas Vesalius of Brussels, 1514–1564* (Berkeley and Los Angeles, 1964), 216–17.

'the Itch, Tremblings, Aches, Gout, &c. It is also very good for a weak Stomack, Head-ache, [and] the Stone in the Bladder proceeding from Cold'.[60] A few decades later, at the end of the 1620s, a Dutch physician resident in the East Indies, Jacobus Bontius, gave personal testimony to its effects, praising China root as a wonderful treatment for the paralysis he endured during one of the sieges of Batavia (now Jakarta), as well as in other complaints.[61] By the later sixteenth century, another root, this one native to the New World, sassafras, was already seen as an alternative to China root, being found to be a very profitable commodity by Sir Walter Raleigh himself (following French and Spanish examples), and it became one of the main export products of the North American English settlements before tobacco and sugar overwhelmed its importance.[62] But it remained one of the commodities sought out in East Asia by the Dutch East India Company (VOC).[63] Well into the later seventeenth century it maintained a reputation for being good in cases of syphilis, as well as for having 'sovereign' properties against 'the Itch, Tremblings, Aches, Gout, &c. It is also very good for a weak Stomack, Head-ache, the Stone in the Bladder proceeding from Cold', and would work without regard to diet or regimen.[64]

The list of new remedies introduced to Europe during the early modern period in this way – through empirical trial on oneself or others, usually in imitation of other peoples, and with implications for profit – is long. Many were held to be specifics against one disease or another while having uses in other cases. Just a few more examples to underline the point. In 1648 an Amsterdam physician, William Piso, published a lavishly illustrated book on the medicine and natural history of Brazil, where he had worked as a physician to Johan Maurits of Naussau during the Dutch period and probed into indigenous medicines. The local people used a root, ipecacuanha, as a remedy for the intestinal flux, and he highly recommended it.[65] It became more widely known after a Dutch empiric, Jean Andrien Schweitzer, who Latinised his name to Helvetius, had great success in using it to cure the French dauphin of dysentery in the

---

[60] Garcia da Orta, *Colloquies on the Simples and Drugs of India*, trans. Clements Markham (1913).

[61] Jacobus Bontius, *Tropische geneeskunde / on Tropical Medicine*, in *Opuscula selecta Neerlandicorum de arte medica* (19 vols., Amstelodami, 1907–48), X, 32–3.

[62] David L. Cowen, 'The British North American Colonies as a Source of Drugs', in *Veröffentlichungen der Internationalen Gesellschaft für Geschichte Der Pharmazie*, ed. Georg Edmund Dann (Stuttgart, 1966), 49–50.

[63] Wittop Koning reports that in 1617 the VOC requested 30,000 'ponds' of fresh radix china: D. A. Wittop Koning, *De handel in geneesmiddelen te Amsterdam tot omstreeks 1637* (Purmerend, 1942), 30–1.

[64] Nieuhof, *Embassy*, 245.

[65] In *Opuscula selecta Neerlandicorum de arte medica*, XIV, 4–17.

mid-1680s; it quickly became known as another specific.[66] A decade later, when a Scotsman named William Cockburn obtained the position of physician to the Blue Squadron, he used his 'blue powder' on the sailors to cure cases of diarrhoea, claiming that his powder was even better than the ipecacuanha made famous by Helvetius. He gained the admiral's blessings to experiment on over 100 sailors with another powder in cases of flux, and had such success that the subsequent Admiral of the Blue, Sir Cloudesley Shovell, ordered it to be purchased in large quantities before he sailed for the Mediterranean. What the lords of the admiralty wanted, explicitly, were simple remedies that would be easy to administer and work successfully in all cases of a particular illness no matter the age or constitution of the patient – in other words, specifics. When the London College of Physicians objected that patients needed to be treated according to their constitutions and the circumstances of the moment, they lost their power to oversee the provisioning of the medical chests.[67]

As such examples indicate, then, conducting medical experiments on animals and humans in the interest of gaining universal remedies was not only common, but had the backing of princes and high-ranking military officers. A final example shows the interconnections: John Colbatch achieved medical fame, wealth and eventually a knighthood in the period following the Glorious Revolution in Britain due to his medical innovations. Beginning as an apprentice to an apothecary of Worcester, gradually rising to the rank of master in the Mercer's Company (to which the apothecaries belonged), he moved from Worcester to London sometime in the early 1690s. By the autumn of 1693, Colbatch was beginning to be known for his proprietary 'Vulnerary Powder' and 'Tincture of the Sulphur of Venus': that is, he was advertising a wound powder to stop bleeding and a tincture of copper sulphate to restore wounded flesh. He claimed to have found them empirically through self-study, chemical experiments and trying things out on 'dogs and other animals'. The London surgical establishment, in the person of William Cowper, undertook a public trial of Colbatch's medicines on a dog, which he reported in the *Philosophical Transactions* of February 1694 as a success. But the subsequent trial on two human inmates of St Bartholomew's Hospital failed. Following an unsuccessful further trial on patients at St Bartholomew's, early in 1694 Colbatch obtained a pass from the government to go to the summer campaign in Flanders, where Major General Sir Henry Bellasis arranged for wounded men to be treated

[66] C. J. S. Thompson, *The Mystery and Art of the Apothecary* (1929), 239–40; Brockliss and Jones, *Medical World*, 313; Helvetius's son became one of the most famous *philosophes* of the eighteenth century.

[67] Harold J. Cook, 'Practical Medicine and the British Armed Forces after the "Glorious Revolution"', *Medical History*, 34 (1990), 1–26.

by Colbatch. He later claimed to have performed 100 experiments in the military hospitals, with only five miscarrying, the latter of which he blamed on his opponents. Colbatch kept the confidence of generals, and when he returned to Flanders again in the summer of 1695, he may even have gained the position of local surgeon-general during the siege of Namur. He obtained his knighthood from George I in 1716.[68] Innovating a specific, proving it with trials on animals and human patients, and gaining fame, wealth and status thereby, was common enough in early modern Britain and Europe to be thought a major problem for the medical establishment.

One of the most powerful attacks on the learned medicine of the period was, therefore, a widespread and growing belief that each disease had a kind of ontological definition that made it distinct from other diseases – there would be no metamorphosis of one set of bodily expressions of illness into others – and that for each of these diseases there would be a regular treatment good in all cases, preferably a specific. The most widely accepted specifics were exotic imports to Europe, but the market was replete with new remedies that claimed to work infallibly and easily, since their producers might hope to obtain wealth and status from them. Clearly, demand for specifics was high. Some of the most powerful figures of the time were also keen on them, and were prepared to pay substantial sums to put them into common use.

But one consequence of this hope for effective universal remedies for particular diseases was that it treated all people alike. Specifics necessarily implied universality of effect. If they worked on hospital inmates, or soldiers and sailors, or ordinary people called to the palace, they would work on European admirals and generals, and well-to-do men and women, young and old, kings and emperors. Trying things out on those who had no voice would be of assistance to those who spoke freely. The emperor's body responded to the bark in the same way as those ordinary people on whom it was first tested in Beijing, in the same way as the indigenous people of northern South America who first used it on themselves. In other words, essaying simple trials of the effectiveness of drugs does not make much sense if each person's body will respond differently according to their particular temperament. (As an aside, it is worth noting that this is still a problem, especially in the make-up of experimental groups of subjects where until recently men were much more common than women, and adults than children, although the manifold problems of experimental trials are now usually addressed by statistics, which of course give probabilities rather than certainties, thus

[68] Harold J. Cook, 'Sir John Colbatch and Augustan Medicine: Experimentalism, Character and Entrepreneurialism', *Annals of Science*, 47 (1990), 475–505.

confusing many modern patients who think that scientific medicine is definitive.[69])

If what I am proposing is correct, and the association between specifics and particular diseases was a common part of 'traditional' or 'folk' medicine in many places in the world, then what we are witnessing in the early modern period is not so much the rise of medical specifics or the universalisation or unitisation of the body as a decline in learned medicine due to market forces, which created commonalities among consumers. This movement toward thinking of people in the market as basically alike can be widely noticed. For instance, there were also changes in regimen. Late sixteenth- and early seventeenth-century medical books, even those in the vernacular, began by offering advice to the reader about how to determine one's temperament according to the system of the four qualities – and sometimes the signs of the sun, moon and planets as well – so that one could begin to think about a proper regimen for the maintenance of health or recovery from illness appropriate to the particular person.[70] But alternatives were beginning to appear as well. For instance, one of the works by a Dutch physician on Java, Jacobus Bontius, *On the Preservation of Health: Or Observations on a Sound Way of Life in the Indies in the Form of a Dialogue* is based on the standard theme of the six non-naturals that effect health and disease – the air, food and drink, evacuations and retentions, motion and rest, sleep and waking, and passions of the mind – but gave recommendations for everyone.[71] He explains, for instance, the effects of the two seasons in the region – the rainy and the comparatively dry one – and the four parts of the day: the morning from dawn until about nine, when the air was temperate and breezy, allowing healthful work and exercise; the dangerous forenoon; the slightly less dangerous early afternoon, when it was best to rest; and the healthful period from about four in the afternoon until nightfall. These periods affected everyone alike, men and women, Europeans, South Asians, East Asians and the locally born Javans. And when it came to diseases such as leprosy, it was clear enough that regimen was not sufficient for treatment – a hospital was established to isolate the infected and to attempt treatment by other means. One of Bontius's successors, the physician Willem ten Rhijne – who first introduced acupuncture to a European audience – heard of a local practitioner from the island of Makassar named Sara Jagera who had a reputation for curing the disease, and in 1691, invited him to come

---

[69] For a fine historical guide, see Harry M. Marks, *The Progress of Experiment: Science and Therapeutic Reform in the United States, 1900–1990* (Cambridge, 1997).

[70] A good vernacular example is Thomas Brugis, *The Marrow of Phisicke. Or, a Learned Discourse of the Severall Parts of Mans Body* (1640).

[71] Jacobus Bontius, *De medicina Indorum* (Lugduni Batav, 1642), 59–106.

to the leprosarium in Batavia to undertake trials on the inmates. Only Jagera's death prevented the experiments from coming to completion.[72]

In other words, long before the so-called clinical revolution in Revolutionary Paris, hospital patients and military servicemen were being used as experimental subjects, while ordinary people, even the powerful and well-to-do, advocated new specifics – and this sense of universal applicability to anyone can be noted in shifting recommendations for regimen as well as in those for medical treatment. Much of the new medicine was based on a love of the exotic and a taste for the novel, something that must be associated to a large extent with the new global commerce of the period. But it also encouraged the desire of ordinary people to hope for a remedy for any ill that could be purchased in the market. All of this implied that what was good for one person was good for anyone else, undercutting the elaborate methods of individualised treatment and regimen so long favoured by the learned physicians. It also favoured not only medical empirics but the scientific virtuosi of the Royal Society and people like the apothecaries, whose reputations depended on their knowledge of the natural particulars they sold to the public. In England, therefore, the beginning of the eighteenth century famously saw the House of Lords decide that apothecaries could legally practise medicine, even if they were not educated in the niceties of learned physic.[73]

A universalised and materialistic humanity was being built from the wheels of commerce and articulated by the new ideas of the so-called scientific revolution. Contemporary medical empiricism included trialling new remedies on experimental subjects, and the connections between empiricism as both an attack on the last vestiges of academic physic and as salesmanship for specific drugs were obvious. The underlying premise coming into focus through such activities was that all people possessed a common biology. Scientific racism would have to find new kinds of distinctions – but that is another story.

A last historiographical reflection, then: since Jacob Burckhardt, modernity has been associated with the rise of expressive individualism; at the same time, his exact contemporary, Karl Marx, who also associated modernity with the rise of the bourgeoisie, considered that what was important was not the individual but the fetters of materialist laws of nature to which all people are subject. More recently, in the contrast between the carnivalesque of Bakhtin and the discipline of knowledge-power found in Foucault there is something similar – to say

[72] J. M. H. van Dorssen, 'Dr. Willem Ten Rhijne and Leprosy in Batavia in the Seventeenth Century', *Janus*, 2 (1897), 257–9.

[73] Harold J. Cook, 'The Rose Case Reconsidered: Physicians, Apothecaries, and the Law in Augustan England', *Journal of the History of Medicine*, 45 (1990), 527–55.

nothing of the frictions between historians of science, medicine and technology who focus on the development of new ideas articulated by individual minds and those who see institutions and social systems at work. One can see both sides of the coin at work, too, in the medicinal empiricism and experimentalism of early modern Europe: both individualist entrepreneurialism and fundamental social change. The coin of which these two sides are emblems was composed of material values evident in worldly wealth generated in part from global commerce, a part of which in turn was the flourishing international trade in medicines. Commerce indeed helped to create the modern body.

Transactions of the RHS 21 (2011), pp. 147–69 © Royal Historical Society 2011
doi:10.1017/S0080440111000077

TROUBLING MEMORIES:
NINETEENTH-CENTURY HISTORIES OF THE
SLAVE TRADE AND SLAVERY

By Catherine Hall

READ 29 OCTOBER 2010 AT THE UNIVERSITY OF YORK

ABSTRACT. This paper explores the memories and histories of the slave trade and slavery produced by three figures, all of whom were connected with the compensation awarded to slave owners by the British government in 1833. It argues that memories associated with slavery, of the Middle Passage and the plantations, were deeply troubling, easier to forget than remember. Enthusiasm for abolition, and the ending of 'the stain' upon the nation, provided a way of screening disturbing associations, partially forgetting a long history of British involvement in the slavery business. Yet remembering and forgetting are always interlinked as different genres of text reveal.

The slave trade and slavery were debated in Britain for at least fifty years between the 1780s and the 1830s. Sometimes, as in the early 1790s or 1830s, there was an intense level of discussion and action; at other times, it was only the committed abolitionists, often the women, who kept the cause alive. Throughout this period, large numbers of Britons, in the West Indies, the Cape and 'at home' continued to enjoy the fruits of slavery, either directly or indirectly. But what happened after emancipation? How were the slave trade and slavery remembered in Britain? Was there a dominant collective memory? Were the memories contested? What was remembered and what was forgotten? In what ways did race and empire figure in these memories? How was the past of the slave trade and slavery constructed in relation to the present of Victorian society?

Much has been written on the attempts to reconstruct memories of the black Atlantic, the complexities of working with slave narratives and their mediated voices, the work of re-remembering done by contemporary artists.[1] Abolitionist histories too have been critically addressed.[2] Much

---

[1] See, for example, Barnor Hesse, 'Forgotten like a Bad Dream: Atlantic Slavery and the Ethics of Postcolonial Memory', in *Relocating Postcolonialism*, ed. David Theo Goldberg and Ato Quayson (Oxford, 2002), 143–73; Stephan Palmié, 'Slavery, Historicism and the Poverty of Memorialization', in Susanna Radstone and Bill Schwarz, eds., *Memory: Histories, Theories, Debates* (New York, 2010), 363–75; Alan Rice, *Creating Memories, Building Identities: The Politics of Memory in the Black Atlantic* (Liverpool, 2010). For visual culture see Marcus Wood, *Blind Memory: Visual Representations of Slavery in England and America 1780–1865* (Manchester, 2000). For a classic work of re-memory see Toni Morrison, *Beloved* (New York, 1997).

[2] J. R. Oldfield, *'Chords of Freedom': Commemoration, Ritual and British Transatlantic Slavery* (Manchester, 2007).

less has been said about the memories and histories of the slave owners and those who benefited from slavery. Three different nineteenth-century accounts provide a way of beginning to explore *their* contemporary imaginings of the slave trade, slavery and abolition. The context for this work is a research project at University College London which is concerned with understanding the legacies of slave ownership.[3] When slavery was abolished in the British Caribbean, Mauritius and the Cape in 1833, the planters and the West India interest in Britain were able to drive a hard bargain. British taxpayers paid £20 million in compensation to the owners (roughly 40 per cent of annual state expenditure at that time) and freed men and women were forced to serve four or six years of 'apprenticeship' – years in which they would 'learn to be free'. Our aim is to trace the ways in which those who received compensation after the abolition of slavery contributed in myriad ways to the formation of modern British society. We are utilising the compensation records, and the work which Nick Draper has already done on them, as a starting point for following the money and the people in Britain who got compensation.[4] Of the c. 29,000 claims, about 10 per cent came from absentee owners or West India merchants – but they received nearly half the money. Of the £20 million approximately £8.2 million stayed in Britain. Some of these slave owners, as for example John Gladstone, William's father, were very rich men. John Gladstone received over £100,000 in compensation for his estates in Demerara and Jamaica and to give some point of comparison for this sum, a well-paid artisan might hope to earn between 25s and 30s a week. Indeed, William Gladstone's first major speech in the House of Commons was against emancipation and he personally went to the compensation office to collect one of the cheques due on the family's West Indian estates. Others received much smaller sums. It is very striking that over 40 per cent of the claimants for compensation were women, hardly our picture of West Indian slavers. Most of them were receiving relatively small payments as would be expected, perhaps on account of an annuity or pension which depended on one or two enslaved women working as domestic servants in Kingston or Bridgetown. Very few received large sums. There are incidents of slave ownership across Britain, not just in the major centres of the slavery business in London, Bristol, Liverpool and Glasgow, but also amongst rural clergy, and in spa towns such as Bath and Leamington, as well as being disproportionately present in Scotland.

---

[3] The Legacies of British Slave Ownership, based in the History Department at UCL, is financed by the Economic and Social Research Council (RES-062–23–1764). We are building a database which will be developed as a web-based encyclopaedia, tracking in as much detail as we can the *c.* 3,000 individuals in Britain who received compensation. This paragraph draws on our research findings to date.

[4] Nick Draper, *The Price of Emancipation: Slave-ownership, Compensation and British Society at the End of Slavery* (Cambridge, 2010).

Our project is attempting to assess the economic effects of this extraordinary injection of capital into the British economy in the 1830s. What part did it play, for example, in the railway boom of the late 1830s and 1840s, or in the turn to India and China? And what was the influence of these men and women in political, social, cultural, and imperial domains? We are also asking, and this is the subject of this paper, what memories surfaced, what histories were constructed and how were these articulated in chronicles, memoirs, poetry or fiction by those who received compensation? How did they contribute to understandings of Britain's role in the slavery business?

One of the most striking aspects of this process of compensation was that, despite the widespread popular support for abolition and the difficulties that those who were opposed to emancipation had in making their case by the 1830s, few opposed the granting of compensation. The principle of private property was so firmly embedded that despite the fact that the campaign for abolition was founded on the moral principle that owning property in people was wrong, indeed sinful in the eyes of God, only the most radical of the emancipationists opposed owners receiving what was deemed to be proper monetary compensation for the enslaved men and women they had owned. 'Thank God', said Wilberforce in his dying days, 'that I should have lived to witness a day in which England is willing to give twenty millions sterling for the Abolition of Slavery.'[5] Justice should be done to the colonists if they suffered injury, for after all, Britain had formerly encouraged the trade. Once compensation was agreed, there was what Nick Draper describes as a 'feeding frenzy' from slave owners.[6] In only one instance have we traced a slave owner who, according to one contemporary report, had not only manumitted his apprentices before emancipation, but also directed that a considerable amount of the compensation money he received should be used for their benefit.[7] What is more, we are finding many instances of links between pro-slavers and abolitionists, which suggests that despite slavery being seen as a 'stain' on the nation, it was not such a stain that it prevented people cooperating on other fronts – acting together in philanthropic organisations, sharing political commitments, living cheek by jowl, worshipping at the same churches, even inter-marrying. In the 1790s, William Wilberforce felt obliged to insist that his daughter break off an engagement with a member of the

---

[5] Robert Isaac Wilberforce and Samuel Wilberforce, *The Life of William Wilberforce: By his Sons Robert Isaac Wilberforce [and] Samuel Wilberforce* (5 vols., 1838), V, 370.

[6] Draper, *The Price of Emancipation*, 4.

[7] Joseph Sturge and Thomas Harvey, *The West Indies in 1837: Being the Journal of a Visit to Antigua, Montserrat, Dominica, St. Lucia, Barbadoes and Jamaica; Undertaken for the Purpose of Ascertaining the Actual Conditions of the Negro Population of those Islands* (1838), 277.

Pinney family, well-known Bristol slavers. In 1834, however, the young Charles Trevelyan, an up-and-coming civil servant in India, married Tom Macaulay's sister Hannah. Hannah was the daughter of an extremely well-known abolitionist, Zachary Macaulay. Trevelyan's widowed mother and several of his uncles had put in claims for compensation on their estates in Grenada at this very time, yet this does not surface in the correspondence over the marriage.[8] Being absentee owners, it was clear, figured very differently from being actively involved in the management of plantations. Property was property, even in people.

Pro-slavers and abolitionists have been constructed as fundamentally divided and they certainly acted in this way in some contexts. The campaign of vilification, for example, that the pro-slavery magazine *John Bull* conducted against Zachary Macaulay, was extensive and long lasting and Gladstone Junior's speech against emancipation was summoned up by his enemies long after. Yet as Emilia da Costa argued in relation to her study on the Demerara rebellion of 1823, planters and abolitionists had much in common.[9] The violent rhetoric utilised on both sides buried deep similarities; the majority belonged to the same ideological universe, sharing a commitment to property rights and profit, alongside a fear of subalterns, whether black or white, and a conviction that with education levels of civilisation could eventually be achieved by 'others' less advanced than ourselves. As was seen in relation to the heated exchanges between the supporters and critics of the actions of Governor Eyre after the events at Morant Bay in Jamaica in 1865, 'Their internecine conflicts were in part associated with what Freud calls "the narcissism of minor differences". It was their closeness in some respects which made it particularly urgent that they demarcate their differences.'[10] There were the exceptions both on the right and the left – those who actively supported the institution of slavery on grounds of racial inferiority, and those radicals who critiqued the institution of private property and believed not only in racial equality but in the value of the cultures of strangers.

In 1808, one year after the abolition of the British slave trade, Thomas Clarkson published his celebrated *The History of the Rise, Progress, and Accomplishment of the Abolition of the African Slave Trade by the British Parliament* in which he documented the growth of a white transatlantic abolitionist movement, inspired by Christian and humanitarian sentiment, and its final triumph, in which he played a key part, the 'establishment of a Magna

---

[8] For the Trevelyan claims see The National Archives, Kew (TNA): HM Treasury Papers, Office of Registry of Colonial Slaves and Slave Compensation Commission Records, T71/880, Grenada, 435,445, 760, 771, 857, 860.

[9] Emilia Viotti Da Costa, *Crowns of Glory, Tears of Blood: The Demerara Slave Rebellion of 1823* (Oxford, 1994), 34.

[10] Catherine Hall, *Civilising Subjects: Metropole and Colony in the English Imagination 1830–1867* (Cambridge, 2002), 435–6.

Charta for Africa in Britain'.[11] 'No evil more monstrous' had ever existed upon earth than the slave trade. The 'great event' of abolition should be recounted, the 'perusal of the history' should afford lessons for posterity. It had become a 'principle in our legislation that commerce itself shall have its moral boundaries . . . the stain of the blood of Africa' no longer poisoned the moral springs of the nation.[12] This was an account which established a framework for thinking about the slave trade and abolition: the triumph was that a movement had unified peoples across different religious and intellectual traditions and by concerted action brought about the ending of the trade.[13] The example could inspire for the future. Similarly, the ending of slavery was seen as a demonstration of the liberal and generous spirit of the British, prepared to contribute £20 million of taxpayers' money to ensure freedom for enslaved Africans. In the *Life* of their father, William Wilberforce, published five years after his death and the passage of Emancipation, Robert and Samuel Wilberforce narrated abolition as their father's triumph, sidelining Clarkson with whom they were locked in an acrimonious competition which continued for years.[14] William Wilberforce was represented as a heroic figure, remarkable for 'the moral sublimity of his Christian character', his sincerity and perseverance, the embodiment of a certain kind of British philanthropy and identity.[15] But more than this, the struggle that was represented was the struggle to win hearts and minds in Britain, not the struggles or the experience of the enslaved, which remained unrepresented. While the *Anti- Slavery Reporter* over years had detailed the horrors of slavery, once it was abolished those could be forgotten. The five-volume account by the Wilberforce brothers of their father's life had little to say about either the trade or the plantations. A 'white mythology' had been inaugurated, one which worked hard to 'deny the possibility of gaining knowledge of the disaster of the Atlantic Slave Trade'.[16] There was a selective forgetting, only parts of the past were to be remembered. The triumph of abolition would screen the horrors and violence of the plantation and the Middle Passage.

Prior to 2007, in so far as there was a collective memory in the United Kingdom on issues of the slave trade and slavery, it was this vision of Britain's pride in having led the world, or so it was thought, in abolition and emancipation. Eric Williams's seminal text, *Capitalism and Slavery*

---

[11] Thomas Clarkson, *The History of the Rise, Progress, and Accomplishment of the Abolition of the African Slave Trade by the British Parliament* (1808) (2 vols., 1968), II, 580. On Clarkson's famous map of the activities of white abolitionists see Wood, *Blind Memory*, 1–6.

[12] Clarkson, *The History*, I, 26–7, II, 583.

[13] David Turley, *The Culture of English Antislavery 1780–1860* (1991), 82.

[14] For an account see Oldfield, '*Chords of Freedom*', 33–55.

[15] Robert Isaac and Samuel Wilberforce, *The Life of William Wilberforce*, V, 376.

[16] Wood, *Blind Memory*, 8.

published in 1944, fundamentally challenged this view, arguing that the industrial revolution was heavily dependent on the slave economy, that after the American Revolution there was a significant decline in this economy and that it was financial and commercial imperatives, the advantages of free labour over enslaved labour in a growing capitalist global market, that lay behind the move for abolition.[17] But his thesis remained extremely controversial, sidelined from mainstream accounts.[18] In the decades since, anti-colonial struggles and the emergence of independent nations, in the Caribbean particularly, have led to new national histories with an emphasis on black agency and resistance. The rebellions of 1823 in Demerara and 1831 in Jamaica are now represented as central to the winning of abolition. These different accounts informed much of the activity in 2007, the bi-centenary of the abolition of the slave trade, when there was an extraordinary level of engagement with British, Caribbean and West African histories. A cornucopia of exhibitions, books, documentaries, theatrical productions and educational initiatives that year explored these issues, sometimes with an emphasis on the black experience – an element which had been so patently ignored in many previous accounts. Orthodox understandings of Britain's role in the slave trade and slavery were contested and the notion that it was the glorious achievement of white Christian men was, at the very least, significantly challenged.

Putting compensation back into the picture adds, I suggest, another element to our thinking. Pride over abolition displaced guilt over slavery. 'The legacy of slavery', as Barnor Hesse argues, became 'the historical record of abolitionism, not the contemporary agenda of racism'.[19] Racial violence and the horrors associated with it were banished in the warm glow of national pride. But it was not simply that slavery was abolished, though this is what was mainly remembered. Compensation of £20 million was paid and this marked a historic compromise, in line with the parliamentary Reform Act of 1832. The Reform Act enfranchised middle-class men, made the ownership of a certain level of property the key to inclusion in the political nation. Compensation confirmed the slave owners' view that their ownership of the enslaved had been legitimate, sanctioned by the law and the state as they had always claimed: they deserved recompense, money for requisitioned property.[20] They were not a stain, there was no need for guilt, they were part of the nation.

[17] Eric Williams, *Capitalism and Slavery* (Chapel Hill, NC, 1944).

[18] A recent study, David Beck Ryden, *West Indian Slavery and British Abolition, 1783–1807* (Cambridge, 2009), convincingly argues that Williams's core thesis was correct.

[19] Hesse, 'Forgotten like a Bad Dream', 143–73.

[20] Compensation for private property requisitioned by the state was a well-established principle. See Julian Hoppit, 'Compulsion, Compensation and Property Rights in Britain, 1688–1833', *Past and Present*, 210 (2011), 93–128. On the recognition of slavery as the nation's

What then of the memories and the histories? Were they troubled? Three examples, each of a well-known figure, offer some insights into the construction of memories. Two of these authors, Lord Holland, a leading Whig peer, and Elizabeth Barrett Browning, a leading woman poet, benefited from compensation. The third, Thomas Babington Macaulay, son of a leading abolitionist and the great historian of England in the mid-nineteenth century, did not himself benefit from compensation, but his beloved sister Hannah did through her marriage. Together, they give some flavour of the complicated legacies of the slave trade and slavery, as they were created after emancipation, across two generations.

Lord Holland

Henry Richard Vassall Fox, Lord Holland, was a leading Whig peer, his uncle Charles James Fox, the great orator, renowned for his defence of civil and religious liberties and his opposition to the slave trade. Fox's grand memorial in Westminster Abbey celebrates his contribution to the abolition of the trade – he lies in the arms of Liberty while at his feet Peace weeps and 'an African negro', in the words of the sculptor, prays.[21] The Whigs, a close-knit group of aristocratic families were committed to the view that they were responsible for securing the liberties of 'the people' against over-mighty monarchs: their particular focus civil and religious liberties. Lord Holland, born in 1773, was orphaned as boy, and brought up by his two uncles. He revered his uncle Charles and saw it as his political responsibility to sustain his values.

In common with many young aristocrats Lord Holland enjoyed a continental tour. In Naples in 1794, he met Elizabeth Vassall, married to Sir Godfrey Webster, a man much older than herself. Holland and Elizabeth fell in love and she refused to return to England with her husband. She was a Jamaican heiress, only child of Richard Vassall. The Vassall family had been in Jamaica since 1672 but it was Elizabeth's grandfather who had made a fortune in the second half of the eighteenth century, the time when Jamaica was truly the jewel in the English crown. Her grandfather left his plantations in trust for her, provided her future husband took on the name of Vassall. Webster divorced Elizabeth and got her fortune including the Jamaica estates – said to be worth £7,000 a year.[22] The Hollands found slave ownership so out of keeping with their

responsibility see Christopher Leslie Brown, *Moral Capital: Foundations of British Abolitionism* (Chapel Hill, NC, 2007).

[21] Madge Dresser, 'Set in Stone? Statues and Slavery in London', *History Workshop Journal*, 64, (Autumn 2007), 162–99.

[22] For an excellent account of Holland's association with Jamaica see V. E. Chancellor, 'Slave-owner and Anti-slaver: Henry Russell Vassall Fox, 3rd Lord Holland, 1800–1840', *Slavery and Abolition*, 5, 3 (Dec. 1980), 263–76.

values that they apparently did not mind her losing her property.[23] As a divorced woman Lady Holland had no rights to her children either; so desperate was she to keep one of her daughters that she faked her illness, death and burial – but this was discovered and the child returned to her father.

In 1800, Webster committed suicide, burdened with heavy gambling debts. The Jamaica property reverted to Elizabeth and Lord Holland, who now took on the name of Vassall. Despite now being a West Indian proprietor Lord Holland supported abolition of the slave trade in 1806, speaking in favour of it in the House of Lords, and seeing this legislation as his beloved uncle's greatest legacy. Wilberforce regarded him at this time as a 'most zealous partisan'.[24] But abolition went alongside substantial measures of tax relief for sugar producers which had been demanded by the West India interest and Lord Holland benefited from these. The two estates in Jamaica were in Westmoreland and were named, extraordinarily inappropriately for plantations of the enslaved, Sweet River and Friendship. One was cattle rearing, the other sugar producing; both were managed by an attorney. Lord Holland had become an absentee proprietor. Up to 1817, he took little interest in the property. But then in the context of his friend Monk Lewis's inspection of the Vassall estates on his celebrated visit to Jamaica, and increasing public discussion of the iniquities of slavery, he began to take more interest. He attempted to encourage a paternalist regime, but like others discovered how difficult this was from afar. Faced with increasing hostility between the abolitionists and the planters he took the view, a classic Whig view in the wake of the American Revolution, that questions relating to colonial property must be subject to the colonial assemblies, for representative government should be protected and there should be no taxation without representation. Jamaica had its own House of Assembly, totally dominated by the planter interest. Holland wanted to avoid a clash between the House of Assembly and the imperial parliament. In 1823, he did not support the abolitionist attempt to challenge slavery, rather aligning with Canning and hoping the colonial assemblies would adopt the policies of amelioration.

As the struggle between the pro-slavers and the abolitionists became more intense, Holland tried to influence both the West India lobby in London and the colonial assemblies towards moderation. Once the Whigs were back in power in 1830, and he was in the cabinet, he maintained these strategies as we know from the careful diary he kept. He regarded the Reform Act of 1832 as necessary to avoid revolution, defend

---

[23] C. J. Wright, 'Fox, Henry Richard, Third Baron Holland of Holland and Third Baron Holland of Foxley (1773–1840)', *Oxford Dictionary of National Biography* (www.oxforddnb.com/view/article10035, accessed 2 July 2010).

[24] Chancellor, 'Slave-owner and Anti-slaver', 263.

aristocratic power and property. At the very same time, he opposed the 'extravagant and impracticable plans' of those in favour of immediate emancipation who had no plan of 'providing for the subsistence or the subordination of the emancipated'.[25] Subordination, in his view, was the proper basis of social and political order, whether 'at home' or in the colonies. Wilberforce, trying to stiffen his sinews, reminded him of the need to uphold his uncle's principles. The new House of Commons after 1832, with its reduced West India interest and increased commitment to abolition, meant that immediate emancipation became inevitable. His role then became to negotiate with Stanley, the colonial secretary, about the terms. He pressed for financial inducements for West Indians to get their agreement, hoping that improving the terms of compensation, from £15 million to £20 million, would secure acceptance by the colonial legislatures as well as the representatives of Liverpool, Bristol, Glasgow and London. His major identification was with the Whigs, he spoke of 'our' government, and 'our' plan, rather than with the West India interest, but he was also fully aware of his identity as a colonial proprietor. Indeed, Wilberforce addressed him in his 'other character as a West India proprietor'.[26] In securing better terms for the slave owners, he was, of course, securing better terms for himself and his wife. He was convinced that the West Indians were unjustly unpopular, that there were undoubtedly cases of cruelty, but that the public was unfairly predisposed against the slave owners. He hoped to mediate between the hothead abolitionists, as he saw them, and the unreasonable plantocracy, and crucially to protect the interests of property. His major fear was of anarchy in the West Indies, just as he had feared in Britain in the stormy days before the Reform Act, particularly after 1831 when rebellion erupted on the Vassall estates in Jamaica. Faced with the terrible reprisals meted out to the rebels while the planters attacked some of the missionaries and their chapels he argued for more military power to uphold 'the various orders of society without which property cannot subsist'.[27]

Three claims were made in the names of Lord and Lady Holland, one of which was contested. The compensation money was divided and the Hollands got over £2,200.[28] Lord Holland continued to try and ensure that the plantations were conducted on paternalistic lines and to influence the Jamaica assembly. He believed that black property owners should get the vote and that it was vital to ensure the future of representative government. It was property that secured order and stability. He died in

---

[25] Abraham D. Kriegel, ed., *The Holland House Diaries 1831–40: The Diary of Henry Richard Vassall Fox, Third Lord Holland, with Extracts from the Diary of Dr. John Allen* (1977), 55.

[26] Chancellor, 'Slave-owner and Anti-slaver', 267.

[27] *Ibid.*, 269.

[28] TNA, T71/871, Jamaica, Westmoreland, 27, 30, 31.

1840, before the notion that the 'great experiment' of emancipation had failed had become widely accepted.

How then did Lord Holland construct the slave trade, slavery and abolition in his *Memoirs of the Whig Party* which dealt with the period up to 1821? The answer is a remarkable silence. But silencing, as the Haitian historian Michel-Rolphe Trouillot argues, is a practice. Questions of silence always raise questions of memory.[29] Who and what has been forgotten? Which peoples and events downplayed? There is 'no memory without forgetfulness, no forgetfulness without memory' and memory is a site of conflict, 'in which many contrary forces converge and in which the interactions between memory and forgetting are contingent as much as they are systematic'.[30] Page after page of Holland's memoirs dealt with issues of foreign politics, while the colonies were ignored. Yet we know from his diary and correspondence that West Indian matters at times occupied much space in his mind. In his history, however, the abolition of the slave trade merited half a paragraph. There was no need to record anything about it, he noted; since it had been extensively dealt with, it could be taken for granted. He merely remarked that it 'put an end to one of the greatest evils to which the human race has ever been exposed, or at least to our share in the guilt of it'.[31] And when it came to considering the failure of efforts to get abolition of the continental slave trade into the peace treaty of 1814, an issue to which Wilberforce and his allies devoted much time and energy, he simply blamed the Tories.[32] In this well-chronicled history, the memories of plantation slavery and the struggles over it had been entirely marginalised. Memories, as Bill Schwarz argues, bring the past into the preset. But they are not histories.[33] Holland chose not to remember slavery as he narrated the doings of the Whig party. It was disturbing, not to be brought into public view. Amnesia was a less troubling condition.

After his death, Thomas Babington Macaulay, one of his young protégés, was asked by Lady Holland to write an appreciation of him in which he was described as 'the planter, who made manful war on the slave trade', his ambivalence about emancipation and his efforts on

---

[29] Michel-Rolphe Trouillot, *Silencing the Past: Power and the Production of History* (Boston, MA, 1995).

[30] Susanna Radstone and Bill Schwarz, 'Introduction: Mapping Memory', in Radstone and Schwarz, eds., *Memory*, 1–9.

[31] Henry Richard Lord Holland, *Memoirs of the Whig Party during my Time*, ed. by his son Henry Edward Lord Holland (2 vols., 1854), II, 158.

[32] Henry Richard Vassall, Third Lord Holland, *Further Memoirs of the Whig Party 1807–1821 with Some Miscellaneous Reminiscences*, ed. Lord Stavordale (1905), 195.

[33] Bill Schwarz, *Memories of Empire*, I (Oxford, 2011) .

behalf of the planters simply erased.[34] In the new *Oxford Dictionary of National Biography*, only recently completed, a 7 page biography of Lord Holland describes him as 'a keen supporter of the abolition of slavery in 1833, despite its adverse effects on his West Indian income' – a very misleading account of a much more complicated picture.[35]

Elizabeth Barrett Browning

If Lord Holland chose effectively to forget his role as an absentee planter, my second figure, Elizabeth Barrett Browning, had a more troubled relationship to her money.

In the summer of 1846, thirteen years after emancipation, she had just secretly married Robert Browning and was about to escape from her dominating and patriarchal father's household. She wrote to Robert about the public announcement that was to be made. 'You might put in the newspaper', she reflected, 'of Wimpole Street and Jamaica, ... or and Cinnamon Hill, Jamaica.'[36] This reference to Jamaica and Cinnamon Hill, the family estate, indicated her powerful, albeit deeply ambivalent, identification with the island where her father had been born, the family's properties were held, members of the family had been buried over generations and from which the family income derived. Browning had his own reasons for complicated feelings about the West Indies. His ancestors 'were in the midst of Jamaican history at its inception', the inception, that is, of British colonialism. His father had himself been so troubled by his family's plantations in St Kitts that, according to his mother's account, he gave up all prospects there.[37]

The first of the Barrett lineage had served on the fleet commanded by Penn and Venables that took Jamaica from the Spanish in 1655.[38] By the eighteenth century the family were established as very significant landholders on the north coast of the island. Elizabeth's great-grandfather, Edward Barrett, built up the family fortunes, named his plantations Oxford and Cambridge and established sugar works near his Great House at Cinnamon Hill. Barrett land was the basis for the development of Falmouth, the major slaving port on the north coast in the eighteenth century. After his death in 1798, his property was left to two grandsons

[34] Thomas Babington Macaulay, 'Lord Holland', *Literary and Historical Essays contributed to the Edinburgh Review* (2 vols., Oxford, 1913), II, 514–24.

[35] Wright, 'Fox, Henry Richard, Third Baron Holland of Holland'.

[36] Elizabeth Barrett Moulton-Barrett (EBMB) to Robert Browning, 17 Sept. 1846, Philip Kelley and Ronald Hudson, eds., *The Brownings' Correspondence* (18 vols., Winfield, KS, c. 1984–2010), XIII, 375.

[37] Jeanette Marks, *The Family of the Barrett: A Colonial Romance* (New York, 1938), x, 554.

[38] On the family history see Marks, *The Family of the Barrett*; R. A. Barrett, *The Barretts of Jamaica: The Family of Elizabeth Barrett Browning* (Winfield, KS, 2000). Laura Fish's novel *Strange Music* (2008) is a powerful account of parts of the Barrett Browning story.

since his three sons had pre-deceased him. Both were the sons of his daughter, Elizabeth Barrett, who had married Samuel Moulton. One was Elizabeth's father, Edward Barrett Moulton, the other her favourite uncle Samuel Barrett Moulton. Both took the paternal Barrett name along with the inheritance so that her father became Edward Barrett Moulton-Barrett. The will, however, was contested by cousins and a long-running legal case drained much of the family resources. In the long term, the cousins Richard Barrett and Samuel Goodin Barrett were to establish more successful branches of the family and they both received compensation for the enslaved on their estates. Samuel Goodin was living in Leamington at the time. Elizabeth's own name, prior to her marriage with Browning, was Elizabeth Barrett Moulton-Barrett.

Elizabeth had contact with Jamaica from her earliest childhood. Her mother, Mary Graham-Clarke came from a rich merchant family in Newcastle.[39] They too had property in Jamaica and were old family friends of the Barretts. Elizabeth's grandparents separated after their marriage and her father, Edward, was taken back by his mother to her family home at Cinnamon Hill. He lived there until he was seven and then was sent to England for his education. His mother, who followed him, could not avoid the traces of slavery after she left Jamaica, and often they were found far too close to home. She was disgusted that her son was in contact with the illegitimate children of her oldest brother George who had at least six children, all of whom he freed, with an enslaved woman, Elissa Peters. Her second brother Henry also had two mixed-race children. George's six children had been sent to England to be educated and their guardian was Mary Graham-Clarke's father. George, all too aware of the discrimination that his mixed-race children would face in Jamaica, hoped that they would 'settle and reside' in a country where 'the distinctions respecting colour (which the policy of the West Indies renders necessary) are not maintained'.[40] In addition to these half-cousins who were an ever-present reminder to the family in England of the pernicious effects of the plantation system Elizabeth's grandmother, who had spent much of her life in Jamaica, was very close to her son's children. Her companion, known as Treppy, was the child of a beleaguered planter and an enslaved woman, and regarded emancipation as a sorrow for the 'poor creatures'.[41]

Elizabeth's father Edward, meanwhile, took an active interest in his Jamaica property and probably went there on business at least once. The estates were very profitable at this highpoint of Jamaica's dominance of

[39] John Charlton, 'Who Was John Graham-Clarke 1736–1818', unpublished paper 2010. Thanks to John Charlton.
[40] Marks, *The Family of the Barrett*, 337.
[41] Barrett, *The Barretts of Jamaica*, 25.

the global sugar market and brought in an estimated income of £4,000 in 1807. Edward Barrett Moulton-Barrett was a paternalistic proprietor. Like Lord Holland, he was a Whig, a supporter of the 1832 Reform Bill and a Wesleyan Methodist. He was influenced by the anti-slavery movement and anxious that the enslaved men and women on his estates should not suffer unduly. In 1823, when debates over emancipation were galvanising people and press in both Britain and Jamaica, he instructed his attorney, who managed his estates, to abolish the whip. Nevertheless, being at a distance from his estates raised problems and it was decided that his brother Samuel, who had also inherited properties from his grandfather but had been living in Yorkshire and was a member of parliament, should move to Jamaica and manage the business himself. This was initially for two years but he settled permanently at Cinnamon Hill and soon some of his nephews, Elizabeth's brothers, were coming to work with him in the hope that they would make their fortunes.

By the early 1830s, the time of abolition, Elizabeth was a young woman in her late twenties and well aware of the implications of abolition for the family fortunes. Yet she was also a supporter of anti-slavery. In 1832, the estate at Hope End on which they had grown up had to be sold, a casualty of the family's legal battles, declining sugar prices, the effects of the 1831 rebellion and the expectation of abolition. Elizabeth wrote to a friend in May 1833, 'The West Indies are irreparably ruined if the bill passes.'[42] Once the bill had passed in September, she wrote 'Of course you know that the late bill has ruined the West Indians. That is settled. The consternation here is very great. Nevertheless, I am glad, and always shall be, that the negroes are – virtually – free.'[43] Any notion of ruin for the West Indians, however, was unduly pessimistic. Edward Moulton-Barrett received £7,800 for 397 enslaved men and women on the Oxford and Cambridge estates.[44]

Concerned about the management of the property in the wake of emancipation, Edward Moulton-Barrett sent his oldest son, known in the family as 'Bro', to Jamaica to work with his Uncle Sam. Elizabeth was anxious about this 'necessary evil'. In September 1834, he was 'still an exile' and wrote cheerfully enough but he 'cannot be happy there', she was convinced, 'among the *white* savages'.[45] Her picture of Jamaica was of a benighted island dominated by the hated system of slavery and capable of hopelessly polluting its white inhabitants. On his return, after 'two years in nearly a solitude – abstractedly from the negroes' he was 'very

[42] EBMB to Julia Martin, 27 May 1833, *The Brownings' Correspondence*, III, 81.
[43] EBMB to Julia Martin, 7 Sept. 1833, *ibid.*, 86.
[44] TNA, TI 71/857 Jamaica, St Ann, 632, Trelawney, 208, 637.
[45] EBMB to Lady Margaret Cocks, 15 Nov. 1833, 14 Sept. 1834, *The Brownings' Correspondence*, III, 328, 101.

very glad to get back to the light of white faces again' and declared he would rather be a stone breaker on English roads than live in Jamaican palaces.[46] Yet there were the family fortunes to consider. In 1836, his younger brother Sam replaced him and lived most of the time with his uncle at Cinnamon Hill while managing the Oxford and Cambridge estates. He, however, succumbed to the vices of the plantocracy, to the great dismay of his family. In 1838, Uncle Sam died, leaving his niece Elizabeth shares in the 'David Lyon', a West India ship named after one of the original proprietors of the West India Dock Company, established in 1799 to build new dock facilities specifically for the Caribbean trade. He also left her some money and this legacy from her favourite uncle made Elizabeth richer than her sisters and able to be independent from her father. She had already inherited £4,000 from her grandmother's properties in 1830.

Sam returned to England for a while, sailing back to Jamaica in 1839 with his younger brother Charles, known as 'Stormie', who was eventually to settle permanently on the island. In 1840, however, to the deep distress of his family, Sam died of fever and was buried at Cinnamon Hill alongside his uncle. Stormie was left to look after the properties. In 1857, at the death of his father he inherited the Jamaica properties according to the terms of his grandfather's will and gave his sisters £5,000 each in compensation. Elizabeth wrote to Henrietta the following year when Stormie was on his way back to the island: 'It is with pain I hear of the departure to Jamaica ... and in that horrid creeping David Lyon too.'[47] Jamaica was contaminated, a dreadful place, and yet so necessary for her family.

Elizabeth expressed her ambivalence about the familial connection with slavery most vividly in the poem that she began in Pisa in 1846 at the request of an American anti-slavery organisation. This was 'The Runaway Slave at Pilgrim's Point' written over a decade after abolition when it was already clear, in the eyes of many, that emancipation was far from an unmitigated success. It may have been easier for her to write about slavery in an American context – a process involving distantiation.[48] The poem told the tragic tale of an enslaved woman, who fell in love with an enslaved man on the plantation. He was killed and she was then raped by her white master. But the white child that she bore 'was far too white ... too white for me' so she suffocated him, to save him from the fate of a

[46] EBMB to Lady Margaret Cocks, Nov. 1835, *ibid.*, 153.

[47] Marks, *The Family of the Barrett*, 611.

[48] Cora Kaplan argues that shifting the scene to US slavery allowed Barrett Browning to use elaborate, melodramatic and violent scenarios – gang rape and child murder – that she simply could not do in a West Indian setting without implicating her family. '"I am black": Aesthetics, Race and Politics in Women's Anti-Slavery Writing from Phyllis Wheatley to Elizabeth Barrett Browning', unpublished paper, 2011.

black mother who could not love him, seeing in him the face of her rapist. Child and mother could only be reconciled in death.

> And he moaned and struggled, as well might be,
> For the white child wanted his liberty –
> Ha, ha! He wanted his master right.

The mother was flogged to death, and she died willingly, a Christ-like figure, yet knowing that as a child murderer there would be no place in heaven for her.

> In the name of the white child, waiting for me
> In the death-dark where we may kiss and agree,
> White men, I leave you all curse-free
> In my broken heart's disdain.[49]

Elizabeth was proud of its anti-slavery content and thought it 'ferocious', possibly too ferocious for the Americans to publish.[50] 'I could not help making it bitter' she told her friend Mary Mitford Russell.[51] Perhaps the scale of the bitterness, as Cora Kaplan has suggested, was possible in part because she was writing about slavery in the US, not the British Caribbean.[52] Furthermore, as Marjorie Stone has convincingly demonstrated, biographical explanations are not enough to account for the militant abolitionist sentiment in the poem. Rather, her inter-textual account of the context for its publication in the *Liberty Bell*, edited by Maria Weston Chapman and closely linked to radical abolitionists and feminists with Garrisonian sympathies, makes sense of Barrett Browning's portrayal of an enslaved black woman, both sexually and racially oppressed. A figure who is martyred for her race and articulates the curse that white slave-holders bring upon themselves.[53] Similarly, Kaplan argues that the poem cannot be explicated only through a family history. Rather, it needs to be seen in relation to the debates about race circulating in Britain as well as the US in the 1840s, and in its revision of earlier feminist antislavery writing, its re-working of familiar tropes and rhetorical challenge to the negative associations of blackness.[54]

Yet, like so much of the anti-slavery discourse of white male and female abolitionists, it was an ambivalent work, speaking for the enslaved woman, the adopted 'I' of the poem, a woman who had no name and who

---

[49] Elizabeth Barrett Browning (EBB), 'The Runaway Slave at Pilgrim's Point', in *Aurora Leigh and Other Poems*, introduced by Cora Kaplan (1978), 392–402.

[50] EBB to Hugh Stuart Boyd, 21 Dec. 1846, *The Brownings' Correspondence*, XIV, 86.

[51] EBB to Mary Mitford Russell, 8 Feb. 1847, *ibid.*, 117.

[52] Kaplan, '"I am black"'.

[53] Marjorie Stone, 'Elizabeth Barrett Browning and the Garrisonians: "The Runaway Slave at Pilgrim's Point", the Boston Female Anti-Slavery Society and Abolitionist Discourse in the *Liberty Bell*', in *Victorian Women Poets*, ed. Alison Chapman (Cambridge, 2003).

[54] Kaplan, '"I am black"'.

could not speak for herself. Elizabeth had had her own historic struggle, to free herself from the authority of her father, which could only be effected through her elopement. He punished her by never speaking to her again. She had been aware from her adolescence of her own 'self-love and excessive passion'. In a manuscript autobiography, written when she was fourteen, she remarked on her 'determined and if thwarted violent disposition'.[55] Her struggle to be an independent creative woman, which meant rejecting her father, has been justly celebrated as one of the success stories of nineteenth-century white feminists. Yet in her poem, the rage of the African woman could only be expressed through the despairing act of killing her child and willingly sacrificing herself. Barrett Browning was claiming freedom for the unfree, yet the only freedom that could be imagined was death. She hated slavery, yet she had lived much of her life on the proceeds of the plantations. Pursued with guilt, she knew her dependence on that tainted money. Her favourite uncle had died an untimely death, her beloved brother was buried at twenty-eight. Jamaica was indeed a dangerous place and 'cursed we are from generation to generation!' she reflected. She wished profoundly that she had 'some purer lineage than that of the blood of the slave'.[56]

In a letter to her friend Anna Jameson some years later, Elizabeth urged her to read *Uncle Tom's Cabin*. 'Is it possible', she asked, 'that you think a woman has no business with questions like the question of slavery?' Then, she continued,

> she had better use a pen no more. She had better subside into slavery and concubinage herself, I think, as in the times of old, shut herself up with the Penelopes in the 'women's apartment', and take no rank among thinkers and speakers. Observe, I am an abolitionist, not to the fanatical degree, because I hold that compensation should be given by the North to the South, as in England. [57]

Property was property, after all. And poetry was a medium through which disturbance could be spoken.

Thomas Babington Macaulay

Thomas Babington Macaulay aimed in his *History of England*, the first two volumes of which were published to huge acclaim in 1848 and established him as **the** great historian of England, to 'civilise subjects', to make Britons aware of their shared history and culture, to bind them to the nation.[58] How did he deal with the slave trade and slavery?

---

[55] Cora Kaplan, 'Wicked Fathers: A Family Romance', in *Sea Changes: Essays on Culture and Feminism* (1986), 197.

[56] EBMB to Robert Browning, 20 Dec. 1845, Barrett, *The Barretts of Jamaica*, 64.

[57] Marks, *The Family of the Barrett*, 628.

[58] This discussion draws on my forthcoming book *Macaulay and Son: Writing Home, Nation and Empire* (2012).

Tom grew up in an abolitionist household. His father Zachary Macaulay was a key figure in the struggle for the abolition of the slave trade and slavery, a tireless lobbyist, collector of evidence, editor and pamphleteer. It was hoped and assumed that Tom, the first born, would become an evangelical Christian like his parents and their friends and neighbours in the Clapham Sect, all of whom were engaged in a wide range of efforts to moralise both the domestic and the imperial world. Tom was educated at a small private school followed by Cambridge. By the early 1820s, a young man in his twenties, he was living at home again in London, hoping initially to make his fortune at the bar. He joined the committee of the new Anti-Slavery Society of which his father was a prime mover and made a powerful impression with his first major public speech at their general meeting in 1824. This was held in the wake of the Demerara rebellion and the death of the missionary John Smith and was an impressive gathering. Tom, naming himself 'a friend of humanity', spoke in support of the Committee's resolutions on the evils of slavery, the failure of amelioration and the need as Christians and as men to work for eventual emancipation. It was the abandonment of proper legal process in Demerara that was a scandal and that endangered social order. Those of us, he said, who had 'always had the happiness of living under the protection of the laws of England' had not had to suffer such wrongs. England had much to glory in: 'her ancient laws ... her magnificent literature ... her long list of maritime and military triumphs ... the vast extent and security of her empire'. But her 'peculiar distinction' was 'not that she has conquered so splendidly – but that she has ruled only to bless, and conquered only to spare'. 'Her mightiest empire', he continued,

> is that of her manners, her language, and her laws; her proudest victories, those which she has achieved over ignorance and ferocity; her most durable trophies, those which she has erected in the hearts of civilized and liberated nations. The strong moral feeling of the English people, their hatred of injustice, their disposition to make every sacrifice, rather than participate in crime – these have long been their glory, their strength, their safety.[59]

The speech was 'rapturously received' and Wilberforce was greatly moved by the spectacle of a new young leader who would carry the baton forward. Tom, however, did not appear on an antislavery platform again. This was Zachary's cause and never his own.

Growing up in an abolitionist household had not made Tom into an enthusiastic abolitionist, indeed far from it. As John Stuart Mill ruefully observed in later years, the sons of abolitionists rarely shared the passions of their fathers.[60] Macaulay Junior liked to poke fun at his father's pieties.

---

[59] *Proceedings of the First Anniversary Meeting of the Anti-Slavery Society Held at the Freemasons Hall, 25 June 1824* (1824), 71–6.
[60] John Stuart Mill, *Autobiography* (1873) (Oxford, 1963), 288.

No doubt the unremitting diet of the horrors of slavery and Zachary's obsessional preoccupation with 'the cause' to the detriment of the family economy was hard to live with. Tom did not share his father's evangelical beliefs though he preferred not to be explicit about this. He did share his understanding of a universal human family and the centrality of culture, education and civilisation to stages of development. Colonising parents must guide their colonised children, raise up their dependants in the hope that one day they would walk alone. In theory, like Zachary, he believed that assimilation should be possible: 'they' would develop the same desires as 'us' and learn to labour accordingly. But while for Zachary the route was Christianity, for Tom a secular notion of civilisation was his key concept. By the nineteenth century, civilisation was increasingly seen as the achievement of certain races and nations. The young Macaulay believed that England and the English had achieved it, though it was never entirely secure. Race and nation were used virtually interchangeably for much of the nineteenth century and 'race' was never just about biology, it was always 'a bricolage of cultural, religious and historical values'.[61] Macaulay Junior did not believe in theory that races were separate and distinct: universalist notions still held sway in his mind. Yet in practice, 'they', whether the 'listless' negroes he imagined to people the West Indies or those he came to identify as 'effeminate Bengalis', were strangers of different kinds, and the language of civilisaational difference could slip into a harsher register of hierarchies. As an avid reader of Scott, Macaulay was deeply familiar with his account of the integration of Saxons and Normans, two hostile races, through a common language: race was invoked only to be sidestepped by an argument for cultural assimilation.[62] This was a way of thinking that was to become common sense to Macaulay.

After leaving Glasgow as a young man, Zachary Macaulay had, like so many of his fellow Scots, sought his fortune in the empire. He spent six years as a book keeper on a Jamaican plantation, and then become governor of the new colony of Sierra Leone in the 1790s. Stories of his father's conflicts with the feisty African-American loyalists who had settled in Sierra Leone left significant negative traces on his son. 'Lord Macaulay had in his youth heard too much about negro preachers, and negro administrators', his nephew recollected, 'to permit him to entertain any very enthusiastic anticipations with regard to the future of the African race.'[63] His friendship for humanity was strictly limited.

By 1833, and his spectacular oratorical successes in the debates over reform when he argued that England's 'peculiar distinction' was its

[61] Robert J. C. Young, *The Idea of English Ethnicity* (Oxford, 2008) 43, 49.
[62] *Ibid.*, 38.
[63] George Otto Trevelyan, *Life and Letters of Lord Macaulay* (1881), 17.

capacity to learn from history and 'reform in time', Macaulay was elected as one of the MP's for Leeds and was appointed to a junior position in the Whig ministry, as secretary of the Board of Control, the government body with responsibility for India. The year 1833 was an extraordinary one in colonial politics, just after the great Reform Act, when distinctions were being made between what worked at home and what was necessary for the empire. Emancipation was being discussed alongside the new Charter Act for India and a Coercion Bill for Ireland. As a member of the government, the difficult negotiations over abolition, with a determined plantocracy on one side and a powerful movement for abolition on the other, were painful for him, caught between his father's principles and his own position in the ministry. Zachary strongly disapproved of some of the clauses in the government's original bill, including the possibility that the enslaved might have to contribute to the costs of compensation to the slave owners. Tom felt that he should support the government especially since the family finances were in a parlous state, and resignation, with the consequent loss of his salary, was an alarming prospect. His own feelings about 'the black man' were apparent in a letter to his sister Margaret, telling her about the constant requests he now received for patronage, including from his father for antislavery employees, 'a clerkship for Mr. Stokes, a place in the excise for Mr. Barnes . . . and he was going on to demand, I suppose, a partnership for the black man, when I stopped him by saying I had nothing to give'.[64] 'I am plagued out of my life', he told his sister Hannah, 'between the Moguls and the Methodists, Rammohun Roy and the Antislavery Agency Society', and he penned a quick poem for her including the lines

> The Niggers in one hemisphere
> The Brahmins in the other
> Disturb my dinner and my sleep
> With 'Ain't I a man and a brother.'.[65]

Deep-seated feelings about racial difference could be shared as secrets with his beloved sisters.[66] 'Niggers', a derogatory term his father, 'the Governor', would never have used, were in his mind those negroes without culture, unknown and nameless, locked in drudgery, to be rescued from 'the foul blot of slavery' and delivered into a society ruled by law.[67] Brahmins and Moguls figured differently. Men such as Rammohun

[64] Thomas Babington Macaulay (TBM) to Mrs Edward Cropper, 21 Jan. 1833, Thomas Pinney, ed., *The Letters of Thomas Babington Macaulay* (1974–81) (6 vols., Cambridge: 2008), II, 225–6.

[65] TBM to Hannah Macaulay, 21 May 1833, Pinney, ed., *Letters*, II, 242.

[66] Avtar Brah, 'The Scent of Memory: Strangers, our Own, and Others', *Feminist Review*, 61 (1999), 4–26.

[67] Hansard, 24 May 1832.

Roy, the leading figure of the Bengal renaissance now visiting London, were cultured in some respects, could give evidence to parliamentary committees and be received in London drawing–rooms, but they were still living in darkness and in need of colonial rule. The West Indies and India were different kinds of colonial spaces, in need of different forms of rule.

The ministry had little enthusiasm for abolition. Macaulay's sense of duty to his father made him decide that he must stand out against the government's proposals on apprenticeship which would have tied freed slaves to twelve years of labour. He was prepared to resign but was led to hope that the cabinet, sympathising with his position, would allow him a free vote. He spoke in support of the principle of abolition and the granting of compensation, which was strongly opposed by the more radical abolitionists, but against the term of apprenticeship, fearing that the effect of the twelve years proposed would be that 'the whole negro population would become inactive, would sink into weak and dawdling inefficiency, and would be much less fit for liberty at the end of the period than at the commencement'.[68] That evocation of 'weak and dawdling inefficiency' evoked a particular view of 'the African'. In the event, Buxton, the abolitionist leader in the House of Commons won the vote, the government cut the term from twelve to six years, and Macaulay's resignation was not accepted.[69] 'I cannot go counter to my father', his nephew reports him as saying, 'he has devoted his whole life to the question, and I cannot grieve him by giving way when he wishes me to stand firm'.[70] To sister Hannah he wrote in a different vein: 'I am glad that you approve of my conduct about the Niggers. I expect, and indeed wish, to be abused by the fools of the Agency Society (the more radical end of the abolitionists). My father is quite satisfied.'[71]

Macaulay introduced the new Charter Act for India on its second reading in the House of Commons. He was particularly proud, he told the House, of the 'noble and benevolent clause': specifying that 'no native of our Indian Empire shall, by reason of his colour, his descent, or his religion, be incapable of holding office'.[72] But this would have to be effected by slow degrees. Just as he believed in theory that enslaved Africans, once freed, might be able to 'become men', so Indians too might be educated into civilisation. He famously looked forward to a day when Indians might be self-governing, for 'to trade with civilised men is infinitely more profitable than to govern savages'.[73] 'To have found a

[68] Hansard, 24 July 1833.
[69] Trevelyan, *Life and Letters*, 223.
[70] *Ibid.*, 222.
[71] TBM to HM, 29 July 1833, Pinney, ed., *Letters*, II, 283.
[72] Thomas Babington Macaulay, *Speeches on Politics and Literature by Lord Macaulay* (1909), 123–4.
[73] *Ibid.*, 124.

great people sunk in the lowest depths of slavery and superstition', 'a race debased by three thousand years of despotism and priestcraft', 'to have so ruled them as to make them desirous and capable of all the privileges of citizens, would indeed be a title to glory all our own'.[74]

The following year Macaulay sailed for India where he stayed for four years, acting as the law member in the governor-general's council. His experience there further convinced him of the gap between 'barbaric peoples' and 'civilised subjects' and of the impossibility of closing that gap quickly. In theory, all positions in the Indian Civil Service should be open to native Indians, in practice, they were not ready. They must toil in the 'waiting room of history', hoping for that day, always delayed, when they would be would be able to represent themselves, rather than being governed by others. While in India, his sister Hannah, who had accompanied him, married Charles Trevelyan, scion of a west country landed family and East India Company official. No mention appears to have been made of the Trevelyan family's West Indian properties, nor of the compensation Charles's widowed mother was successfully seeking along with her Trevelyan relatives.[75] The taint of slave ownership was cleansed by abolition.

A decade later, when Macaulay was busy writing his history of England, West Indian sugar producers were still trying to maintain their privileged position, complaining bitterly that emancipation had ruined them and the government owed them recompense. But the protection of West Indian sugar became a divisive issue, even for abolitionists, in the context of a strong movement for free trade.[76] Macaulay was a free trader and spoke in the House of Commons in favour of a reduction in sugar duties. This speech provided him with an occasion to reassert his antislavery credentials with an attack on the particularly horrible practices of the southern states of the US, where slaves were being bred for sale. This was the slave trade in its worst form, to his mind, and it was 'a trade as regular as the trade in pigs between Dublin and Liverpool, or as the trade in coals between the Tyne and the Thames'.[77] Slavery in the US was peculiarly horrible, for it was rooted in 'the antipathy of colour'. Here was Macaulay, the opponent of distinctions based on colour, a position which he had consistently maintained formally, while undermining informally on the basis of culture and history. The job of liberal reformers was to remove restraints on individual freedom and

---

[74] *Ibid.*, 126.

[75] The Trevelyan claims are discussed in John Charlton, *Hidden Chains. The Slavery Business and North East England* (Newcastle upon Tyne, 2008), 126–34.

[76] As Richard Huzzey convincingly argues, both protectionists and free traders were against slavery, 'Free Trade, Free Labour, and Slave Sugar in Victorian Britain', *Historical Journal* 53, 2 (2010), 359–79.

[77] TBM, *Speeches*, 259.

to ensure access to the rule of law. Inequalities of gender, of race and of ethnicity were not their concern for they were universalists. Exclusion and equality were wedded together in the liberal imperial state.[78] Macaulay had felt himself bound in the past, as 'a British legislator', whatever the cost to himself and his constituents, 'to remove a foul stain from the British laws'.[79] But once slavery was ended in the British empire, he no longer felt the same responsibility. The great struggle for negro freedom had been won in Britain, the nation had been cleansed. This was the legacy of his father's generation and it had freed his generation. With slavery gone, race was no longer a problem for the English in his mind. 'I hate slavery from the bottom of my soul', Macaulay recorded in his journal, 'and yet I am made sick by the cant and the silly mock reasons of the Abolitionists ... the nigger driver and the negrophile – are two odious things to me.'[80]

Like Dickens, who, he judged, 'hated slavery as heartily as I do', Macaulay hated slavery as an institution, because it was the antithesis of the freedom he valued so highly.[81] Yet, again like Dickens, he felt only contempt for Africans and their defenders. Macaulay's liberal ambivalence, so characteristic of liberalism, rested on a contradiction. A formal and legalistic universalism was underpinned by an acceptance of inequality, whether of race, ethnicity, class or gender, as the necessary foundation for any stable society. Slavery was a denial of human freedom, but freed slaves were not 'like us'. Skin colour was irrelevant to appointments in the Indian Civil Service, yet Indians were never ready for those senior appointments.

Macaulay's *History of England* focused on the late seventeenth century. Yet it had nothing to say about the development of the slave trade and slavery, the Royal African Company and the royal patronage of Charles II and James II, the expansion of London and its docks, the slave ships in Bristol, the merchants who made their fortunes in that trade and became key players in the new global financial markets. Nor about the sugar which gradually became part of the consumer revolution, bringing sweetness to those teas, coffees and chocolates which were arriving from the empire. Nor about the ways in which race was imagined in England – in written and visual culture, in the plays of Shakespeare or Aphra Behn, or the paintings of the enslaved serving the wealthy. Nor about the ways in which colonists in the West Indies constructed new legal codes

---

[78] Saidiya V. Hartman, *Scenes of Subjection: Terror, Slavery and Self-making in Nineteenth-century America* (1997).

[79] TBM, *Speeches*, 265.

[80] TBM, *The Journals of Thomas Babington Macaulay*, ed. William Thomas (5 vols., 2008), V, 188–9.

[81] TBM to Napier, 19 Oct. 1842, Pinney, ed., *Letters*, IV, 61.

that enshrined their freedom and rights to property and representative government, while at the same time denying others their rights to their own bodies and labour. The silence is striking: his father's lifetime work had been to expose the horrors of slavery. Yet the history of England as Macaulay imagined it could be told outside of empire; the nation was self-determining, the logic of its development one of constitutionalism, a story of peaceful incorporation and assimilation, no irreconcilable class conflict, no question of gender trouble, no racial tremors. Abolition had cleansed the nation of any racial taint, Britain's hands were clean. There was no need to return to these troubling subjects. The empire was a reforming empire – one that refused slavery, saw peoples of colour as British subjects with rights to the rule of law, and believed, as Macaulay did, that one day, in the future, it might be possible for those imperial subjects to become 'brown Englishman', enjoying the same liberties and freedoms as the English.

But putting slavery aside meant deliberately avoiding and forgetting: disavowal. Macaulay was well aware of the extent to which slavery had sustained the economy and society. He was a member of the government that negotiated compensation to the slave owners: he knew what the payment of £20 million meant.

In her wonderful long essay, *Playing in the Dark*, Toni Morrison dissects the ways in which the canon of white American literature disavowed, knew but did not know, the African-American presence whilst constructing the white American man in relation to his silenced black other. Yet, she argued, read with a certain eye, the 'tremors' were there, the slippages that spoke, the ghosts that haunted, the spectres that disrupted.[82] Lord Holland forgot, Barrett Browning remembered, Macaulay disavowed. The challenge is to grasp how the slave trade, slavery and race are present in the absences and silences, the particular forms of remembering and forgetting, of nineteenth-century histories. What contribution did this make to 'island stories'? And how might this be re-imagined in the present?

---

[82] Toni Morrison, *Playing in the Dark: Whiteness and the Literary Imagination* (1993).

Transactions of the RHS 21 (2011), pp. 171–91 © Royal Historical Society 2011
doi:10.1017/S0080440111000089

THE MEANINGS OF 'LIFE': BIOLOGY AND BIOGRAPHY IN THE WORK OF J. S. HALDANE (1860–1936)

By Steve Sturdy

READ 14 APRIL 2010 AT GLASGOW CALEDONIAN UNIVERSITY

ABSTRACT. In the course of his somewhat unorthodox career in science, the physiologist John Scott Haldane occasionally turned to biography to portray the aims and values that he associated with such a career. But the same concerns can also be discerned in his scientific writings which drew, in large part, on experiments he conducted on himself. For Haldane, biology, as the science of life, was inseparable from biography, as the depiction of a life in science; and he embodied both these enterprises in his own autobiological investigations. Analysing these connections in Haldane's work serves to illuminate the contested role of science in the growth of professional society and the emergence of the intellectual aristocracy.

British science underwent a process of professionalisation from about the mid-nineteenth century onwards, with the growth of new employment opportunities and the establishment of new career pathways. But exactly what a scientific career should look like, and particularly what status and purpose should be accorded to academic science, remained an open question until well into the twentieth century. This is evident in the career of the physiologist John Scott Haldane (1860–1936). Haldane is now chiefly remembered for his groundbreaking research into the delicate biological mechanisms underlying the regulation of breathing rate and other physiological processes, and he is often credited as one of the founders of the modern concept of homeostasis. But his scientific work ranged far more widely, to include research into health and safety in industrial workplaces and elsewhere, and Haldane would eventually withdraw from academic life to spend the rest of his career in the service of government and industry.

Haldane's life in science was thus in itself something of an experiment: an exploration of the kinds of opportunities and activities that might be open to a professional scientist. He would occasionally reflect on the nature of such a life in short biographical writings, some of which I will examine in this paper. But I will go on to argue that his thinking about the social role of science and scientists was not confined to his biographical writings alone. We can trace the same concerns in another, more important aspect of Haldane's work, namely his physiological research. For Haldane as for many of his contemporaries, such research involved an investigation into the nature of life. I will argue that Haldane's concern to understand life in the biological sense was continuous with his understanding of life in a biographical sense. My contention is that Haldane's research into how living organisms maintain their functional integrity in a changing physical environment also provided a way of thinking about his own career as a scientist working in a changing social environment. This convergence of biology with biography is all the more evident for the fact that Haldane performed the vast majority of his experiments on himself or on his colleagues; he was at once the subject and the object of his own research, and his life as a scientist involved a constant examination of his life as a living organism. Haldane's pursuit of a scientific career, and the choices he made about how to live life as a scientist, were thus inseparable from his embodied experience of his own biological life; in effect, autobiography was indistinguishable in Haldane's work from what we might call 'autobiology'.

Haldane's career in context

Let me start by briefly outlining Haldane's career.[1] He was born in 1860, into a minor branch of the Scottish aristocracy. At sixteen he matriculated at Edinburgh University, taking a general MA degree in 1879. He then moved on to study medicine, graduating MB, CM in 1885. Rather than practice medicine, however, he began looking for a career in scientific research and teaching. The opportunities for making a living by this kind of work were at that time very limited, with only a handful of full-time posts available in British universities and medical schools. But Haldane's ambitions were encouraged by his uncle, John Burdon Sanderson, one of the first generation of full-time academic medical scientists in England, who in 1882 had been appointed to the newly created Wayneflete Chair of Physiology at the University of Oxford.[2] In 1887, Haldane moved south to become Demonstrator in the Oxford School of Physiology. Once in post, he gave ample proof of his ability as a teacher and researcher. Promoted to lecturer in 1894 and reader in 1907, he would dominate the development

---

[1] Basic details of Haldane's life and scientific work can be found in C. G. Douglas, 'John Scott Haldane 1860–1936', *Obituary Notices of Fellows of the Royal Society*, 2 (1936), 115–39. For more extended biographical studies, see Steve Sturdy, 'A Co-ordinated Whole: The Life and Work of John Scott Haldane' (Ph.D. thesis, University of Edinburgh, 1987); Martin Goodman, *Suffer and Survive: The Extreme Life of Dr. J. S. Haldane* (2007).

[2] Terrie M. Romano, *Making Medicine Scientific: John Burdon Sanderson and the Culture of Victorian Science* (Baltimore, 2002).

of physiological research in Oxford from the early 1890s to the outbreak of the First World War.

Despite his evident ability, however, Haldane's career in the Department of Physiology did not proceed entirely as he had hoped. The difficulties can be traced to his understanding of the purpose of medical science, and especially of physiology, which differed significantly from that of many of his contemporaries. Many of those who championed the establishment of medical science as an occupation in its own right took the view that this could best be achieved by claiming independence from the practical expectations of doctors and others, and by insisting instead on the value of science for its own sake. 'Pure' science, untainted by the need to demonstrate immediate practical benefits, offered the best means of generating authoritative knowledge of the natural world, they argued.[3] Physiology, concerned with elucidating fundamental processes occurring in living organisms, and increasingly identified by the pursuit of specialised programmes of experimental research, lent itself well to the idea of pure science; and physiologists were accordingly in the vanguard of the movement to establish independent careers in medical science.[4] Practical benefits could still be expected to follow from the application of the knowledge they produced, but most physiologists argued that the realisation of such benefits was better delegated to subaltern 'applied' disciplines such as pathology or public health or indeed medicine itself.

Haldane shared his colleagues' desire to see the creation of full-time positions for medical research and teaching, and agreed that physiology was in the vanguard of that movement. But instead of endorsing a strategy of academic purity and abstraction, he held that physiology should demonstrate its worth by looking beyond the academic laboratory and engaging directly with the practical concerns of government and

---

3 Robert F. Bud and Gerrylynn K. Roberts argue that the language of 'pure' and 'applied science' acquired particular salience in the Royal Commission on Scientific Instruction and the Advancement of Science (Devonshire Commission) appointed in 1870: *Science Versus Practice: Chemistry in Victorian Britain* (Manchester, 1984), 140–51. The rhetorical use of that language in late nineteenth-century Britain is also discussed in Thomas Gieryn, 'Boundary-Work and the Demarcation of Science from Non-Science: Strains and Interests in Professional Ideologies of Scientists', *American Sociological Review*, 48 (1983), 781–95. On parallel developments in the USA, see Ronald Kline, 'Construing "Technology" as "Applied Science": Public Rhetoric of Scientists and Engineers in the United States, 1880–1945', *Isis*, 86 (1995), 194–221.

4 The literature on the growth of physiology as a scientific discipline at this time is correspondingly large. See, *inter alia*, Gerald L. Geison, *Michael Foster and the Cambridge School of Physiology: The Scientific Enterprise in Late Victorian Society* (Princeton, 1978); Stella V. F. Butler, 'Centres and Peripheries: The Development of British Physiology, 1870–1914', *Journal of the History of Biology*, 21 (1988), 473–500; Stewart Richards, 'Conan Doyle's "Challenger" Unchampioned: William Rutherford F.R.S. (1839–99), and the Origins of Practical Physiology in Britain', *Notes and Records of the Royal Society of London*, 40 (1985–86), 193–217.

industry. His own research work was consistent with this view. Throughout his career, he would spend much of his time in industrial workplaces, investigating the problems of industrial health and safety that were arousing widespread concern at that time. This did not mean that he was uninterested in advancing knowledge of fundamental biological processes; indeed, he is generally remembered for doing just that. Rather, Haldane took the view that no meaningful distinction could be drawn between pure and applied science. His own scientific work reflected this: many of his most apparently abstract physiological researches were directly stimulated by practical problems he encountered in mines and factories, and revealed a fruitful dialectic between his efforts to elucidate the fundamental processes of respiration and his concern to promote safe and healthy working conditions in industry.[5] At the same time, his research was informed by an overtly philosophical understanding of the nature of life that was at odds with the reductionist and mechanistic perspective that most other biologists of that time adopted, either implicitly or explicitly.[6] Haldane's heterodox understanding of the nature and aims of physiology would have adverse consequences for his academic career.

In 1895, Burdon Sanderson resigned from the Chair of Physiology to take up the post of Regius Professor of Medicine, as part of his larger strategy to build a complete medical school at Oxford. Haldane applied for the vacant Chair of Physiology, but the post went instead to Francis Gotch, a one-time assistant to Burdon Sanderson who had gone on to become the first full-time professor of physiology at University College, Liverpool. Meanwhile, Burdon Sanderson tried to steer Haldane towards research and teaching in hygiene and public health – a more clearly 'applied' field of science for which he evidently felt his nephew's talents were more suited.[7] In the event, Haldane remained within the Department of Physiology, where his abilities as a researcher and teacher effectively eclipsed Gotch's largely undistinguished efforts.[8] On Gotch's death in 1913, Haldane again applied for the Chair of Physiology, and was again passed over, this time in favour of the neurophysiologist C. S. Sherrington.[9] Sherrington was undoubtedly brilliant, and would go on

---

[5] Douglas, 'John Scott Haldane', 135; Sturdy, 'A Co-ordinated Whole', *passim*.

[6] Steve Sturdy, 'Biology as Social Theory: John Scott Haldane and Physiological Regulation', *British Journal for the History of Science*, 21 (1988), 315–40.

[7] Sturdy, 'A Co-ordinated Whole', 251–6.

[8] See for instance, Anon., 'The Oxford Medical School', *British Medical Journal*, 1 (1906), 1479–91, which characterises Gotch as 'an original investigator ... an inspiring teacher', but considers Haldane to be 'universally recognised as one of the first of living physiologists' (1486). It is telling that although Gotch was a Fellow of the Royal Society, no obituary of him was ever published in the Society's *Proceedings*.

[9] Sturdy, 'A Co-ordinated Whole', 271–3.

to win the Nobel Prize for his work on the physiology of nervous reflexes. But as we shall see, his selection over Haldane owed as much to the latter's views on the nature and purpose of physiology as to Sherrington's own achievements as a researcher.

On being rejected for the second time, Haldane resigned his position in the Oxford University Department of Physiology. He retained a Research Fellowship at New College, Oxford, and he continued to collaborate with university colleagues in the laboratory he had built at his home. But other than this, he would pursue the remainder of his career largely outside academia, promoting the value of scientific expertise in the solution of problems of industrial regulation and management: as a Gas Referee, employed by the Board of Trade to regulate the production of town gas; as director of a coal industry laboratory charged with promoting safety measures in mines; as president of the Institution of Mining Engineers; and as an expert member of various Royal Commissions and other official investigations.[10]

These basic events of Haldane's career locate him at a point in British history when the proper nature and social role of professional science was still subject to negotiation and contestation. But the emergence of the professional scientist at that time was part of a much wider process of social transformation. This was the period when the new professional middle class consolidated their position as key figures in the maintenance and management of an increasingly differentiated and organised industrial society.[11] The world was shifting from one dominated by an old elite of inherited wealth and aristocratic status, to one increasingly mediated by technical, managerial and other forms of expertise. Such expertise was commonly certified by academic training. Consequently, as part of this process, the British university system was itself professionalised and expanded in the decades from the mid-nineteenth century onwards. Salaried university professorships, along with an insistence on peer evaluation as the main criterion for career advancement, served to secure

[10] Apart from the work he undertook during the first world war, which is described in detail in Sturdy, 'A Co-ordinated Whole', 276–355, and in Goodman, *Suffer and Survive*, 268–328, Haldane's career after resigning his Oxford University readership has received only incidental scholarly attention. His contribution to the development of diving suits and high-altitude pressure suits is discussed at length in Alexander von Lünen, 'Under the Waves, Above the Clouds: A History of the Pressure Suit' (Ph.D. dissertation, Technische Universität Darmstadt, abridged version, 2010), and his role in debates over miners' lung diseases in Arthur McIvor and Ronald Johnston, *Miners' Lung: A History of Dust Disease in British Coal Mining* (Aldershot, 2007), 69–73.

[11] Harold Perkin, *The Rise of Professional Society: England since 1880* (1989).

the autonomy of the emerging profession, leaving academics free to foster new kinds of scholarship, including a greater emphasis on the pursuit of research as one of the main aims of academic life.[12] Haldane's own discipline of physiology was at the forefront of the professionalisation process. Not only was it one of the leading disciplines in the struggle for salaried academic posts and the promotion of research; it was also central to the establishment of academic training as a necessary basis for admission to the medical profession.[13]

Haldane was thus a transitional figure in a broad and far-reaching social transformation. Indeed, as a member of an old landed family who chose to cultivate a professional career, he was at once actor and exemplar in the shift from an aristocratic towards a more professional social order. The Haldanes were prominent within that small group of families – mostly descended from the lesser aristocracy – identified by Noel Annan as playing a disproportionately influential role in the intellectual and professional life of twentieth-century Britain.[14] As is clear from the success of this 'intellectual aristocracy' in founding its own dynasties, the new professional society did not represent a complete break with the culture of an earlier ruling class; at least in part, it involved a transformation within the ruling class and its means of ruling.[15] As Haldane's troubled trajectory makes clear, however, there was no single view on what the new social order should look like, let alone on the role that scientists should occupy in that order. Haldane, like all those who endeavoured at that time to build professional careers, was engaged in a project to create a new polity in which their own special skills and abilities would enjoy particular authority. For the time being, the outcome of that project remained unclear. Professional science, in particular, did not develop along pre-determined lines. How scientific expertise should be constituted, what kind of authority it should assert and how scientists might best contribute to the organisation and governance of modern society, were all still being worked out.

---

[12] R. D. Anderson, *Universities and Elites in Britain since 1800* (1992); A. J. Engel, *From Clergyman to Don: The Rise of the Academic Profession in Nineteenth-Century Oxford* (Oxford, 1983); Sheldon Rothblatt, *The Revolution of the Dons: Cambridge and Society in Victorian England* (1968). The role of science in that transformation is examined in T. W. Heyck, *The Transformation of Intellectual Life in Victorian England* (1982).

[13] Thomas Neville Bonner, *Becoming a Physician: Medical Education in Britain, France, Germany, and the United States, 1750–1945* (New York and Oxford, 1995), 236–79.

[14] Noel G. Annan, 'The Intellectual Aristocracy', in *Studies in Social History*, ed. J. H. Plumb (1955), 241–87.

[15] Perry Anderson, 'Components of the National Culture', *New Left Review*, 50 (1968), 3–57, at 15–16; William Whyte, 'The Intellectual Aristocracy Revisited', *Journal of Victorian Culture*, 10 (2005), 15–45.

Recasting auto/biography

The growth of the professional middle class was reflected in the changing conventions of the literary genre of biography. Writing in the 11th edition of the *Encyclopaedia Britannica*, Edmund Gosse – a personal friend, incidentally, of the Haldane family – meditated on recent developments in the genre. Where earlier forms of biography had treated the life of the individual primarily as a personification of 'certain definite moral qualities', Gosse argued, modern writings tended to reflect 'the true conception of biography as the faithful portrait of a soul in its adventures through life'.[16] More recent scholars have elaborated on this insight. Early nineteenth-century biography was characterised by a predominantly biblical hermeneutic, concerned with charting the career of individual souls in their journey from sin to salvation. By the time Gosse came to write his own autobiography in *Father and Son*, this pietism had given way to a more relativistic view of individual development as an open-ended process of personal self-realisation.[17] This implied a shift in the social message that readers should find in a biography. By showing how personal salvation was to be sought by living a life of virtue within the constraints of birth and station, earlier pietistic biography had taught primarily how one should accept one's place within a preordained religious and social order. By contrast, the more open-ended narratives favoured by Gosse were concerned with the problems of finding a place and a role within a changing social order. As such, they conveyed a more functional understanding of social virtue.

Gosse was himself aware of this shift in the exemplary aim of biography: 'The only remnant of the old rhetorical purpose of "lives" which clearer modern purpose can afford to retain is the relative light thrown on military or intellectual or social genius by the achievement of the selected subject.'[18] Gosse's use of the word 'genius' is significant. In his 1869 study of *Hereditary Genius*, Francis Galton – himself a member of the intellectual aristocracy – had attributed it to those individuals who achieved the highest social distinction for their 'originality of conception, for enterprise, for activity and energy, for administrative skill, for various acquirements, for power of literary expression, for oratory, and much besides of general values, as well as for more specially professional merits'.[19] In effect, Galton relativised genius by recasting it, not simply as intellectual brilliance, but

---

[16] Edmund Gosse, 'Biography', *Encyclopaedia Britannica*, 11th edn (Cambridge, 1910), III, 952–4, at 952.
[17] Linda H. Peterson, *Victorian Autobiography* (New Haven, 1986), 156–91.
[18] Gosse, 'Biography', 953.
[19] Francis Galton, *Hereditary Genius: An Inquiry into its Laws and Consequences* (1869), 7.

as the ability to play an animating role in society.[20] Gosse took this a step further, locating genius in precisely those spheres of activity – military, intellectual, social – where the new professionals were most actively seeking to assert their influence. As conceived by Galton and Gosse, the notion of 'genius' served the purposes of the new professional middle class in ways that the notion of a life redeemed by Christ's blood did not. It reflected the idea that lives should be valued, not for their exemplification of transcendental moral values, but for their influence on the development of society and culture. Biography, as a chronicle of a soul's 'adventures through life', provided a way of illuminating and exemplifying the role that the new professional class was coming to play in society.[21] That is not to say that biography did not continue to present a vision of a moral life. But late nineteenth- and early twentieth-century biography reworked earlier moral tropes in ways that were more appropriate to a professionalising society. Hard work, self-sacrifice and the importance of 'character' all continued to be idealised as moral virtues, but now inflected by a new stress on the importance of independent thought, self-determination and social leadership.[22] As Robbie Gray observed in his analysis of Victorian autobiography, 'Middle-class men were concerned to present themselves as makers of the world they inhabited.'[23] Special virtue was often accorded to those whose personal convictions led them to sacrifice their own advancement to the advancement of some greater social good: a life well lived was a life devoted to a particular social aim or mission.

Complementing this concern with social mission was an almost ethnographic interest in the particular fields or domains of activity in which such a mission might be pursued. This was particularly evident in the burgeoning sub-genre of collective biography, itself a notably successful division of the Victorian biographical enterprise.[24] Tellingly, the *Dictionary of National Biography* – the most monumental achievement of that sub-genre – listed its subjects' occupations before detailing their parentage, in a move which epitomised the ascendancy of profession

[20] Cf. Simon Schaffer, 'Genius in Romantic Natural Philosophy', in *Romanticism and the Sciences*, ed. Andrew Cunningham and Nicholas Jardine (Cambridge, 1990), 82–98.

[21] David Amigoni looks at how a new generation of professional academic historians sought to wrest biography from the hands of gentlemanly 'men of letters', and thereby to assert their own authority over the training of young minds for public service: *Victorian Biography: Intellectuals and the Ordering of Discourse* (Hemel Hempstead, 1993).

[22] Ira Bruce Nadel, *Biography: Fiction, Fact and Form* (1984), 13–38. See also Stefan Collini, *Public Moralists: Political Thought and Intellectual Life in Britain, 1850–1930* (Oxford, 1991).

[23] Robbie Gray, 'Self-made Men, Self-narrated Lives: Male Autobiographical Writing and the Victorian Middle Class', *Journal of Victorian Culture*, 6 (2001), 288–312, at 307. See also Donna Loftus, 'The Self in Society: Middle-class Men and Autobiography', in *Life-Writing and Victorian Culture*, ed. David Amigoni (Aldershot, 2006), 67–86.

[24] Nadel, *Biography*, 13–66.

over birth.[25] But the convergence of biography with occupational differentiation found its most intense expression in another sub-genre of biography, namely the professional obituary. As distinct professional groups began to establish themselves as the guardians of particular social functions, so the publication of obituaries in professional journals came to serve the purpose of representing these new occupations to their members and to the public at large. Scientific obituaries were a case in point. The practice of publishing obituary notices of eminent scientists dated back to later eighteenth-century France.[26] British scientists were initially slow to follow suit, reflecting the relatively unprofessionalised state of British science at that time.[27] Towards the end of the nineteenth century, however, the number of obituaries published in the *Proceedings of the Royal Society*, and the number of words devoted to each obituary, began to increase rapidly. By the 1930s the Society judged this undertaking sufficiently important to warrant the publication of separate volumes of obituary notices. The same period also saw an enormous growth in professional journals devoted to specific scientific disciplines, many of which also carried obituary notices. Such obituaries were principally concerned with exemplifying the activities and values that defined a particular science; the information they provided was overwhelmingly about the contributions the subject had made to the advancement of their discipline, while those aspects of the subject's life that did not relate directly to professional concerns were clearly relegated to second place. The writing of scientific lives – both in obituaries but also in a growing number of longer biographies of particularly important scientists – thus epitomises the way that the exemplary function of biography came, by the early twentieth century, to subserve the project of professional consolidation and advancement.[28]

---

[25] David Amigoni, 'Life Histories and the Cultural Politics of Historical Knowing: The *Dictionary of National Biography* and the Late Nineteenth-century Political Field', in *Life and Work History Analyses: Qualitative and Quantitative Developments*, ed. Shirley Dex, Sociological Review Monograph 37 (1991), 144–66.

[26] Charles B. Paul, *Science and Immortality: The Éloges of the Paris Academy of Sciences (1699–1791)* (Berkeley, Los Angeles and London, 1981).

[27] Biographies of individual scientists did become increasingly common during the early nineteenth century, but these were usually iconic founder-figures rather than more ordinary practitioners. See e.g. Richard Yeo, 'Genius, Method, and Morality: Images of Newton in Britain, 1760–1860', *Science in Context*, 2 (1988), 257–84; L. S. Jacyna, 'Images of John Hunter in the Nineteenth Century', *Medical History*, 21 (1983), 85–108.

[28] Given the interest that historians of science have taken both in the professionalisation of science and the function of scientific biography, it is surprising to find that they have scarcely considered the relationship between the two. See, for instance, Michael Shortland and Richard Yeo, eds., *Telling Lives in Science: Essays on Scientific Biography* (Cambridge, 1996); Thomas Söderqvist, ed., *The History and Poetics of Scientific Biography* (Aldershot, 2007).

Haldane's biographical reflections

Even as science gained in professional solidarity and social influence, there remained room for disagreement over just what form that influence should take. Scientific biography was one site where individuals could exemplify their different visions of what science should be. Haldane was among those who availed themselves of the opportunity to do so, making several contributions to the biographical literature of his chosen profession. While these writings celebrated such general scientific values as dedication to the pursuit of new knowledge, they also served to illustrate and endorse the particular approach to science that Haldane himself favoured.

A case in point is the obituary he wrote of the German pathologist and early advocate of the germ theory, Max von Pettenkofer.[29] Haldane published this piece in the first volume of the *Journal of Hygiene*, of which he was himself one of the founding editors. The new journal reflected Haldane's views on the practical value of science. Rather than championing a particular line of disciplinary research, it provided a common outlet for scientists from different disciplines who were keen to advance the practice of public health. 'With a view to increasing the general usefulness of the *Journal of Hygiene*', the editors declared, 'we propose not to limit the contributions entirely to reports of original observations and experiments, but to accept and encourage discussions of administrative and practical questions, the importance of which is apt to be overlooked in scientific journals.'[30] The *Journal* was an attempt to establish a programme of inquiry defined more by the sphere of social action to which it was addressed than by any narrowly disciplinary concerns with scientific purity. In his memoir, Haldane portrayed Pettenkofer as a tragic hero of this kind of practically oriented science.

Trained as a chemist, from the 1850s Pettenkofer turned his scientific skills to public health work. Despite his chemical background, he was alert to the biological aspects of disease causation, favouring a form of germ theory over the miasmatic views that had dominated German public health measures in the first half of the century. However, his particular conception of germ theory and of its implications for sanitary practice was challenged by Robert Koch in the 1880s. Pettenkofer held that the virulence of disease germs depended on the natural and human environment in which they found themselves; consequently, he favoured an approach to public health that focused on understanding

---

[29] J. S. Haldane, 'The Work of Max von Pettenkofer', *Journal of Hygiene*, 1 (1901), 289–94.
[30] George H. F. Nuttall, John Haldane and Arthur Newsholme, 'Introduction', *Journal of Hygiene*, 1 (1901), 1–2.

and improving that environment. Koch, by contrast, sought first to elucidate the behaviour of germs isolated in the laboratory, and only secondarily to apply that knowledge to matters of public health; control the germ, through measures such as quarantine and the development of vaccines, and you controlled the disease. Pettenkofer fared badly in the ensuing controversies, as Koch's theories and ideas of practice won favour among public health administrators. Pettenkofer became an increasingly marginal figure in German medical science, and committed suicide in 1901.[31] Haldane's commemoration of Pettenkofer in the *Journal of Hygiene* signalled the new journal's commitment to a more holistic, environmentally oriented conception of public health than the laboratory-centred bacteriological reductionism favoured by Koch and his followers. It also celebrated Pettenkofer's exemplary devotion to his scientific mission. In 1892, Pettenkofer had publicly drunk a culture of cholera microbes sent to him by Koch, in order to prove that germs alone did not cause disease. Recalling this event, Haldane reproduced Pettenkofer's statement that he was prepared to 'die in the service of Science as a soldier on the field of battle ... The man who wills to stand higher than an animal must be ready to sacrifice even life and health for a higher ideal good.'[32] Pettenkofer had survived that particular battle, but lost the war for recognition in his own lifetime. Haldane's obituary vindicated Pettenkofer, and announced his determination to carry forward the programme of practically engaged science that his life exemplified.

Biography thus provided Haldane with a way to reflect on his own position as a scientist. It offered consolation for the difficulties of his own career;[33] it vindicated his commitment to views that were unpopular among his peers; and it served to exemplify and validate the particular professional project that he pursued. It also offered an outlet for Haldane's reflections on the role of professional service more generally. In 1929, one of his cousins published a family history which traced the Haldane line back to its first appearance in the thirteenth century, and included brief biographies of the more noteworthy members of the family. In many respects, this volume can be read as a straightforward example of the older genre of genealogy, which identified social status with the patrilineal inheritance of titles and property. But in a short essay that he contributed

---

[31] The most comprehensive account of Pettenkofer's rise and fall can be found in Richard J. Evans, *Death in Hamburg: Society and Politics in the Cholera Years 1830–1910* (Oxford, 1987), 237–75, 490–507.

[32] Haldane, 'Max von Pettenkofer', 294.

[33] This consolatory function is even more apparent in the biography he published of J. J. Waterson, a Scottish scientist who, far more than Pettenkofer, was marginalised in his lifetime and only recognised some years after his death: J. S. Haldane, 'Memoir of J. J. Waterston', in *The Collected Scientific Papers of John James Waterston*, ed. J. S. Haldane (Edinburgh, 1928), xiii–lxviii.

to this work, Haldane recast these earlier notions of inheritance in a more modern and functionalised form.[34]

Haldane's essay was informed by the ideas of the economist Henry George, whose work he had read and approved as a young man. In the 1880s, George had mounted a well-publicised challenge to prevailing legal notions of landed property. For George, land belonged not to those individuals or families who had historically laid claim to it, but to the communities who lived on it. Land in private hands should be regarded, not as private property, but as a loan from the community, to be paid for in rent or taxes rendered back to the community. That rent could be generated by putting the land to productive use, or it might be raised from elsewhere, for instance in the pursuit of a remunerative career. Possession of land was not a right to be inherited but a privilege to be earned. In effect, George functionalised the notion of ownership by linking it to the fulfilment of a productive or otherwise valued role in the life of the community.[35] In his essay on the heredity of the Haldanes, Haldane reiterated his own support for George's idea of land tax:

> Since the value of all property is dependent on the community within which it is held, that community seems perfectly justified in gradually taking back an equivalent of the interest on this value, with the result that, unless the holder of property can himself earn the equivalent of that interest, the value of the property returns ultimately to the community.[36]

He went on to argue that those views actually served to ratify the Haldane family's ownership of estates in Scotland.

'Family "influence" and unpaid public service are powerless against [taxation and death duties]', Haldane told his readers, 'so that those who have inherited must, if they are to maintain the old position, adopt some sufficiently lucrative profession or employment.'[37] That was precisely what the Haldanes had done. Pointing to his family's long history of public service, initially to patrons from the higher ranks of the aristocracy and latterly in the professions, he observed that it was not just property alone that had passed from father to son. There was also transferred a 'conscious and growing tradition, developing with the civilisation in contact with it'.[38] It was the inheritance of this tradition – of work, of professional service and of social and cultural leadership – rather than any mere legal fiction of heredity that had enabled one Haldane after another

---

[34] J. S. Haldane, 'The Heredity of the Gleneagles Family', in J. Aylmer L. Haldane, *The Haldanes of Gleneagles* (Edinburgh, 1929), 269–72.

[35] Warren J. Samuels, Kirk D. Johnson and Marianne F. Johnson, 'The Duke of Argyll and Henry George: Land Ownership and Governance', in *Henry George's Legacy in Economic Thought*, ed. John Laurent (Cheltenham, 2005), 99–147.

[36] Haldane, 'Heredity of the Gleneagles Family', 270.

[37] *Ibid.*

[38] *Ibid.*, 269.

to earn the rent on their land.[39] Haldane found vivid proof of this claim in his own family history. Patrick Haldane, an eighteenth-century lawyer, had earned a reputation for harsh and unpopular judgements. As a result, his business had suffered, and his estates would have passed out of the family had it not been for the intervention of a more prudent brother, whose own success in the service of the East India Company enabled him to redeem the lands. Haldane interpreted this story as evidence that the continuity of family inheritance could only be sustained by continuously adapting to new forms of public service: 'Where there is failure in this development', he concluded, 'the direct family line suffers disaster, and is replaced by other family lines.'[40]

Haldane thus recast the older genre of genealogy in ways that were consistent with new professional ideals of social achievement as the proper basis of social standing. In so doing, he mirrored at the level of family history the same shift as Gosse had observed at the level of individual biography. For Haldane, what mattered was not the inheritance of fixed qualities of property or status but rather a developing and adaptable tradition of work and service that had enabled his family to sustain its identity and integrity on its journey through changing historical circumstances. At the level of the family as of the individual, functional adaptation and achievement were the guarantors of personal virtue and social success. Continuing eminence in social life was a matter of constant self-making, in productive interaction with the world they inhabited and helped to shape. As a member of the family whose cultural heredity he described, Haldane plainly saw his own scientific activities as contributing to this project of professional self-realisation.

Haldane's science of life

Haldane's reflections on professional life, and on his own life and role as a professional scientist, were not confined to his biographical writings. They are also evident in the work for which he is better known, namely his research into life in the biological sense. Haldane's interest in the nature of life had initially developed during his undergraduate studies at the University of Edinburgh, when he had become immersed in the

[39] Haldane's emphasis on the inheritance of tradition, rather than biological traits, effectively set him apart from the efforts of Frances Galton, among others, to naturalise inheritance as a biological phenomenon.

[40] Haldane, 'Heredity of the Gleneagles Family', 269. Haldane was not alone in arguing thus. Mrs Humphry Ward, herself a member of the intellectual aristocracy through her family connection to Matthew and Thomas Arnold, worked similar arguments into her best-selling novel *Marcella*. Her literary success had recently enabled her to acquire an estate in Hertfordshire. John Sutherland, *Mrs Humphry Ward, Eminent Victorian, Pre-eminent Edwardian* (Oxford, 1991), 141–2.

philosophical idealism that dominated British philosophy at that time.[41] His decision to study medicine was inspired by that philosophy: 'I had become interested in questions, the answer to which can only be obtained from the study of the processes of life', he later explained.[42] His reflections on those questions would be published in the explicitly philosophical articles and books that he published throughout his life. But they also informed his pioneering research into the processes of physiological regulation, and his explanation of how such processes enable living organisms to maintain their integrity in the face of constantly changing circumstances.

Haldane was not alone in seeking to understand the phenomena of physiological regulation and integration. For instance C. S. Sherrington, who secured the Oxford Chair of Physiology to which Haldane had aspired, devoted much his career to addressing the same questions.[43] But Haldane and Sherrington differed markedly in the kinds of answers they offered. Sherrington, like most other physiologists of the time, held that regulatory phenomena were ultimately reducible to physical and chemical processes that could be understood in purely mechanistic terms; and he saw his own research into the nervous coordination of muscular action as validating this view of the living body as an exquisite machine.[44] Sherrington acknowledged that his research was guided in part by ideas of function and purpose which 'trench on a kind of teleology ... We cannot but feel that we do not obtain due profit from the study of any particular type-reflex unless we can discuss its immediate purpose as an adapted act.'[45] But he held that his own elucidation of reflex processes effectively eliminated teleology by showing how everything that occurred in the nervous system could be understood purely in terms of cause and effect. 'You thought Nature intelligent, even wise', he concluded. 'You now know her devoid of reason ... How can she have reason or purpose being pure mechanism?'[46]

[41] Sturdy, 'A Co-ordinated Whole', 12–75.

[42] Anon. [J. S. Haldane], *Letter to the Edinburgh Professors by a Medical Student – Edited, with Preface, by a Graduate of Eminence* (1890), 1.

[43] Garland Allen includes both Sherrington and Haldane among those who effected a shift from the 'mechanistic materialism' of mid-nineteenth-century physiology to a position that he calls 'holistic materialism': Garland E. Allen, *Life Science in the Twentieth Century* (Cambridge, 1978), 74, 88–94, 97. See also Donna Jeanne Haraway, *Crystals, Fabrics and Fields: Metaphors of Organization in Twentieth-Century Developmental Biology* (New Haven, 1976).

[44] The most detailed historical study of Sherrington's scientific work is still Judith P. Swazey, *Reflexes and Motor Integration: Sherrington's Concept of Integrative Action* (Cambridge, MA, 1969).

[45] C. S. Sherrington, *The Integrative Action of the Nervous System*, 2nd edn (New Haven, 1947), 236, 238.

[46] C. S. Sherrington, *Man on his Nature: The Gifford Lectures, Edinburgh 1937–8*, 2nd edn (Cambridge, 1951), 290.

Haldane rejected this mechanistic understanding of vital phenomena. Teleology was not simply a convenient fiction to guide physiological investigation, he argued; rather, it was an irreducible aspect of biological reality itself. Those who, like Sherrington, dismissed the idea of purpose and adaptation as nothing more than a trick of the mind betrayed their own metaphysical prejudices. From the viewpoint of idealist philosophy, by contrast, it was evident that living processes really did involve a kind of purposiveness. '[T]he distinguishing feature of vital activity is self-preservation, or the conservation of the organism in a state of functional activity', Haldane declared in the first paper he ever published.[47] Biology, he later insisted, necessitated a view of living organisms as 'expressing and preserving their own identity'.[48] Far from explaining away the appearance of teleology, detailed physiological investigation simply showed that biological processes were functional through-and-through. 'The more delicate and definite the physiological regulations which the advance of experimental physiology is constantly discovering', he declared, 'the stronger the case for vitalism.'[49] Haldane saw his own research into the regulation of breathing as a case in point: 'The idea which gives unity and coherence to the whole of the physiology of respiration is that of the organic determination of the phenomena', he argued.[50] And not just his own research: he saw Sherrington's work on reflex phenomena as proving the same point. According to Haldane, the latest research into reflex action showed that 'It is the end obtained, and not the physical response, which is simple and definite . . . A mechanism which attains ends in this way is inconceivable . . . even in the case of the complex activities of the nervous system the teleological conception is the only one which is ultimately capable of rendering the phenomena intelligible.'[51] For all that he might protest to the contrary, Haldane argued, Sherrington's research

---

[47] R. B. Haldane and J. S. Haldane, 'The Relation of Philosophy to Science', in *Essays in Philosophical Criticism*, ed. Andrew Seth and R. B. Haldane (1883), 41–66, at 54.

[48] J. S. Haldane, 'Life and Mechanism', *Guy's Hospital Reports*, 60 (1906), 89–123, at 104.

[49] J. S. Haldane, *Organism and Environment as Illustrated by the Physiology of Breathing* (New Haven, 1917), 16–17. By 'vitalism', Haldane did not mean the kind of dualistic vitalism that supposed that some kind of immaterial vital principal was super-added to a mechanical body. Such a view involved 'a breach, or rather innumerable breaches, in the intelligibility of the universe', he argued: J. S. Haldane, *Religion and the Growth of Knowledge* (1924), 14. His own view was determinedly monistic, and late in life he would complain that 'It has always been difficult for me to prevent confusion between the ideas which I had adopted and the old fashioned Vitalism': J. S. Haldane, 'Autobiographical Notes' (n.d.), National Library of Scotland, MS 20235, fo. 181.

[50] J. S. Haldane, *Mechanism, Life and Personality: An Examination of the Mechanistic Theory of Life and Mind* (1913), 88.

[51] Haldane, 'Life and Mechanism', 118, 121.

served to demonstrate that 'here, as elsewhere in recent physiology, the fact of co-ordination has been the keynote of recent work'.[52]

Haldane's teleological understanding of regulatory processes also had implications for where in the living body those processes should be seen to reside. Sherrington's view of nervous integration and coordination was hierarchical and centralised, locating ultimate control over the organs of the body in the central nervous system.[53] For Haldane, by contrast, organic regulation was radically decentralised; it was an essential property of all the parts equally. Each part was exquisitely adapted to fulfil its function within the organism as a whole, and tended naturally to act in such a way as to maintain the functional integrity of that whole. While the nervous system had an important role to play in mediating communication and coordination between the various parts, it was still only one organ among many, each of which contributed in its own way to the maintenance of the whole. It was not even the dominant organ of internal communication. For Haldane, delicate shifts in the constitution of the blood conveyed far subtler messages about the changing state of the body, which served to regulate even the actions of the nervous system.[54] Where Sherrington saw a centralised hierarchy of nervous control mechanisms, Haldane saw a collaborative effort by the community of organs to maintain their collective identity and function.

This disagreement between Haldane and Sherrington over the nature of biological regulation had implications beyond the sphere of physiology itself. It also reflected the way they tended to envisage the processes of social regulation. The use of physiological metaphors to think about society, and of social metaphors to think about biology, was commonplace at that time. Indeed, as Roger Smith has argued, it involved more than just explicitly metaphorical or analogical reasoning: talk about biological processes often slipped seamlessly into talk about society, in ways that elided any clear distinction between biological and social discourse.[55] Ideas about the integrative action of the nervous system, in particular, were commonly mobilised in discussions of social coordination and integration. Just as the nervous system served to coordinate bodily action

---

[52] J. S. Haldane, *The Sciences and Philosophy: The Gifford Lectures, University of Glasgow, 1927 and 1928* (1929), 50.

[53] Roger Smith, *Inhibition: History and Meaning in the Sciences of Mind and Brain* (1992), 179–90.

[54] See for instance his *chef d'œuvre*, *Respiration* (Oxford, 1922), which emphasised the mediating role of the blood in regulating a host of organic functions, and which ended with a chapter of 'General Conclusions' arguing that the facts of respiration made clear the impossibility of a mechanistic account of life.

[55] Roger Smith, 'Biology and Values in Interwar Britain: C. S. Sherrington, Julian Huxley and the Vision of Progress', *Past and Present*, 178 (2003), 210–42. See also Gregg Mitman, 'Defining the Organism in the Welfare State: The Politics of Individuality in American Culture, 1890–1950', in *Biology as Society, Society as Biology: Metaphors*, ed. Sabine Maasen, Everett Mendelsohn and Peter Weingart (Dordrecht, 1995), 249–78.

by synthesising and communicating information about the state of the body and its environment, so social action was seen to be coordinated through the synthesis and communication of appropriate knowledge of society and the world. Sherrington's hierarchical, centralised model of reflex integration and coordination mirrored widely held views about government as a hierarchically organised, centralised 'sensorium' gathering social intelligence and using it to enact and administer appropriate legislative and bureaucratic controls.[56] It was a vision that appealed to many scientists, who were inclined to see themselves as part of that central sensorium, working in their laboratories to produce pure, disinterested knowledge of the world and how best to act on it.[57]

Haldane dissented from this view of government, and of scientists' role in relation to it. Like many others who criticised 'mechanical' accounts of social progress, he was suspicious of claims that social order could be imposed through central legislation.[58] Top-down compulsion was ultimately incapable of imposing order where the members of society were unable or unwilling to do what was demanded of them. Effective government must proceed organically, in keeping with the disparate abilities and expectations of the various members of the social organism. Just like physiological regulation, Haldane took the view that social regulation should be understood in radically decentralised terms – a teleologically arranged, adaptive process of self-adjustment that took place throughout society, and that thereby conduced to the maintenance of the social organism as a whole. This was no mere metaphor. From the perspective of philosophical idealism, Haldane saw the teleological processes of self-regulation that made possible the continuing integrity of a living organism as identical with those involved in the day-to-day coordination of social life.[59]

---

[56] See J. A. Hobson, 'The Re-statement of Democracy', *Contemporary Review*, 81 (1902), 262–72, for an instance of such reasoning by neurological metaphor.

[57] For an earlier view of scientists, and intellectuals more generally, as belonging to the social sensorium, see Elizabeth Green Musselman, *Nervous Conditions: Science and the Body Politic in Early Industrial Britain* (Albany, 2006); Christopher J. Lawrence, 'The Nervous System and Society in the Scottish Enlightenment', in *Natural Order: Historical Studies of Scientific Culture*, ed. Barry Barnes and Steve Shapin (1979), 19–40.

[58] Those whose political ideas were informed by philosophical idealism, in particular, were inclined to denounce both the 'mechanical' economics of laissez-faire liberalism and the 'mechanical' socialism of the Fabians and others further to the left, and to urge instead what Andrew Vincent and Raymond Plant call a 'moralised capitalism' that located the impetus to social betterment in the shared sentiments of citizens: *Philosophy, Politics and Citizenship: The life and Thought of the British Idealists* (Oxford, 1984), 31–3, 83–7.

[59] Sturdy, 'Biology as Social Theory'. Haldane's elevation of humoral over nervous regulation, and the preference for decentralised rather than centralised government that he associated with it, has interesting parallels with the view of Arthur Keith and Morley Roberts, discussed in Rodhri Hayward, 'The Biopolitics of Arthur Keith and Morley Roberts', in

This had implications for how he envisaged the role of scientists, in particular. Rather than withdrawing into laboratories remote from the rest of the world, they should involve themselves directly in society in all its parts. His own work on the health conditions of workplaces showed why and how. Physiological phenomena elicited in the laboratory were not necessarily the same as those that occurred under the ordinary circumstances of life. Consequently, if physiologists were to address the problems occurring in the workplace, it was no use handing down recommendations based solely on knowledge won in the laboratory, since these would rarely prove applicable to local circumstances. Rather, scientists should work directly with those affected to develop a proper appreciation of problems they faced and to help them devise viable and appropriate means of alleviating their problems. Rather than seek to influence society through the agency of central government alone, scientists should involve themselves in the local processes of social self-regulation. It was just such a role that Haldane sought to fulfil through his own engagement with the problems of industry.[60]

Conclusion: self-experimentation, autobiology and autobiography

Haldane's research into the nature of physiological regulation thus reflected – indeed, served in effect to naturalise – the ideas about the social function of the professional classes, and in particular the role of professional scientists, in his occasional biographical writings. This was precisely the kind of scientific life that he himself sought to live. In this regard, it is striking to note that his biological view of life was in large part based on experiments that he conducted on himself. Throughout the course of his career in physiology and industrial health, Haldane performed his physiological research almost exclusively on himself or on other human subjects; whether investigating the minute regulation of breathing or the effects of poisonous gases on miners, he was always his own favourite guinea-pig. In effect, he used his own biological life to demonstrate the principles of physiological regulation that he saw as informing his chosen biographical life.[61]

Regenerating England: Science, Medicine and Culture in Inter-war Britain, ed. Christopher Lawrence and Anna-K. Mayer (Amsterdam, 2000), 251–74.

[60] Haldane's views on how to effect reforms in industrial practice, and the limits of legislation to do so, are discussed in Sturdy, 'A Co-ordinated Whole', 160–3, 174–83.

[61] On the relationship of science, authority and identity in the practice of self-experiment during the late eighteenth and early nineteenth centuries, see Simon Schaffer, 'Self-Evidence', in *Questions of Evidence: Proof, Practice, and Persuasion across the Disciplines*, ed. James Chandler, Arnold I. Davidson and Harry Harootunian (Chicago, 1994), 56–91; Noel B.

In part, Haldane's preference for self-experimentation had a methodological basis. He took the view that vivisectional experiments on animals, of the kind favoured by Sherrington and most other experimental physiologists, inevitably abstracted from and often distorted the normal processes of regulation. If the physiologist's aim was to understand normal biology, it would be better to investigate a whole, conscious human being than an anaesthetised and vivesected animal. Moreover, self-experimentation added an extra dimension to his physiological observations by enabling him to take note, not just of objective phenomena, but also of subjective experiences that might alert him to subtle biological responses that were not registered by the particular methods of observation and measurement that he happened to be employing at the time.[62] Physiology, for Haldane, was the science of life, and all aspects of life, including the subjective, were grist to the physiological mill.

More than this, however, physiology was an intimate part of the way Haldane experienced himself as a biographical individual. His scientific researches did not just elucidate biological life in the abstract; they illuminated life as he himself lived it. Indeed, physiology – and especially the teleological aspect of physiology that he himself stressed – had direct practical consequences for how he chose to live. In his thirties, he developed an irregular heart beat. The dominant cardiological wisdom of the day dictated that anyone suffering from such a condition should live as a semi-invalid, lest any sudden exertion precipitate a complete cardiac collapse. But Haldane chose to consult J. S. Mackenzie, a general practitioner from Burnley who had undertaken physiological research into the action of the heart, and who was just beginning to make a name for himself as a consultant cardiologist. Mackenzie's understanding of physiology was similar in important respects to Haldane's, with its emphasis on adaptation and the self-maintenance of vital function. Mackenzie took the view that in many cases of heart disease, the heart was able to adjust its action to compensate for whatever damage or disruption it had suffered. In such cases, patients need not retire from active life, but could continue to function as normal. Haldane heeded Mackenzie's advice, and went on to enjoy thirty more years of vigorous scientific and professional activity.[63] His functional understanding of physiological life

Jackson, 'Critical Conditions: Coleridge, "Common Sense", and the Literature of Self-Experiment', *ELH*, 70 (2003), 117–49.

[62] Haldane's experimental style is discussed further in Sturdy, 'A Co-ordinated Whole', 201–41.

[63] J. B. S. Haldane, 'The Scientific Work of J. S. Haldane', in *Penguin Science Survey 1961*, ed. S. A. Barnett and Anne MacLaren (Harmondsworth, 1961), Part 2, 11–33, at 19. McKenzie's contribution to the physiological redefinition of heart disease is described in Christopher J.

was thus instrumental in enabling him to pursue his social function as a scientist and a citizen.

Haldane's life can thus be seen as a protracted biological experiment – a study of the processes by which a living body responds, over days and years, to the circumstances in which it finds itself. His physiological researches served both to deepen his understanding of those processes and to inform the life he lived: self-experimentation was not just a means of scientific observation, but a way of experiencing life itself. Haldane literally embodied his own knowledge of physiology,[64] while his elucidation of physiological processes can be seen, in a very real sense, as a form of autobiography.[65] At the same time, Haldane's career was also an experiment in the kind of life that might be lived by a professional biologist, and his self-experiments served to dramatise the virtues that he associated with such a life. In the course of his researches in mines and factories, he repeatedly put himself in physical danger, and even the experiments he conducted in the relative safety of his own laboratory often involved a considerable degree of discomfort and sometimes risk. Haldane's approval of Pettenkofer's willingness to 'die in the service of Science as a soldier on the field of battle' found a peculiar resonance his own life, particularly during the First World War when he undertook research into poison gases for the War Office. In the course of this work, he repeatedly risked exposure to dangerous concentrations of gas. His health was impaired as a result, leaving him bent and often breathless. For the rest of his life he would bear the stigmata of his devotion to science and to the social purpose that he saw science as serving.[66]

For Haldane, physiology was thus a way of experiencing and expressing some of the most intimate aspects of his very self; in effect, life as autobiology was inseparable from life as autobiography. Physiological investigation of his own body provided a means of addressing and answering a multiplicity of questions about how he should live his life. It helped him to understand his own health and his own capabilities; it provided him with tools for investigating and managing industrial life; it exemplified the principles of physiological and social regulation that he believed should inform the role of science in the modern world; and it

Lawrence, 'Moderns and Ancients: The "New Cardiology" in Britain 1880–1930', *Medical History*, Supplement No. 5 (1985), 1–33.

[64] Christopher Lawrence and Steven Shapin, eds., *Science Incarnate: Historical Embodiments of Natural Knowledge* (Chicago and London, 1998).

[65] Cf. Thomas Söderqvist, *Science as Autobiography: The Troubled Life of Niels Jerne*, trans. David Mel Paul (New Haven, 2003), for a more psychologistic approach to science as self-realisation.

[66] The risks Haldane ran in the course of his work are well described in Goodman, *Suffer and Survive*, passim.

provided an opportunity to enact the values that he saw as central to his own professional identity.

As we have seen, this physiological understanding was at odds, on practically every count, with the way that most leading physiologists of his generation envisaged their own professional identity.[67] Small wonder, then, that he lost out to Sherrington in his bid to lead the Oxford Department of Physiology. This was undoubtedly a blow to his professional ambitions – but perhaps less so than it would have been for many of his colleagues. Haldane was nothing if not adaptable, as his self-experiments made abundantly clear, and the university laboratory was only one of a number of environments in which he saw himself pursuing a scientific life. His decision to withdraw from academia was far from the end of his career, and he continued to pursue an active life in science and industry. His resignation removed him from the mainstream of professional science, however, and thereby from the purview of scientific biography; his later career was largely glossed over in the obituaries written on his death, and has received little attention from historians of science. Haldane continued to live life on his own terms, but in the end, those terms meant little to those who determined what an exemplary life in science should look like.

---

[67] Cf. Roger Smith, 'The Embodiment of Value: C. S. Sherrington and the Cultivation of Science', *British Journal for the History of Science*, 33 (2000), 283–311.

Transactions of the RHS 21 (2011), pp. 193–215 © Royal Historical Society 2011
doi:10.1017/S0080440111000090

THE DEMISE OF THE ASYLUM IN LATE TWENTIETH-CENTURY BRITAIN: A PERSONAL HISTORY*

By Barbara Taylor

READ 24 SEPTEMBER 2010

ABSTRACT. Mental health care in Britain was revolutionised in the late twentieth century, as a public asylum system dating back to the 1850s was replaced by a community-based psychiatric service. This paper examines this transformation through the lens of an individual asylum closure. In the late 1980s, I spent several months in Friern mental hospital in north-east London. Friern was the former Colney Hatch Asylum, one of the largest and most notorious of the great Victorian 'museums of the mad'. It closed in 1993. The paper gives a detailed account of the hospital's closure, in tandem with my personal memories of life in Friern during its twilight days. Friern's demise occurred in an ideological climate increasingly hostile to welfare dependency. The transfer of mental health care from institution to community was accompanied by a new 'recovery model' for the mentally ill which emphasised economic independence and personal autonomy. Drawing on the Friern experience, the paper concludes by raising questions about the validity of this model and its implications for mental healthcare provision in twenty-first century Britain.

Historians of the recent past often witness its remnants disintegrating around them; sometimes they even participate in the process. This happened to me in the late 1980s, when I was a patient in Friern mental hospital, in north-east London. In 1988 and 1989 I had three stints in Friern, totalling some eight months. The hospital closed four years later. Today it is a luxury apartment complex inhabited mostly by

* Many people assisted me with the preparation of this article. For discussing their experiences and ideas with me, my grateful thanks to Janet Alldred, Bobby Baker, Peter Barham, Annie Brackx, Annette de la Cour, Jackie Drury, Rosalind Furlong, Ian Griffiths, David Jones, Adah Kay, Elaine Murphy, Diana Rose, David Taylor, Bill Travers, Wendy Wallace and John Wilkinson. Special thanks to Felicity Callard, Norma Clarke, Kate Hodgkin and Denise Riley for reading and commenting on earlier drafts. I learned much from all these people; nonetheless the opinions expressed here, as well as any errors of fact or interpretation, remain entirely my responsibility.

City employees (the nearby train station is on a direct line to London's financial district).

Friern was not just any loony bin. Entering it for the first time in July 1988, I found myself in what was once England's largest and most advanced mental institution: the Middlesex County Pauper Lunatic Asylum at Colney Hatch, or 'Colney Hatch' as it was universally known until the mid-twentieth century. A few days after my admission, my friend the historian Raphael Samuel came to visit me. He looked around the vast drab ward with undisguised fascination and embraced me. 'Darling Barbara! What a privilege for you, as a historian, to be present at the demise of one of the last great Victorian institutions!' I was annoyed and amused, but he was right of course – and I dedicate this paper to him.

The closure of Friern, along with the rest of Britain's great asylums, was first intimated in 1961, by the then minister of health, Enoch Powell, in his famous 'Water Tower' speech. 'There they stand', Powell told his audience at the annual conference of National Association for Mental Health (now MIND): 'Isolated, majestic, imperious, brooded over by [the] gigantic water-tower[s] ... the asylums which our forefathers built with such immense solidity to express the notions of their day.' But this day had passed: 'For the great majority of these establishments there is no appropriate future use.'[1] Later that year the MP for Finchley and Friern Barnet, one Margaret Thatcher, spoke at a nurses' prize-giving ceremony at Friern. The young MP praised the state of mental health services in the UK. 'We lead Europe in our approach to mental health', she declared, 'and it is delightful with the coming of the Common Market that this is something for which Europe was coming to Britain.' If a chill wind blew down the hospital corridors as she spoke, no one recorded it.[2]

In 1962, Powell issued his Hospital Plan which provided for the replacement of the mental hospitals by acute-care psychiatric wards in general hospitals and community-based services for non-acute and

---

[1] The full text of Powell's speech is available on www.studymore.org.uk/xpowell.htm. Powell's decision to close the asylums was strongly influenced by a 1961 study forecasting a steady fall in the need for psychiatric beds (Trevor Turner, 'The History of Deinstitutionalisation and Reinstitutionalisation', *Psychiatry*, 3, 9 (2004), 1). In fact, the proportion of the population admitted to inpatient psychiatric institutions grew steadily between 1945 and 1990; what declined was the average length of these admissions, which decreased rapidly from the mid-1950s (James Raftery, 'Decline of Asylum or Poverty of Concept?', in *Asylum in the Community*, ed. Dylan Tomlinson and John Carrier (1996), 18–30; Peter Barham, *Closing the Asylum: The Mental Patient in Modern Society* (1997), 11–12, 158). The admission rate to Friern Hospital increased by 40 per cent between 1956 and 1961, but with an accelerating shift toward short-stay patients (letter from Friern Hospital Group Medical Advisory Committee, to group secretary, 4 July 1962: London Metropolitan Archives (LMA), H/12/CH/A/30/1).

[2] Margaret Thatcher, 'Speech at Friern Hospital', 9 Oct. 1961: www.margaretthatcher/org/speeches/displaydocument.asp?docid=101111.

after-care. But it was to be another two decades before Friern's closure was formally announced, and a decade more before the hospital shut its doors for the last time.[3] By then, most of the old asylums had closed and the number of psychiatric beds in England had fallen from its 1954 high of 152,000 to 43,000, a drop of 72 per cent.[4] Today these great 'museums of the mad',[5] once such a familiar sight on the outskirts of cities and towns across the UK, have either vanished or metamorphosed into business parks, leisure centres or – as in the case of Friern – up-market housing developments.[6] Their former residents are back with their families, or living in group homes or social housing; or they have vanished into the netherworld of the urban homeless.

Why did the asylums die, and what died with them? The question is controversial. From the 1960s, when Michel Foucault's jeremiad against the 'Great Confinement' of European lunatics lent intellectual muscle to the anti-psychiatry movement, historians of the Asylum Age have divided between critics who regard the asylums as primarily instruments of social control and defenders who stress the humanitarian motives of the asylum founders while acknowledging – insufficiently, critics contend – the abuses and suffering that went on in them.[7] Their demise has also been contentious, with some historians portraying 'deinstitutionalisation' as a progressive policy response to the failings of hospital care, facilitated by the development of new drug therapies,[8] while others emphasise

---

[3] Friern's closure is described in Elaine C. Stewart, 'Community Care in the London Borough of London Borough of Islington for Former Short Stay and Long Stay Patients Following the Decision to Close Friern Hospital' (Ph.D. thesis, University of London, 1999).

[4] Sarah Payne, 'Outside the Walls of the Asylum? Psychiatric Treatment in the 1980s and 1990s', in *Outside the Walls of the Asylum: The History of Care in the Community, 1750–2000*, ed. P. Bartlett and D. Wright (1999), 247. In 1960, there were 130 mental hospitals in England; by the time Friern closed, there were 41 (Joan Busfield, 'Restructuring Mental Health Services in Twentieth Century Britain', in *Cultures of Psychiatry and Mental Health Care in Postwar Britain and the Netherlands*, ed. Marijke Gijswijt-Hofstra and Roy Porter (Amsterdam, 1998), 22).

[5] Andrew Scull, *Museums of Madness: The Social Organisation of Insanity in Nineteenth-Century England* (New York, 1979); enlarged and revised as *The Most Solitary of Afflictions: Madness and Society in Britain, 1700–1900* (1993).

[6] For the fate of the old asylums, see Anna Lowin, Martin Knapp and Jennifer Beecham, 'Uses of Old Long-Stay Hospital Buildings', *Psychiatric Bulletin*, 22 (1998), 129–30; SAVE, *Mind over Matter: A Study of the Country's Threatened Mental Asylums*, SAVE Britain's Heritage (1995).

[7] Michel Foucault, *The History of Madness*, trans. Jonathan Murphy and Jean Khalfa (2006). The most influential spokesman for the social control thesis has been the American sociologist Andrew Scull: see *Most Solitary of Afflictions*, 376–81, for his sophisticated version of the argument. For a nuanced defence of the asylum system, see Kathleen Jones, *Asylums and After: A Revised History of the Mental Health Services from the Early Eighteenth Century to the 1990s* (1993).

[8] As studies from Britain and elsewhere show, the introduction of new drug therapies did not cause deinstitutionalisation, which was already well underway before the new medications came into use, but it fuelled optimism and played an important role in shaping

'the attractiveness of community care to policy-makers concerned about ever-rising costs of health care within a capitalist welfare system'.[9] The arguments are fiercer for having been strongly politicised, as historians find themselves caught up in the policy battles raging around welfare provision over the last half century.

I do not intend to adjudicate these disagreements (although I have more to say about them further on). I am not a historian of mental health policy and anyway my own concerns are rather different. I am interested neither in loading more opprobrium on the defunct hospitals, nor in defending them (although my experience revealed some things that warrant defending); rather, I want to explore the ideals behind the asylum, and what has become of them in recent times. The birth of the asylum witnessed the emergence of a paradigm conflict still evident in mental health circles. This conflict maps loosely onto the historic opposition between psychological and biomedical models of madness, but terms such as near versus far, interactive versus passive, subject versus object, probably tell us more about it. How close to madness does one need to get to treat it effectively? One paradigm shows us madness practitioners proffering remedies to madness sufferers across a gulf of professional expertise and objectivity; the other shows sufferer and healer drawn together in a therapeutic partnership which, in the strongest versions of this tradition, directly implicates the healer's own psyche in the treatment process (an approach recently described by the leading forensic psychotherapist, Dr Gwen Adshead, as 'mak[ing] your mind available to somebody else, to help them recover').[10] The pioneers of the Asylum Age initiated the second tradition, creating an up-close therapeutic regimen based on personal rapport, moral example and the utilisation of other-regarding emotions ('social affections' in the vocabulary of the day) as remedial agents. This psycho-relational paradigm was known as 'moral treatment', and was strongly resisted by many mad-doctors at the time, accustomed to dispensing biophysical remedies – blood-letting, purging, drugs, psychosurgery, etc. – from a professional distance.[11] The demise of the asylum, I argue below, has reconfigured this conflict without

community-care policy (Jed Boardman, *New Services for Old – an Overview of Mental Health Policy*, Sainsbury Centre for Mental Health (2005), 29).

9 John Welshman, 'Rhetoric and Reality: Community Care in England and Wales, 1948–74', in *Outside the Walls*, ed. Bartlett and Wright, 205. As John Raftery and others note, the deinstitutionalisation of mental health care also needs to understood as part of a long-term government drive to curtail public health expenditure by shifting provision toward the private and voluntary sectors: Raftery, 'Decline of Asylum', 20; Turner, 'History of Deinstitutionalisation', 3–4.

10 'Desert Island Discs', BBC Radio 4, 16 July 2010.

11 See below, pp. 202–7, for a more detailed discussion of this.

diminishing it, and it continues to reverberate throughout mental health services.

Here in the UK, asylumdom entered its terminal phase with the foundation of the National Health Service. The decision to incorporate mental health services into the NHS, thereby drawing them into the medical mainstream, effectively signed the execution warrant for the old 'bins'.[12] But socialised medicine was not the sole or even the main factor behind deinstitutionalisation. The transfer of mental health care from asylum to community was a general western phenomenon, occurring more or less simultaneously in countries with medical systems as diverse as those of Britain, Italy and the USA. From the 1960s onward, asylums across Europe and North America faced a host of enemies: anti-psychiatrists who damned them as 'total institutions' and 'carceral cities'; public purseholders keen to reduce health costs; welfare reformers and campaigning journalists shocked by conditions in the infamous 'back wards'; and, increasingly, patients themselves, organised into a growing 'consumer' movement.[13] The most radical of these opponents (in the UK, R. D. Laing and his followers) regarded themselves as psychiatric insurgents, but the times favoured them.[14] Asylum populations were changing: voluntary patients had been admitted since 1930, and in the wake of the 1959 Mental Health Act (which abolished the distinction between psychiatric and general hospitals) the ratio of voluntary to detained patients rose dramatically: a transformation that made the custodial regimen of the old asylums appear gratuitously oppressive as well as out-dated.[15] Outpatient psychiatric services had expanded throughout the 1950s and 1960s, as new drug treatments made it possible to treat increasing numbers of people in their homes. By the early 1970s, asylums everywhere were recording a steady shrinkage in their resident numbers.[16] Moreover, many of the buildings housing these old

---

[12] Jones, *Asylums*, 146–8; Douglas Bennett, 'The Drive towards the Community', in *150 Years of British Psychiatry, 1841–1991*, ed. G. Berrios and Hugh Freeman (1991), 326–7; Elaine Murphy, *After the Asylums: Community Care for People with Mental Illness* (1991), 10–11, 13. The provision of social welfare benefits and public housing was also crucial in enabling the unwaged mentally ill to live outside asylums, although generally in very straitened circumstances.

[13] For the deinstitutionalisation of mental health services internationally, see *International Journal of Mental Health*, 11, 4 (1982/3) (entire issue); Walid Fakhoury and Stefan Priebe, 'Deinstitutionalisation and Reinstitutionalisation: Major Changes in the Provision of Mental Health Care', *Psychiatry*, 6, 8 (2007), 313–16.

[14] R. Boyers and R. Orrill, eds., *Psychiatry and Anti-Psychiatry* (Harmondsworth, 1972); Peter Sedgwick, *Psycho Politics* (1982).

[15] Bennett, 'Drive towards Community', 327.

[16] Admission rates (including repeated admissions: the notorious 'revolving-door' syndrome) were higher than ever by the end of the 1960s, but these admissions were increasingly short term (see n. 1 for references).

hospitals were crumbling. Refurbishing them would be hugely costly: an unwelcome prospect to governments, especially during the fiscal crisis of the seventies. And then there were the scandals. In the UK, there were a series of these in the 1960s and 1970s – several involving Friern hospital – which gave the *coup de grâce* to the Asylum Age. Who could defend institutions that handled people like 'human trash'? as one journalist demanded in the wake of a major exposé of the treatment of the demented elderly at Friern in the late 1960s.[17]

This constellation of anti-asylum forces could be found, with variations, in most western nations. But deinstitutionalisation also had a deeper root, in resurgent free-market ideology and the correlative attack on welfare 'dependency'. The last quarter of the twentieth century saw the post-war welfare settlement coming under sustained assault from free-marketeers, with a commensurate growth in hostility toward people reliant on state support. The opprobrium was initially directed against those traditional bogeys of the liberal (now 'neoliberal') imagination – the idle, the shiftless, the 'undeserving poor' – but quickly expanded to include new categories such as single mothers and, inevitably, the chronically mad:

> The punitive sentiments directed against those who must feed from the public trough extend only too easily to embrace those who suffer from the most severe forms of psychiatric misery ... those incapacitated by psychiatric disability all too often find themselves the targets of those who would abolish social programs because they consider any social dependency immoral.[18]

Today the discourse of mental health 'providers' is all about autonomy and independence. The language of dependency is almost entirely negative. Its primary referents are to drug and alcohol addiction, but the pejorative connotations extend across most varieties of neediness, including for basic care and support. To need other people on a day-to-day basis (unless you are very young, very old or very disabled) is seen as inherently pathological; independence is a *sina qua non* of mental health.[19] The motives behind this philosophy are, in many respects, honourable: to treat mentally ill people as full adults, capable of making valid life decisions; to prevent emotional exploitation; to promote self-confidence and reduce stigmatisation. But the ideal of personal autonomy driving the agenda is, Elizabeth Bott has argued in a classic study of hospital care,

---

[17] Barbara Robb, *Sans Everything: A Case to Answer* (1967). Robb's book caused a furor. An independent committee of inquiry was established to investigate her allegations of abuse and neglect; for its findings (which many commentators at the time decried as a 'whitewash'), see www.sochealth.co.uk/history/Friern.htm.

[18] Andrew Scull, 'Historical Reflections on Asylums, Communities, and the Mentally Ill', *Mentalities*, 11, 2 (1997), 14–15.

[19] For examples of this policy language see Department of Health, *Independence, Well-Being and Choice* (2005); Department of Health, *From Segregation to Inclusion: Commissioning Guidance on Day Services for People with Mental Health Problems* (2006).

illusory: 'autonomous is just what most mental . . . patients are not. Either they are social isolates, or they are locked in dependent but conflict-ridden relationships with relatives'.[20]

If Bott is right about this – and I suspect most people with mental disorders, or people who work with people with mental disorders, would endorse her description – what are the care implications? Today, in Britain, 'choice' is the watchword in mental health services, as it is throughout the NHS. In 2006, the Department of Health initiated a website, 'Our Choices in Mental Health'. Launching the site, a DoH spokesperson declared that 'patients should know that they now have the powers to choose their own path through services and keep control of their lives. They have the preference to choose how, when, where or what treatments they receive.'[21] (The following year the government introduced Community Treatment Orders, which compel previously detained patients to take their medication under threat of re-hospitalisation if they refuse.) This 'logic of choice' is the focus of a recent book by the Dutch philosopher Annemarie Mol, who contrasts it to a 'logic of care'. 'Choice', Mol shows, interpellates the patient as an autonomous consumer selecting from an array of treatment options, while the 'logic of care' sees patient and carer interacting for the patient's benefit. Mol illustrates the difference between the two logics with an anecdote about a man in a mental hospital who refuses to leave his bed. A group of ethicists and psychiatrists meet to discuss how the man should be treated. The ethicists argue for non-intervention: the patient, they say, is harming no one by staying in bed; it's his choice to be there; he should be left alone. A discussion of what choice means for someone with severe mental illness ensues; eventually a psychotherapist cuts across it. The question, he says, cannot be decided outside its institutional context. Does the hospital have plenty of staff? If so, a nurse should be assigned to sit by the patient's bed and find out *why* he doesn't want to get up.

> 'Maybe his wife is not coming for a visit that afternoon, maybe he feels awful and fears he will never be released from hospital. Take time for him, let him talk.' Someone who does not want to get up, says the psychotherapist, needs care. Offering him the choice of staying in bed is as much a way of neglecting him as is forcing him to get up.[22]

---

[20] Elizabeth Bott, 'Hospital and Society', *British Journal of Medical Psychology*, 49 (1976), 126. Bott's classic essay is more than three decades old, but problems of social isolation and family conflict among people with serious mental illness appear to be ongoing: see Brendan D. Kelly, 'Structural Violence and Schizophrenia', *Social Science and Medicine*, 61 (2005), 721–30; J. Boydell, K. McKenzie, J. Van Os and R. M. Murray, 'The Social Causes of Schizophrenia', *Schizophrenia Research*, 53 (Suppl.) (2002), 264; J. Leary, E. C. Johnstone and D. C. Owens, 'Social Outcome', *British Journal of Psychiatry*, 159 (Suppl. 13) (1991), 13–20.

[21] For the announcement of the website launch see www.e-health-insider.com/news/itemcfm?ID = 2246. The website www.mhchoice.org.uk appears to be defunct.

[22] Annemarie Mol, *The Logic of Care: Health and the Problem of Patient Choice* (2008), x–xi.

'Choice' in mental health care is usually contrasted to force: 'is care a soft form of force', Mol asks, 'or might it be something different?'[23] The view of psychiatric care as a 'soft form of force' was popular in libertarian circles in the 1960s and 1970s, and still has many proponents. But what was once an anti-Establishment stance has now leached into official policy. Alongside choice, mental health policy-makers today are increasingly preoccupied by risk: a concern that focuses primarily on safety risks to the public from aggressive patients,[24] but which runs too in the opposite direction: toward the potential risks to patient autonomy from carers and care institutions. Minimising these latter risks is a core aim of the 'recovery model', a healthcare approach which means living with a chronic illness as if one doesn't have it.[25] Services everywhere are becoming geared to this model, which requires patients (service users as they are now known) to pass through the system as quickly as possible; open-ended care – whether on an outpatient or inpatient basis – is a no-no.[26] Even

---

[23] *Ibid.*, xii.

[24] Risk leapt to the forefront of UK government mental health policy after the widely publicised murder of Jonathan Zito by the schizophrenic Christopher Clunis in 1992. The public inquiry that followed revealed care failures that were deemed to necessitate a more risk-oriented policy approach. 'Risk minimisation' became the must-do, dominating day-to-day decision-making, albeit in ways that sat very uneasily alongside the 'choice' agenda. As John Wilkinson, a former manager of mental health services in East London, writes: 'The very people who stalk the nightmares of tabloid editors and Heath Ministers and who must be policed in thought and act, at one and the same time are Consumers, who must exercise Choice and must assess the Performance of those providing them with services. The very people who must be subject to community orders and who must demonstrate Compliance – with treatment, with care plans – must grasp those opportunities made available to them through the new Recovery perspective!' (John Wilkinson, 'The Politics of Risk and Trust in Mental Health', *Critical Quarterly*, 46, 3 (2004), 83).

[25] The recovery model is a complex policy initiative. It has received strong impetus from the service-users movement, which sees in it a rejection of psychiatric paternalism in favour of a service that treats its users as persons rather than patients, and affords them a greater voice over their treatments and care. Critics however – which includes both users and practitioners – argue that the model has been 'hijacked' by mental health managers as a way of legitimating service cuts. For a government statement of the model see Mental Health Division Department of Health, *New Horizons: A Shared Vision for Mental Health* (HMSO, 2009); for service-users' perspectives see www.psychminded.co.uk, and a host of other internet sources. For a detailed discussion of the model see Geoff Shepherd, Jed Boardman and Mike Slade, *Making Recovery a Reality*, Sainsbury Centre for Mental Health (2008).

[26] Most inpatient admissions are now strictly time-limited; getting a patient 'off the books' – if only by shunting him or her onto another part of the service – is the goal. Outpatient services which do not fit into the new recovery model, such as rehabilitation programmes and day centres, are disappearing everywhere. For the decline in rehabilitation services see Debbie Mountain, Helen Gillaspy and Frank Holloway, 'Mental Health Rehabilitation Services in the UK in 2007', *Psychiatric Bulletin*, 33 (2009), 215–18. For day centre closures, see www.communitycare.co.uk, and scores of internet-based protests against local day centre closures.

NHS psychological treatments like cognitive behaviour therapy are time-limited in order to encourage 'client self-management' and to mitigate 'dependency issues'.[27] The ideal of the autonomous self underpinning these policies is so radically individuated that it begins to approximate to Melanie Klein's account of psychotic aloneness, although in this case the anxieties driving the fantasy belong to the professionals rather than the mad.[28] It is as if the terrible loneliness of madness, which Klein describes so well, has flooded the entire mental health establishment. Cognitive behaviour therapy, for example, can now be done on the NHS without any human contact at all, sitting alone at one's computer with an online CBT package – and this despite the fact that a host of studies have shown that it is the quality of the relationship with the therapist that determines the outcome of CBT, as it does all therapeutic encounters.[29]

I interviewed a number of mental health managers for this lecture. All, with one exception, repeated the anti-dependency mantra; all, *without* exception, spoke passionately about the need for emotional rapport between care-workers and users, and – in the spirit of Mol's psychotherapist – gave examples of up-close, sympathetic care relationships as instances of best practice. These contradictions, a London psychiatrist explained to me, are not incidental but endemic to a system

[27] The British Association for Behavioural and Cognitive Therapies describes the therapeutic relationship in CBT as a 'partnership' that aims to promote client independence: 'The approach ... relies on the therapist and client developing a shared view of the individual's problem. This then leads to identification of personalised, usually time limited therapy goals and strategies which are continually monitored and evaluated. The treatments are inherently empowering in nature, the outcome being to focus on specific psychological and practical skills ... aimed at enabling the client to tackle their problems by harnessing their own resources ... Thus the overall aim is for the individual to attribute improvement to their own efforts, in collaboration with the psychotherapist' (Katy Grazebrook, Anne Garland and the Board of BABCP, *What are Cognitive and/or Behavioural Psychotherapies?* (2005)). For the need to time-limit CBT in order to avoid 'dependency issues', see Ceri Evans, 'Cognitive Behavioural Therapy with Older People', *Advances in Psychiatric Treatment*, 13 (2007), 111–18.

[28] Melanie Klein, 'On the Sense of Loneliness', in her *Envy and Gratitude and Other Works, 1946–1963* (1988), 300–13.

[29] M. Lambert and D. E. Barley, 'Research Summary on the Therapeutic Relationship and Psychotherapy Outcome', *Psychotherapy*, 38, 4 (2001), 357–61; Paul Gilbert and Robert L. Leahy, eds., *The Therapeutic Relationship in Cognitive Behavioural Therapies* (Hove, 2007). In 1962, Denis Martin, the physician superintendent of Claybury Hospital in Essex, criticised psychiatric institutions for failing to develop strong relationships between patients and practitioners: 'Lack of channels of communication seems to be the fundamental barrier to constructive change and fosters a very ... superficial kind of personal relationship [between practitioner and patient]' (Denis Martin, *Adventures in Psychiatry* (Oxford, 1962), 15, quoted in Barham, *Closing the Asylum*, 7). Today this is a failing which many service managers – keen to avoid 'dependency-generative relationships' – seem to regard as a strength, while mental health staff who continue to emphasise the value of the therapeutic relationship are 'dismissed as self-serving and mystifying' (Wilkinson, 'Politics of Risk', 95).

that requires mental health professionals to respond empathically to patient suffering while simultaneously defending themselves against this suffering lest it draw them into care relationships that violate the anti-dependency imperative. These emotional defences are also meant to keep the craziness on the patient's side, well away from professional sanity . . . although this isn't always so easy. Mental health workers must get close enough to their clients' misery to comprehend it; keeping too far away, as one service manager complained to me, makes them callous. 'So how do you stay sane?' I asked a long-time psychiatrist. 'I don't always', he told me. 'I don't think I should.'

These paradoxes are stark today, but they are not new: the underlying issues stretch back to the beginnings of the asylum age. 'I used to be astonished', the leading Victorian psychiatrist John Conolly wrote in 1856, 'to see humane physicians going daily round the wards of asylums, mere spectators of every form of distressing coercion, without a word of sympathy, or any order for its mitigation.'[30] But now, Conolly claimed, things were changing. In the 1840s, Conolly had been the superintendent of Hanwell Asylum in Middlesex, an institution whose medical officer was 'really intimate with the insane'. 'He is constantly with the patients', Conolly wrote of this practitioner: 'their characters are intimately known to him; he watches the effects of all the means of cure to which he resorts; and his own character gives the tone to the whole house'.[31] As a result, 'wherever they [inmates] go they meet kind people and hear kind words; they are never passed without some recognition, and the face of every officer is the face of a friend'.[32]

The sympathetic relationships described by Conolly were the linchpin of moral treatment, the foundational regimen of the public asylum system. Moral treatment, which was pioneered at the end of the eighteenth century by Phillipe Pinel in France and the Tuke family in England, was a portmanteau term for therapeutics directed at the minds and emotions of lunatics (their 'moral' characteristics) rather than any supposed organic cause of insanity.[33] At a minimum, moral treatment meant managing

[30] John Conolly, MD, *The Treatment of the Insane without Mechanical Restraints* (1856; 1973), 13.

[31] John Conolly, MD, *A Letter to Benjamin Rotch Esq . . . on the Plan and Government of the Additional Lunatic Asylum for the County of Middlesex, About to be Erected at Colney Hatch* (1847), 20.

[32] Conolly, *Treatment of the Insane*, 58.

[33] For moral treatment at the York Retreat see Charles L. Cherry, *A Quiet Haven: Quakers, Moral Treatment and Asylum Reform* (Rutherford, NJ, 1989); Anne Digby, *Madness, Morality and Medicine: A Study of the York Retreat, 1796–1914* (Cambridge, 1985); Louis C. Charland, 'Benevolent Theory: Moral Treatment at the York Retreat', *History of Psychiatry*, 18, 1 (2007), 61–79; Samuel Tuke, *Description of the Retreat: An Institution near York, for Insane Persons of the Society of Friends* (1813; Milton Keynes, 2010). For Pinel see Philippe Pinel, *A Treatise on Insanity* (1806); Jan Goldstein, *Console and Classify: The French Psychiatric Profession in the Nineteenth Century* (Chicago, 2001); Dora B. Weiner, '*La Geste de Pinel*: the History of a Psychiatric Myth', in *Discovering the History of Psychiatry*, ed. Mark Micale and Roy Porter (Oxford, 1994), 232–49.

lunatics without recourse to 'mechanical restraints' such as chains or manacles, or to the ineffectual and often brutal physical remedies favoured by mad-doctors of the period. In its stronger versions, it was a psycho-therapeutic that utilised the asylum environment and staff/inmate relationships as healing agents. Phillipe Pinel was physician-in-chief at the Salpêtrière asylum from 1795. There he engaged his patients in 'repeated, probing, personal conversations', taking detailed notes as they spoke.[34] Pathological ideas and emotions (the 'secrets of the heart') were identified and, where possible, gently challenged.[35] Pinel and the Tukes were passionate believers in the efficacy of *douceur*, 'judicious kindness' in Samuel Tuke's phrase,[36] and their curative optimism was very strong. Prior to the eighteenth century, lunacy had been anathematised as a debased, reprobate or even bestial state. Enlightened opinion in the eighteenth century reconceived it as an ailment to which any person – even a king, as in the case of George III – might succumb. Now moral therapists insisted that the disease was only partial, that lunatics retained intellectual and moral powers which, if properly acted upon in a supportive environment, would replace 'morbid feelings . . . [with] healthy trains of thought'.[37] Ordinary life, especially family life, was full of travails and 'excitements' that wracked the fragile mind.[38] A well-conducted asylum was a sanctum where demented minds could be soothed into sanity:

> calmness will come; hope will revive; satisfaction will prevail. Some unmanageable tempers, some violent or sullen patients, there must always be; but much of the violence, much of the ill-humour, almost all the disposition to meditate mischievous or fatal revenge, or self-destruction will disappear . . . .and despair itself will sometimes be found to give place to cheerfulness or secure tranquility. [The asylum is] where humanity, if anywhere on earth, shall reign supreme.[39]

At the York Retreat – the Quaker asylum founded in 1796 by the philanthropist William Tuke and made famous by his grandson Samuel in his 1813 *Description of the Retreat* – there were no high walls or window bars. Inmates were treated as members of the Quaker 'family' and

---

[34] Weiner, '*La Geste de Pinel*', 235.

[35] Goldstein, *Console and Classify*, 88.

[36] Tuke, *Description of the Retreat*, 168.

[37] Scull, 'Historical Reflections', 3. See also Tuke, *Description of the Retreat*, 133–4.

[38] Arguing for the institutional confinement of the insane, some early champions of the asylum system claimed that removal from family life was, for many lunatics, a prerequisite to recovery (Scull, 'Historical Reflections', 3). Historians have tended to dismiss such arguments as self-serving, but it seems very likely, as Elizabeth Bott suggests, that for some inmates the asylum served as a refuge from miserable homes. Bott tells the story of one female patient who, during a period of turmoil in her hospital, remarked to Bott: 'There are so many changes and upsets here now that I might as well go home' ('Hospital and Society', 128).

[39] Conolly, quoted in Scull, 'Historical Reflections', 4.

encouraged to participate in the religious life of the community.[40] Whipping and manacling were banned, although milder forms of restraint were permitted as a last resort. Bleeding, purging, drugging and other popular medical treatments were mostly eschewed in favour of rational conversation (to wean patients away from mad ideas) and appeals to the patient's moral sensibility. Like Pinel, the Tukes were agnostic about whether madness had a biophysical component but, as William Tuke testified to the 1815 Select Committee on lunacy, experience had demonstrated that treatments directed at the body had 'very little effect' in 'cases of mental derangement'.[41]

Mad-doctors, pushed onto the back foot, were generally hostile.[42] But lay reformers and legislators were more persuadable, and by the mid-nineteenth century a dilute version of moral treatment, combining non-restraint with some traditional medical remedies, had become public policy.[43] In 1845, the government made it mandatory for local authorities across England and Wales to provide institutional care for pauper lunatics, then mostly languishing in workhouses. A Lunacy Commission was created to regulate all institutions catering to the insane. In 1847, the commissioners reported very favourably on the 'substitution of mild and gentle treatment in place of the old method of mechanical coercion', and by 1854, twenty-seven of the thirty county asylums in England and Wales had abandoned mechanical restraints.[44] Visitors to the Hanwell Asylum, where Conolly had pioneered non-restraint in the 1840s, were delighted to witness the inmates gardening, attending chapel and even dancing at a Christmas party without 'a single circumstance occurring to mar [their] happiness'.[45]

These happy times did not last long, as we shall see. But how happy were they? Like other aspects of asylum history, the moral treatment tradition has been contentious. Critics have raised questions about the continued use of physical restraints, the quality of nursing staff, the uneasy balance between care and custodialism.[46] The psycho-relational method pioneered in the moral-treatment asylums has also come in for criticism – most famously from Michel Foucault, who in an excoriating attack on the

[40] Digby, *Madness*, 37–50.
[41] Scull, *Most Solitary*, 192.
[42] *Ibid.*, 190–3.
[43] Leonard Smith, *Cure, Comfort and Safe Custody: Public Lunatic Asylums in Early Nineteenth Century England* (Leicester, 1999), 275–6.
[44] John Walton, 'Pauper Lunatics in Victorian England', in *Madhouses, Mad-doctors and Madmen: The Social History of Psychiatry in the Victorian Era*, ed. Andrew Scull (Philadelphia, 1981), 168.
[45] Harriet Martineau, *A History of the Peace* (1858), book 3, 304; *London Illustrated News*, Jan. 1848.
[46] See Walton, 'Pauper Lunatics', 182–92, for a detailed account of these concerns as they arose in relation to conditions in Lancaster Asylum between 1816 and 1870.

up-close therapeutics practised by Pinel and the Tukes, charged them with fostering a malign complicity between the madman and the practitioner who 'begin to form a strange sort of couple, an undivided unity . . . the root cell of madness'.[47] This therapeutic coupling, Foucault went on to argue, paved the way to Freudian psychoanalysis, in which 'all the structures integrated by Pinel and Tuke into confinement' became 'concentrated' in the analytic relationship. 'All the powers that had been shared out in the collective existence of the asylum' were 'appropriated' by the analyst, Foucault fulminated, in a 'gigantic moral imprisonment'. Freud thereby 'freed the patient from . . . asylum existence' only to bring the spirit of the asylum into the 'psychoanalytic situation': a paradox that Foucault clearly relished even as he decried it.[48] In fact, the differences between moral treatment and psychoanalysis were manifold, but Foucault was right to draw a connection.[49] I want now to look at this in more detail.

Foucault's critique of moral treatment, in the penultimate chapter of the *History of Madness*, took him far beyond asylum history, or even madness history as it is generally conceived, into a set of profound meditations on the vicissitudes of human subjectivity. The chapter brought to a head all the paradoxes and inversions that made this extraordinary book such a treasure trove for contrarians. In an anticipation of what he would later describe as subjectification, Foucault denounced Pinellian *douceur* as psychological authoritarianism. But the authority that moral therapists imposed on the lunatic, Foucault argued, was not external but internal; it was the lunatic's own psyche 'in thrall to the pedagogy of good sense, truth and morality'.[50] What moral treatment inflicted on the madman, via his relationship with his would-be healer (which, in the case of moral-treatment asylums, was more often a lay attendant than a medical physician), was a new agony of self-awareness about his mental state and its impact on others. For William Tuke, Foucault wrote

> the liberation of the alienated, the abolition of constraints . . . were mere justifications . . . In fact, Tuke created an asylum where he substituted the stifling anguish of responsibility for the free terror of madness; the fear was no longer of what lay on the other side of the prison door, but what raged instead beneath the seals of conscience.[51]

[47] Foucault, *History of Madness*, 507.
[48] *Ibid.*, 510–11.
[49] For a brief discussion of these differences in relation to therapeutic practices at the York Retreat, see Roy Porter, *Mind-Forg'd Manacles: A History of Madness in England from the Restoration to the Regency* (1987), 225–6. As Porter says, the Tukes were not concerned with exploring the unconscious minds of their patients but in 'making them want to be good'. However, like most historians of moral treatment Porter underestimated the innovativeness of the Tukes' emphasis on the therapeutic relationship as a curative agent.
[50] Foucault, *History of Madness*, 483.
[51] *Ibid.*, 484–5.

Here Foucault arraigned Tuke's Quaker convictions, but the argument was not about religious guilt but about self-judgement in general, the 'mind-forg'd manacles' of conscience. Within the lunatic/attendant couple, where the madman's subjectivity became lodged, shackles gave way to self-restraint, surveillance and coercion to self-policing. The inmates of the York Retreat were continuously observed and monitored, but under Tuke's moral ministrations this external gaze became an inward gaze, until these lunatics could not 'fail to see themselves for what they were'.[52]

There is much more to Foucault's critique of moral treatment than this, a good deal of which is historically inaccurate.[53] But his emphasis on the therapeutic relationship as the locus of what Andrew Scull calls the 'curative utopianism' of moral treatment is surely right, although Foucault missed the intellectual roots of this optimism. Pinel and Tuke's faith in the healing power of the patient/practitioner interaction was an Enlightenment product, an offshoot of enlightened moral sentimentalism. Moral sentimentalists – who included such luminaries as David Hume, Adam Smith and Jean-Jacques Rousseau – posited a natural sympathy between human beings, an innate fellow-feeling variously dubbed 'sensibility', 'benevolence', or 'social affection'.[54] Pinel and Tuke, and Conolly after them, believed that even the most demented mind retained 'unextinguished remains' of such 'valuable feelings',[55] which they sought to reignite through a combination of moral example and the exercise of their own sympathetic capabilities.[56] Pinel revered Rousseau and was an enthusiastic reader of Adam Smith's *Theory of Moral Sentiments*, a bible of enlightened sentimentalism.[57] The Tukes were devout believers in the healing powers of Christian love, combining this with Pinellian *douceur* and enlightened sentimentalism to produce a model of individualised care delivered in an atmosphere of quasi-familial intimacy.[58] Their success rate was said to be high, demonstrating, Samuel Tuke claimed, 'the almost infinite power of judicious kindness and sympathy on disordered minds'.[59]

This power could be coercive. Some madmen evinced no social feeling, Pinel conceded, and in such cases 'it is necessary to subjugate first,

---

[52] *Ibid.*, 499.

[53] Porter, *Mind-Forg'd Manacles*, 5–9; Andrew Scull, *Insanity of Place/the Place of Insanity* (Abingdon, 2006), 42.

[54] Adam Phillips and Barbara Taylor, *On Kindness* (2009), 26–38.

[55] Conolly, *Treatment of the Insane*, 115.

[56] According to Samuel Tuke, one of the most important qualifications for an asylum manager was 'a ready sympathy with man, and a habit of conscientious control of the selfish feelings and passions' (quoted in Digby, *Madness*, 27).

[57] Goldstein, *Console and Classify*, 97; Aubrey Lewis, 'Philippe Pinel and the English', *Proceedings of the Royal Society of Medicine*, 48, 8 (1955), 584.

[58] Digby, *Madness*, 37, 51, 58–61.

[59] *Ibid.*, 105.

and encourage them afterward'. For '[w]hat good could come of ... *douceur*' with lunatics who 'regarded other men as particles of dust?'[60] Like previous generations of mad-doctors, Pinel was proud of his ability to gain emotional sway over his patients, while insisting that such domination must be 'exempt from feelings of animosity or anger'.[61] The Tukes similarly aimed to 'domineer for good purposes', using techniques of punishment and reward adapted from Quaker childrearing practices (although Samuel Tuke also warned against treating lunatics 'in a childish manner').[62] So Foucault's diatribe against moral treatment contains a kernel of truth, encased in a Dionysian fantasy of madness as untamed libido and psychotherapy as inherently carceral – a 'confinement without confinement' as Derrida later described psychoanalysis.[63] But one does not need to be mad, or to be a card-carrying Freudian, to know that madness is at bottom a self-incarceration. The therapeutic relationship that Foucault excoriates may not be as gentle or ethically unambiguous as the moral therapists imagined (or as transcendently illuminating as some psychoanalytic enthusiasts fondly believe), but the guilt and pain that it releases are the patient's own; what Foucault derides as the 'miracle cure' of the disclosed self has nothing miraculous about it.[64] 'To know the worst about oneself', the psychoanalyst Marion Milner once wrote, '[is] like the breaking down of a prison wall'.[65]

The moral treatment phase of British asylum history was shortlived. In the second half of the nineteenth century, asylum populations rose rapidly, as pauper lunatics crowded in from the workhouses, and the wards 'silted up' with the 'chronically crazy'.[66] Moral therapy collapsed under the combined pressures of overcrowding, 'cheeseparing economies, overworked medical superintendents ... untrained, undersupervised nursing staff'.[67] By the late 1860s, most asylums had reintroduced straitjacketing and other physical restraints.[68] By the end of the nineteenth century, the curative optimism of the asylum pioneers had vanished entirely, to be replaced by a hereditarian determinism as gloomy as the decaying buildings housing the 'degenerates' and 'defectives' that lunatics had now become.[69] Care collapsed into custodialism, as the mad were

---

[60] Goldstein, *Console and Classify*, 86.
[61] *Ibid.*, 86, 99. See also Patrick Vandermeersch, '"*Les Mythes d'Origine*" in the History of Psychiatry', in *Discovering the History of Psychiatry*, ed. Micale and Porter, 222.
[62] Digby, *Madness*, 61; Tuke, *Description of the Retreat*, 59.
[63] Joel Whitebook, 'Against Interiority: Foucault's Struggle with Psychoanalysis', in *The Cambridge Companion to Foucault*, ed. Gary Cutting, 2nd edn (2005), 323.
[64] Foucault, *History of Madness*, 506–11.
[65] Joanna Field [Marion Milner], *On Not Being Able to Paint* (Los Angeles, 1957), 92.
[66] Scull, *Insanity of Place*, 82.
[67] Walton, 'Pauper Lunatics', 91.
[68] Murphy, *After the Asylums*, 37.
[69] Scull, *Insanity of Place*, 82.

pronounced irredeemable, 'tainted persons', and the asylums became their prisons.[70]

The fate of Colney Hatch asylum – *my* asylum, as I cannot help thinking of it – illustrates well this sad collapse of vision. Even before construction began on Colney Hatch, John Conolly was warning the Middlesex officials that the asylum's projected size of 1,000 inmates would militate against the 'close and intimate' care that lunatics required. Wards would be unvisited, patients neglected and 'many good principles ... hopelessly given up'.[71] In 1849, the foundation stone was laid in a flurry of moral-treatment propaganda. No hand or foot would be bound at Colney Hatch, the chairman of the Middlesex magistrates declared at the ceremony, for here was no mere gaol but 'a *curative* institution, and ... we anticipate that, with the advantages which this asylum can command, it will soon acquire a European reputation'.[72] The asylum opened in 1851, the year of the Great Exhibition. People coming to London for the Exhibition were urged to visit, to admire the asylum's lovely grounds and elaborate Italianate frontage, to peer down its endless corridors (the main corridor was a third of a mile, the longest in Europe) and to witness at first hand the happy condition of its inmates, labouring peaceably in the communal farms, gardens and craft workshops.[73] A decade later, such visitors could, if they wished, attend a 'lunatic ball' (fifteen of these were held in 1868 alone, along with magic lantern exhibitions, concerts, lectures and plays) or the ever-popular summer fête. So idyllic did all this seem that it left more than one early visitor convinced that Colney Hatch was a model environment for the sane as well as the insane. The only anxiety was that patients enjoying a steady diet of such delights would never want to leave.[74]

Yet almost as soon as Colney Hatch opened, the Lunacy Commission was expressing concern about overcrowding and insanitation, its dark prison-like wards and poor structural condition. By 1865, the asylum's population had doubled, mechanical restraints were in use, and the overall atmosphere, especially in the 'refractory wards', was so oppressive that the commissioners were moved to declare that '[i]t would be difficult to instance more perfect examples of what the wards of an asylum ... should not be, than are presented here'.[75] The downward spiral continued relentlessly through the rest of the century and into the next, through two world wars and the foundation of the NHS. The arrival of the NHS put

---

[70] Barham, *Closing the Asylum*, 75–7; Murphy, *After the Asylums*, 36–41.

[71] Conolly, *Letter to Benjamin Rotch*, 21, 14, 12.

[72] Richard Hunter and Ida Macalpine, *Psychiatry for the Poor: 1851 Colney Hatch Asylum-Friern Hospital 1973* (1974), 24.

[73] *Ibid.*, 25–9.

[74] *Ibid.*, 44–5.

[75] *Ibid.*, 86; Barham, *Closing the Asylum*, 2.

the medical staff of the asylum – now renamed Friern Mental Hospital – on an equal footing with doctors and nurses in general hospitals, but otherwise effected few changes.[76] The mid-1950s saw admissions into UK mental hospitals reach a new high, including admissions into Friern which were running at three times the pre-war rate.[77] The succeeding decade saw some improvements to the hospital, including the introduction of psychotherapeutic treatments;[78] but in 1966, Friern was hit by a major scandal when Barbara Robb, a campaigner for the elderly, revealed serious abuses in the care of the demented elderly there. Robb's report, and the publicity and government inquiry that followed, led to calls for closure, although no official action was taken until over a decade later.[79]

Not all mental hospitals were faring so badly. In the 1950s and 1960s, a wave of innovative energy swept throughout the asylum system, with the introduction of new treatments and rehabilitation programmes, the unlocking of wards and a revitalisation of moral therapy, especially among psychiatrists with a psychodynamic bent.[80] David Clark, the psychoanalytically trained medical superintendent of Fulbourne Mental Hospital, was a leader in this moral-treatment renaissance, introducing psychosocial therapies that soon became very influential under the banner of the 'therapeutic community' movement.[81] In his memoir of Fulbourne, Clark recalled the transition from custodialism to the therapeutic-community regimen: 'It was more satisfying to intelligent and sensitive staff and was more humane and dignified. However, it did require more staff and it was perplexing and exhausting work. To open oneself fully to the tortured feelings of the deeply mentally ill is very disturbing.'[82]

[76] *Ibid.*, 84. Despite its integration into the NHS, patient costs at Friern for the remaining decades of its existence were kept well below levels at general hospitals (Stewart, 'Community Care', 308).

[77] Bott, 'Hospital and Society', 97, 102, 103, 106; Stewart, 'Community Care', 27.

[78] In 1969, the Head of Nursing Services at Friern noted proudly that 'all treatments available in the psychiatric field' were currently at use in the hospital, including individual and group psychotherapy (but not psychoanalysis, which was judged 'too expensive of time to be a viable proposition') (*Nursing Mirror*, Oct. 1969). The psychotherapeutic treatments were mostly delivered in Halliwick House, a small inpatient unit located in a separate building on the Friern grounds. Unlike the vast majority of Friern inmates, Halliwick patients tended to be drawn from the professional middle class.

[79] Robb, *Sans Everything*; Stewart, 'Community Care', 279–80. The uncatalogued files from Friern deposited in the Royal Free Hospital Archives Centre at the time of the hospital's closure include files pertaining to the Robb scandal.

[80] Peter Barham, 'From the Asylum to the Community: The Mental Patient in Postwar Britain', in *Cultures of Psychiatry*, ed. Gijswift-Hofstra and Porter, 224–6.

[81] David H. Clark, *Social Therapy* (1974); David H. Clark, *The Story of a Mental Hospital: Fulbourn 1858–1983* (1996).

[82] Clark, *Story of a Mental Hospital*, 180.

Similar developments were occurring in other UK mental hospitals, and the sector was gripped by a resurgent curative optimism.[83] It was at this point that the government, in the person of Enoch Powell, announced its intention to close the hospitals – a timing later described by Roy Porter as a 'rich irony': 'our age, which has seen the agitation for the closing of traditional asylums come to fruition, has also been the time when many of them have been, at long last, most therapeutically innovative and successful'.[84]

By the late 1970s, asylums everywhere were running down, with wards closing and their former inhabitants out on the street. By the mid-1980s, the hospital population had declined by two-thirds: a truly astonishing rate of reduction when one realises that it was achieved, as Peter Sedgwick wrote at the time, 'through the creation of a rhetoric of "community care facilities" whose influence over policy in hospital admission and discharge has been particularly remarkable when one considers that they do not, in the actual world, exist'.[85] Opposition MPs declared community care a 'catastrophe': a judgement later endorsed by a leading figure in UK mental health politics, Baroness Elaine Murphy, who titled her account of community care between 1962 and 1990, 'The Disaster Years'.[86]

Friern's closure was announced in the midst of this debacle. In July 1983, the hospital learned its fate from a televised news announcement.[87] Staff were very shocked. Significant improvements had been made to the hospital in the wake of the Robb scandal, and doctors and nurses had no inkling of any closure plans.[88] In 1980, the Hospital Management Team had even issued a glossy brochure, *Friern 2000*, celebrating the hospital's achievements and looking forward to the next millennium.[89] But the North East Thames Regional Health Authority had done its feasibility studies and added up its sums, and Friern faced the axe. The decade that followed was a wretched one for the staff, some of whom mounted a robust anti-closure campaign but were soon outgunned by their opponents.[90]

---

[83] Bott, 'Hospital and Society', 104–5.

[84] Roy Porter, 'Introduction', in Clark, *Story of a Mental Hospital*, x.

[85] Sedgwick, *Psycho Politics*, 192–3. Sedgwick's assessment of the situation was endorsed by a Parliamentary Select Committee, which reported in 1985 that 'the pace of removal of hospital facilities for mental illness has far outrun the provision of services in the community to replace them' (cited in Barham, *Closing the Asylum*, xii). 'Any fool can close a long-stay hospital', the Committee went on to comment, but 'it takes more time and trouble to do it properly and compassionately'.

[86] Murphy, *After the Asylums*, 60–85.

[87] Stewart, 'Community Care', 291.

[88] *Ibid.*, 293.

[89] LMA, H/12/CH/A/30/6.

[90] Writing about the situation in Friern in 1985, the Chair of its Medical Committee, Rosalind Furlong, described plummeting staff morale: 'When such staff are already working under pressure in adverse conditions, this can have a profound effect' (Rosalind C. Furlong,

'We were quite a militant group', Doris Hollander, a consultant on my ward who led the campaign, later recalled: '[but] [t]here were other powerful organisations saying "It has got to happen now" . . . There was no shortage of people who could point to all the terrible things in the old hospitals and disregard their positive side.'[91] Hollander's views were aired in parliament, where in July 1990, the Labour MP for Islington North, Jeremy Corbyn, described a state of 'panic' among patients at Friern, and demanded assurance that the hospital's closure would not proceed unless adequate accommodation for its inmates could be guaranteed.[92] A few of these patients and former patients made their voices heard, attending meetings with Friern managers where they expressed support for the hospital's closure mixed, however, with strong concern about post-closure provision.[93] Even the local vicar got in on the act, collecting fifty signatures on an anti-closure petition.[94]

Meanwhile, in 1985, a team of researchers moved into Friern, under the aegis of a government-funded study into the impact of the hospital's closure on its former residents. The Team for the Assessment of Psychiatric Services (TAPS) researchers followed the progress of inmates into staffed group homes over a five-year period and reported, for the most part positively, on their lives there.[95] The people being studied, however, had been selected for their capability while many others, more disabled and harder to place, remained in hospital; some were still there on the night before Friern closed.[96] Moreover – and more important for the long-term consequences of the hospital's closure – over a third of the

'Closure of Large Mental Hospitals – Practicable or Desirable?', *Bulletin of the Royal College of Psychiatrists*, 9 (1985), 130–4).

[91] 'In Conversation with Doris Hollander', *Psychiatric Bulletin*, 28 (2004), 18; Stewart, 'Community Care', 294.

[92] House of Commons Debates, 6 July 1990, 1.15pm (www.theyworkforyou.com/debates).

[93] No one involved in the hospital's closure seems to have made any systematic effort to ascertain the patients' views. Those patients who met with management wanted to see the hospital shut down, but were very anxious about what would become of ex-inmates; some, like the service-user activist and academic Diana Rose, became actively involved in supporting patients through the transition into community care (Dr Diana Rose, personal communication).

[94] Dylan Tomlinson, *Utopia, Community Care and the Retreat from the Asylums* (Milton Keynes, 1991), 135.

[95] Tomlinson, *Utopia*; Julian Leff, ed., *Care in the Community: Illusion or Reality?* (Chichester, 1997); Julian Leff, 'Why is Care in the Community Perceived as a Failure?', *British Journal of Psychiatry*, 179 (2001), 381–3; Dylan Tomlinson and John Carrier, eds., *Asylum in the Community* (1996); Christine McCourt Perring, *The Experience of Psychiatric Hospital Closure* (Avebury, Aldershot, 1993); Barham, *Closing the Asylum*, 21–4.

[96] 'Friern Hospital Decommissioning Report', Royal Free Hospital Archives Centre (uncatalogued papers relating to Friern Hospital's closure).

decanted patients required readmission during the five-year follow-up.[97] Alternative inpatient provision was radically insufficient, and seriously ill patients entering the hospital in its twilight days faced an accelerating crisis of resources. Many of these 'new long-stay' patients, as they were awkwardly dubbed, did not qualify for the new community facilities: what was to become of them, when Friern's doors closed for the last time?[98]

In 1989, I was a likely candidate for 'new long stay' status, or at least that was certainly how I saw myself when I entered Friern for the third time and remained there for over six months. My stints in Friern came midway through the closure process, and the evidence of this was everywhere. Most of the ward nurses had left and been replaced by agency staff.[99] The ward across the stairwell from mine was empty, having been burned out in a major fire shortly before I arrived. Corridors were sealed off, therapy rooms locked up, the old apple orchard was choked with weeds. The kiln in the pottery workroom broke down and was not repaired; a little pot that I left in the firing queue was thrown away.

Yet for me Friern was truly an asylum. I entered it on my knees: I could no longer do ordinary life, and giving up the struggle was an incalculable relief. My home in the hospital was a locked acute ward with a deservedly violent reputation: a Dickensian barrack of crumbled brickwork and peeling walls, reeking with fag smoke and teeming with ghosts; but for me it was a sanctuary. I settled in quickly, got to know people, acquired a lot of new survival skills (some of which have proven surprisingly useful since, especially in university committees). I was very wretched most of the time, and often frightened, but I felt safe from what I feared the most: myself. This was a huge plus, and I wanted to stay forever.

People like me who end up in the bin – that is, educated, middle-class people – if they write about the experience later on, often sound a bit like tourists on an alien planet. But I was no tourist. By the end of the 1980s, I was deeply embedded in the world of the chronically mentally ill. I had lost my home, and was living in a psychiatric hostel. When I was not in Friern, I was at the Whittington day hospital (later made notorious by Clare Allen in her bestselling novel *Poppy Shakespeare*) or at the Pine Street Day Centre in Finsbury. I still had friends and connections from earlier days, but I spent most of my time with other mental health users with whom I often felt more comfortable than with old chums (although

[97] Julian Leff, 'The TAPS Project: A Report on 13 Years of Research, 1985–1998', *Psychiatric Bulletin*, 24 (2000), 165.

[98] G. Thornicroft, O. Margolius and D. Jones, 'The TAPS Project 6: New Long-Stay Psychiatric Patients and Social Deprivation', *British Journal of Psychiatry*, 161 (1992), 621–4; Rosalind Furlong, 'Haven Within or Without the Hospital Gate: A Reappraisal of Asylum Provision in Theory and Practice', in *Asylum*, ed. Tomlinson and Carrier, 158–62.

[99] Stewart, 'Community Care', 294–7.

I should add here that old chums were wonderfully kind and supportive). It wasn't a good life, but it was a do-able life: and in its best moments it yielded feelings of care and belonging which were new to me. 'I think it will be good for you to stay here for a while', my Friern psychiatrist told me in the summer of 1989, 'you will discover that you can be looked after, and that will be important to you.' She was right on both counts.

Mental hospitals like Friern were places of horror for many. Recorded testimony from former Friern inmates speaks of coercion and neglect: of nurses punishing awkward patients with violent drug injections; of beatings; of psychiatrists ignoring or deriding patients.[100] I witnessed abuses like these, especially of 'sectioned' patients (those legally detained under the terms of the 1983 Mental Health Act). My voluntary status and, even more, my middle classness protected me from the worst of such cruelties, although I too was briefly targeted by a sadistic nurse who made my life hell for a time. No one who has ever been subjected to such behaviours is likely to wax nostalgic about the asylum system, or to mourn its demise – and I do not.

And yet: I also received a lot of very effective looking-after during my years as a mental patient. Living in the bin was tough, but it gave me some shelter from my darkest self and, very importantly, the friendship of other patients, which made my days tolerable. My psychiatrist, who was psychoanalytically oriented, was intelligent and kind. During the three plus years I was under her care, I was also seeing a psychoanalyst five times a week. Like many severely ill people in psychoanalysis, I became abjectly dependent on my analyst. This dependence, and the painful therapeutic dialogues to which it gave rise, were the means by which I learned the sources of my misery, and gradually made my peace with them.

In 1990, this therapeutic education went through a crisis which proved to be a turning-point. The following year, I left my last day centre, and in 1992, I was discharged from the UK mental health system.

Friern closed in April 1993. Two years later it reopened as Princess Park Manor, 'a supremely elegant' residence of some 200 apartments. The gorgeous asylum frontage and part of the grounds were retained, but otherwise all traces of the old asylum were obliterated – bar the original commemorative plaque, which now overlooks the glossy reception area outside the Manor's gym.

In 1996, a group of film-makers came to Princess Park Manor to interview the first batch of apartment owners.[101] They brought with them a few former patients, including one whom I knew slightly – a bright, pugnacious Mind activist. The film that resulted is riveting. As the

---

[100] 'Testimony: Inside Stories of Mental Health Care', British Sound Library Archive.

[101] The film, *Asylum*, directed by Rebecca Frayn for Cutting Edge, was screened by Channel 4 in March 1999.

two groups of inhabitants chatter to camera, a slow movement toward each other occurs. The patients are thoughtful, humorous, fluent. One, a former theatre-worker, describes the hospital as having been 'hell on earth'. Finding himself in the gutted main hall, he abruptly opens his mouth and sings his heart out. 'I can go now', he tells the camera. 'I'm not frightened any more.' Another, an elderly man, looks wistfully at the carcase of his ward, my 'second home', and reminisces about his time on the Friern football team. Meanwhile, a feng shui consultant is busy tapping for energy sources in the walls. 'Phew!' she cries, knocking hard, 'Something sure was going on here!' Are they afraid of ghosts? the film-makers ask the new residents. None will admit to this, but all emphasise their sympathy for the mentally ill. 'My friends say I should have been in an institution like this long ago', one man chortles. Quizzed about their reasons for choosing the Manor, some become remarkably self-revealing, one retired man describing the 'mad' world beyond its gates as too stressful for him, while a divorcée admits that she hopes such a self-contained housing development – with its fancy leisure facilities, café and private bus service to the train station and shops – will bring her new friends and romances. She had been feeling pretty suicidal before she moved in, she confides. How ironic, my Mind acquaintance comments to the camera, that people are now willing to pay large sums of money to live in a place that advertises itself as somewhere that you 'never need to leave'. With its manned security gate, high tech locking systems and omnipresent surveillance cameras, Princess Park Manor aims to keep out what Friern was meant to keep in: but not all the devils that beset individuals are so easily contained. Yet it is good to be reminded, as this lovely film does, of the miseries and frailties common to all humankind, whether hopefully mad or hopelessly sane.[102]

I was fortunate not to need an asylum by the time Friern closed. I would not like to have been left to the tender mercies of 'the community'. Reading mental health policy documents today – with their warm talk of 'connected communities' and 'shared visions'[103] – it would be easy to imagine that the up-close therapeutic regimen pioneered by Pinel and the Tukes, and revived by the therapeutic-community movement in the 1950s, was once again in the ascendant. In fact, nothing could be further from the truth. In the quick-fix, drug-based culture of present-day psychiatry, the community, in Peter Barham words, 'possesses null value':[104] it is not a site of belonging and support; it is just where people go when they are sufficiently 'recovered' to negotiate daily life without posing a

---

[102] An earlier version of this account of the filming of Princess Park Manor appeared in the *London Review of Books*, 8 May 2003 (under the pseudonym 'Eve Blake').
[103] Mental Health Division Department of Health, *New Horizons* (see n. 25).
[104] Barham, *Closing the Asylum*, 13.

danger to themselves or others. The notion that decanting people from institutions automatically improves their lives is a convenient myth. 'There is an assumption', the TAPS researchers wrote in the run-up to Friern's closure, 'that the quality of life for those who are relatively independent in the community is by definition greater than the quality of life for those . . . in asylum-type settings. This assumption is not easily supported.'[105]

In the UK today, community mental health services are delivered to their recipients as 'care packages'. Care is individuated and disconnected from any communal body; the enforced sociality of the asylum has been replaced by the insularity of the healthcare consumer. Sociability among service users is not encouraged: day centres of the kind that I attended, and where I made some very close friends, are now mostly closed.[106] Service users are meant to integrate into the community, which for people with serious mental disorders can be a cruelly daunting ambition. The much-touted independence of the community-based user thus often equals a life of lonely isolation, with a television for companionship.[107] It is an extraordinary fact that – in a modern world acknowledged by all to be fragmented, anomic, and psychologically demanding of even the most capable – mentally ill people are increasingly expected to thrive (to achieve 'wellness' in another buzzword) with a minimum of day-to-day support. Most people in twenty-first century Britain spend most of their lives in institutions of one sort or another – schools, offices, factories, universities – and few of us could manage emotionally without the sense of belonging that these institutions provide. The old mental hospitals had plenty wrong with them – horribly wrong, in many cases – but they nurtured communities of their own whose disappearance has been painful for many. People, with or without mental disorders, depend on other people to lead a decent life: we do not really need history to tell us this, but history can show what happens when we forget it. The asylum story is not a good one, but if the demise of the asylum means the death of effective and humane mental health care, then this will be more than a bad ending to the story: it will be a tragedy.

---

[105] D. W. Jones, D. Tomlinson and J. Anderson, 'Community and Asylum Care: *plus ça change*', *Journal of the Royal Society of Medicine*, 84 (May 1991), 253.

[106] See n. 26.

[107] On the television as a 'friend', see Tomlinson, *Utopia*, 165–6. One ex-inmate, who spent his days alone in his flat in front of the television, told a researcher that it was just like living in a hospital ward 'but with nobody else there' (Dr Felicity Callard, personal communication).

ROYAL HISTORICAL SOCIETY
REPORT OF COUNCIL
SESSION 2010–2011

Officers and Council

- At the Anniversary Meeting on 26 November 2010 the Officers of the Society were re-elected.
- The Vice-Presidents retiring under By-law XVII were Mr R Fisher and Professor D M Palliser. Dr R Baldock, BA, PhD and Professor C Kidd, BA, DPhil were elected to replace them.
- The Officers retiring under By-law XV were Professor J P Parry, Honorary Treasurer and Professor M Cragoe, Honorary Director of Communications. Professor M J Hughes, BA, MSc, PhD and Dr E Griffin, BA, MA, PhD were elected, respectively, to replace them.
- A new Office was created under By-law XV of Honorary Academic Editor (BBIH). Professor S J C Taylor, MA, PhD was elected to this Office.
- The Members of Council retiring under By-law XX were Professor S Connolly, Professor T Hitchcock, and Professor N Miller. Professor D Feldman, MA, PhD, Professor A Musson, MA, MusB, LLM, PhD and Dr A Thacker, MA, DPhil, FSA were elected in their place.
- The Society's administrative staff consists of Sue Carr, Executive Secretary and Melanie Ransom, Administrative Secretary.
- Kingston Smith LLP were re-appointed auditors for the year 2010–2011 under By-law XXXIX.
- Brewin Dolphin Securities were re-appointed to manage the Society's investment funds.

Activities of the Society during the year

The Annual Report contains individual reports of the activities of the seven Committees which support the work of Council: Research Policy, Education Policy (formerly Teaching Policy), General Purposes, Publications, Finance, Membership and Research Support. The remarks which now follow are a preface to these more detailed reports.

Throughout the year the Society has maintained its prominent role in defending and advancing the interests of the discipline and the profession.

As noted last year, the government's research funding strategy, announced in April 2009, protected science funding and seriously disadvantaged some high-scoring History Departments and their institutions. In 2009–10 we saw individual institutions' reactions to the difficult financial situation, including threats to posts in History and related disciplines. In 2010–11 these concerns were overtaken by fears for the whole HE Humanities sector, following the Browne report (October 2010) and the consequent fierce debate about funding and student fees. Neither the short- nor the long-term effects of these drastic changes in the structure of funding on the study of History at universities and the university system as a whole can be clearly forecast. Of similar concern to Council and the Society is the increasing focus on 'strategic' research funding, and the cutbacks, by several different funders, of the small grants schemes vital to much independent, curiosity-driven historical research. The President, Vice-Presidents, Officers and Councillors have contributed to public and private debate on these issues, and are seeking to develop contacts with government to pursue these concerns.

While the Historical Association takes the lead on History in schools, this is another important concern of the Society (curriculum, content, teacher training, continuing professional development of teachers). The President, Professor Peter Mandler, Vice-President and Chair of the Education Policy Committee, and other members of Council met with representatives from several UK examination boards on 29 September 2010, to discuss recent developments in the A-Level History curricula and examinations. This was the latest in a series of annual meetings. On 22 November 2010, the President hosted a dinner with Michael Gove MP, Secretary of State for Education, and a number of distinguished historians. The A-Level syllabus was one topic of discussion. Mr Gove promised to attend a future event organised by the Society. Council also later discussed The Royal Society of Edinburgh Advice Paper: The Teaching of History in Scottish Schools, and its usefulness to the English debate.

The shape of HEFCE's future Research Excellence Framework (REF 2014) has become clearer, and the membership of panels and sub-panels has been announced. An ad-hoc subcommittee of Council led by the President and Ms Joanna Innes, Vice-President and Chair of the Research Policy Committee, worked very hard making nominations to these panels, many of which were accepted. The contribution of publications, research environment, and 'impact' to the overall REF assessment was settled but aspects of the assessment criteria and the working methods of the panels are still being worked out; consultation with HEIs closed on 5 October 2011, and the Society has made a detailed response.

The Society is maintaining its contacts with AHRC, and has responded to a number of developments and policy statements. The announcement of further devolution of BGP funding (in this case for research students' travel and research expenses) to HEIs, at a flat rate of £200 per student, arouses concern that unless institutions put in place policies to guard against it, this could disadvantage those History research students who need significant sums for overseas travel and research. Research Support Committee has noted a rise in applications to the Society for travel grants and is seeking to ensure that HEIs are meeting their obligations to their own students. AHRC announced a reduction, allocated by HEI and not by discipline or subject, in the previously-notified numbers of funded students for 2011. AHRC has also decided to phase out its smaller research grant schemes, in favour of larger grants and a focus on 'research leadership'. Inside and outside Council there has been considerable discussion of government's role in directing research activity, the Haldane principle, and the incorporation of themes such as 'the Big Society' into research council policy statements. In all these areas the Society's representatives have been active and vocal. The annual meetings formerly held between representatives of ESRC and a group of relevant History societies, led by the Economic History Society, have been revived and the first meeting is scheduled for November 2011.

The society maintains good relations with The National Archives through formal and informal meetings, especially between the President and the CEO of TNA, Mr Oliver Morley, although the Society is not formally represented on the Lord Chancellor's Advisory Council on National Records and Archives. Collaboration with TNA also continues in the form of the Gerald Aylmer seminar, held this year on 25 February at the Institute of Historical Research, focusing on the understanding and use of medieval and early modern archives, with two panel discussions and an attendance of some fifty people. The IHR's support for the event was very welcome, and it is hoped that the organisation of the seminar will in future become a wider partnership.

The online Bibliography of British and Irish History, in partnership with the Institute of Historical Research and Brepols, has now been running on a subscription basis for over a year, with a very encouraging level of subscriptions. Professor Stephen Taylor was elected to the new honorary post of Academic Editor of the BBIH.

Following initiatives suggested last year, the Society has begun to record and podcast its lectures. Discussions of the Society's website, and the ways in which it can be made more useful and attractive to Fellows, are continuing. Dr Emma Griffin was elected Honorary Director of Communications, in succession to Professor Matthew Cragoe, and her first edited newsletter has appeared.

In accordance with normal practice, Council appointed two subcommittees to search for the next President of the Society, in succession to Professor Jones, who retires from office in November 2012, and the Honorary Secretary, in succession to Professor Harding, who retires in November 2011. The Presidential subcommittee comprised Dr Baldock (in the chair), the Honorary Secretary, the Honorary Treasurer, and Professor Fincham. After consultation and discussion they nominated Professor Peter Mandler, currently a Vice-President and formerly Honorary Secretary, and the nomination was unanimously approved by Council at its May meeting. The second subcommittee comprised Professor Bernard (in the chair), Professor Dixon, Dr Lewis and the President; after similar consultation and discussion, they nominated Dr Adam Smith, UCL, and the nomination was unanimously approved by Council.

Officers and members of Council made two visits this year on behalf of the Society, to the University of York on 29 October 2010 and to Lancaster University on 16–17 June 2011. At York, Council members held meetings with academic and research staff and postgraduate research students in the Department of History, and the visit concluded with a very well-attended and well-received lecture by Professor Catherine Hall, UCL. At Lancaster, Council members held a meeting with postgraduate research students of the History Department and the President chaired a plenary session at the symposium sponsored by the Society 'Edges of Europe: Frontiers in Context'.

The Society continues to work closely with the IHR and its Director, Professor Miles Taylor, on a number of issues, most notably the Bibliography of British and Irish History. Termly meetings of representatives of the Society, the IHR, the HA, and History UK have been held at the IHR. The Honorary Secretary participated in the interviews for Postgraduate Fellowships at the IHR in June, including the Society's Centenary and Marshall Fellowships. A joint reception was held following the Prothero Lecture on 29 June 2011.

Council and the Officers record their gratitude to the Society's administrative staff: the Executive Secretary, Sue Carr and the Administrative Secretary, Melanie Ransom. We thank them for their expert and dedicated work on the Society's many activities.

RESEARCH POLICY COMMITTEE, 2010–11

It is not obvious how most effectively to intervene in public policy discussions in the current rather ideological policy climate, in which moreover bodies in receipt of public money tend to be 'captured' by a government agenda, to which they feel compelled to defer, limiting their ability to reflect back to policymakers the views of their own constituencies. The Committee continues to discuss this, as well as how it can best work together with other bodies such as History HE UK and the Historical Association in this connection, and in what terms it is best to contest the many problematic elements of public discourse. It has noted with interest the establishment in the United States of a National Commission on the Humanities and Social Sciences, charged with identifying 'the top ten actions that Congress, state governments, universities, foundations, educators, individual benefactors, and others should take now to maintain national excellence in Humanities and social scientific scholarship and education, and to achieve long-term national goals for our intellectual and economic well-being; for a stronger, more vibrant civil society; and for the success of cultural diplomacy in the 21st century?' (http://www.humanitiescommission.org). It will monitor the proceedings of this Commission, to see whether it might provide a useful reference point.

The Committee was pleased to learn that, following an initiative from Dr Tristram Hunt MP, the All-Party Group on Archives is extending its remit to become the Group on Archives and History.

A meeting held at the British Academy on the subject of the Haldane Principle was attended by Professor Peter Mandler on behalf of the Society.

The Committee continues to monitor the activities of the AHRC and ESRC, informed by comments from Fellows and Council and the Society's representatives on its panels and committees. The President submitted comments on the future of the AHRC's Block Grant scheme for funding doctoral research on behalf of the Society. The President has also critically discussed with the AHRC the effects of devolving funding for research expenses to universities. The fact that this is done on a per capita basis means that funding is not necessarily effectively channelled to students for whose research it is crucial, particularly those whose research necessitates trips abroad. University policy is also a matter of concern: it is crucial that universities carefully consider the arrangements they have in place for distributing these funds. The Committee will attempt to monitor this, and make further representations to the AHRC if necessary.

AHRC policies for funding academic research, within the envelope set by the Department of Business, Innovation and Skills, have also been critically discussed. The Committee is concerned about the planned increase in the share of funding to be devoted to thematic research strands, and about plans to reshape research leave with an emphasis on training future research leaders. It seems that increasingly the AHRC regards it as the role of other bodies, such as Leverhulme, to fund individual, curiosity-driven research. Although it is clear that the intention is to define the prioritised themes broadly, they are not all encompassing; furthermore there is tension between their very breadth and the proclaimed aim of fostering cutting edge research that will advance the discipline in selected areas. Even supposing it were right to target research funding, it is questionable whether a small number of decision-makers within the AHRC has the competence to identify appropriate targets.

The Committee continues to follow REF arrangements carefully. After consultation with the membership, the Committee submitted an extended list of nominations for the Humanities and History panels; most of those ultimately appointed appeared on the panel's list (of course, many of these were no doubt also nominated by other subject associations). The Chair of the History Panel, Chris Wickham, held a special meeting with the Society's Council to discuss the consultation papers circulated in connection with the REF (these can be seen on the REF website at http://www.hefce.ac.uk/research/ref/pubs/). Members were invited to send in comments to inform discussion at this meeting.

The Committee has also continued to develop its relationship with the British Library, which faces 15% cuts. A meeting was held in October attended by the President and others, at which relations between the Library and HE institutions, and also the Library's archival collection strategy, were especially discussed.

The Committee has continued to nurture its relationship with TNA, and is pleased that the acting CEO has indicated his interest in continuing to meet informally with subject representatives. TNA this year faces a 25% budget cut; savings it made last year will help it to accommodate this. TNA's supervisory role in relation to local government archives is a particularly important one in a period when local archives are also under significant pressure as a result of budget cuts.

The Committee has also considered the Society's relationship with the new Archives and Records Association (replacing the former National Council on Archives). The Committee agreed to consult Councillor Dr David Thomas (of TNA) about the implications for archivists of the bill for reform of the Law of Defamation (consultation on the draft bill closed in July 2011).

According to practice first established last year, a joint meeting with Education Policy Committee was held in July. At this, the general issue of how best to contribute to public policy debate, and the AHRC's research-funding policy, were discussed.

EDUCATION POLICY COMMITTEE 2010–11

The Education Policy Committee considers all aspects of History in education from schools to postgraduate level, although naturally it relies very much on other organisations to take the lead in areas where they have specific expertise, for example, the Historical Association for schools and History UK (HE) for universities. To this end the Committee co-opts representatives from the HA, History UK and also from the Higher Education Academy's History Subject Centre, so that it might serve as a meeting-point for the various bodies that share an interest in this area. The Society is grateful to Dr Andrew Foster, Dr Jason Peacey and Dr Sarah Richardson for acting in this capacity.

This year was one of unprecedented upheaval in all aspects of education, with the government's announcements of a new system of higher education funding (which very largely replaces the system of direct grants for teaching with an income stream from student fees), a review of the national curriculum and a reconsideration of the entire regulatory framework for both schools and universities. The Committee worked hard to keep up with the pace of events.

On the place of History in the schools, the Committee was grateful for the expert advice of Dr Michael Maddison HMI, Ofsted's specialist adviser for History, who spoke at two of our meetings this year, including our annual joint meeting with the Research Policy Committee. His cool and clear appraisal of the state of history in the schools, 'History for All', was published in March 2011, and while it is not alarmist about the prospects for History – GCSE and A-Level numbers remain stable – it identifies important points of weakness (in primaries, at KS3, in academies). The Committee can also recommend the Royal Society of Edinburgh's January 2011 advice paper, 'The Teaching of History in Scottish Schools', for some interestingly parallel remarks. The Committee's lines of communication to the examination boards – organized through our annual meeting with chief history examiners – provided additional valuable information on patterns of uptake at GCSE and A-Level. It was decided not to contribute to the first phase of the government's national curriculum review, which was limited to very general principles, but the Committee now feels well prepared to contribute to the second phase in 2012 where the content of national curriculum subjects, including History, will be considered. The meeting that the President organised in November 2010 with the Secretary of State for Education, Michael Gove, also provided an opportunity for an early airing of historians' views.

The impact of the new system of higher education funding will not be clear until admissions for the 2012–13 academic year are further advanced. The Committee worked with the President to monitor closely pre-emptive moves that might be taken by university administrations, and proposals to end the teaching of History at the University of Cumbria and London Metropolitan University were followed closely and with great concern. A particular worry is that opportunities for less able students to study History both at school and at university are shrinking most rapidly.

Among the first effects of government reform of the regulatory system has been the closure of the History Subject Centre. The Committee is working closely with History UK and others to consider how some of the Subject Centre's most important functions might be carried on by others.

One focus of the joint meeting with the Research Policy Committee was a discussion of how the Society might best contribute to some of the policy-forming roles that the Subject Centre undertook. The impact of other regulatory changes – questions of the future of the Quality Assurance Agency for Higher Education, the closure of the Qualifications and Curriculum and Development Agency, and the reconfiguration of the HE funding bodies – remain obscure at the time of writing. But it is clear that learned societies will be called upon by government for more aid and advice in future, and be needed more to speak up in a disinterested way for scholarship and learning, and the Committee anticipates as crowded an agenda next year as this.

GENERAL PURPOSES COMMITTEE, 2010–11

The remit of this Committee ranges across many activities of the Society. It receives suggestions from Fellows and Council for speakers and makes recommendations to Council on the Card of Session, taking into account the need for a balanced programme in terms of chronological and geographical spread. In addition to the regular sessions held at UCL and outside London, it is also responsible for the Prothero Lecture, the Colin Matthew Lecture and the Gerald Aylmer Seminar.

The programme of lectures and visits for 2011 was confirmed, including visits to Lancaster University in June and the University of Glamorgan in November. Proposals for 2012 have been discussed and speakers invited. Regional symposia and visits to Sheffield and Southampton will take place in 2012. The Committee continues to review the purpose and success of both lectures and visits, and to consider ways of increasing their reach, for example through podcasting and repeat lectures. The Committee was pleased to receive several proposals for regional symposia, and would like to encourage more departments to make such proposals. The 2011 Gerald Aylmer Seminar was held in February on 'Training and research skills in the use of early (medieval and early modern) archives' (reported above) and discussions with TNA and the IHR for the 2012 seminar are under way.

The Committee is also responsible for the appointment of assessors for the Society's prizes, and receives their reports and proposals for award winners. It regularly reviews the terms and conditions of the awards. It is grateful to members of Council for their hard work in reading entries and selecting the prize winners.

Meetings of the Society

Six papers were given in London this year.

At the ordinary meetings of the Society the following papers were read:

'The Media Revolution in Early Modern England: An Artist's Perspective', Professor Dror Wahrman (30 June 2010: Prothero Lecture)

'The Demise of the Asylum in Late Twentieth Century Britain: A Personal History' Professor Barbara Taylor (24 September 2010)

At the Anniversary Meeting on 26 November 2010, the President, Professor Colin Jones delivered his second address on 'French Crossings II: Laughing over Boundaries.

'Negotiating the medieval and the modern', Professor Janet Coleman (4 February 2011)

'After 1848: The European Revolution in Government', Professor Christopher Clark (6 May 2011)

The Colin Matthew Memorial Lecture for the Public Understanding of History was given on Wednesday 11 November 2010 by Professor Amanda Vickery 'Fashion, Time and Place in Georgian England'. These lectures continue to be given in memory of the late Professor Colin Matthew, a former Literary Director and Vice-President of the Society.

Prizes

The Society's annual prizes were awarded as follows:

The Alexander Prize for 2010 attracted thirteen entries and was awarded to:

Richard Huzzey for his article 'Free trade, free labour, and slave sugar in Victorian Britain' in *Historical Journal*, 53, 2 (2010).

The *judges'* citation read:

> This is a sophisticated and impressively researched essay, which draws on a wide range of sources to re-examine the controversy over the sugar duties in the early Victorian period and what the debate reveals about attitudes towards slavery. The main focus of Huzzey's attention is the relationship between religion – above all, evangelicalism – and political economy. This has hardly been a neglected theme in writing on nineteenth-century British history in recent years. What is really impressive about this essay, therefore, is not simply its understanding of the controversy or its ability to locate it within the current historiography, but rather the way in which it succeeds in taking the historical debate forward. Huzzey's key argument is that the sugar duties debate needs to be understood as 'a reckoning between two contradictory traditions within the movement for abolition and emancipation'. He has produced a remarkably mature and persuasive essay, which makes an important contribution to our knowledge of both free trade and abolitionism in the nineteenth century and will be a key point of reference in future debate.

The judges nominated a proxime accessit:

Erika Hanna, 'Dublin's north inner city, preservationism and Irish modernity in the 1960s', in *Historical Journal*, 53, 4 (2010).

The David Berry Prize for an article on Scottish history for 2010 attracted seven entries and was awarded to:

Alasdair Raffe for his article 'Presbyterians and Episcopalians: The Formation of Confessional Cultures in Scotland, c. 1660–1715', in *English Historical Review*, 125 (2010).

The judges' citation read:

'Presbyterians and Episcopalians: The Formation of Confessional Cultures in Scotland, 1660–1715' persuasively argues that the late seventeenth and early eighteenth centuries saw Scottish religious life coalesce around two increasingly divergent (and oppositional) confessional cultures. Rejecting the standard view that few fundamental theological differences divided Scottish Episcopalians and Presbyterians, the author deploys a wealth of material drawn from pamphlet debates, sermons and Scottish archival sources to identify widening disagreements over a range of issues that included predestination, conversion and liturgical worship. Further compounded by growing disparities in Presbyterian and Episcopalian approaches to church government, these debates served to consolidate opposing confessional cultures that in turn underpinned distinctive political identities. Clearly written and abundantly supported with evidence, the article makes a substantial and welcome addition to recent literature on religious adherence in a crucial period of Scottish history.

The Whitfield Book Prize for a first book on British history attracted forty-four entries.

The Prize for 2010 was awarded to:

Arnold Hunt, *The Art of Hearing: English Preachers and their Audiences, 1590–1640* (Cambridge University Press, 2010).

The judges' citation read:

This year's Whitfield Prize attracted all in all a pretty strong field of entries spanning the eleventh to the twentieth centuries. From these, the judges were unanimous in awarding the prize to Arnold Hunt. This book addresses a well-worn subject – the impact of protestant preaching in the later stages of the Reformation – but does so with entirely new perspectives and intriguing findings. Hunt is interested in the sermon as performance, and demonstrates that printed texts are only an approximate and polished version of what would have been heard from the pulpit. He also explores the reception of sermons among the congregation, a crucial component of the dissemination of the new faith, hitherto largely ignored by historians, which he analyses through a careful study of sermon notes taken by hearers. It transpires that what preachers laboured to emphasise was not always that on which parishioners fastened. Three case-studies (in Chapter Five) expose the crudity of our current understanding of the expectations of protestant congregations, and here he sets a new post-Haighian agenda. The final chapter also convincingly demonstrates the importance of the theology of predestination at popular level, against historians who have claimed that it was a rarified subject beyond the ken of most people. The book offers a series of sophisticated, linked arguments which will have a real impact on the field. It is also meticulously researched and written in clear, authoritative English.

The Gladstone Book Prize for a first book on non-British history attracted sixteen entries.

The Prize for 2010 was awarded to:

Natalie A Zacek, *Settler Society in the English Leeward Islands, c. 1670–1776* (Cambridge University Press, 2010).

The judges' citation read:

The dominant tendency among the historiography of Britain's West Indian colonies has been to depict the plantation societies of the Caribbean in dark, deeply negative hues. The sugar planters who settled in that region have been variously characterised as grasping capitalists, moral degenerates and cultural philistines, whose get-rich-quick mentality militated against the creation of stable societies committed to the preservation of a common English identity. In her sparkling study of the Leeward Islands (Antigua, Montserrat, Nevis and St. Kitts) from their independence from Barbados in 1670 to the outbreak of the American Revolution, Natalie Zacek challenges the notion that the English colonies of the West Indies were in any way failed societies. While she in no way downplays the centrality of black slavery to the economy of the Leewards, Zacek is primarily interested in exploring the complex dynamics of settler society and in doing so engages with a wide range of themes, including topography, migration, slavery, religion, ethnicity, gender and the family. The picture that emerges is of colonists who, while ready and able to adapt to an unfamiliar and sometimes hostile environment, were equally determined to uphold English social and cultural ideals. Subtle, reflective and elegantly written, this enlightening analysis not only rescues the Leewards from the margins of colonial studies, but is an important contribution to the wider discussion about the character of British colonial settlement in America.

The Society's Rees Davies Essay Prize for the best article based on a conference paper delivered by a recipient of a Royal Historical Society travel grant attracted seven entries.

The Prize for 2010 was awarded to:

Elizabeth Hunter for her article '"The Black Lines of Damnation": Melancholia and Reprobation in Reformation England'.

The judges' citation read:

This elegant paper negotiates the literature of Calvinist counsel and treatises on melancholy to tease out the varying positions on the relationship between despair, predestination, and melancholia. In doing so it contributes to our understanding both of godly pastoral counsel and of the confessional conflicts of the later sixteenth and early seventeenth centuries.

In order to recognise the high quality of work now being produced at undergraduate level in the form of third-year dissertations, the Society continued, in association with *History Today* magazine, to award an annual prize for the best undergraduate dissertation. Departments are asked to nominate annually their best dissertation and a joint committee comprised of representatives from the Society and *History Today* select, in the autumn, the national prize-winner from among these nominations. The prize also recognizes the Society's close relations with *History Today* and the important role the magazine has played in disseminating scholarly research to a wider audience. Thirty submissions were received.

The Prize for 2010 was awarded to:

Alexander Baggallay (University of Edinburgh) for his essay 'Myths of Mau Mau expanded: the role of rehabilitation in detention camps during the state emergency in Kenya, 1954–60'.

A runner up was nominated:

David Kenrick (University of Liverpool) for his essay 'Identity and the politics of survival: White Rhodesia, 1965–1980'.

An article by the prize-winner presenting his research will appear in *History Today* in 2011.

The German History Society, in association with the Royal Historical Society, awards a prize to the winner of an essay competition. The essay, on any aspect of German history, including the history of German-speaking people both within and beyond Europe, was open to any postgraduate student either currently registered for a degree or having submitted their thesis within the last twelve months, at a university in either the United Kingdom or the Republic of Ireland.

The Prize for the winning essay in 2010 was awarded to:

Natalie Kwan (St Antony's College, Oxford), for her essay 'Woodcuts and witches: Ulrich Molitor's *De lamiis et pythonicis mulieribus*, 1489–1669'.

The Frampton and Beazley Prizes for A-Level performances in 2010 were awarded to the following nominations from the examining bodies:

Frampton Prize:

Edexcel:	Claire Smith (Wallington County Grammar School)
OCR:	Anna Glendenning (Prince Henry's Grammar School, West Yorkshire)

Beazley Prize:

SQA:	Zara Reid (The Glasgow Academy)
CCEA:	Amy Taylor (Coleraine High School)

The Director of the Institute of Historical Research announced the winner of the Pollard Prize 2011 awarded annually to the best postgraduate student paper presented in a seminar at the IHR. The Pollard Prize for 2011 was awarded to Siobhan Talbott (University of Manchester) for her paper '"If you were hier you could gaine what you please, for thereis many English and severall Scots that you might deall with": British Commercial Interests on the French Atlantic Coast, c. 1560–1713' given to the Economic and Social History of the Premodern World, 1500 – 1800 seminar. The article will appear in *Historical Research* in 2012.

Publications

PUBLICATIONS COMMITTEE, 2010–11

At the beginning of 2011 Dr Ian Archer resigned as Academic Editor of the Bibliography of British and Irish History (BBIH), having guided the project successfully for over a decade and overseen the transition to our new publisher. Professor Stephen Taylor was elected to the new position of Honorary Academic Editor (BBIH). The new publication arrangements with Brepols continue to bed down well and there continues to be a good take up of subscriptions, particularly among British higher education institutions. Progress has been made in negotiations about a reduced rate subscription for Fellows and Members of the Society, which will become available in the course of 2012. We have again exceeded our annual target for new records, adding over 15,000 to the Bibliography during the year 2010–11; the total number of records in the database now stands at over 500,000. Dr Jason McElligott has taken over as the section editor for the modern Irish material.

The updating of the Society's website has coincided with an overhaul of the lists of local record society publications (formerly known as *Texts and Calendars*). The updates were previously made available through the Bibliography, but the lists are now being maintained separately by the Executive Secretary, ensuring that this resource remains free to end users.

The Publications Committee remains responsible for the ongoing programme. Professor Arthur Burns represents the Society's interests on the *Studies in History* Editorial Board, while Dr Ian Archer edits *Transactions*, and they share responsibility for Camden volumes.

Transactions, Sixth Series, Volume 20 was published during the session, and *Transactions*, Sixth Series, Volume 21 went to press.

In the Camden, Fifth Series, *The Life of John Rastrick, 1650–1727*, ed. Andrew Cambers (vol. 36) and *British Envoys to Germany 1816–1866, Vol. IV: 1851–1866* eds. Markus Mösslang, Chris Manias and Torsten Riotte (vol. 37) were published during the session.

The Making of the East London Mosque, 1910–1951, ed. Humayun Ansari (vol. 38), *The Papers of the Hothams: Governors of Hull during the Civil War*, ed. Andrew Hopper (vol. 39) and *A Monastic Community in Local Society: the Beauchief Cartulary*, eds., David Luscombe, David Hey and Lisa Liddy (vol. 40) went to press for publication in 2011–12.

The *Studies in History* Editorial Board continued to meet throughout the year. The Second Series continues to produce exciting volumes. Dr Jon Lawrence retired from and Professor Barry Doyle joined the Editorial Board. The following volumes were published, or went to press, during the session:

○ *The Scottish Middle March, 1573 to 1625*, Anna Groundwater

- *Samuel Rawson Gardiner and the Idea of History*, Mark Nixon
- *Time and the French Revolution: the Republican Calendar, 1789 – Year XI*, Matthew Shaw
- *Poverty, gender and life-cycle under the English Poor Law, 1760–1834*, Samantha Williams
- *Liberalism and Local Government in Early Victorian London*, Ben Weinstein
- *English Catholic Exiles in Late Sixteenth-Century Paris*, Katy Gibbons
- *Religion, Atheism and Enlightenment in Pre-Revolutionary Europe*, Mark Curran
- *Conquest and land in Ireland: the transplantation to Connacht, 1649–1690*, John Cunningham

As in previous subscription years, volumes in the *Studies in History* Series were offered to the membership at a favourably discounted price. Many Fellows, Associates and Members accepted the offer for volumes published during the year, and the advance orders for further copies of the volumes to be published in the year 2011–2012 were encouraging.

The Society acknowledges its gratitude for the continuing subventions from the Economic History Society and the Past and Present Society to the *Studies in History* series.

Finance

FINANCE COMMITTEE 2010–11

The Finance Committee approves the Society's accounts each financial year and its estimates for the following year. This year, as before, the accounts were professionally audited by Kingston Smith LLP. They are presented later in *Transactions*, together with the Trustees' Annual Report.

The Society's expenditure was broadly in line with estimates. Income was considerably greater than anticipated, however, largely due to a greater than expected income from the joint publishing agreement with Cambridge University Press (due to on-going sales of the new digital archive).

The Society has run a surplus for a number of years, which has allowed it to build up a cash reserve in its COIF account and Barclays current account. The Finance Committee recognises that the coming years are likely to be more challenging financially than recent years, particularly as income from the digitisation component of the publishing agreement with Cambridge University Press will decline sharply. It is for this reason that the Society anticipates continuing to hold a substantial cash reserve in the expectation that it will be drawn down in future years to cover in-year deficits.

The value of the Society's investments rose to £2.54 million in June 2011 from £2.16 million in June 2010. The total return was well ahead of the return for the APCIMS Balanced (Total Return) index against which performance is benchmarked. The portfolio continues to be managed by Brewin Dolphin Securities for the longer term and is now practically fully invested. Dividend income declined slightly in 2010–11, in part because of a slight shift away from the very defensive investment strategy that had been pursued in recent years, although it still covered almost all the society's 'draw-down'.

Mr Adam Broadbent kindly agreed to become an external member of the Finance Committee, joining Dr Nick Draper, and we are grateful to them for their help and advice throughout the year.

- Council records with gratitude the benefactions made to the Society by:
  - Professor M Arnoux
  - Dr G Bakker
  - The Bibliographical Society
  - Dr S J G Blair, OBE
  - Dr C M K Bowden
  - Professor C R Cole
  - Professor J R Cramsie
  - Professor J E Cronin
  - Dr S W Davies
  - The Economic History Society
  - Professor Sir Geoffrey Elton
  - The Estate of Vera London
  - Professor F F R Fernandez-Armesto
  - Mr P J C Firth
  - Professor H W G Gneuss
  - Dr R P Hallion
  - Miss B F Harvey
  - The History of Parliament Trust
  - Professor P M Kennedy
  - Dr P C Lowe
  - Dr M Lynn
  - Professor R G Maber
  - Dr E Magennis
  - Professor P J Marshall
  - Mr L J McLoughlin
  - Mr S A Murray
  - Professor Dame J L Nelson
  - Professor H Ono
  - Professor D M Palliser
  - Past & Present Society
  - Reverend N R Paxton
  - Sir George Prothero

o Lieutenant Colonel Dr H E Raugh
o Dr L Rausing
o Miss E M Robinson
o Professor Lord Smith of Clifton
o Professor D P Smyth
o Dr A F Sutton
o Dr G P Tapsell
o Dr E R Turton
o Mr T V Ward

Membership

MEMBERSHIP COMMITTEE, 2010–11

The Committee reviews all applications for Fellowship and Membership received by the Society, and makes recommendations to Council. The Committee is keen to encourage applications for Fellowship on the basis of scholarly achievement in history, whose definition is not limited to traditional forms of publication, but also includes, for example, the curatorship of exhibitions and publication in newer media. The Committee is glad to receive applications to join the Society in either the Fellowship or Membership category, and emphasises that it favours a broad view of what constitutes history when assessing candidates.

The Committee would also like to draw the attention of supervisors and postgraduate students to the new category of Postgraduate Member. The first intake of Postgraduate Members started their Membership in the July 2010 - June 2011 subscription year. Postgraduate Members apply in the same way as regular Members but if they are current research postgraduates (UK or overseas) they are entitled to their first two years' subscription at £10 (with all the same benefits of regular Membership), after which they automatically revert to normal Member status. The discounted first two years still applies even if the students finish their degree during that time. The Society does require proof of postgraduate research student status, but only at the time of election.

The following were elected to the Fellowship:

Kevin J Alban, MA, MTh, PhD
Henrice Altink, BA, MA, MA, PhD
Gerben Bakker, MSc, PhD
Ian Barnes, BA, MA, PhD
Laura D Beers, AB, MA, PhD
Gill Bennett, MA
Andrea Benvenuti, MA, DPhil
Kate Bradley, BA, MA, PhD

Harald E Braun, MA, DPhil
Alex Bremner, BA, MArch, PhD
Thom Brooks, BA, MA, MA, PhD
Alan P Caddick-Adams, BA, PhD
Jane Cartwright, BA, PhD
Alison Cathcart, BA, PhD
Stephen J Catterall, BA, MA, DPhil
Andrew M Chandler, BA, PhD
William H Clements, LLB
John P D Cooper, BA, MA, DPhil
Edward Coss, PhD
Peter J A Crooks, BA, PhD
James W Daniel, BA, MA
Robin H Darwall-Smith, BA, MA, DPhil
Christopher Davies, BA, MA
Peter Dorey, BA, MA, PhD
Nicholas A Draper, BA, MBA, MA, PhD
Heiko Feldner, MA, PGCE
Graeme A Garrard, BA, MA, DPhil
Brian Girvin, BA, MA, PhD
William Godsey, MA, PhD
Caroline Goodson, PhD
Claire Gorrara, BA, MSt, DPhil
Matthew Grant, BA, MA, PhD
James M Gratton, BA, MEd, PhD
Janet Greenlees, BA, MA, DPhil
Allan Greer, BA, MA, PhD
Carl J Griffin, BSc, PhD
Richard P Hallion, BA, PhD
Matthew Hammond, BA, MA, PhD
David Hein, BA, MA, PhD
David Hendy, MA, PhD
David M Hopkin, BA, MA, PhD
Jonathan House, AB, MA, MMAS
Mark M Hull, PhD, JD
Joanna Huntington, BA, MA, PhD
Anthony J G Insall, BA, PhD
John A Irving, BMus, PhD
Ben Jackson, BA, MA, DPhil
David H Jenkins, MA, MA, MA, PhD
Matthew T Jenkinson, BA, MSt, DPhil
Paul R Jennings, BA, MPhil, PhD
Peter H G Joseph, BSc, MSc, MSc
Sarah Knott, DPhil

William W J Knox, MA, PhD
Mary R Laven, BA, MA, MA, PhD
Rebekah Lee, BA, MPhil, DPhil
Timothy Leunig, BA, MPhil, DPhil
Donald M Lewis, BA, DPhil
Andreas Loewe, BA, MA, MPhil, PhD
Scott H Mandelbrote, MA
Steve Marsh, BA, PhD
Ted McCormick, BA, MA, MPhil, PhD
Charles McKean, BA, Hon D.Litt
Leslie J McLoughlin, BA, BA, MA
David Milne, BA, MA, PhD
Joseph P Moran, BA, MA, PhD
Peter J Morden, BA, BD, MPhil, PhD
Simon J Morgan, BA, MA, DPhil
Axel E W Muller, MA
Lucy Noakes, BA, DPhil
Ralph O'Connor, BA, MA, MPhil, PhD
Sinead O'Sullivan, BA, MA, DPhil
Richard G Parry, LLB, PhD
Sarah J K Pearce, BD, DPhil
John R Peaty, BA, MA, PhD
Andrew C Perchard, BA, MPhil, PhD
Dilwyn Porter, BA, PhD
Maria Power, BA, MA, PhD
John M J Reay
Duncan E M Redford, BA, MA, PhD
Rebecca A C Rist, PhD
Michael B Roberts, BA, MA
Richard G Rodger, MA, PhD
Jan Rueger, MA, PhD
Paul A Scott, BA, MA, PhD
Jill A Shefrin, BA, MLS
Ales Skrivan, PhD
Philip J Smith, BA, MA, PhD
Stephanie Spencer, BA, MA, PhD
Andrew D Stewart, BA, PhD
Ingrid J Sykes, PhD
Richard Talbot, MPhil
Annie Tindley, MA, MSc, PhD
Isabelle S L Tombs, PhD
Marius Turda, BA, MA, PhD
Colin Tyler, BA, MA, DPhil, MA
Diane Urquhart, BA, MA, PhD

Nicola Verdon, BA, MA, PhD
Malcolm Walsby, BA, PhD
Thomas Weber, MSt, DPhil
Helen Weinstein, BA
Anna Whitelock, BSc, MPhil, PhD
Emma L Wild-Wood, BD, MTh, PhD
Louise J Wilkinson, BA, MA, PhD
Paul Williamson, BA, MPhil, LittD
Gwenyth A Yarker, BA, MA

The following were announced in the Queen's Honours Lists during the year:

Professor Rosemary Crampton – Fellow – D.B.E. for services to Scholarship.
Dr Simon Thurley – Fellow – C.B.E. for services to Conservation.
Dr Allen Warren – Fellow – O.B.E. for services to Higher Education.
Professor Thomas James - Fellow - M.B.E. for services to Higher Education.

Council was advised of and recorded with regret the deaths of 10 Fellows, 19 Retired Fellows, 3 Corresponding Fellows and 2 Associates.

These included:

Professor M Altschul – Retired Fellow
Mr A S Baxendale – Associate
Professor R W Beachey – Retired Fellow
Professor R A Chapman – Retired Fellow
Professor B Coward – Retired Fellow
Mr R S Craig – Fellow
Professor O Crisp – Retired Fellow
Reverend Dr R W D Fenn – Fellow
Dr J B Fitzpatrick – Fellow
Dr R L Frazier – Retired Fellow
Mr R K Gilkes – Retired Fellow
Professor J A S Grenville – Retired Fellow
Mr P Heath – Retired Fellow
Dr F Hull – Fellow
Professor K Ingham – Retired Fellow
Mr D L Jones – Fellow
Professor T R Judt – Fellow
Professor B G Kohl – Retired Fellow
Professor D Kosary – Corresponding Fellow
Mr J B Lewis – Associate
Dr W A Maguire – Retired Fellow
Professor J F McMillan – Fellow

Professor S Nagy – Corresponding Fellow
Canon T J Prichard – Retired Fellow
Professor A J R Russell-Wood – Retired Fellow
Mr H F Starkey – Retired Fellow
Dr A T Q Stewart – Retired Fellow
Professor D M Tanner – Fellow
Mrs D K G Thompson – Retired Fellow
Professor F M Turner – Fellow
Professor W V Wallace – Retired Fellow
Professor Wang Jufei – Corresponding Fellow
Dr A W A White – Retired Fellow
Professor W N Yates – Fellow

Over the year ending on 30 June 2011, 105 Fellows and 102 Members were elected, and the total membership of the Society on that date was 3,042 (including 1,909 Fellows, 683 Retired Fellows, 15 Honorary Vice-Presidents, 81 Corresponding and Honorary Fellows, 45 Associates and 309 Members).

The Society exchanged publications with 15 societies, British and foreign.

Representatives of the Society

- The representation of the Society upon other various bodies was as follows:
    - Dr Julia Crick on the Joint Committee of the Society and the British Academy established to prepare an edition of Anglo-Saxon charters;
    - Professor Claire Cross on the Council of the British Association for Local History; and on the British Sub-Commission of the Commission Internationale d' Histoire Ecclesiastique Comparée;
    - Professor Mark Ormrod on the Archives and Records Association Consultative Forum;
    - Professor Richard Rathbone on the Court of Governors of the University of Wales, Swansea;
    - Professor Colin Jones on the board of the Panizzi Foundation and the Advisory Council of the Committee for the Export of Objects of Cultural Interest;
    - Professor Chris Whatley on the Court of the University of Stirling

Grants

RESEARCH SUPPORT COMMITTEE, 2010–11

The Committee met five times in the course of the year to distribute research funds to early career historians (primarily research students but also recent PhDs not yet in full-time employment) through a process of peer review. In total, the Committee made 134 awards to researchers at over forty UK institutions, of which 11 grants were to support research within the UK, 34 to support research outside the UK, 46 to support attendance at conferences to deliver papers, 43 to allow conference organisers to subsidise attendance of early career researchers at their event, one (the Martin Lynn Scholarship) to support research within Africa. The broad range of topics funded by the Committee attests both to the vibrancy of the discipline in sub-fields that extend from medieval European religious history to contemporary South African history. Successful applicants' end-of-award reports confirm that RHS funding significantly enhances postgraduate students' opportunities to conduct substantial archival research projects and to hone their ensuing dissertation chapters and first publications through participation in national and international workshops and conferences. The calibre of applicants continues to be high, with significantly more qualified applicants than the Committee is able to fund - a circumstance that recent and impending reductions of research funding at both university and Research Council-level will likely exacerbate in the coming year. Further, to ensure that its limited funds are allocated to the most appropriate candidates, the Committee devoted considerable time this year to clarifying and streamlining its application process and criteria.

The Royal Historical Society Centenary Fellowship was awarded in the academic year 2010–2011 to Robert Priest (New College, Oxford) for work on 'The Production, Reception and Legacy of Ernest Renan's *Vie de Jésus* in France', and to Jan Machielsen (Lady Margaret Hall, Oxford) for work on 'Demons & Letters; The Life and Works of Martin Delrio (1551–1608)'.

The Society's P J Marshall Fellowship was awarded in the academic year 2010–2011 to Alexander Russell (Jesus College, Oxford) for work on 'England and the general councils (1409–1562)'.

• Grants during the year were made to the following:

Travel to Conferences (Training Bursaries):

o Nicholas Barnett, Liverpool John Moores University
Cold War Cultures: Transnational and Interdisciplinary Perspectives, University of Texas, 30th September – 3rd October 2010
o Adam Burns, University of Edinburgh
The 4th Annual Conference for Historians of the Twentieth-Century United States, University of Oxford, 7th-9th July 2011
o James Cameron, University of Cambridge
Society for Historians of American Foreign Relations Annual Meeting, Virginia, US, 23rd-25th June 2011

o Thomas Carter, University of Oxford
  Reformation Studies Colloquium, Biennial Conference, St Andrews, 7th-9th September 2010
o Rory Cox, Aberystwyth University
  The History PhD: Past, Present and Future, Institute of Historical Research, 28th January 2011
o Alex Fairfax-Cholmeley, Queen Mary, University of London
  Consortium on the Revolutionary Era, 1750–1850, Tallahassee, Florida, 3rd-5th March 2011
o Nicholas Grant, University of Leeds
  New Perspectives on African American History and Culture, University of North Carolina, 19th-20th February 2011
o Alix Green, University of Hertfordshire
  The History PhD: Past, Present and Future, Institute of Historical Research, 28th January 2011
o Katherine Harvey, King's College London
  International Medieval Congress 2011, Leeds, 11th-14th July 2011
o Simon Hill, Liverpool John Moores University
  British Scholar, Conference 2011, University of Texas, 31st March – 2nd April 2011
o William Jewell, Liverpool John Moores University
  6th European Society for Environmental History: Encounters of Sea and Land, Turku, Finland, 28th June – 2nd July 2011
o Fiona Kao, University of Cambridge
  The 1st St Andrews Graduate Conference for Biblical and Early Christian Studies, St Andrews, 15th-16th June 2011
o Lionel Laborie, University of East Anglia
  57th Annual Meeting of the Society for French Historical Studies, Charleston, 10th-12th February 2011
o Jan Lanicek, University of Southampton
  American Responses to the Holocaust: Transatlantic Perspectives, Middelburg and Antwerp, 15th-17th June 2011
o Daniel Lee, University of Oxford
  The Association for Jewish Studies: 42nd Annual Conference, Boston, USA, 19th-21st December 2010
o Marie-Louise Leonard, University of Glasgow
  Annual Meeting of the Renaissance Society of America, Montreal, 24th-26th March 2011
o Sarah Lynch, University of Leeds
  46th International Congress on Medieval Studies, Kalamazoo, 12th-15th May 2011
o Ruselle Meade, University of Manchester

The Fourth Asian Translation Traditions Conference, Hong Kong, 15th-17th December 2010

o Matthew Mesley, University of East Anglia
Haskins Society Conference, Boston, USA, 4th-7th November 2010

o Stephen Miles, University of Glasgow
9th International Conference on History: From Ancient to Modern, Athens, Greece, 1st-4th August 2011

o Richard Mills, University of East Anglia
The North American Society for Sports History, Annual Conference 2011, Texas, US, 27th-30th May 2011

o Rhys Morgan, Cardiff University
English and Welsh Diaspora: Regional Cultures, Disparate Voices, Remembered Lives, Loughborough University, 13th-16th April 2011

o Stuart Morrison, University of Stirling
Encounters of Sea and Land: 6th Conference of the European Society for Environmental History, Turku, Finland, 28th June – 1st July 2011

o Christian O'Connell, University of Gloucestershire
Jazz and Race, Past and Present, Open University, Milton Keynes, 11th-12th November 2010

o Daniel Peart, UCL
Society for Historians of the Early American Republic (SHEAR), Philadelphia, USA, 14th-17th July 2011

o Tamson Pietsch
The History PhD: Past, Present and Future, Institute of Historical Research, 28th January 2011

o Stefan Ramsden, University of Hull
35th Annual Social Science History Association Conference: 'Power and Politics', Chicago, 18th-21st November 2010

o Lowri Rees, Aberystwyth University
The North American Association for the Study of Welsh Culture and History International Conference on Welsh Studies, Washington D.C., 22nd-24th July 2010

o Fern Riddell, King's College London
Politics, Performance and Popular Culture in Nineteenth-Century Britain, Lancaster, 7th-9th July 2011

o Daniel Roach, University of Exeter
46th International Congress on Medieval Studies, Kalamazoo, 12th-15th May 2011

o Euryn Roberts, Bangor University
30th Annual Harvard Celtic Colloquium, Harvard University, 7th-10th October 2010

o Tashia Scott, Oxford Brookes University

The Canadian Association for the History of Nursing Congress 2011, New Brunswick, Canada, 28th-30th May 2011

o Carolanne Selway, King's College London
Australia & New Zealand Association of Medieval & Early Modern Studies Eighth Biennial Conference, Dunedin, 2nd-5th February 2011

o William Smiley, University of Cambridge
Byzantine and Ottoman Civilizations in World History, Istanbul, Turkey, 21st-24th October 2010

o Jean Smith, University of California, Santa Barbara
The History PhD: Past, Present and Future, Institute of Historical Research, 28th January 2011

o Marjolein Stern, University of Nottingham
7th International Symposium on Runes and Runic Inscriptions: Runes in Context, Oslo, 9th-13th August 2010

o Emma Sutton, UCL
The American Philosophical Association (Eastern Division) Annual Meeting, Boston, 27th-30th December 2010

o Tom Symmons, Queen Mary, University of London
International Association of Media and Film History Conference 2011, Copenhagen, Denmark, 6th-9th July 2011

o Nimrod Tal, University of Oxford
Civil War, Global Conflict, Charleston, 3rd-5th March 2011

o Tina Tamman, University of Glasgow
The History PhD: Past, Present and Future, Institute of Historical Research, 28th January 2011

o Deborah Toner, University of Warwick
Food and Drink: Their Social, Political and Cultural Histories, Preston, 15th-17th June 2011

o Daniel Travers, University of Huddersfield
2nd Island Dynamics Conference, Valletta, Malta, 11th-15th May 2011

o Patrick Wadden, University of Oxford
The 29th International Conference of the Charles Homer Haskins Society, Boston, USA, 5th-7th November 2010

o Emma Wells, University of Durham
New Approaches to Medieval Religious Cultures: Concepts, Perceptions and Practices of Piety and Charity, London, 16th December 2010

o Sara Wolfson, University of Durham
The 57th Annual Meeting of the Renaissance Society of America, Montreal, 24th-26th March 2011

o Akhila Yechury, University of Cambridge
Association for Asian Studies and International Convention of Asian Scholars Special Joint Conference, Honolulu, 31st March – 3rd April 2011

Research Expenses Within the United Kingdom:

o Jonathan Atherton, Newman University College
  Archives in London, 7th-21st March 2011
o Andras Becker, University of Southampton
  Archives in London, January – February 2011
o Eva Blomqvist, King's College London
  Archives in Yorkshire, Manchester and Aberdeen, March – May 2011
o Miriam Cady, University of Leicester
  Archives in Northern Ireland, 7th-16th February 2011
o Carolyn Donohue, University of York
  Archives in London, July – August 2011
o Stephen Etheridge, University of Huddersfield
  Archives in London, 9th-12th March 2011
o Aaron Hope, UCL
  Archives in Lincoln, Winchester, Oxford and Cambridge, June 2011
o Fiona Kao, University of Cambridge
  Latin Summer School, Durham, 14th-26th August 2011
o Eleni Liapi, University of York
  Archives in London, July 2011
o Linsey Robb, University of Strathclyde
  Archives in Reading, May 2011
o Andrew Senter, University of Essex
  Archives in Essex and London, April – October 2011

Research Expenses Outside the United Kingdom:

o Michael Aeby, University of Sheffield
  Archives and interviews in Cape Town, South Africa, May – June 2011
o Dawn Berry, University of Oxford
  Archives in Ottawa, New York and Washington D.C., 8th-29th August
  2010
o Olga Bertelsen, University of Nottingham
  Archives in Kharkiv and Kiev, Ukraine, June – August 2011
o James Boyd, Cardiff University
  Archives in Germany, 19th January – 26th February 2011
o Matthew Carnell, University of Sheffield
  Archives in Washington D.C. and Yale, 19th July – 9th August 2010
o Benjamin Coombs, University of Kent
  Archives in Ottawa, Canada, May – June 2011
o Caroline Cornish, Royal Holloway, University of London
  Archives in West Bengal and Uttar Pradesh, India, September 2011
o Rabia Dada, University of Leeds

Archives in Karachi, Lahore and Islamabad, 15th October – 30th November 2010

o Thomas Davies, University of Leeds
  Archives in California, May – July 2011
o Christopher Dennis, Cardiff University
  Archives in France, 17th-21st April 2011
o Julie Farguson, University of Oxford
  Archives in Amsterdam, 13th-22nd September 2010
o Oliver Godsmark, University of Leeds
  Archives in New Delhi and Mumbai, India, July – October 2011
o Aaron Graham, University of Oxford
  Archives in California, 6th December 2010 – 11th January 2011
o Mark Hay, King's College London
  Archives in the Netherlands, 3rd-30th January 2011
o Asa McKercher, University of Cambridge
  Archives in Maryland, Massachusetts, Texas and Kansas, USA, July – September 2011
o Monica Merlin, University of Oxford
  Archives in China, March – September 2011
o Christopher Minty, University of Stirling
  Archives in Michigan, USA, July – September 2011
o Christopher Moffat, University of Cambridge
  Archives and interviews in New Delhi, Patiala and Chandigarh, India, October 2011 – May 2012
o John Mueller, University of Cambridge
  Archives in Germany and Switzerland, January – October 2011
o Emilie Murphy, University of Nottingham
  Archives in Moscow, 1st September – 8th November 2010
o Timothy Rogan, University of Cambridge
  Archives in New York and Washington, D.C., USA, August – November 2011
o Aidan Russell, University of Oxford
  Archives in Paris, Brussels and Bordeaux, 16th August – 16th September 2010
o David Sandifer, University of Cambridge
  Archives in California, 28th September – 23rd October 2010
o Pamela Schievenin, Queen Mary, University of London
  Archives in Rome, 28th April -31st July 2011
o Christian Schneider, University of Durham
  Archives in Italy, 6th January – 26th February 2011, Archives in Madrird, 29th March – 14th May 2011
o Louise Seaward, University of Leeds
  Archives in Paris, September 2010 – September 2011

- o Amal Tarhuni, London School of Economics
  Archives in Michigan, Georgia, California, Tripoli, Damascus, Cairo, London and Cambridge, February – December 2011
- o Andrew Tillman, University of Cambridge
  Archives in Venezuela, 15th January – 15th May 2011
- o Peter Whitewood, University of Leeds
  Archives in Moscow, February – May 2011
- o Rebecca Williams, University of Warwick
  Archives in New Delhi and Punjab, 15th October 2010 – 29th April 2011
- o Christopher Wilson, University of Exeter
  Archives in Rome, December 2010
- o Rachel Wilson, Queen's University Belfast
  Archives in Dublin, Ireland, June – July 2011
- o Lisa Wotherspoon, University of Aberdeen
  Old Irish Summer School, Limerick, Republic of Ireland, 20th June – 1st July 2011
- o William Young, University of Glasgow
  Archives in Berlin, Germany, August – September 2011

Conference Organisation (Workshop):

- o Christopher Abel
  "The Theme of Independence in Latin American History"
  UCL, 27th-28th October 2011
- o Olly Ayers
  "South-East Hub for History Postgraduate Conference: 'Why Study the Past?'"
  University of Kent, 15th June 2011
- o Emily Baughan
  "Empires and Humanitarianism"
  University of Bristol, 20th May 2011
- o Anke Bernau
  "Gender and Punishment"
  University of Manchester, 11th-13th January 2012
- o Lucy Bland
  "'Looking Back – Looking Forward': The Twentieth Annual Women's History Network Conference"
  The Women's Library, 9th-11th September 2011
- o Caroline Bowden
  "Identities, organisations and exile: Towards a History of Women Religious of Britain and Ireland"
  Queen Mary, University of London, 24th-25th June 2011
- o Christina Brindley
  "Third History Lab North West Postgraduate Workshop"

Manchester Metropolitan University, 1st June 2011

- Alison Carrol
"Society for the Study of French History Annual Conference"
University of Cambridge, 13th-15th July 2011
- Imogen Clarke
"British Society for the History of Science Postgraduate Conference"
University of Manchester, 4th-6th January 2011
- Krista Cowman
"Women in British Politics 1890–2000"
University of Lincoln, 6th-7th May 2011
- Surekha Davies
"The Global Dimensions of European Knowledge, 1450–1700"
Birkbeck, University of London, 24th-25th June 2011
- Simon Ditchfield
"Conversion Narratives in the Early Modern World"
University of York, 9th-11th June 2011
- Jill Francis
"Gardens and Gardening in Early Modern Britain"
Birmingham & Midland Institute, 18th June 2011
- Julie Gottlieb
""The Aftermath of Suffrage": What happened after the vote was won?"
University of Sheffield, 24th-25th June 2011
- Aaron Graham
"A British Military Revolution, 1500–1700?"
University of Oxford, 7th May 2011
- Kate Hammond
"Law, Violence and Social Bonds, c.900–1250"
University of St Andrews, 17th-19th June 2011
- Karen Heath
"Historians of the Twentieth Century United States, Fourth Annual Conference"
University of Oxford, 7th-9th July 2011
- Kate Hill
"Travel in the C19th: Narratives, Histories and Collections"
University of Lincoln, 14th-15th July 2011
- David Hitchcock
"'Idle and Disorderly Persons': The representations and realities of the mobile poor in Early Modern England"
University of Warwick, 12th March 2011
- Laura Ishiguro
"Imperial Relations: Families in the British Empire"
Institute of Historical Research, 5th-6th September 2011

- Sushma Jansari
  "West meets East: Contact and Interaction between India and the Mediterranean World from the Hellenistic period to late Antiquity" UCL, 20th June 2011

- Simon John
  "Deviance and Orthodoxy"
  Swansea University, 23rd-24th June 2011

- Bronach Kane
  "The Experience of Neighbourliness in Europe, c.1000–1600" Queen Mary, University of London, 17th-18th May 2012

- Kevin Killeen
  "The Bible in the C17th: The AV Quatercentenary (1611–2011)" University of York, 7th-9th July 2011

- Alan Kissane
  "New Perspectives on Medieval Lincolnshire"
  University of Lincoln, 2nd-3rd September 2011

- Catriona Macdonald
  "Real and Imagined Communities: Reshaping Historical Landscapes" University of Strathclyde, 3rd-4th June 2011

- Giulio Marchisio
  "Evolution, Revolution or Devolution? Reflections on the Italian Right, 1861–2011"
  Durham University, 4th-5th November 2011

- Matthew Mesley
  "Contextualizing Miracles in the Christian West, 1100–1500: New Historical Approaches"
  University of Cambridge, 16th April 2011

- Linne Mooney
  "Out of Bounds: Mobility, Movement and Use of Manuscripts and Printed Books, 1350–1550"
  University of York, 3rd-7th July 2011

- Julie Mumby
  "Revealing Records III"
  King's College London, 27th May 2011

- Jade Munslow Ong
  "Why Allegory Now?"
  University of Manchester, 1st April 2011

- Miles Pattenden
  "Renaissance Italy and the Idea of Spain"
  University of Oxford, 9th-10th January 2012

- Jonathan Phillips
  "The Crusades, Byzantium and Islam"
  German Historical Institute London, 8th-9th July 2011

- o Valentina Pugliano
  "Colonial Science and its Histories. The Workshop"
  Institute of Historical Research, 14th January 2011
- o Carole Rawcliffe
  "Fifteenth-Century Conference 2011: Society in an Age of Plague"
  University of East Anglia, 1st-3rd September 2011
- o Matthew Stevens
  "Medieval Urban Life: 'Facts' and 'Fictions'"
  Swansea University, 17th-18th June 2011
- o Siobhan Talbott
  "British Migration, 1560–1760"
  University of Manchester, 23rd March 2012
- o Andrea Thomson
  "Scotland in Motion"
  Glasgow, 6th-7th May 2011
- o Bjorn Weiler
  "Plantagenet Britain and its Neighbours, 1180–1330"
  Aberystwyth and Lampeter, 5th-8th September 2011
- o Jane Whittle
  "Tawney's Agrarian Problem 100 Years On: Landlords and Tenants in Rural England c.1400–1750"
  University of Exeter, 11th-12th July 2011
- o Mark Williams
  "Europe, Empire and Public Opinion: Debate and Consensus in Britain and Ireland, 1660–1763"
  University of Oxford, 15th-16th July 2011

Martin Lynn Scholarship:

- o Vincent Hiribarren, University of Leeds
  Archives in Kaduna and Maiduguri and interviews in Ngala, Fotokol, Namasak and Diffa, June – August 2010

Royal Historical Society Postgraduate Speakers Series (RHSPSS):

- o University of Northampton
- o Universities of Durham and Newcastle

23 September 2011

FINANCIAL STATEMENTS
FOR THE YEAR ENDED
30 JUNE 2011

THE ROYAL HISTORICAL SOCIETY REFERENCE AND ADMINISTRATIVE INFORMATION

Members of Council:

Professor C D H Jones, BA, DPhil, FBA	President - Officer
Professor V A Harding, MA, PhD	Honorary Secretary – Officer
I W Archer, MA, DPhil	Literary Director - Officer
Professor R A Burns, MA, DPhil	Literary Director - Officer
Professor M J Hughes, BA, MSc, PhD	Honorary Treasurer (from November 2010)
Professor J P Parry, MA, PhD	Honorary Treasurer – Officer (to November 2010)
Professor M F Cragoe, MA, DPhil	Honorary Director of Communications – Officer (to November 2010)
E Griffin, BA, MA, PhD	Honorary Director of Communications – Officer (from November 2010)
Professor S J C Taylor, MA, PhD	Honorary Academic Editor - BBIH (from November 2010)
R Baldock, BA, PhD	Vice President (from November 2010)
Professor G W Bernard, MA, DPhil	Vice President
R K Fisher, MA	Vice-President (to November 2010)
Professor M C Finn, BS, PhD	Vice-President
J M Innes, MA	Vice President
Professor C C Kidd, BA, DPhil	Vice President (from November 2010)
Professor P Mandler, BA, AM, PhD	Vice President
Professor D M Palliser, MA, DPhil	Vice-President (to November 2010)
Professor S F Barton, BA, MA, DPhil	Councillor
Professor S Connolly, DPhil	Councillor (to November 2010)
Professor J M Cornwall, PhD	Councillor
Professor S Dixon, MA, PhD	Councillor
Professor D M Feldman, BA, PhD	Councillor (from November 2010)
Professor K C Fincham, MA, PhD	Councillor
Professor C Given-Wilson, MA, PhD	Councillor
Professor T Hitchcock, AB, DPhil	Councillor (to November 2010)
J J Lewis, BA, PhD	Councillor
Professor N A Miller, PhD	Councillor (to November 2010)
Professor A J Musson, BA, MusB, LLM, PhD	Councillor (from November 2010)
Professor M Ormrod, BA, DPhil	Councillor
A T Thacker, MA, DPhil, FSA	Councillor (from November 2010)
D Thomas, PhD	Councillor
Professor C A Whatley, BA, PhD	Councillor

Executive Secretary:	S E Carr, MA
Administrative Secretary:	M F M Ransom, BA
Registered Office:	University College London Gower Street London WC1E 6BT
Charity registration number:	206888
Auditors:	Kingston Smith LLP Chartered Accountants Devonshire House 60 Goswell Road London EC1M 7AD
Investment managers:	Brewin Dolphin 12 Smithfield Street London EC1A 9BD
Bankers:	Barclays Bank Plc 27 Soho Square London W1A 4WA

THE ROYAL HISTORICAL SOCIETY
REPORT OF THE COUNCIL (THE TRUSTEES)
FOR THE YEAR ENDED 30 JUNE 2011

The members of Council present their report and audited accounts for the year ended 30 June 2011. The information shown on page 1 forms a part of these financial statements.

STRUCTURE, GOVERNANCE AND MANAGEMENT

The Society was founded on 23 November 1868 and received its Royal Charter in 1889. It is governed by the document 'The By-Laws of the Royal Historical Society', which was last amended in June 2010. The elected Officers of the Society are the President, six Vice-Presidents, the Treasurer, the Secretary, the Director of Communications, not more than two Literary Directors and the Honorary Academic Editor (BBIH). These officers, together with twelve Councillors constitute the governing body of the Society, and therefore its trustees. The Society also has two executive officers: an Executive Secretary and an Administrative Secretary.

Appointment of Trustees

The identity of the trustees is indicated above. All Fellows and Members of the Society are able to nominate Councillors; they are elected by a ballot of Fellows. Other trustees are elected by Council.

The President shall be *ex-officio* a member of all Committees appointed by the Council; and the Treasurer, the Secretary, the Director of Communications, the Literary Directors and the Honorary Academic Editor shall, unless the Council otherwise determine, also be *ex-officio* members of all such Committees.

In accordance with By-law XVII, the Vice-Presidents shall hold office normally for a term of three years. Two of them shall retire by rotation, in order of seniority in office, at each Anniversary Meeting and shall not be eligible for re-election before the Anniversary Meeting of the next year. In accordance with By-law XX, the Councillors shall hold office normally for a term of four years. Three of them shall retire by rotation, in order of seniority in office, at each Anniversary Meeting and shall not be eligible for re-election before the Anniversary Meeting of the next year.

At the Anniversary Meeting on 26 November 2010, the Vice-Presidents retiring under By-law XVII were Mr R Fisher and Professor D Palliser. Dr R Baldock and Professor C Kidd were elected to replace them. The Members of Council retiring under By-law XX were Professor S Connolly and Professor T Hitchcock. Professor N Miller retired in accordance with By-law XXII. In accordance with By-law XXI, Professor D Feldman, Professor A Musson and Dr A Thacker were elected in their place.

Trustee training and induction process

New trustees are welcomed in writing before their initial meeting, and sent details of the coming year's meeting schedule and other information about the Society and their duties. They are advised of Committee structure and receive papers in advance of the appropriate Committee and Council meetings, including minutes of the previous meetings. Trustees are already Fellows of the Society and have received regular information including the annual volume of *Transactions of the Royal Historical Society* which includes the annual report and accounts. They have therefore been kept apprised of any changes in the Society's business. Details of a Review on the restructuring of the Society in 1993 are available to all Members of Council.

MEMBERSHIP COMMITTEE:	Professor C Kidd – Chair (from November 2010)
	Professor D Palliser – Chair (to November 2010)
	Professor S Barton (from November 2010)
	Professor C Given-Wilson
	Professor C Whatley
RESEARCH SUPPORT COMMITTEE:	Professor M Finn – Chair
	Professor S Barton (to November 2010)
	Professor M Cornwall (from November 2010)
	Dr D Feldman (from November 2010)
	Professor K Fincham
	Dr A Thacker (from November 2010)
	Professor N Miller (to November 2010)

Risk assessment

The trustees are satisfied that they have considered the major risks to which the charity is exposed, that they have taken action to mitigate or manage those risks and that they have systems in place to monitor any change to those risks.

OBJECTS, OBJECTIVES, ACTIVITIES AND PUBLIC BENEFIT

The Society has referred to the guidance in the Charity Commission's general guidance on Public Benefit when reviewing its aims and objectives and in planning its future activities. In particular, the trustees consider how planned activities will contribute to the aims and objectives they have set.

The Society remains the foremost society in Great Britain promoting and defending the scholarly study of the past. The Society promotes discussion of history by means of a full programme of public lectures and conferences, and disseminates the results of historical research and debate through its many publications. It also speaks for the interests of history and historians for the benefit of the public.

The Society offers grants to support research training, and annual prizes for historical essays and publications. It produces (in conjunction with Brepols Publishers and the Institute of Historical Research) the Bibliography of British and Irish History (BBIH), a database of over 500,000 records, by far the most complete online bibliographical resource on British and Irish history, including relations with the empire and the Commonwealth. The Bibliography is kept updated, and includes near-comprehensive coverage of works since 1901 and selected earlier works.

The Society's specific new objectives for the year are set out in 'Plans for Future Periods' below.

The Society relies on volunteers from among its Fellows to act as its elected Officers, Councillors and Vice-Presidents. In many of its activities it also relies on the goodwill of Fellows and others interested in the study of the past. It has two salaried staff, and also pays a stipend to the Series Editor of Studies in History and to certain individuals for work on BBIH.

ACHIEVEMENTS AND PERFORMANCE

Grants

The Society awards funds to assist advanced historical research, by distributing grants to individuals. A wide range of people are eligible for these research and conference grants, including all postgraduate students registered for a research degree at United Kingdom institutions of higher education (full-time and part-time). The Society also considers applications from individuals who have completed doctoral dissertations within the last two years and are not yet in full-time employment. It operates five separate schemes, for each of which there is an application form. The Society's Research Support Committee considers applications at meetings held regularly throughout the year. In turn the Research Support Committee reports to Council. This year the grants budget was raised to £35,000, and this was fully allocated, though the accounts show a lower sum expended, as grants paid after last year's travel are also included.

The Society was also able to award its Centenary and Marshall Fellowships this year. Those eligible are doctoral students who are engaged in the completion of a PhD in history (broadly defined) and who will have completed at least two years' research on their chosen topic (and not more than four years full-time or six years part-time) at the beginning of the session for which the awards are made. Full details and a list of awards made are provided in the Society's Annual Report.

Lectures and other meetings

During the year the Society held meetings in London and at universities outside London at which papers are delivered. Lectures are open to the public and are advertised on the website. In 2010–11 it sponsored sessions at the University of York and Lancaster University. It continues to sponsor the joint lecture for a wider public with Gresham College. It meets with other bodies to consider teaching and research policy issues of national importance. Together with The National Archives, it organised the annual Gerald Aylmer seminar, between historians and archivists, in March. Full details are provided in the Annual Report.

Publications

This year, as in previous years, it has delivered an ambitious programme of publications – a volume of *Transactions*, two volumes of edited texts in the *Camden* Series and six further volumes in the *Studies in History* Series have appeared. It has increased its financial support for the Bibliography of British and Irish History, in its new format as a Brepols publication from January 2010. The Bibliography is offered to all universities at institutional rates, and made available free to members consulting it at the Institute of Historical Research.

Library

The Society continues to subscribe to a range of record series publications, which, with its other holdings, are housed either in the Council Room or in the room immediately across the corridor, in the UCL History Library. A catalogue of the Society's private library holdings and listings of record series and regional history society publications (Texts and Calendars) have been made available on the Society's website.

Membership services

In accordance with the Society's 'By-laws', the membership is entitled to receive, after payment of subscription, a copy of the Society's *Transactions*, and to buy at a preferential rate copies of volumes published in the *Camden* series, and the *Studies in History* series. Society Newsletters continue to be circulated to the membership twice annually, in an accessible format. The membership benefits from many other activities of the Society including the frequent representations to various official bodies where the interests of historical scholarship are involved.

Investment performance

The Society holds an investment portfolio with a market value of about £2.54 million at 30 June 2011 (2010: £2.16 million)]. It has adopted a "total return" approach to its investment policy. This means that the funds are invested solely on the basis of seeking to secure the best total level of economic return compatible with the duty to make safe investments, but regardless of the form the return takes.

The Society has adopted this approach to ensure even-handedness between current and future beneficiaries, as the focus of many investments moves away from producing income to maximising capital values. The total return strategy does not make distinctions between income and capital returns. It lumps together all forms of return on investment – dividends, interest, and capital gains etc, to produce a "total return". Some of the total return is then used to meet the needs of present beneficiaries, while the remainder is added to the existing investment portfolios to help meet the needs of future beneficiaries.

During the year Brewin Dolphin plc continued to act as investment managers. They report all transactions to the Honorary Treasurer and provide regular reports on the portfolios, which are considered by the Society's Finance Committee which meets three times a year. In turn the Finance Committee reports to Council. A manager from Brewin attends two Finance Committee meetings a year.

The Society assesses investment performance against the FTSE APCIMS Balanced (Total Return) index. Investment returns on the Society's portfolio were well ahead of the benchmark in 2010–11 (against a slight underperformance in 2009–10). Fees are 0.5% of the portfolio. The Society has a policy of not drawing down more than 4% of the market value of the portfolio (valued over a 3-year rolling period). The drawdown in 2010–11 was less than 3.1% (measured against the portfolio value at year end).

FINANCIAL REVIEW

Results

The Society generated a surplus of £42,189 (£2009–10: 27,222). Income from the joint publishing agreement with Cambridge University Press remained very buoyant in 2010–11 and was well ahead of expectations due to ongoing sales of the new digital archive. Subscription income was slightly increased over the previous year. There was a slight decline in investment income compared with 2009–10. Expenditure in 2010–11 was slightly higher than the previous year. The Society continues to bear substantial costs for the production of the Bibliography of British and Irish History. The cost to the Society is estimated to average £25,000 per year over the next two years. The Society maintains a significant cash reserve as a result of the accumulated surplus of the previous few years. It is anticipated that the Society will use some of this money in future years in order to meet rising costs and potential new initiatives.

Fixed assets

Information relating to changes in fixed assets is given in notes 5 and 6 to the accounts.

Reserves policy

Council has reviewed the reserves of the Society. To safeguard the core activities in excess of the members' subscription income, Council has determined to establish unrestricted, general, free reserves to cover three years' operational costs (approximately £650,000). Unrestricted, general, free reserves at 30 June 2011 were around £2.5 million (after adjusting for fixed assets). Council is satisfied with this level.

The Society's restricted funds consist of a number of different funds where the donor has imposed restrictions on the use of the funds which are legally binding. The purposes of these funds are set out in notes 11–13.

PLANS FOR FUTURE PERIODS

Council plans to develop its website in order to improve communication with both Fellows and the General Public. Council will also continue to monitor closely how policy and funding changes at the national level are likely to impact on the work of historians. It will also continue to monitor the challenges currently faced by local archives in an uncertain funding environment. Council is also paying considerable attention to current policy initiatives that affect the teaching of History in schools and colleges. It will continue to offer support for wide-ranging seminar/lecture events outside London each year, some to be held at universities, and some run by consortia of local universities and other academic institutions. Council will continue to review the role, function, and membership of its committees, focusing first on the Teaching Policy and Research Policy Committees.

The Society intends to maintain the level of its current financial support to postgraduate and other young historians. It will continue to support the stipends for the Centenary and Marshall Fellowships (and will continue to be involved in the selection procedure for the Fellowships, organised by the Institute of Historical Research).

STATEMENT OF COUNCIL'S RESPONSIBILITIES

The Council members are responsible for preparing the Trustees' Report and the financial statements in accordance with applicable law and United Kingdom Accounting Standards (United Kingdom Generally Accepted Accounting Practice.)

The law applicable to charities in England & Wales requires the Council to prepare financial statements for each financial year which give a true and fair view of the state of the affairs of the charity and of the incoming resources and application of resources of the charity for that period. In preparing these financial statements, the trustees are required to:

- select suitable accounting policies and then apply them consistently;
- observe the methods and principles in the Charities SORP;
- make judgements and estimates that are reasonable and prudent;
- state whether applicable accounting standards have been followed, subject to any material departures disclosed and explained in the financial statements;
- prepare the financial statements on the going concern basis unless it is inappropriate to presume that the charity will continue in business.

The Council is responsible for keeping proper accounting records that disclose with reasonable accuracy at any time the financial position of the charity and enable them to ensure that the financial statements comply with the Charities Act 1993, the Charity (Accounts and Reports) Regulations 2008 and the provisions of the Royal Charter. It is also responsible for safeguarding the assets of the charity and hence for taking reasonable steps for the prevention and detection of fraud and other irregularities.

In determining how amounts are presented within items in the statement of financial activities and balance sheet, the Council has had regard to the substance of the reported transaction or arrangement, in accordance with generally accepted accounting policies or practice.

AUDITORS

Kingston Smith LLP were appointed auditors in the year. They have indicated their willingness to continue in office and a proposal for their re-appointment will be presented at the Anniversary meeting.

By Order of the Board

Honorary Secretary

Professor V Harding

23 September 2011

THE ROYAL HISTORICAL SOCIETY
INDEPENDENT AUDITORS' REPORT TO THE TRUSTEES
OF THE ROYAL HISTORIAL SOCIETY

We have audited the financial statements of The Royal Historical Society for the year ended 30 June 2011 which comprise the Statement of Financial Activities, the Balance Sheet and the related notes. The financial reporting framework that has been applied in their preparation is applicable laws and United Kingdom Accounting Standards (United Kingston Generally Accepted Accounting Practice).

This report is made solely to the charity's trustees, as a body, in accordance with regulations made under section 43 of the Charities Act 1993. Our audit work has been undertaken so that we might state to he charity's trustees those matters we are required to state to them in an auditor's report and for no other purpose. To the fullest extent permitted by law, we do not accept or assume responsibility to any party other than the charity and charity's trustees as a body, for our audit work, for this report, or for the opinion we have formed.

Respective responsibilities of trustees and auditor
As explained more fully in the Trustees' Responsibilities Statement, the trustees are responsible for the preparation of financial statements which give a true and fair view. We have been appointed as auditors under section 43 of the Charities Act 1993 and report in accordance with regulations made under section 44 of that Act. Our responsibility is to audit the financial statements in accordance with applicable law and International Standards on Auditing (UK and Ireland). Those standards require us to comply with the Auditing Practices Board's Ethical Standards for Auditors.

Scope of the audit of the financial statements
An audit involves obtaining evidence about the amounts and disclosures in the financial statements sufficient to give reasonable assurance that the financial statements are free from material misstatement, whether caused by fraud or error. This includes an assessment of: whether the accounting policies are appropriate to the charity's circumstances and have been consistently applied and adequately disclosed; the reasonableness of significant accounting estimates made by the trustees; and the overall presentation of the financial statements. In addition we read all the financial and non-financial information in the Annual Report to identify material inconsistencies with the audited financial statements. If we become aware of any apparent material misstatements or inconsistencies we consider the implications for our report.

Opinion on the financial statements
In our opinion:

- give a true and fair view of the state of the charity's affairs as at 30 June 2011 and of the charity incoming/outgoing resources and application of resources for the year then ended; and
- have been properly prepared in accordance with United Kingdom Generally Accepted Accounting Practice applicable to Smaller Entities; and
- have been prepared in accordance with the requirements of the Charities Act 1993.

Matters on which we are required to report by exception
We have nothing to report in respect of the following matters where the Charities Act 1993 requires us to report to you if, in our opinion:

- the information given in the Annual Report is inconsistent in any material respects with the financial statements; or
- sufficient accounting records have not been kept; or
- the financial statements are not in agreement with the accounting records and returns; or
- we have not received all the information and explanations we require for our audit

Devonshire House
60 Goswell Road   **Kingston Smith LLP**
London EC1M 7AD   Statutory auditor

Date:

Kingston Smith LLP is eligible to act as auditor in terms of Section 1212 of the Companies Act 2006.

THE ROYAL HISTORICAL SOCIETY
STATEMENT OF FINANCIAL ACTIVITIES
FOR THE YEAR ENDED 30 JUNE 2011

	Note	Unrestricted Funds £	Endowment Funds £	Restricted Funds £	Total Funds 2011 £	Total Funds 2010 £
INCOMING RESOURCES						
Incoming resources from generated funds						
Donations, legacies and similar incoming resources	2	15,545	–	1,000	16,545	10,792
Investment income	6	72,715	–	2,229	74,994	78,689
Incoming resources from charitable activities						
Grants for awards		–	–	11,000	11,000	10,000
Grants for publications		5,000	–	–	5,000	8,000
Subscriptions		106,657	–	–	106,657	103,146
Royalties		64,810	–	–	64,810	53,986
Other incoming resources		124	–	–	124	666
TOTAL INCOMING RESOURCES		264,851	–	14,229	279,080	265,279
RESOURCES EXPENDED						
Cost of generating funds						
Investment manager's fees		11,184	–	346	11,530	10,779
Charitable activities						
Grants for awards	3	52,642	–	13,990	66,632	69,486
Lectures and meetings		12,336	–	–	12,336	14,900
Publications		74,038	–	–	74,038	71,643
Library		5,405	–	–	5,405	5,161
Membership services		48,271	–	–	48,271	47,781
Governance		18,679	–	–	18,679	18,309
TOTAL RESOURCES EXPENDED	4a	222,555	–	14,336	236,891	238,059
NET INCOMING/(OUTGOING) RESOURCES BEFORE TRANSFERS		42,296	–	(107)	42,189	27,221
Gross transfers between funds		(740)	–	740	–	–
NET INCOMING/(OUTGOING) RESOURCES BEFORE GAINS		41,556	–	633	42,189	27,221
Other recognised gains and losses						
Net (loss)/gain on investments	6	377,237	11,668		388,905	202,705
NET MOVEMENT IN FUNDS		418,793	11,668	633	431,094	229,926
Balance at 1 July		2,199,518	62,276	3,595	2,265,389	2,035,462
Balance at 30 June		2,618,311	73,944	4,228	2,696,483	2,265,389

The notes on pages 257–261 form part of these financial statements.

THE ROYAL HISTORICAL SOCIETY

BALANCE SHEET AT 30 JUNE 2011

	Note	2011 £	2011 £	2010 £	2010 £
FIXED ASSETS					
Tangible assets	5		681		794
Investments	6		2,535,967		2,162,298
COIF Investments			115,302		57,671
			2,651,950		2,220,763
CURRENT ASSETS					
Debtors	7	6,156		46,901	
Cash at bank and in hand		82,646		30,916	
		88,802		77,817	
LESS: CREDITORS					
Amounts due within one year	8	(44,269)		(33,191)	
NET CURRENT ASSETS			44,533		44,626
NET ASSETS			2,696,483		2,265,389
REPRESENTED BY:					
Endowment Funds	10				
A S Whitfield Prize Fund			49,475		41,697
The David Berry Essay Trust			24,469		20,579
Restricted Funds	11				
A S Whitfield Prize Fund			1,806		1,551
P J Marshall Fellowship			–		–
The David Berry Essay Trust			1,422		1,044
The Martin Lynn Bequest			1,000		1,000
Unrestricted Funds					
Designated – E M Robinson Bequest	12		126,798		108,115
General Fund	13		2,491,513		2,091,404
			2,696,483		2,265,389

The accounts have been prepared in accordance with the Financial Reporting Standard for Smaller Entities (effective April 2008).

The notes on pages 257–261 form part of these financial statements.

The financial statements were approved and authorised for issue by the Council on 23 September 2011 and were signed on its behalf by:

. . . . 　　　　　　　　　. . . . .

Professor C Jones – **President**　　　　　　　Professor M J Hughes – **Honorary Treasurer**

THE ROYAL HISTORICAL SOCIETY

NOTES TO THE FINANCIAL STATEMENTS FOR THE YEAR ENDED 30 JUNE 2011

1. ACCOUNTING POLICIES

Basis of Accounting
The financial statements have been prepared under the historical cost convention, as modified to include the revaluation of fixed assets including investments which are carried at market value, in accordance with the Statement of Recommended Practice (SORP 2005) "Accounting and Reporting by Charities", published in March 2005, with applicable accounting standards and the Financial Reporting Standard for Smaller Entities (effective April 2008).

Depreciation
Depreciation is calculated by reference to the cost of fixed assets using a straight line basis at rates considered appropriate having regard to the expected lives of the fixed assets. The annual rates of depreciation in use are:

Furniture and equipment   10%
Computer equipment   25%

Stock
Stock is valued at the lower of cost and net realisable value.

Library and Archives
The cost of additions to the library and archives is written off in the year of purchase.

Subscription Income
Subscription income is recognised in the year it became receivable with a provision against any subscription not received.

Investments
Investments are stated at market value. Any surplus/deficit arising on revaluation is included in the Statement of Financial Activities. Dividend income is accounted for when the Society becomes entitled to such monies.

Donations and Other Voluntary Income
Donations and other voluntary income are recognised when the Society becomes legally entitled to such monies.

Royalties
Royalties are recoginised on an accruals basis in accordance with the terms of the relevant agreement.

Grants Payable
Grants payable are recognised in the year in which they are approved and notified to recipients.

Funds
Unrestricted: these are funds which can be used in accordance with the charitable objects at the discretion of the trustees.
Designated: these are unrestricted funds which have been set aside by the trustees for specific purposes.
Restricted: these are funds that can only be used for particular restricted purposes defined by the benefactor and within the objects of the charity.
Endowment: permanent endowment funds must be held permanently by the trustees and income arising is separately included in restricted funds for specific use as defined by the donors.
The purpose and use of endowment, restricted and designated funds are disclosed in the notes to the accounts.

Allocations
Wages, salary costs and office expenditure are allocated on the basis of the work done by the Executive Secretary and the Administrative Assistant.

Pensions
Pension costs are charged to the SOFA when payments fall due. The Society contributed 12.5% of gross salary to the personal pension plan of two of the employees.

Governance costs
Governance costs of the charity include the costs of running the charity such as audit, staff costs and statutory compliance.

2. DONATIONS AND LEGACIES

	2011 £	2010 £
Donations via membership	1,487	1,254
Gladstone Memorial Trust	600	600
Vera London	4,696	–
Lisbet Rausing trust	5,500	5,000
Martin Lynn scholarship	1,000	1,000
Sundry income	–	–
Gift Aid reclaimed	3,262	2,938
	16,545	10,792

3. GRANTS FOR AWARDS	Unrestricted Funds £	Restricted Funds £	Total funds 2011 £	Total funds 2010 £
RHS Centenary Fellowship	13,200	–	13,200	10,000
Research support grants (see below)	28,632	1,000	29,632	34,019
A-Level prizes	400	–	400	300
AS Whitfield prize	–	1,000	1,000	1,000
E M Robinson Bequest				
Grant to Dulwich Picture Library	–	–	–	4,000
Gladstone history book prize	1,000	–	1,000	1,000
P J Marshall Fellowship	–	11,740	11,740	10,670
David Berry Prize	–	250	250	250
Alexander Prize	500	–	500	–
Rees Davies Prize	100	–	100	–
Staff and support costs (Note 4a)	8,810	–	8,810	8,247
	52,642	13,990	66,632	
30 June 2010	56,479	13,007		69,486

During the year Society awarded grants to a value of £29,632 (2010 - £34,019) to 127 (2010 - 131) individuals.

GRANTS PAYABLE	2011 £	2010 £
Commitments at 1 July	8,069	1,300
Commitments made in the year	57,822	61,238
Grants paid during the year	(58,586)	(54,469)
Commitments at 30 June	7,305	8,069

Commitments at 30 June 2011 and 2010 are included in creditors.

4a. TOTAL RESOURCES EXPENDED	Staff costs £	Support costs £	Direct costs £	Total £
Cost of generating funds				
Investment manager's fee	–	–	11,530	11,530
Charitable activities				
Grants for awards (Note 3)	6,062	2,748	57,821	66,631
Lectures and meetings	6,063	1,374	4,899	12,336
Publications	10,778	5,496	57,764	74,038
Library	2,694	1,374	1,337	5,405
Membership services	33,680	13,741	850	48,271
Governance	8,083	2,748	7,848	18,679
Total Resources Expended	67,360	27,481	142,049	236,890
30 June 2010	65,441	23,573	149,041	238,055
	(Note 4b)	**(Note 4c)**		

4b. STAFF COSTS	2011 £	2010 £
Wages and salaries	55,030	53,360
Social security costs	5,570	5,390
Other pension costs	6,760	6,691
	67,360	65,441

4c. SUPPORT COSTS	2011 £	2010 £
Stationery, photocopying and postage	15,382	12,669
Computer support	392	490
Insurance	951	920
Telephone	287	254
Depreciation	113	113
Other	10,356	9,126
	27,481	23,573

The average number of employees in the year was 2 (2010 - 2). There were no employees whose emoluments exceeded £60,000 in this year or in the previous year.

During the year travel expenses were reimbursed to 16 (2010: 20) Councillors attending Council meetings at a cost of £3,866 (2010 - £3,311). No Councillor received any remuneration during the year (2010 - £Nil).

Included in governance is the following:

	2011 £	2010 £
Auditors Remuneration - current year	7,848	7,461
Auditors Remuneration - in respect of prior years	–	88
Auditors Remuneration for non-audit services	–	550

5. TANGIBLE FIXED ASSETS

	Computer Equipment £	Furniture and Equipment £	Total £
COST			
At 1 July 2010	33,224	2,307	35,531
Disposal	–	(1,173)	(1,173)
At 30 June 2011	33,224	1,134	34,358
DEPRECIATION			
At 1 July 2010	33,224	1,513	34,737
	–	(1,173)	(1,173)
Charge for the year	–	113	113
At 30 June 2011	33,224	453	33,677
NET BOOK VALUE			
At 30 June 2011	–	681	681
At 30 June 2010	–	794	794

All tangible fixed assets are used in the furtherance of the Society's objects.

6. INVESTMENTS

	General Fund £	Designated Robinson Bequest £	Whitfield Prize Fund £	David Berry Essay Trust £	Total £
Market value at 1 July 2010	1,989,312	108,115	43,248	21,623	2,162,298
Additions	378,730	20,642	8,817	4,658	412,847
Disposals	(393,837)	(21,404)	(8,562)	(4,280)	(428,083)
Net gain on investments	357,792	19,445	7,778	3,890	388,905
Market value at 30 June 2011	2,331,997	126,798	51,281	25,891	2,535,967
Cost at 30 June 2011	1,909,040	103,752	41,501	20,750	2,075,043

	2011 £	2010 £
UK Equities	1,831,858	999,392
UK Government Stock and Bonds	–	551,602
Overseas Equities	659,937	575,604
Uninvested Cash	44,173	35,700
	2,535,968	2,162,298
Dividends and interest on listed investments	74,294	78,092
Interest on cash deposits	650	597
	74,944	78,689

7. DEBTORS

	2011 £	2010 £
Other debtors	4,056	2,261
Royalty debtor	1,162	42,366
Prepayments	938	2,274
	6,156	46,901

8. CREDITORS: Amounts due within one year

	2011 £	2010 £
Sundry creditors	17,080	13,486
Taxes and social security	1,566	1,210
Subscriptions received in advance	7,416	6,345
Accruals and deferred income	18,207	12,150
	44,269	33,191

Included within Sundry creditors is an amount of £577 (2010: £398) relating to pension liabilities.

9. LEASE COMMITMENTS

The Society has the following annual commitments under non-cancellable operating leases which expire:

	2011 £	2010 £
Under 1 year	3,282	–
Within 1 - 2 years	–	9,846

10. ENDOWMENT FUNDS

	Balance at 1 July 2010 £	Investment Gain £	Balance at 30 June 2011 £
A S Whitfield Prize Fund	41,697	7,778	49,475
The David Berry Essay Trust	20,579	3,890	24,469
	62,276	11,668	73,944

A S Whitfield Prize Fund

The A S Whitfield Prize Fund is an endowment used to provide income for an annual prize for the best first monograph for British history published in the calendar year.

The David Berry Essay Trust

The David Berry Essay Trust is an endowment to provide income for annual prizes for essays on subjects dealing with Scottish history.

11. RESTRICTED FUNDS

	Balance at 1 July 2010 £	Incoming Resources £	Outgoing Resources £	Transfers £	Balance at 30 June 2011 £
A S Whitfield Prize Fund	1,551	1,486	(1,231)	–	1,806
P J Marshall Fellowship	–	11,000	(11,740)	740	–
The David Berry Essay Trust	1,044	743	(365)	–	1,422
Martin Lynn Bequest	1,000	1,000	(1,000)	–	1,000
	3,595	14,229	(14,336)	740	4,228

A S Whitfield Prize Fund Income

Income from the A S Whitfield Prize Fund is used to provide an annual prize for the best first monograph for British history published in the calendar year.

P J Marshall Fellowship

The P J Marshall Fellowship is used to provide a sum sufficient to cover the stipend for a one-year doctoral research fellowship alongside the existing Royal Historical Society Centenary Fellowship at the Institute of Historical Research.

The David Berry Essay Trust Income

Income from the David Berry Trust is to provide annual prizes for essays on subjects dealing with Scottish history.

The Martin Lynn Bequest

This annual bequest is used by the Society to give financial assistance to postgraduates researching topics in African history.

12. DESIGNATED FUND	Balance at 1 July 2010 £	Incoming Resources £	Outgoing Resources £	Investment Gain £	Transfers £	Balance at 30 June 2011 £
E M Robinson Bequest	108,115	3,715	(4,477)	19,445	–	126,798

E M Robinson Bequest

Income from the E M Robinson Bequest is to further the study of history and to date has been used to provide grants to the Dulwich Picture Gallery.

13. GENERAL FUND	Balance at 1 July 2010 £	Incoming Resources £	Outgoing Resources £	Investment Gain £	Transfers £	Balance at 30 June 2011 £
	2,091,403	261,137	(218,079)	357,792	(740)	2,491,513

14. ANALYSIS OF NET ASSETS BETWEEN FUNDS

	General Fund £	Designated Fund £	Restricted Funds £	Endowment Funds £	Total £
Fixed assets	681	–	–	–	681
Investments	2,331,997	126,798	3,228	73,944	2,535,967
COIF investments	115,302	–	–	–	115,302
	2,447,980	126,798	3,228	73,944	2,651,950
Current assets	87,802	–	1,000	–	88,802
Less: Creditors	(44,269)	–	–	–	(44,269)
Net current assets/(liabilities)	43,533	–	1,000	–	44,533
Net Assets	2,491,513	126,798	4,228	73,944	2,696,483